CATIA V5-6R2017: Advanced Assembly Design & Management

Learning Guide

1st Edition

ASCENT - Center for Technical Knowledge®

CATIA V5-6R2017: Advanced Assembly Design & Management

1st Edition

Prepared and produced by:

ASCENT Center for Technical Knowledge
630 Peter Jefferson Parkway, Suite 175
Charlottesville, VA 22911

866-527-2368
www.ASCENTed.com

Lead Contributor: Scott Hendren

ASCENT - Center for Technical Knowledge is a division of Rand Worldwide, Inc., providing custom developed knowledge products and services for leading engineering software applications. ASCENT is focused on specializing in the creation of education programs that incorporate the best of classroom learning and technology-based training offerings.

We welcome any comments you may have regarding this learning guide, or any of our products. To contact us please email: feedback@ASCENTed.com.

AS-56CAT17-AAD1-SG // RS-56CAT17-AAD1-SG

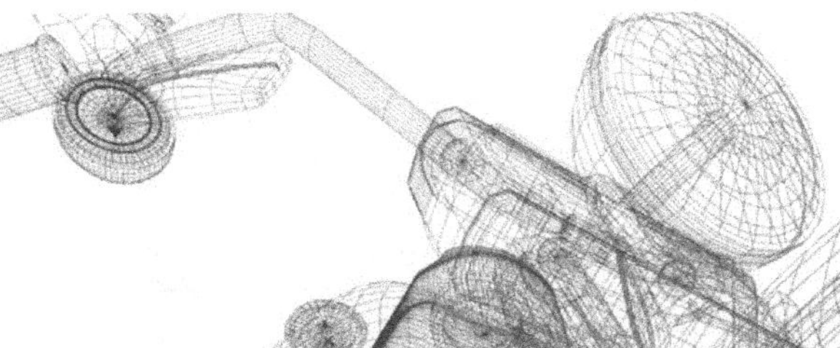

Contents

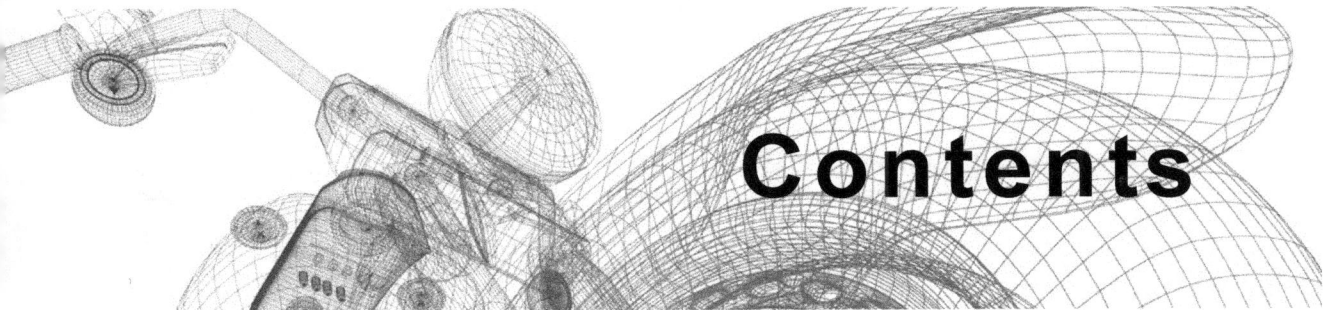

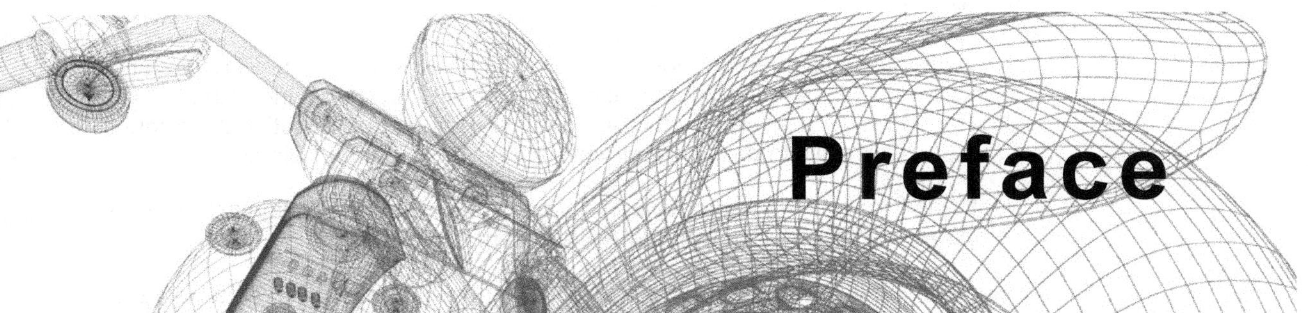

Preface

The *CATIA V5-6R2017: Advanced Assembly Design & Management* learning guide builds on the assembly functionality introduced in the *CATIA: Introduction to Modeling* course. Students gain a full understanding of how to design and manage a complex assembly in the CATIA software while concentrating on techniques that maximize the capabilities of the Assembly workbench. This extensive hands-on course contains numerous labs focused on process-based practices to give you practical experience and improve design productivity.

Topics Covered

- Assembly operations (reconnecting constraints, specification tree customization, save operations, Desk Command, etc.)
- Skeleton Modeling
- Contextual Design
- Publications
- Link Management
- Collaborative Design
- Component Degrees of Freedom
- Assembly Duplication (multi-instantiation, component symmetry, reuse patterns, etc.)
- Assembly analysis (measurements, clash, sectioning a model, etc.)

Note on Software Setup

This learning guide assumes a standard installation of the software using the default preferences during installation. Lectures and practices use the standard software templates and default options for the Content Libraries.

This course was developed against CATIA V5-6R2017, Service Pack 1.

Lead Contributor: Scott Hendren

Scott Hendren has been a trainer and curriculum developer in the PLM industry for almost 20 years, with experience on multiple CAD systems, including Pro/ENGINEER, Creo Parametric, and CATIA. Trained in Instructional Design, Scott uses his skills to develop instructor-led and web-based training products.

Scott has held training and development positions with several high profile PLM companies, and has been with the Ascent team since 2013.

Scott holds a Bachelor of Mechanical Engineering Degree as well as a Bachelor of Science in Mathematics from Dalhousie University, Nova Scotia, Canada.

Scott Hendren has been the Lead Contributor for *CATIA: Advanced Assembly Design & Management* since 2013.

In this Guide

The following images highlight some of the features that can be found in this Learning Guide.

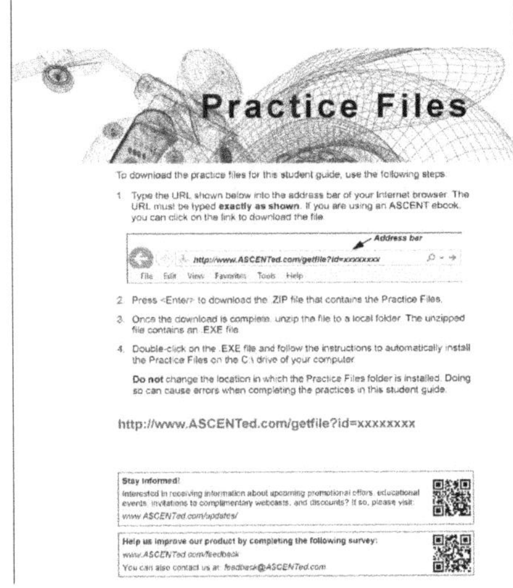

Practice Files

To download the practice files for this student guide, use the following steps:

1. Type the URL shown below into the address bar of your Internet browser. The URL must be typed **exactly as shown**. If you are using an ASCENT ebook, you can click on the link to download the file.

   Address bar
   http://www.ASCENTed.com/getfile?id=xxxxxxxx
   File Edit View Favorites Tools Help

2. Press <Enter> to download the .ZIP file that contains the Practice Files.
3. Once the download is complete, unzip the file to a local folder. The unzipped file contains an .EXE file.
4. Double-click on the .EXE file and follow the instructions to automatically install the Practice Files on the C:\ drive of your computer.

   Do not change the location in which the Practice Files folder is installed. Doing so can cause errors when completing the practices in this student guide.

http://www.ASCENTed.com/getfile?id=xxxxxxxx

Stay Informed!
Interested in receiving information about upcoming promotional offers, educational events, invitations to complimentary webcasts, and discounts? If so, please visit:
www.ASCENTed.com/updates/

Help us improve our product by completing the following survey:
www.ASCENTed.com/feedback
You can also contact us at: *feedback@ASCENTed.com*

FTP link for practice files

Practice Files

The Practice Files page tells you how to download and install the practice files that are provided with this learning guide.

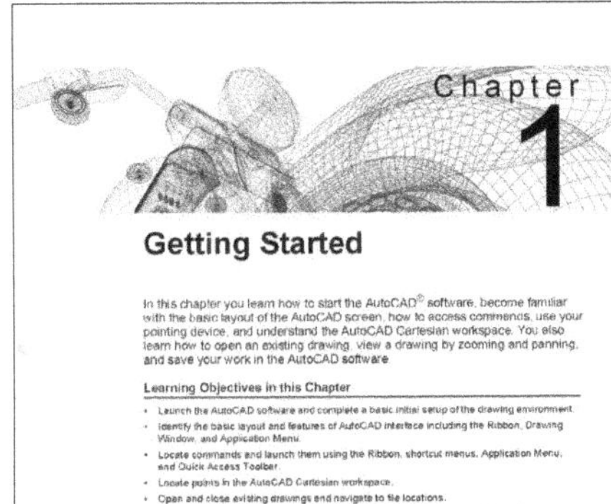

Chapter 1

Getting Started

In this chapter you learn how to start the AutoCAD® software, become familiar with the basic layout of the AutoCAD screen, how to access commands, use your pointing device, and understand the AutoCAD Cartesian workspace. You also learn how to open an existing drawing, view a drawing by zooming and panning, and save your work in the AutoCAD software.

Learning Objectives in this Chapter

- Launch the AutoCAD software and complete a basic initial setup of the drawing environment.
- Identify the basic layout and features of AutoCAD interface including the Ribbon, Drawing Window, and Application Menu.
- Locate commands and launch them using the Ribbon, shortcut menus, Application Menu, and Quick Access Toolbar.
- Locate points in the AutoCAD Cartesian workspace.
- Open and close existing drawings and navigate to file locations.
- Move around a drawing using the mouse, the **Zoom** and **Pan** commands, and the Navigation Bar.
- Save drawings in various formats and set the automatic save options using the **Save** commands.

Learning Objectives for the chapter

Chapters

Each chapter begins with a brief introduction and a list of the chapter's Learning Objectives.

Side notes

Side notes are hints or additional information for the current topic.

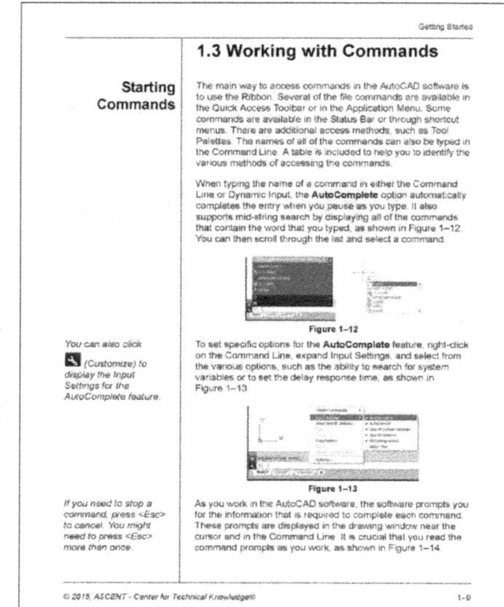

Getting Started

1.3 Working with Commands

Starting Commands

The main way to access commands in the AutoCAD software is to use the Ribbon. Several of the file commands are available in the Quick Access Toolbar or in the Application Menu. Some commands are available in the Status Bar or through shortcut menus. There are additional access methods, such as Tool Palettes. The names of all of the commands can also be typed in the Command Line. A table is included to help you to identify the various methods of accessing the commands.

When typing the name of a command in either the Command Line or Dynamic Input, the **AutoComplete** option automatically completes the entry when you pause as you type. It also supports mid-string search by displaying all of the commands that contain the word that you typed, as shown in Figure 1–12. You can then scroll through the list and select a command.

Figure 1–12

You can also click (Customize) to display the Input Settings for the AutoComplete feature.

To set specific options for the **AutoComplete** feature, right-click on the Command Line, expand Input Settings, and select from the various options, such as the ability to search for system variables or to set the delay response time, as shown in Figure 1–13.

Figure 1–13

If you need to stop a command, press <Esc> to cancel. You might need to press <Esc> more than once.

As you work in the AutoCAD software, the software prompts you for the information that is required to complete each command. These prompts are displayed in the drawing window near the cursor and in the Command Line. It is crucial that you read the command prompts as you work, as shown in Figure 1–14.

© 2015, ASCENT - Center for Technical Knowledge® 1-9

Instructional Content

Each chapter is split into a series of sections of instructional content on specific topics. These lectures include the descriptions, step-by-step procedures, figures, hints, and information you need to achieve the chapter's Learning Objectives.

Practice Objectives

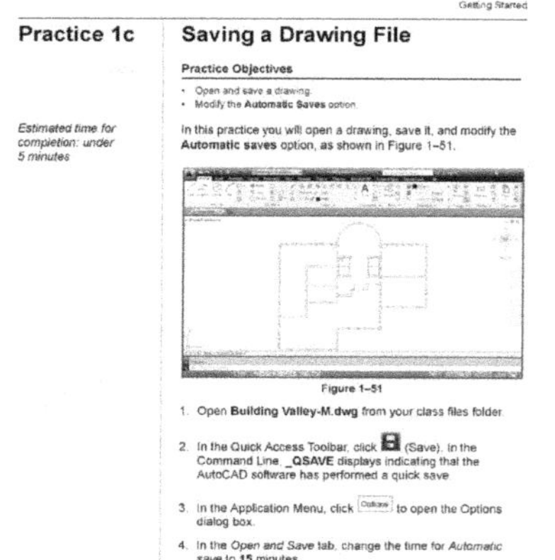

Getting Started

Practice 1c Saving a Drawing File

Practice Objectives

- Open and save a drawing.
- Modify the **Automatic Saves** option.

Estimated time for completion: under 5 minutes

In this practice you will open a drawing, save it, and modify the **Automatic saves** option, as shown in Figure 1–51.

Figure 1–51

1. Open **Building Valley-M.dwg** from your class files folder.
2. In the Quick Access Toolbar, click (Save). In the Command Line, **_QSAVE** displays indicating that the AutoCAD software has performed a quick save.
3. In the Application Menu, click Options to open the Options dialog box.
4. In the *Open and Save* tab, change the time for *Automatic save* to **15** minutes.

Practices

Practices enable you to use the software to perform a hands-on review of a topic.

Some practices require you to use prepared practice files, which can be downloaded from the link found on the Practice Files page.

To download the practice files for this learning guide, use the following steps:

1. Type the URL shown below into the address bar of your Internet browser. The URL must be typed **exactly as shown**. If you are using an ASCENT ebook, you can click on the link to download the file.

2. Press <Enter> to download the .ZIP file that contains the Practice Files.
3. Once the download is complete, unzip the file to a local folder. The unzipped file contains an .EXE file.
4. Double-click on the .EXE file and follow the instructions to automatically install the Practice Files on the C:\ drive of your computer.

   Do not change the location in which the Practice Files folder is installed. Doing so can cause errors when completing the practices in this learning guide.

http://www.ASCENTed.com/getfile?id=coccinellidae

Stay Informed!

Interested in receiving information about upcoming promotional offers, educational events, invitations to complimentary webcasts, and discounts? If so, please visit:

www.ASCENTed.com/updates/

Help us improve our product by completing the following survey:

www.ASCENTed.com/feedback

You can also contact us at: *feedback@ASCENTed.com*

Assembly Operations

The Assembly Design workbench enables you to explore various design configurations and locate missing files. Operations, such as assembly constraints and constraint creation modes, help you to create a flexible assembly. This chapter introduces operations in the Assembly Design workbench, and compares top-down design techniques to bottom-up design techniques when creating assemblies.

Learning Objectives in this Chapter

- Review the Assembly Design Workbench and assembly related terms and definitions.
- Understand the Assembly Specification Tree.
- Learn how to work with assembly annotations.
- Learn how to work with assembly constraints.
- Understand the Save operations and the Desk command.

1.1 Assembly Design Workbench

When designing parts in the Part Design workbench, features are created and positioned parametrically with respect to each other and to other reference features. Parts that belong to an assembly can be assembled and positioned parametrically in a CATProduct file using the Assembly Design workbench.

Accessing the Assembly Design Workbench

By default, CATIA opens in the Assembly Design workbench. You can also activate the Assembly Design workbench by selecting **Start>Mechanical Design>Assembly Design** or **File>New>Product**.

When the Assembly Design workbench is activated, various assembly-specific toolbars open. The Product Structure toolbar shown in Figure 1–1 enables you to assemble components, create part and product files in context, replace components, manage an assembly, and multi-instantiate components.

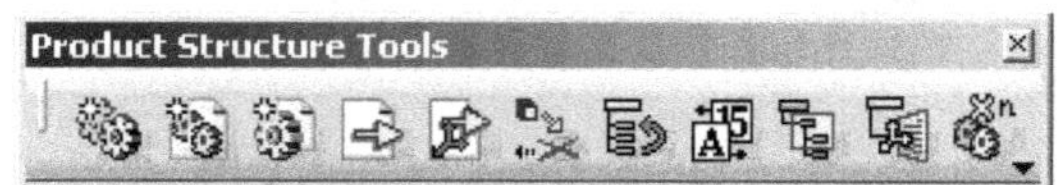

Figure 1–1

1.2 Terms and Definitions

Skeleton

A skeleton is a CATIA part model that is used to aid the construction of a complex assembly model. The part is used as a storage location for any critical design information, such as industrial design surfaces (e.g., A-side or masterline surfaces), and location and sizing information. The skeleton information is shared with the other components in the assembly to drive the design. The skeleton model is always the first component in an assembly and should only contain wireframe and surface geometry so that assembly mass properties are not affected.

Contextual Design

Contextual design involves the creation of part-level geometry in the context of an assembly. By visualizing all of the components of an assembly while building a part, it is possible to share critical design information between components and ensure that components do not interfere with each other.

The contextual design approach is driven by the creation of external references between assembly components. These links add an extra level of complexity to the assembly and must be maintained throughout the design process to obtain maximum benefits. Building an assembly contextually requires good communication in the design team and a clear reference structure in the assembly.

Bottom-Up Design

In a traditional bottom-up design approach, part geometry is created independent of the assembly or any other component. Any design criteria established before the part is modeled are not shared between models. Once all of the part models are completed, they are brought together for the first time in the assembly. At this point in the design, problems often result with the assembly because engineering information is not correctly shared or communicated. Problems can include interference between components, misalignment between components, or incomplete design. In addition, any modifications to components must be manually propagated throughout the assembly.

Top-Down Design

The top-down design approach places critical information in a top-level assembly and then communicates that information to lower levels of the product structure. The first step in creating a top-down design model is to create an initial assembly structure. Design information is placed in this assembly through the use of skeleton models and parameters that are controlled by design tables. Any changes made to the top-level information are automatically propagated to all affected components.

Top-down design techniques simulate a design team and facilitate concurrent engineering. The top-down design approach forces you to consider all areas of a final model before creating any geometry. Consider the following questions when using this technique:

- What does the assembly do?
- How does a specific model interface with other components in the assembly?
- What are the inputs and outputs of the assembly?

Planning the assembly using the top-down design approach helps to create clean, reusable geometry that interfaces correctly with the rest of the assembly.

Collaborative Design

Collaborative design involves two or more people simultaneously developing geometry for an assembly. For example, when designing a car, several departments contribute to the finished product.

A major concern in a collaborative environment is the loss of data or duplication of efforts. If two people open a part model at the same time, the last person to save defines the latest revision, while the first person's modifications are lost. Communication is one defence against these types of setbacks. Another solution is to install a Product Data Management (PDM) application.

Product Data Management

Product Data Management (PDM) is a type of software that organizes and manages files in a database. Files in a PDM system are related to the development of a product. These files are stored on a server commonly referred to as the vault. From here, you can open files and save them back to the server. The PDM system keeps track of and controls all file operations. Only one person can work on a file at a time. All other users can only display the file, but not make changes to it.

Common capabilities of a PDM system include:

- Tracking revisions of a document.
- Advanced tools to search documents in the database.
- Viewing file information.
- Managing change orders.
- Managing bill of materials.
- Permissions control over files.

1.3 Assembly Specification Tree

This section discusses the following methods of customizing the specification tree for a CATIA Product:

- Node Customization
- Graph Tree Reordering

Node Customization

When working in the Assembly Design workbench, the specification tree displays component part numbers and instance numbers by default.

Select **Tools>Options** to open the Options dialog box. Expand **Infrastructure** and select **Product Structure** in the tree. Select the *Nodes Customization* tab. The nodes of the specification tree can be customized to report information, such as **Description**, **Revision**, and **Source** (vendor information).

Figure 1–2 shows the *Nodes Customization* tab.

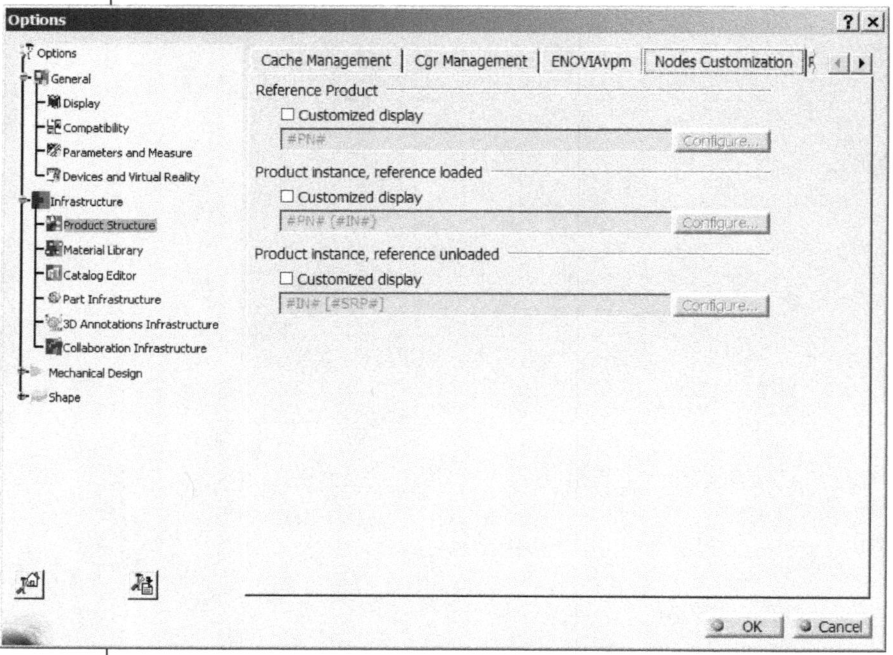

Figure 1–2

Graph Tree Reordering

You can reorder the children of the top level product or any of its subassemblies.

The Graph tree reordering element is useful for reordering components of a product.

How To: Reorder Parts in a Product

1. In Product Structure Tools toolbar, click (Graph tree reordering) and select the product whose children are to be reordered. The Graph tree reordering dialog box opens as shown in Figure 1–3.

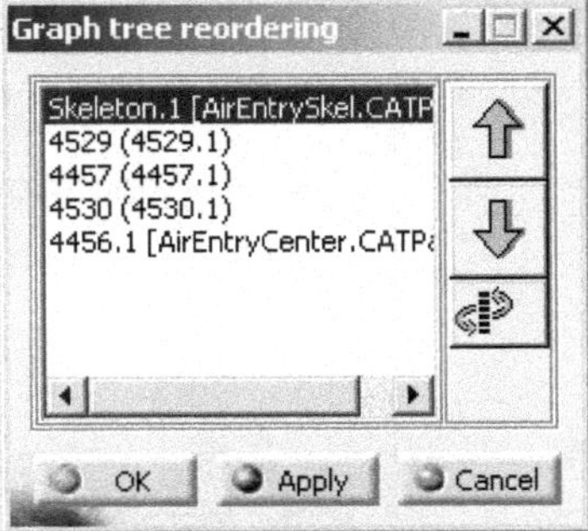

Figure 1–3

2. Use the following options to reorder components:
   - Click to move the selected components up one step in the product specification tree.
   - Click to move the selected component down one step in the product specification tree.
   - Click and another component to switch its position in the specification tree.
3. Click **Apply** to apply changes.
4. Click **OK** to complete the Graph tree reordering feature.

1.4 Assembly Annotations

Annotations can be added to an assembly to identify various parts and components. The Annotations toolbar is shown in Figure 1–4. The following types of annotations can be created:

- Weld Feature
- Text with Leader
- Flag Note with Leader
- Front View/Annotation Plane
- 3D-Annotation-Query Switch On/Switch Off

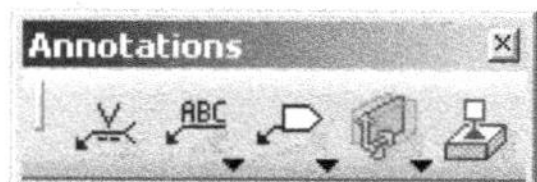

Figure 1–4

Click (Text with Leader) to create a text note and then select an element to attach the leader. The Text Editor dialog box opens as shown in Figure 1–5 in which you can enter text.

To add another line of text to a note, press <Shift>+<Enter>.

Figure 1–5

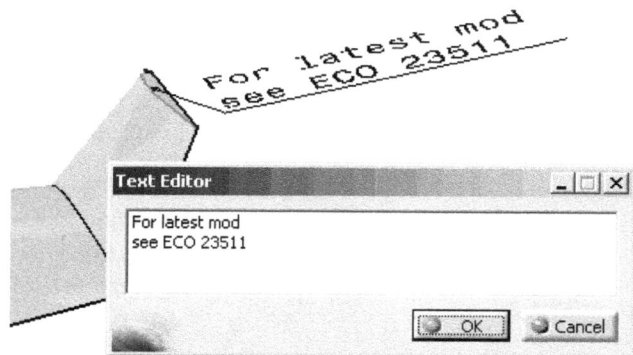

Views can be hidden.

Annotation features are added under the Annotation node in the specification tree. For example, a front view is automatically created with annotations, as shown in Figure 1–6.

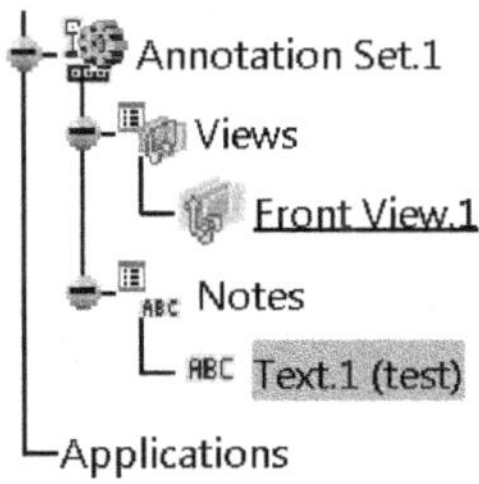

Figure 1–6

Multiple notes can be associated with a single view. A view is useful for displaying all of the notes with one model orientation setting.

1.5 Assembly Constraints

When creating features for part models, parent/child relationships result from geometrical, dimensional, and depth option references between features. When working with parts in a Product file, parent/child relationships are established through assembly constraints.

Assembly constraints are created using the Constraints toolbar shown in Figure 1–7.

Figure 1–7

The constraints are described as follows:

Icon	Description
	Coincidence: Aligns axes, planar surfaces, planes, and points.
	Contact: Mates two planar surfaces and can force curved surfaces to touch.
	Offset: Specifies an offset distance between two planar elements.
	Angle: Permits a keyed-in value between planar selections. Parallel and perpendicular can also be specified.
	Fix: Constrains a component in 3D space. This option constrains all six degrees of freedom.
	Fix Together: Prompts you for a name and applies a Fix constraint between two or more components.
	Quick Constraint: Enables the system to automatically select the constraint to use, based on your selection. This constraint can be changed later.

To change the type of existing constraint, click (Change Constraint) and select the new constraint type in the Possible Constraints dialog box, as shown in Figure 1–8.

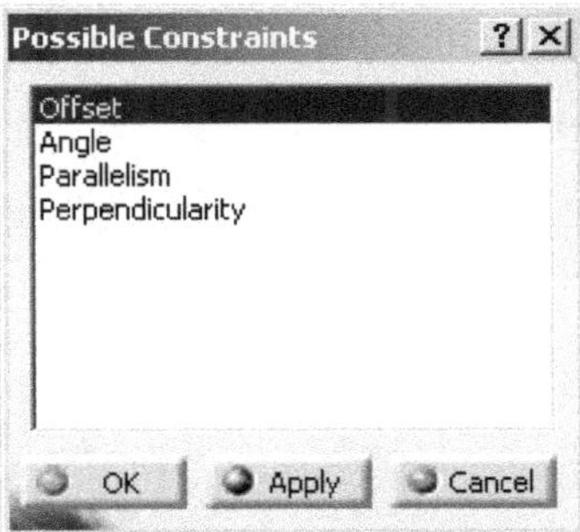

Figure 1–8

Constraint Creation

Three different constraint creation modes can be activated. The system stays in the selected mode until a different mode has been selected. The Constraint Creation toolbar is shown in Figure 1–9.

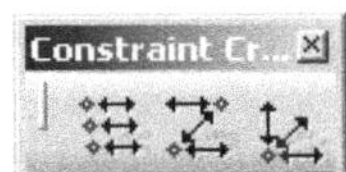

Figure 1–9

The three constraint creation modes are described as follows:

Mode	Description
	Default mode: Selects references selected between two components.
	Chain mode: Selects references from multiple components to be incrementally offset.
	Stack mode: Selects a common reference for multiple components.

1.6 Reconnecting Constraints

If an incorrect constraint reference is selected or if the design requires a change to the references of an existing constraint, the constraint must be reconnected. Two components with constraints that need to be reconnected are shown in Figure 1–10.

Figure 1–10

General Steps

Use the following general steps to reconnect a constraint:

1. Edit the constraint.
2. Select new reference(s).
3. Update the assembly.

Step 1 - Edit the constraint.

Double-click on the constraint in the specification tree. Click **More** in the Constraint Definition dialog box, as shown in Figure 1–11.

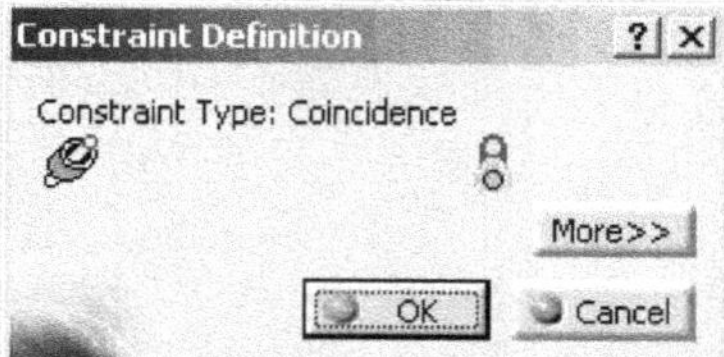

Figure 1–11

Double-click on the *Connected in the Status* column of the reference to be changed. The Plane reference of Fuselage part is being redefined, as shown in Figure 1–12.

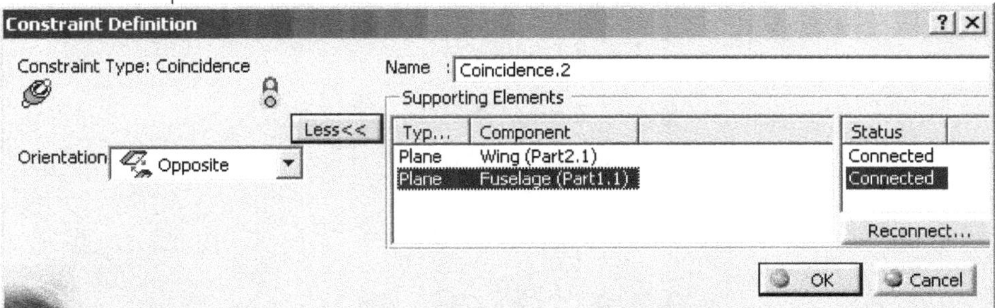

Figure 1–12

Step 2 - Select new reference(s).

Select a new element to be referenced in the specification tree or on the display. Click **OK** to complete the constraint definition.

Step 3 - Update the assembly.

Click (Update All) to update the assembly constraints. The updated assembly displays as shown in Figure 1–13.

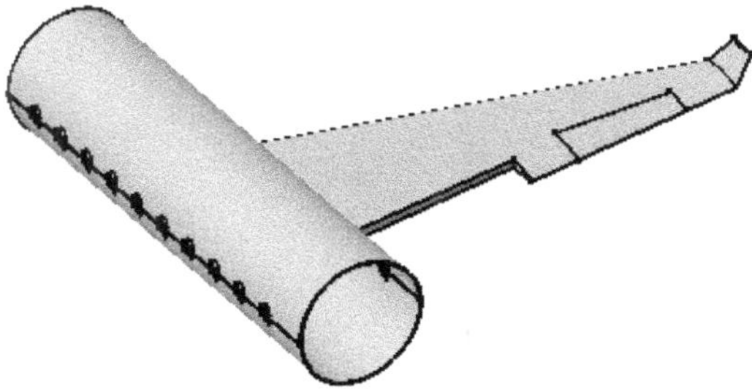

Figure 1–13

1.7 Save Operations

New or modified files should be saved frequently to prevent data loss. Files can be saved using a variety of options:

- Save
- Save As
- Save All
- Save Management
- Send To

Save

To save a file without renaming it, click (Save) in the Standard toolbar or select **File>Save**. Using this option requires no further input from you.

Save As

If the file is being saved for the first time, the **Save As** option is performed automatically. You can also use this option to rename a file or save a file to another format. Select **File>Save As** to open the Save As dialog box, as shown in Figure 1–14. The current name of the file displays in the *File name* field. To rename the file, replace the name in the *File name* field with the required name. Click **Save** to save the file to the hard drive.

By default, the file is saved as a .CATProduct file. You can change the type of file by selecting the file format in the ***Save as type*** *drop-down list.*

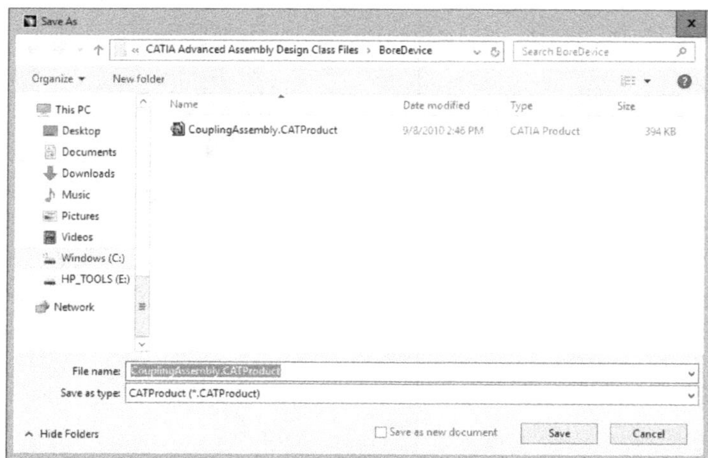

Figure 1–14

Save All

The **Save All** option performs the **Save** command on all open modified documents. This option enables you to save several open documents simultaneously. To perform the operation, select **File>Save All**. If the **Save** operation can be performed on the documents without any user input, a prompt box opens as shown in Figure 1–15. Click **Yes** to save all of the modified open documents.

If any of the files to be saved requires additional user input, the prompt box shown in Figure 1–16 opens. Click **OK** to continue.

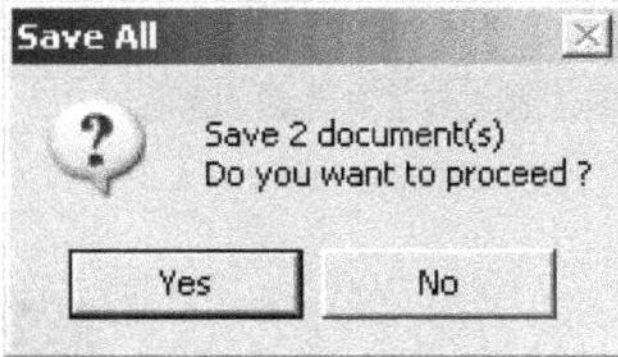

Figure 1–15

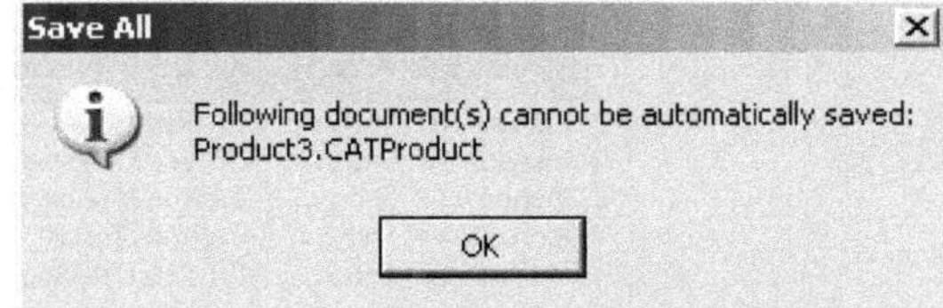

Figure 1–16

If documents cannot be automatically saved, the Save All dialog box opens. It lists all of the open modified files that require additional input to be saved. For example, in Figure 1–17 two files require additional input before they can be saved. The first file is a new file, indicating that it has never been saved to the hard drive. The second file is a read-only file and cannot be saved to the same location with the same name. In both cases, select the file and click **Save As** to perform a Save As operation on the selected file. Once all of the files listed in the window have had a **Save As** performed on them, click **OK** to complete the **Save All**.

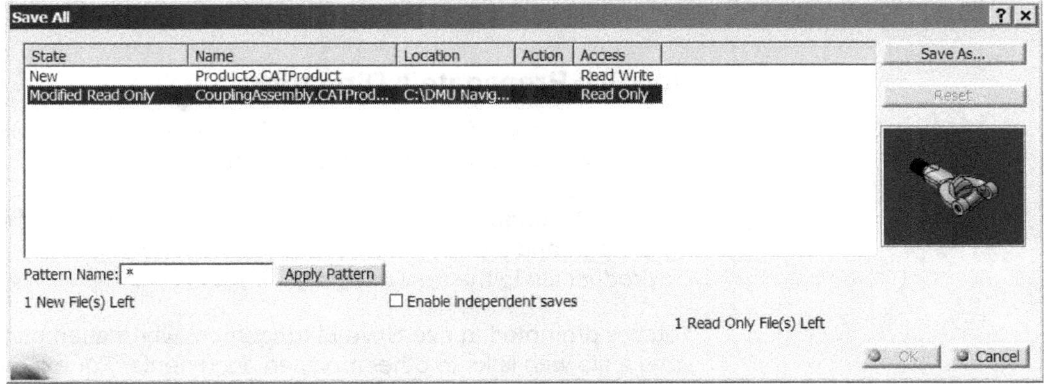

Figure 1–17

Save Management

The **Save Management** option enables you to control where all open files are saved. This option is useful when you need to rename multiple files.

How To: Rename the Part Files of a Product

1. Select **File>Save Management**.
2. Select the part file in the Save Management dialog box, as shown in Figure 1–18.

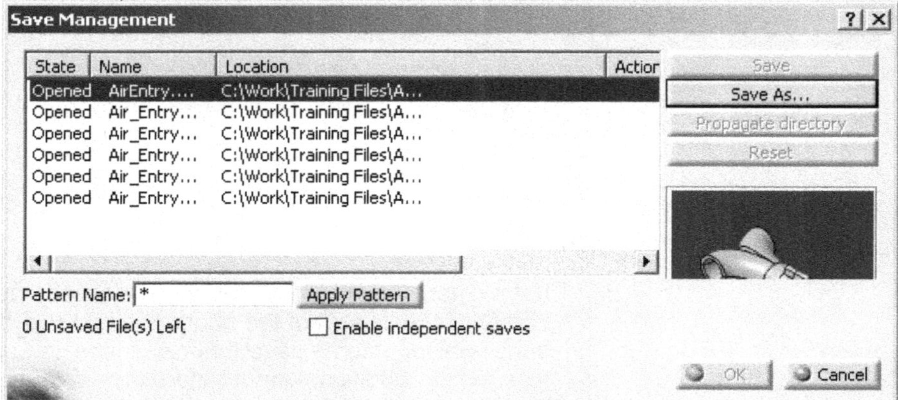

Figure 1–18

3. Click **Save As** and enter new name for the part file.

Save Management is also useful for exploring an alternative product development path. **Propagate directory** enables you to create a copy of a complete assembly in a different directory. The part and product files from the new directory can then be modified and re-configured without affecting the original product and part files.

How To: Propagate a Directory

1. Select a product file in the Save Management dialog box.
2. Click **Save As**. Specify a different directory to save the product file.
3. Click **Propagate directory**. The system saves a copy of all of the part and product files associated with the selected product file to the new directory.

You are prompted to use Save Management when attempting to save a file with links to other modified documents. For example, when a product is saved and contains a part that has been altered, the prompt box shown in Figure 1–19 opens.

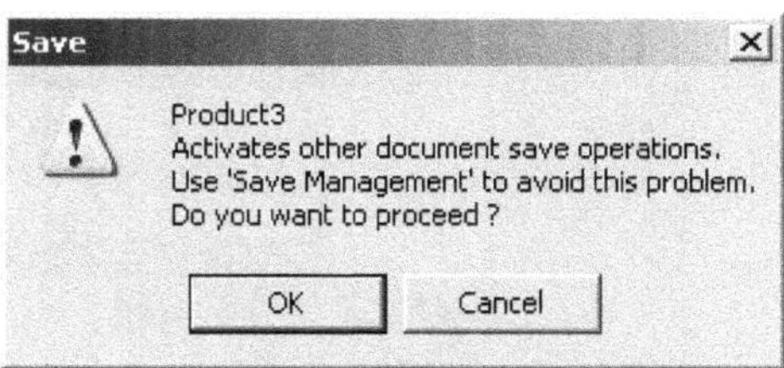

Figure 1–19

If you proceed with the **Save** option, only the selected document is saved and not the other modified documents. Instead, try clicking **Cancel** to abort the **Save** option and then using the **Save Management** or **Save All** option to avoid problems.

Send To

The **Send To** option copies a product and all of its linked files to a specified directory or attaches them to an e-mail. This option ensures that all of the files required to open a product file are included in an e-mail or moved with the product file.

How To: Perform a Send To Operation

*In this example, **Send To Directory** was selected. The Send To Mail dialog box is the same but does not have the Copy to field at the bottom of the dialog box.*

1. Select **File>Send To>Mail** or **File>Send To>Directory**. The Send to dialog box opens. The top window lists the selected product file and all of the files linked to it, as shown in Figure 1–20.

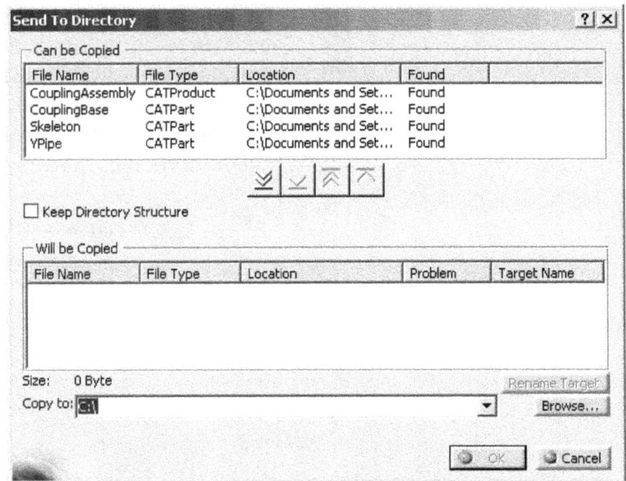

Figure 1–20

2. Click to copy the product and all of its associated files to the *E-mail* directory. The files move from the top window to the bottom window, as shown in Figure 1–21.

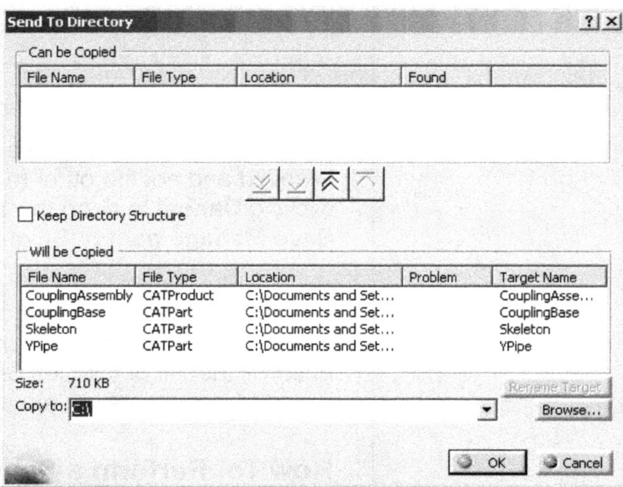

Figure 1–21

3. If the **Send To Directory** operation is performed, the files are copied to the directory indicated in the *Copy to* field. To change the directory, click **Browse** and locate the correct directory. The *Copy To* field updates to reflect the change.
4. Click **OK** to complete the copy.
5. If you have selected to **Send To Mail**, an e-mail opens with the copied files attached. If you have selected **Send To Directory**, a message window opens, notifying you that the copy was successful, as shown in Figure 1–22.

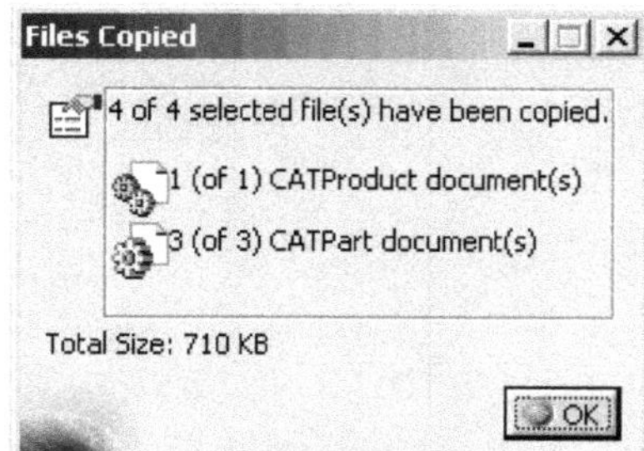

Figure 1–22

1.8 Desk Command

When a CATIA product model is created, file paths to component files (e.g., *.CATPart and *.CATProduct) are written to the Product file. If the system cannot locate these files during retrieval, a message window opens, similar to the one shown in Figure 1–23.

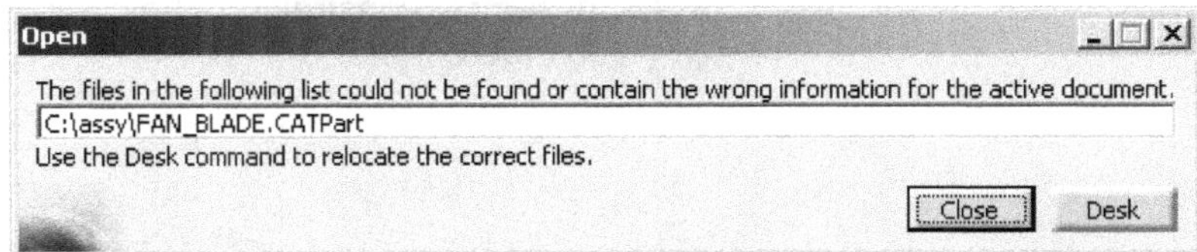

Figure 1–23

If **Close** is clicked, the system does not include the missing component in the assembly.

If **Desk** is clicked, a Desk window opens, displaying the assembly and its components in a tree. Any missing components are highlighted in red. To locate the missing component, right-click on it in the tree and select **Find**, as shown in Figure 1–24.

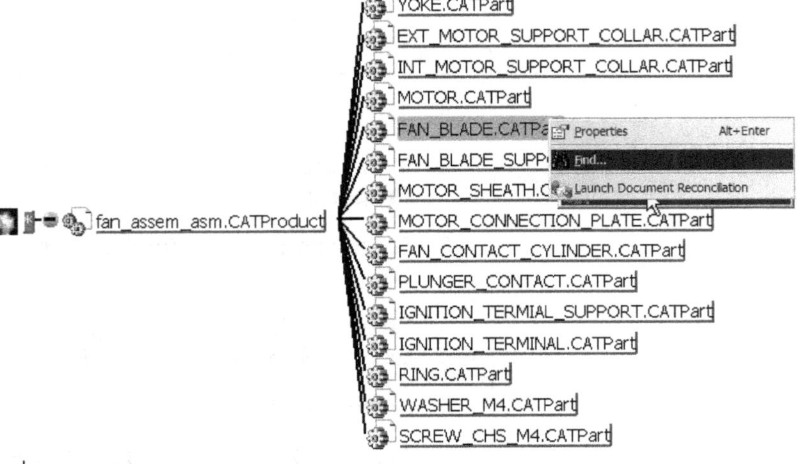

Figure 1–24

6. The system then opens a File Selection dialog box for you to browse for the missing component. Once the component has been located, the Desk window can be closed.

Practice 1a Assembly Creation

Practice Objectives

- Create a Product file.
- Assemble components.

In this practice, you will create an assembly using a variety of assembly constraints. The completed model displays as shown in Figure 1–25.

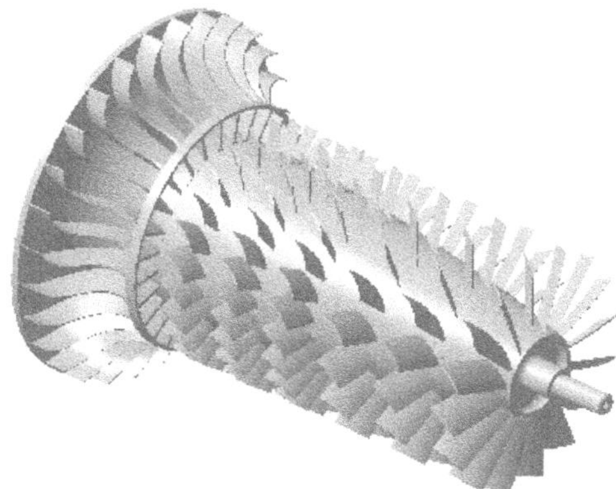

Figure 1–25

Task 1 - Create a Product file.

1. Select **File>New** and create a new Product file.
2. In the specification tree, right-click on **Product1** and select **Properties**.
3. For the part number for the product, enter **71499** and click **OK**.
4. Select **Tools>Options** to open the Options dialog box. Expand **General** and select **Parameters and Measure**.
5. Select the *Units* tab.
6. Set *units for length* to **Millimeters(mm)**.
7. Save the product in the Turbine directory with the name **CompressorRotor**.

Task 2 - Assemble Impeller.CATPart.

1. Ensure that the Assembly Design workbench is active. If not, select **Start>Mechanical Design>Assembly Design**.

2. Click (Existing Component). In the specification tree, select **71499**.

3. In the *Turbine* directory, select **Impeller.CATPart**.

4. In the Constraints toolbar, click (Fix Component) and select the **Impeller** model. The component displays with the fix component anchor symbol, as shown in Figure 1–26.

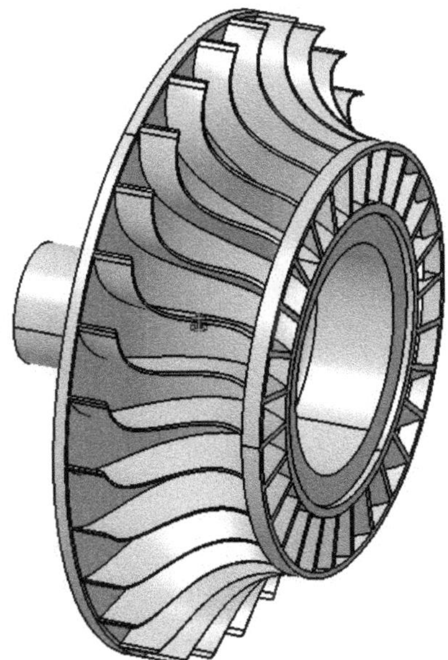

Figure 1–26

Task 3 - Define Node Customization for the specification tree.

1. Select **Tools>Options** to open the Options dialog box.

2. Expand **Infrastructure** and select **Product Structure**.

3. Select the *Nodes Customization* tab. The Options dialog box opens as shown in Figure 1–27.

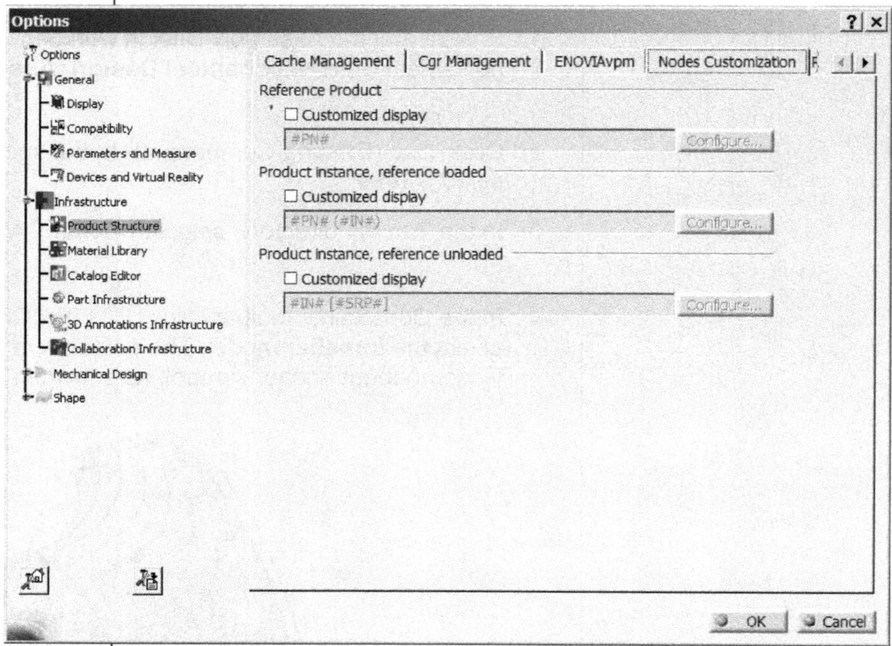

Figure 1–27

4. In the *Product instance, reference loaded* field, select **Customized display**, as shown in Figure 1–28.

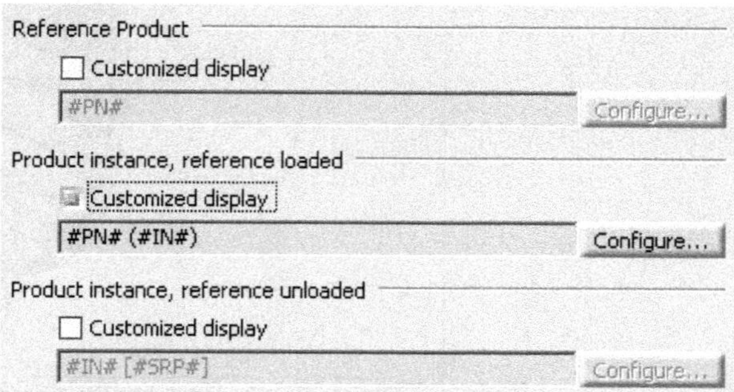

Figure 1–28

5. Click **Configure**. The Configure customized display dialog box opens as shown in Figure 1–29.

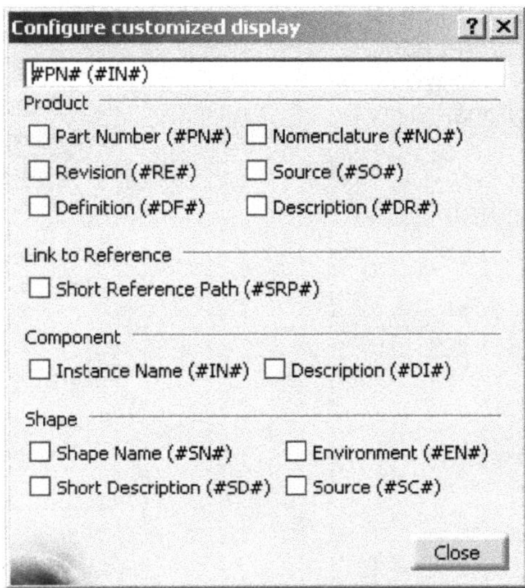

Figure 1–29

6. Clear the contents in the upper field, as shown in Figure 1–30.

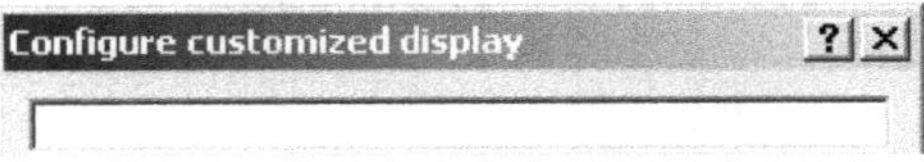

Figure 1–30

7. Select the **Part Number (#PN#)**

8. Add a left side bracket and select **Short Description (#SD#)**.

9. Add a right side bracket. The *Display* field displays as shown in Figure 1–31.

The Short Description is the filename of the part. Products do not have short descriptions.

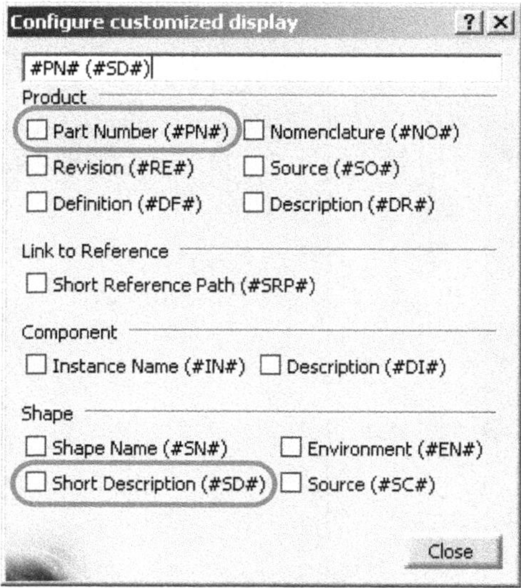

Figure 1–31

10. Click **Close** to close the Configure customized display dialog box.

11. Click **OK** to close the Options dialog box. The specification tree displays as shown in Figure 1–32.

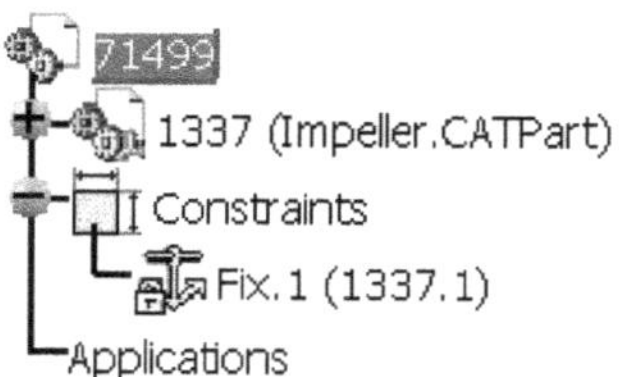

Figure 1–32

Task 4 - Assemble 6thStage.CATPart.

1. In the specification tree, right-click on **71499** and select **Components>Existing Component**.

2. Open **6thStage.CATPart**. The model displays in its default location on top of the impeller.

3. Use the compass to reposition **6thStage**. Right-click on the red box on the compass and select **Snap Automatically to Selected Object**.

4. In the specification tree, select **1296**. The compass snaps to the component.

5. Drag the compass to reposition **6thStage**, as shown in Figure 1–33.

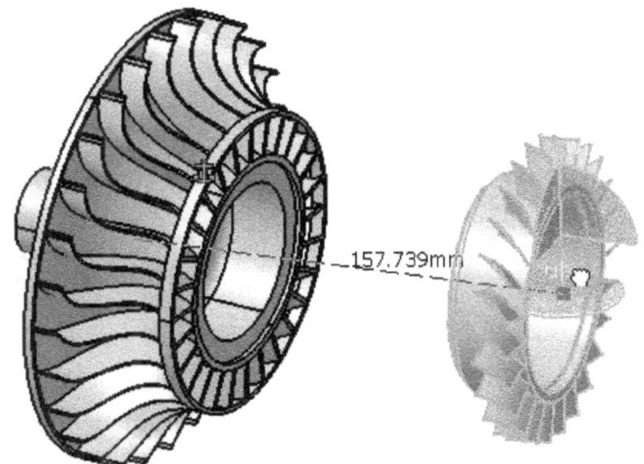

Figure 1–33

6. Drag the compass off **6thStage**.

7. Click (Coincidence Constraint).

8. Select the implicit axis of **6thStage** and the **Impeller**, as shown in Figure 1–34.

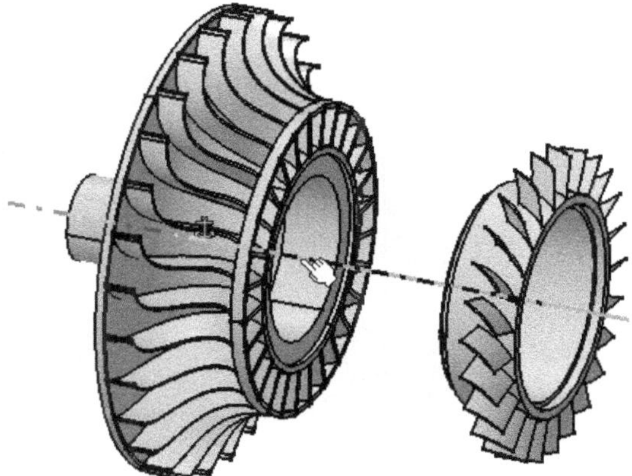

Figure 1–34

9. Click (Contact Constraint).

10. Select the surface on **Impeller** shown in Figure 1–35.

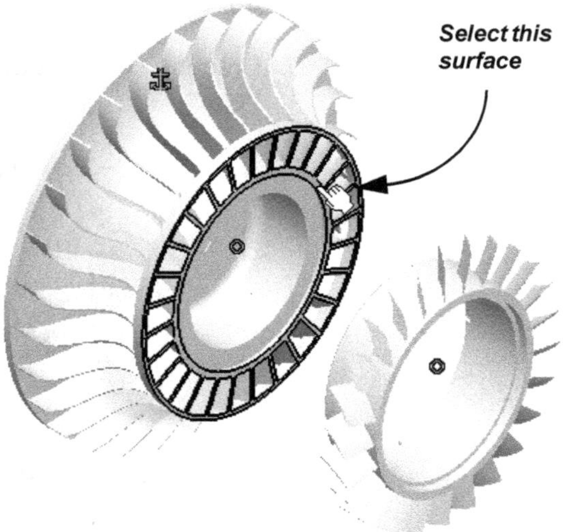

Figure 1–35

11. Reorient the model and select the surface on **6thStage**, as shown in Figure 1–36.

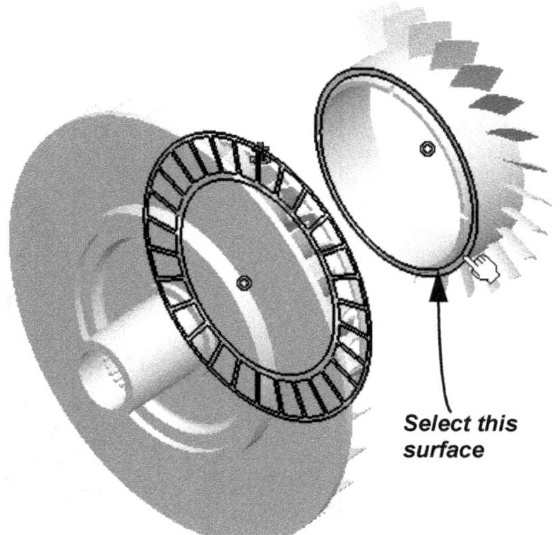

Figure 1–36

12. Click (Update All) to update the assembly, as shown in Figure 1–37.

Figure 1–37

Task 5 - Assemble 5thStage.CATPart.

1. Insert the **5thStage.CATPart**.
2. Use the compass to reposition **5thStage**.
3. Create a Coincidence constraint between the implicit axis of **5thStage** and **6thStage**.
4. Create a Contact constraint between the two surfaces shown in Figure 1–38.

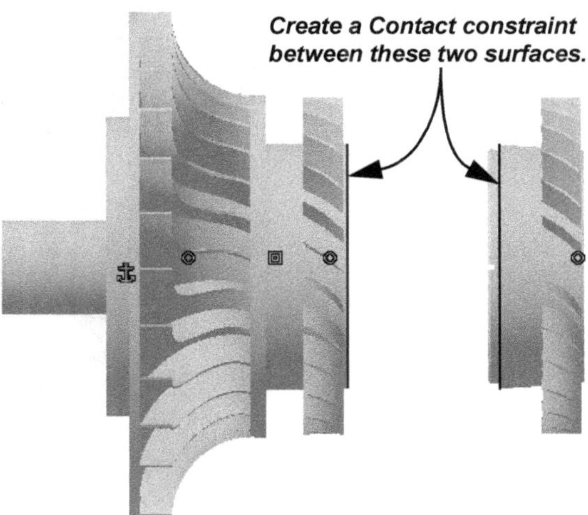

Figure 1–38

5. Add a third constraint to orient **5thStage**. Zoom in on the locating tab of **6thStage**, as shown in Figure 1–39.

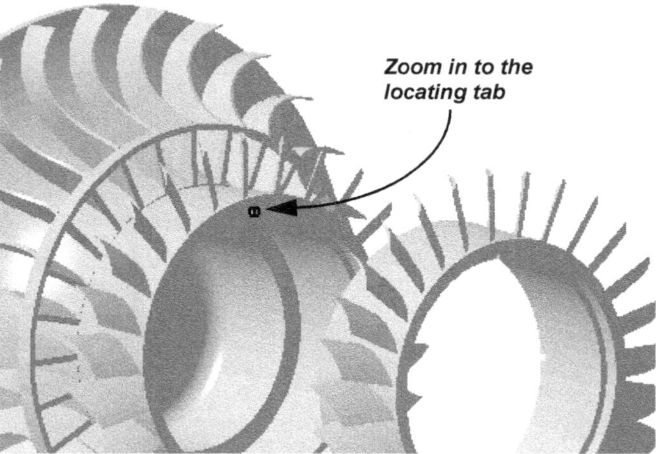

Figure 1–39

6. Click (Angle Constraint) and create a Parallelism constraint between the surface of **6thStage** shown in Figure 1–40 and the surface of **5thStage** shown in Figure 1–41. Ensure that the *Orientation* is set to **Same**.

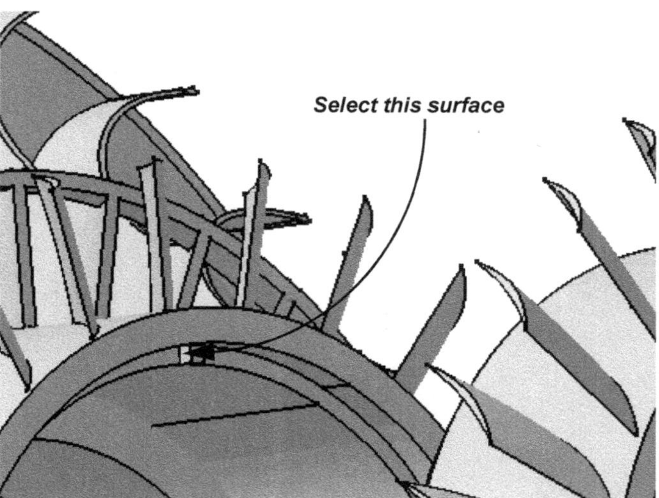

Figure 1–40

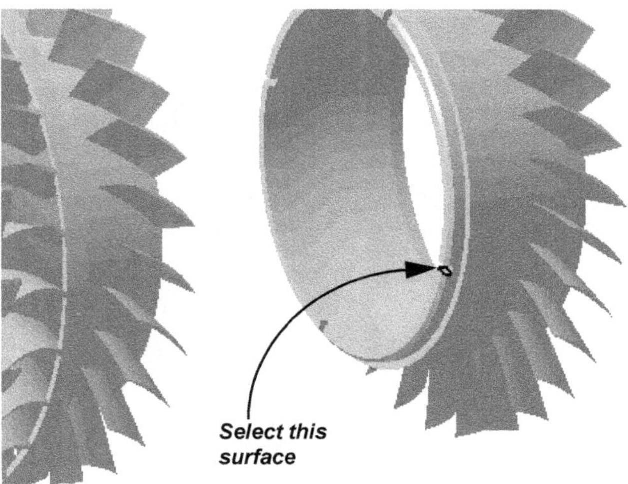

Figure 1–41

7. Click (Update All).

8. Click (Isometric View).

   The assembly displays as shown in Figure 1–42.

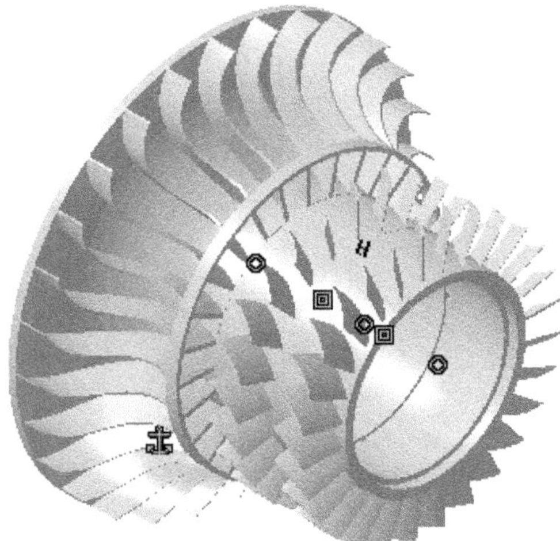

Figure 1–42

Task 6 - Assemble the remaining turbine wheel components.

1. Insert the remaining components of the assembly. When selecting the components to open, use <Ctrl> to select **4thStage**, **2nd3rdStage**, and **1stStage**.

2. Use the compass to drag each component out to new locations, as shown in Figure 1–43.

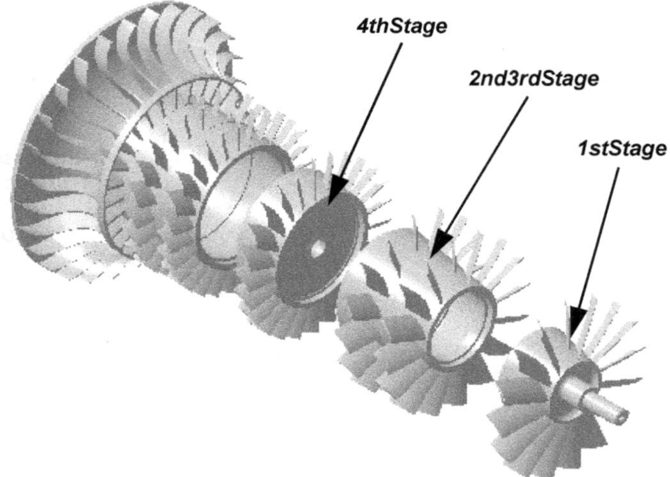

Figure 1–43

Task 7 - Change the constraint creation mode.

1. In the Constraint Creation toolbar, click (Stack Mode).

2. Double-click on (Coincidence Constraint).

3. Select the axis of **1337**, as shown in Figure 1–44.

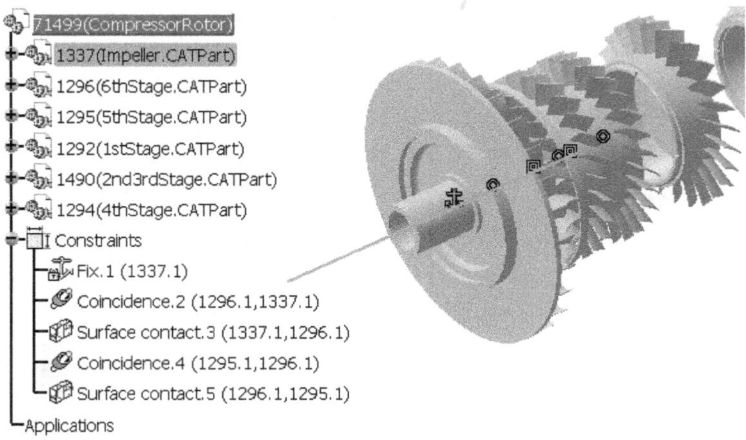

Figure 1–44

4. Select the axes of the three turbine wheels, as shown in Figure 1–45.

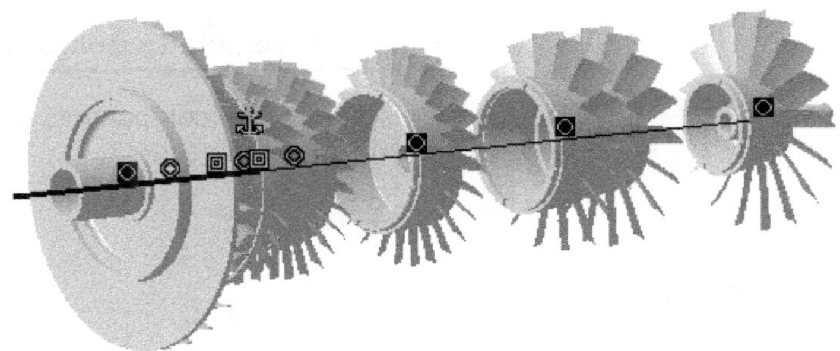

Figure 1–45

5. Set the constraint creation mode to (Default).
6. Create three Parallelism constraints between the turbine wheels.
7. Create three Contact constraints between the turbine wheels.
8. Click (Update All).

9. In the specification tree, right-click on the Constraints node and select **Hide/Show**. The updated model displays as shown in Figure 1–46.

Figure 1–46

Task 8 - Assemble TieBolt.CATPart.

1. Hide all of the components except **Impeller** and **1stStage**, as shown in Figure 1–47.

When selecting components to hide, select them in the specification tree, otherwise you might only hide the PartBody and not the complete instance of the part.

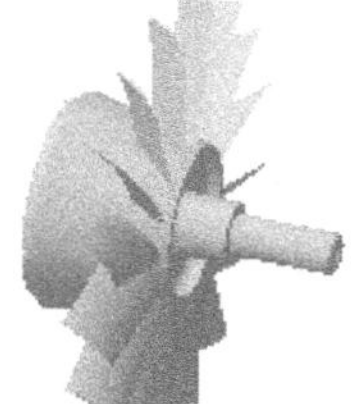

Figure 1–47

2. Insert **TieBolt.CATPart**.

3. Apply a Contact constraint to the surface of **TieBolt**, as shown in Figure 1–48 and to the back surface of **Impeller**, as shown in Figure 1–49.

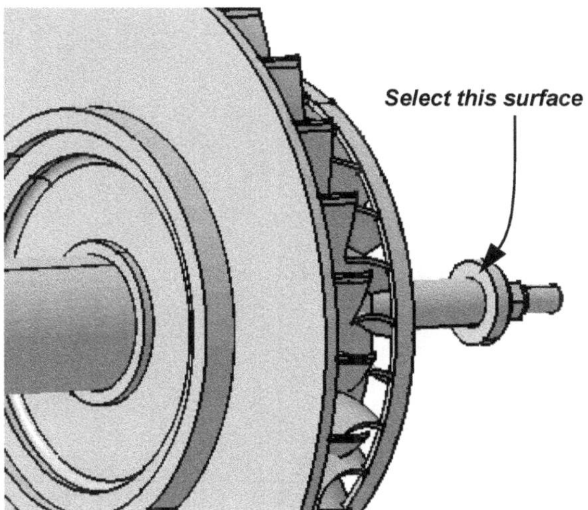

Figure 1–48

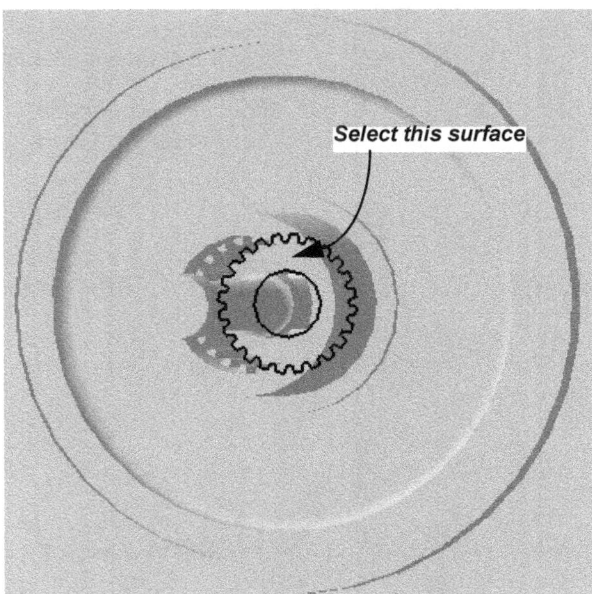

Figure 1–49

4. Constrain the axes of **TieBolt** and **Impeller** and update the assembly. The assembly displays as shown in Figure 1–50.

Figure 1–50

Task 9 - Change update options and assemble Coupling.CATPart.

1. Select **Tools>Options**. Expand Mechanical Design and select **Assembly Design**.
2. Select the *General* tab and select the **Automatic** option in the *Update* area, as shown in Figure 1–51.

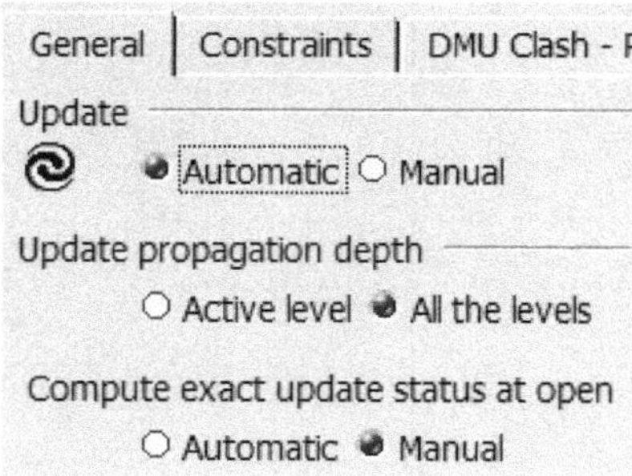

Figure 1–51

3. Click **OK** to close the Options dialog box.
4. Hide the **Impeller (1337)**.

5. Assemble **Coupling.CATPart** to the impeller end of the tiebolt, as shown in Figure 1–52.

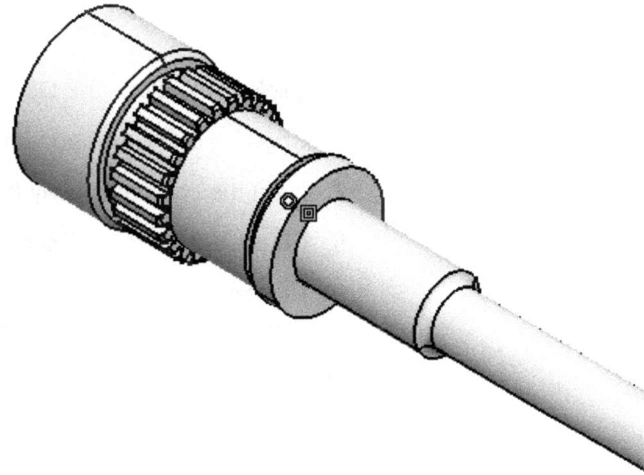

Figure 1–52

Note that the system automatically updates the constraints on creation.

Task 10 - Restore options.

1. Select **Tools>Options**. The Options dialog box opens, displaying the *General* tab in **Assembly Design**.

2. Click (Reset parameters values to default ones). The Reset dialog box opens as shown in Figure 1–53.

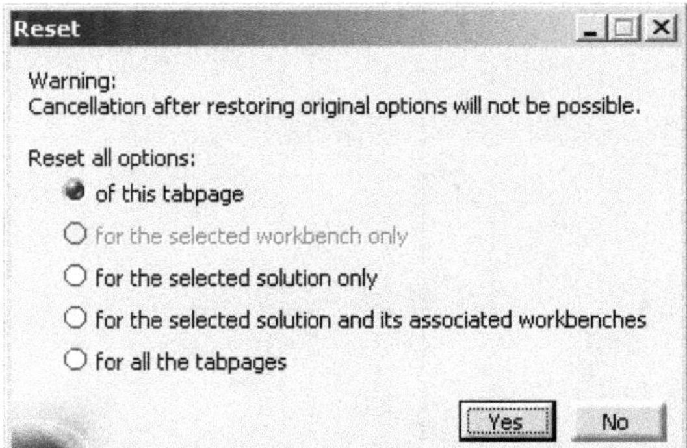

Figure 1–53

3. Click **Yes** to restore the options in the *General* tab.
4. Select **Infrastructure>Product Structure>***Nodes Customization* **tab** and repeat Steps 2 and 3 to restore the settings.
5. Click **OK** to close the Options dialog box.
6. Show all of the components,
7. Drag the compass away from the parts.
8. Select **View>Reset Compass**.
9. Right-click on the compass and clear the **Snap Automatically to Selected Object** option.
10. Save the model and close the file.

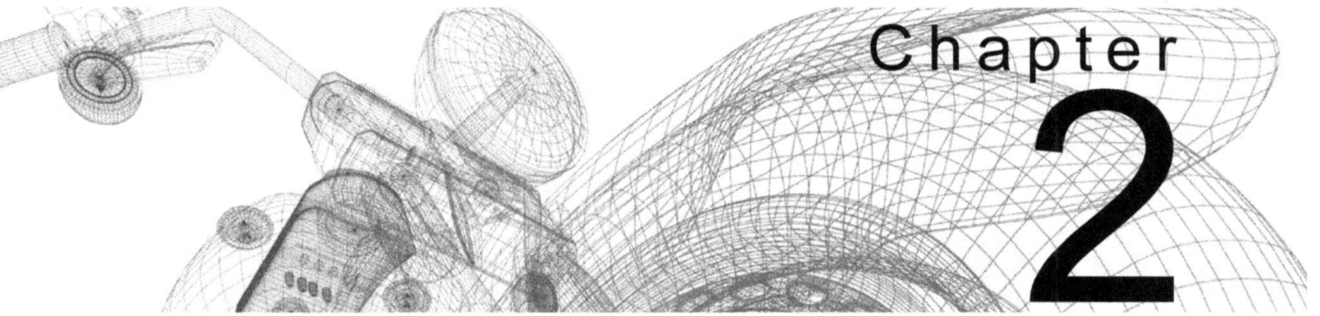

Designing with Skeletons

Skeleton models are part files that only contain surfaces and reference geometry. Skeleton models help maintain the design intent of a model by including all of the vital volume requirements of components in a product. When using the top-down design method, skeletons are an intricate step.

Learning Objectives in this Chapter

- Understand the use of Skeleton models.
- Understand how contextual design is used to create part geometry in the context of an assembly model.
- Use publications to identify and select elements to be externally referenced.
- Use skeleton models to share parameters between assemblies and components.
- Create a skeleton.

2.1 Skeleton Modeling

Skeleton models create an underlying structure for product files. The skeleton model is a standard CATPart file. This file acts as a three-dimensional layout of an assembly to facilitate a top-down design.

Skeleton models generally consist of wireframe features, surface features, and parameter information. Parts are then constrained to or created from them.

Parent/Child Relationships

Constraining parts to a skeleton model instead of to other parts reduces unwanted parent/child relationships. Deleting and replacing parts is also easier because fewer dependency relationships exist between parts.

Volume Control

Creating parts from a skeleton model ensures that they fit the location and volume requirements of the product. Skeleton models can be used to create a conceptual part that defines a region of a product. This region represents the volume to be occupied or avoided by one or more parts that have yet to be created. The skeleton model can then be referenced during the creation of these parts to ensure that they fit the location and volume limitations. For example, when designing a car, the frame or body is designed around the engine. The space claimed by the engine can be represented by a skeleton and the frame and body data can be designed around the constraint.

Styling Data

The skeleton model is also a central location for all of the styling data that is created. The surfaces or curves can then be used across a number of different components in the assembly to control their shape.

2.2 Contextual Design

To better understand how skeleton models facilitate the development of assembly geometry, this section introduces contextual design methods. Contextual design is the process of creating part geometry in the context of an assembly model. This provides the advantage of being able to reference the geometry of other part and assembly models while developing geometry for the active part. Contextual design is the mechanism through which skeleton geometry can be used throughout the assembly.

When designing parts in context, you must be aware of any external references being created. An external reference can be created when a reference outside the active part is selected. When you select geometry from Part A to create a feature in Part B, a dependency is generated. The feature in Part B cannot be modified or updated unless Part A is present. Therefore, it is important to only generate external references when they are required to drive the design intent of the model.

An external reference can be created in the following cases:

- Selecting a support
- Creating geometrical constraints
- Creating dimensional constraints
- Specifying a depth option requiring a selection
- Projecting 3D or silhouette edges

General Steps

Use the following general steps to create components in context:

1. Set external reference options.
2. (Optional) Publish elements.
3. Activate or create a part file.
4. Develop geometry in the context of the assembly.
5. Save the part.

Step 1 - Set external reference options.

Select **Tools>Options>Infrastructure>Part Infrastructure**. Select the *General* tab and activate the required options.

External Reference Settings

You can control how external references are created and handled. A company standard that requires everyone to use the same options is recommended to promote consistency.

To set external reference options, select **Tools>Options> Infrastructure>Part Infrastructure**. Select the *General* tab as shown in Figure 2–1.

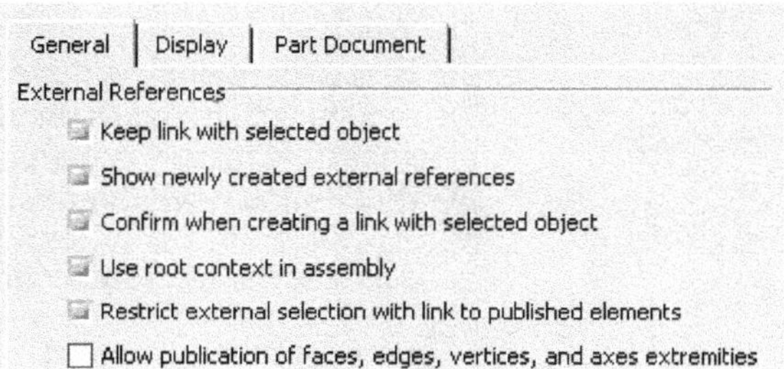

Figure 2–1

You can set the following options for external references:

- **Keep link with selected object:** Maintains a link between the source part and the target part. If this option is cleared, reference elements are copied to the target part as a geometrical set and do not associatively update.
- **Show newly created external references:** Displays external references that are created. If this option is cleared, external references are automatically hidden in the target part.
- **Confirm when creating a link with selected object:** Causes the Selection In Context warning dialog box to open, as shown in Figure 2–2.

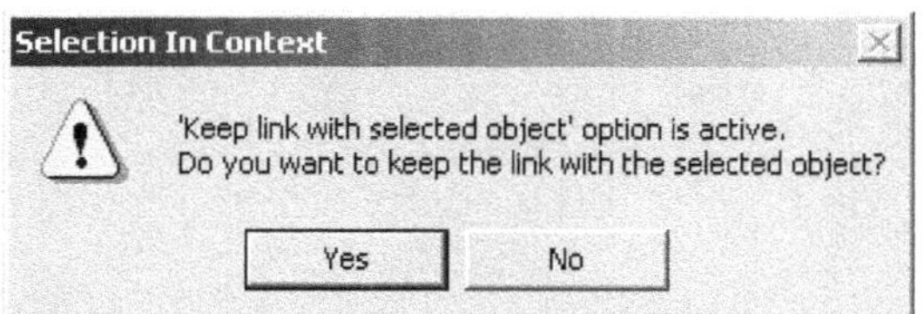

Figure 2–2

This dialog box indicates that a link is created when selecting an external reference. At this point, you can disable the **Keep link with selected object** option by clicking **No**.

- **Use root context in assembly:** Determines the assembly level used to develop a contextual link between two parts. When this option is selected, the top-level assembly is always used to develop a contextual link, regardless of the level of the two parts. When the option is cleared, the subassembly closest to the two parts is used.

  This setting impacts a designer when they are trying to update or modify the contextual links that have been developed. Consider the following rules:

1. You cannot create links between two parts that are at a different context level.
2. You cannot update links if the assembly context they were created in is not in session.

   Therefore, with the option selected, the top-level assembly must be loaded to update the links no matter how far down the hierarchical tree the links were created. However, with the option cleared, links cannot be created between components of two different subassemblies because it would fall outside the context.

The *Update* area in the *General* tab is shown in Figure 2–3. If the **Synchronize all external references when updating** option is selected, the system searches for any modifications to the source part and updates the target part accordingly. Selecting this option ensures that you are working with the latest version of the source part. However, this option also increases update time.

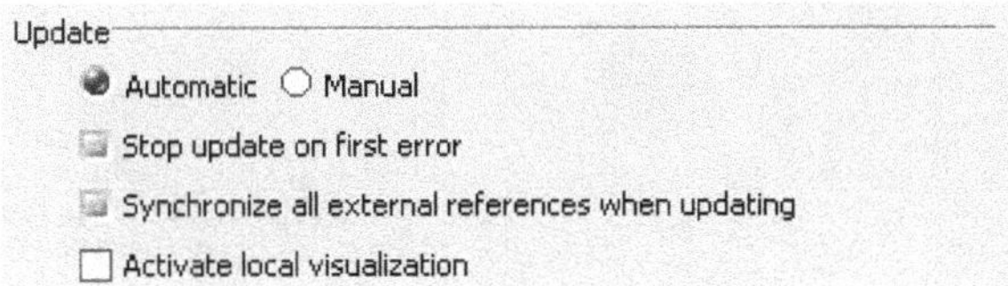

Figure 2–3

Select the *Display* tab and select **External References** from the list of options, as shown in Figure 2–4, to display the external reference branch in the specification tree.

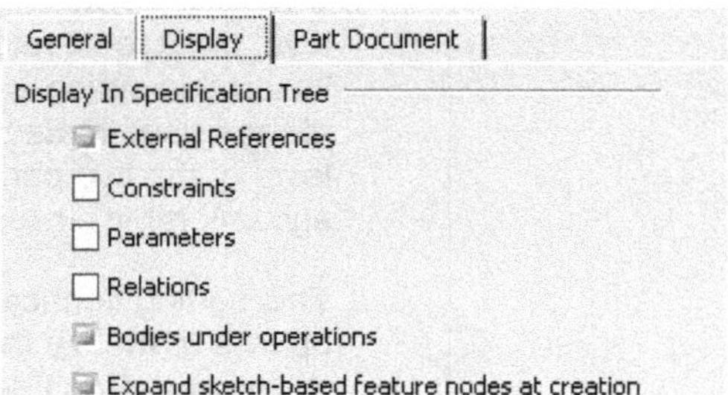

Figure 2–4

Step 2 - (Optional) Publish elements.

Publish elements of a component that you want to be used for external references.

Step 3 - Activate or create a part file.

Activate an existing part or click (Part) to create a part. If the part is being created, the origin of the new part must be specified using the New Part: Origin Point dialog box, as shown in Figure 2–5.

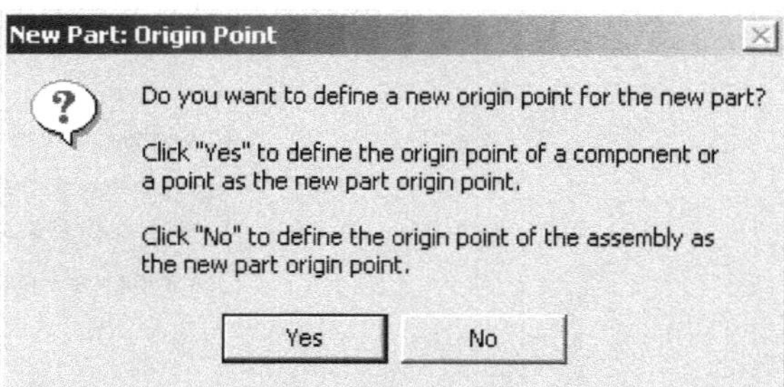

New Part: Origin Point
Do you want to define a new origin point for the new part?
Click "Yes" to define the origin point of a component or a point as the new part origin point.
Click "No" to define the origin point of the assembly as the new part origin point.
Yes
No

Figure 2–5

Step 4 - Develop geometry in the context of the assembly.

Once the part has been activated from the assembly, the system launches one of the part modeling workbenches (e.g., Part Design or Generative Shape Design), enabling you to use these modeling tools to add geometry to the active part.

When working in the context of a large assembly, it is a common practice to bring all of the required external references into the design part. Therefore, the part can be developed without needing to load the assembly.

For example, a sketch created in context is shown in Figure 2–6. The geometrical and dimensional constraints that have been developed between the sketch and the surrounding geometry. With this sketch created in the assembly context, the part can now be opened in a separate window and completed.

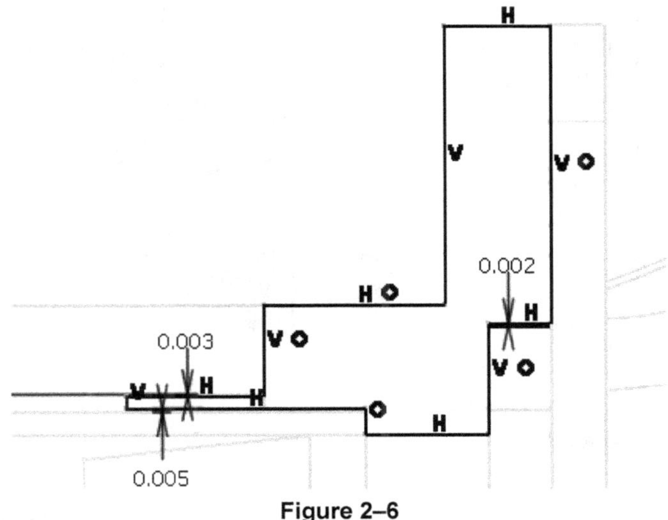

Figure 2–6

Step 5 - Save the part.

Once the external reference information is captured, enter a part number if the part is new, and save it with a descriptive name. Open the part in the Part Design workbench and create geometry to complete the design.

2.3 Publications

A publication is an organizational and reference management tool that is used to identify and select elements to be externally referenced. When an element is published, it is added to a new Publications branch in the specification tree and can be renamed so that it can be easily identified and selected by other designers.

For example, the dashboard surface of an automobile has been published in the **DashSkel** component shown in Figure 2–7. This publication is then externally referenced by any of the dashboard components, such as the HVAC vent bezel or the storage compartment lid, to define their shape.

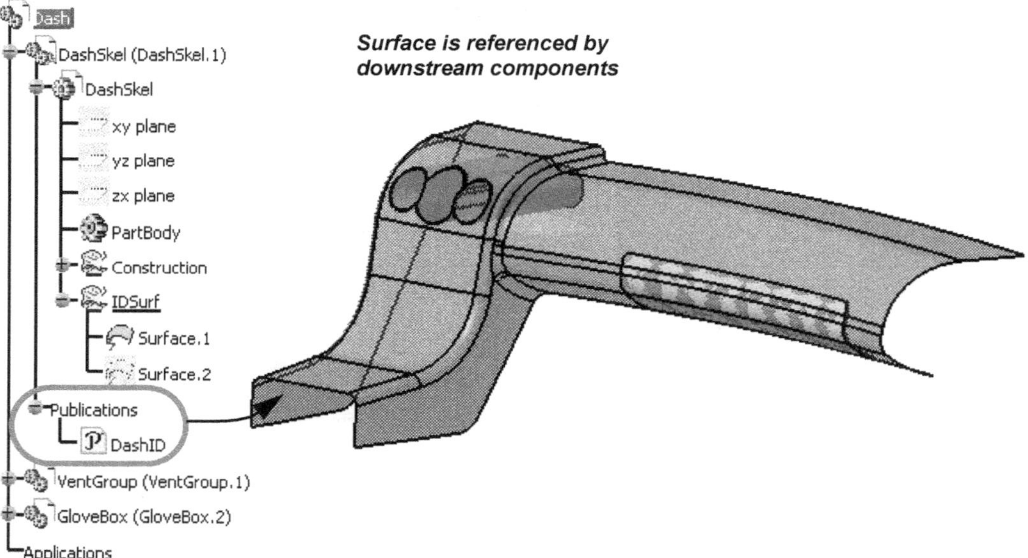

Figure 2–7

Creating this contextual link between elements ensures that the shapes of the dashboard components always match the defined design intent of the published surface. The use of publications in performing this operation acts as a controlling mechanism that defines the geometry that can be externally referenced and facilitates its selection by placing it in a separate branch in the tree.

Another benefit of publishing data is seen when integrating with a data management system, such as LCA, VPM, or SmarTeam. During the lifecycle process of data creation, links can become disconnected from their references for a number of reasons. The use of publications places the geometry at a higher level of importance by giving the publication feature its own UUID. Therefore, the publication is viewed with the same weight as an actual part file. This facilitates the management of links through the use of publications.

You can publish the following types of elements:

- Reference elements, such as points, planes, lines, and splines
- Features
- Sketches
- Bodies
- Surfaces
- Parameters
- Sub-elements, such as faces, edges, and axes

General Steps

Use the following general steps to publish elements:

1. Access the Publication settings.
2. Select elements to publish.
3. Rename published elements.
4. Complete the operation.
5. (Optional) Define options for published elements.

Step 1 - Access the Publication settings.

Before publishing elements, activate the model(s) in which you want to create published elements. In the example of the car dashboard, the **DaskSkel.CATPart** component should be activated to publish elements in the part.

Select **Tools>Publication**. The Publication dialog box opens as shown in Figure 2–8.

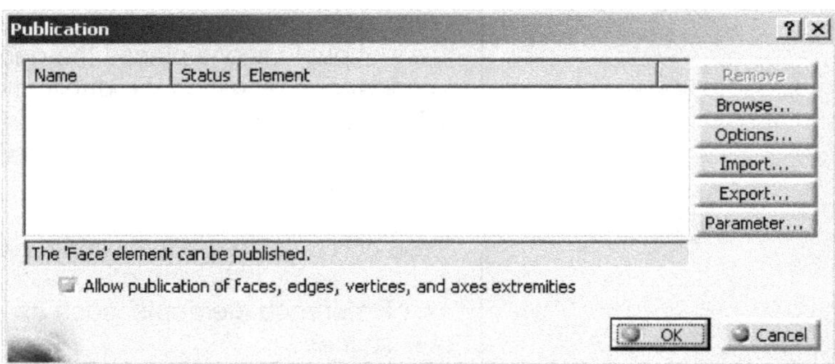

Figure 2–8

The Publication dialog box options are described as follows:

Option	Description
Remove	Removes the selected element from the Publication list.
Browse	Displays the file path and status of a publication. This option is only available at the assembly level.
Options	Sets renaming options. Enables the use of features for publication.
Import	Imports the publication names from a *.TXT ASCII file.
Export	Exports the publication names from a *.TXT ASCII file.
Parameter	Publishes a parameter.

Step 2 - Select elements to publish.

To publish an element, select it in the model or specification tree. In the car dashboard example, the Surface.1 styling surface is published. Once selected, the surface is added to the Publications dialog box, as shown in Figure 2–9.

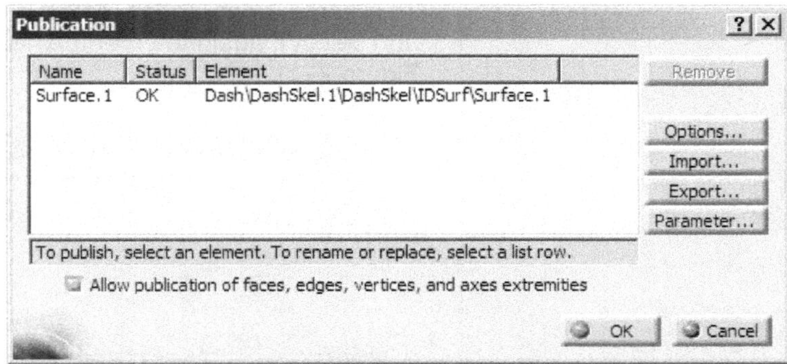

Figure 2–9

If the appropriate elements do not exist, they must be created before publishing. For example, the model in Figure 2–10 requires an element representing a rotational axis. You can publish an implicit axis by right-clicking on the cylindrical face and selecting **Other Selection**. Alternatively, you can create and publish a reference line to represent the axis.

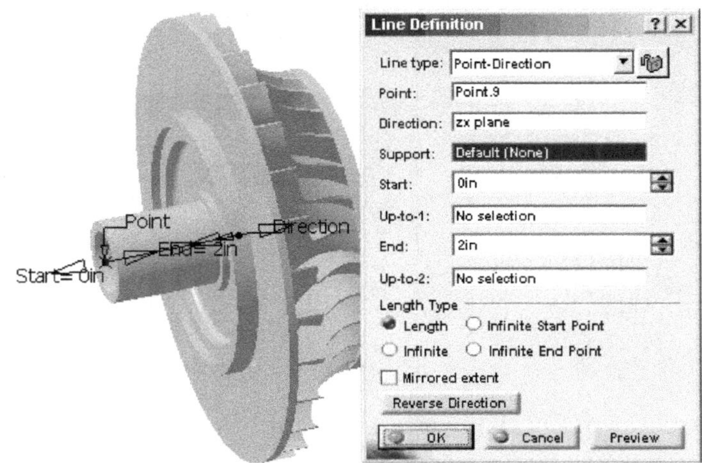

Figure 2–10

Step 3 - Rename published elements.

By default, a published element assumes the name of the element that it represents. It is a recommended that you rename either the published element or the publication, so that the end user can identify the element in the tree.

To rename a publication, select it in the Publication dialog box and select it again to enter the new name, as shown in Figure 2–11.

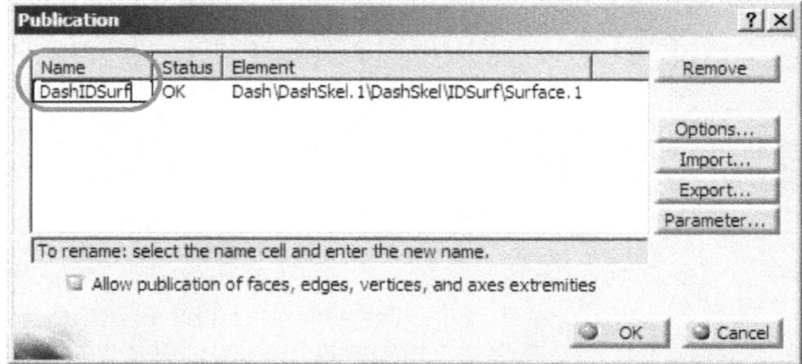

Figure 2–11

By default, the published feature is not renamed to match the name given to the publication element. If you want to rename the published feature, click **Options** and select **Ask**. Then select the cell under the *Name* column and enter the new name, as shown in Figure 2–12.

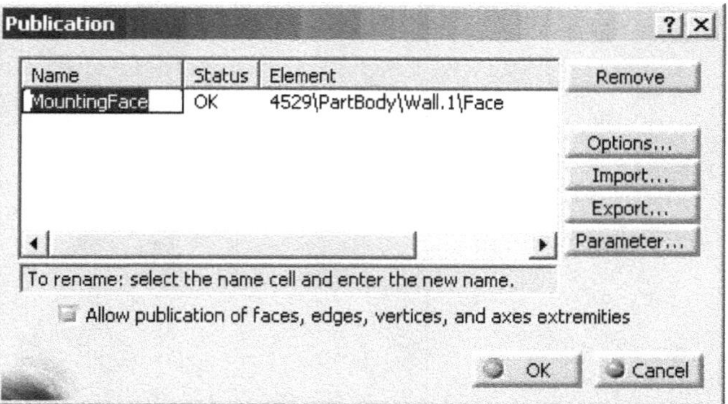

Figure 2–12

*A publication can have a different name than the feature that it represents. Click **Yes** to rename the source feature being published with the same name entered for the publication.*

When you enter the new name and press <Enter>, the Rename Element dialog box opens as shown in Figure 2–13.

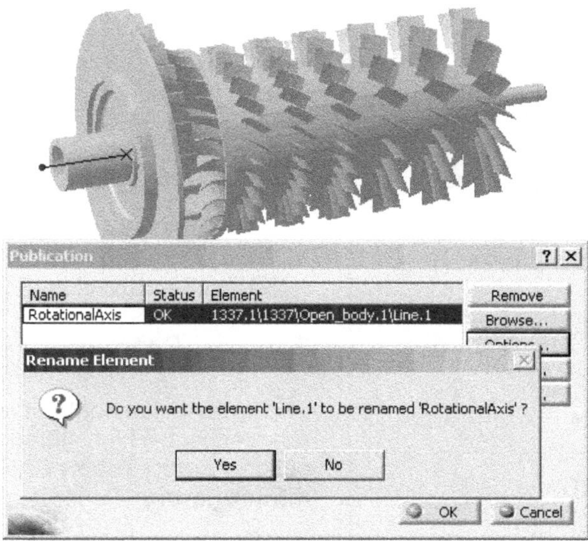

Figure 2–13

Step 4 - Complete the operation.

Once you have finished publishing the required elements, click **OK** to close the Publication dialog box. The system adds the published element to a new Publications branch in the specification tree, as shown in Figure 2–14.

Figure 2–14

Step 5 - (Optional) Define options for published elements.

Many companies enforce a design standard stating that any element to be externally referenced must first be published. This is done to ensure that no unwanted parent-child relationships are developed.

There are two ways to make reference selection:

- External References
- Constraint Creation

External References

The options that control the use of publications for external references are highlighted in Figure 2–15. To access these options, select **Tools>Options>Infrastructure>Part Infrastructure>***General* tab.

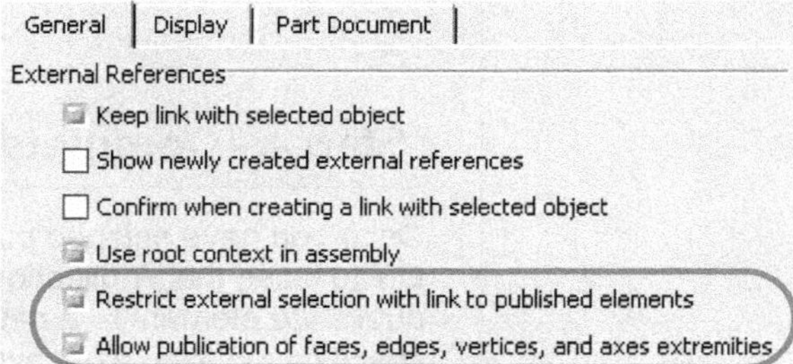

Figure 2–15

Option	Description
Restrict external selection with link to published elements	With this option enabled, external references can only be developed by selecting a published element.
Allow publication of faces, edges, vertices, and axes extremities	This option must be enabled to publish individual sub-elements of features, such as the face, edge, or vertex of a Pad. When disabled, sub-elements cannot be published, thus restricting you from making boundary representation selections.

Constraint Creation

Assembly constraint options can be set to enable only the published elements to be referenced, as shown in Figure 2–16. To access this option, select **Tools>Options>Mechanical Design>Assembly Design>**_Constraints_ tab.

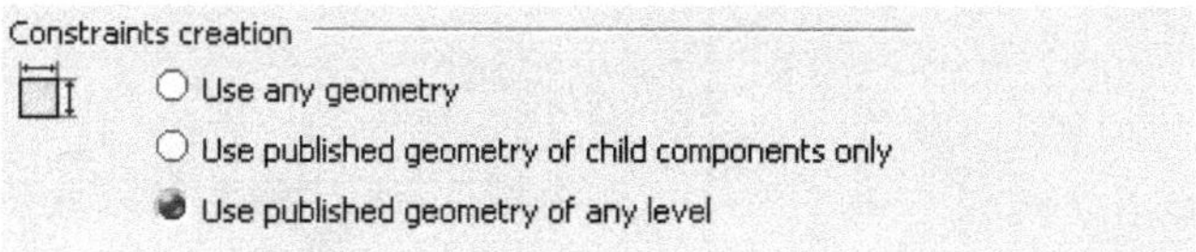

Figure 2–16

Replacing a Published Element

Another advantage of using Publications is that all external references are linked to the published element and not directly to the feature. As long as there is a publication with the same name, the link is valid and updated. This simplifies the replacement of data, because the referenced geometry can be replaced through the publication so that all of the references are automatically updated.

How To: Replace a Publication with a New Reference

1. Activate the component containing the publication and select **Tools>Publication**.
2. In the Publication dialog box, select the published element to be replaced.
3. Select the replacing element in the model or specification tree. The system prompts you to confirm the modification, as shown in Figure 2–17.

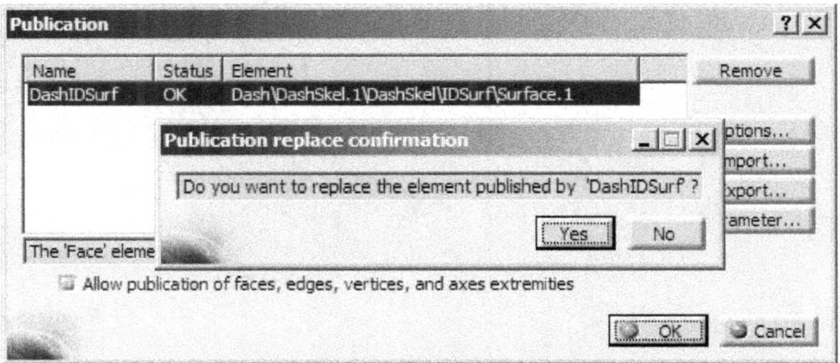

Figure 2–17

4. Click **Yes** to complete the operation. The system updates the Publication dialog box to display the new pointed element, as shown in Figure 2–18.

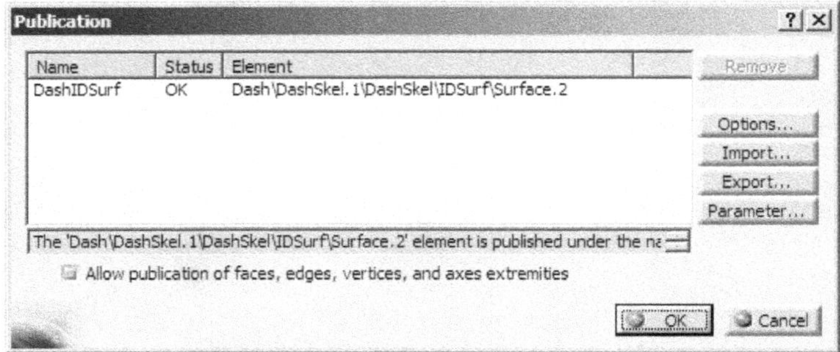

Figure 2–18

5. Activate the assembly and update the model to propagate the changes. The dash assembly using the original and new styling surface displays as shown in Figure 2–19.

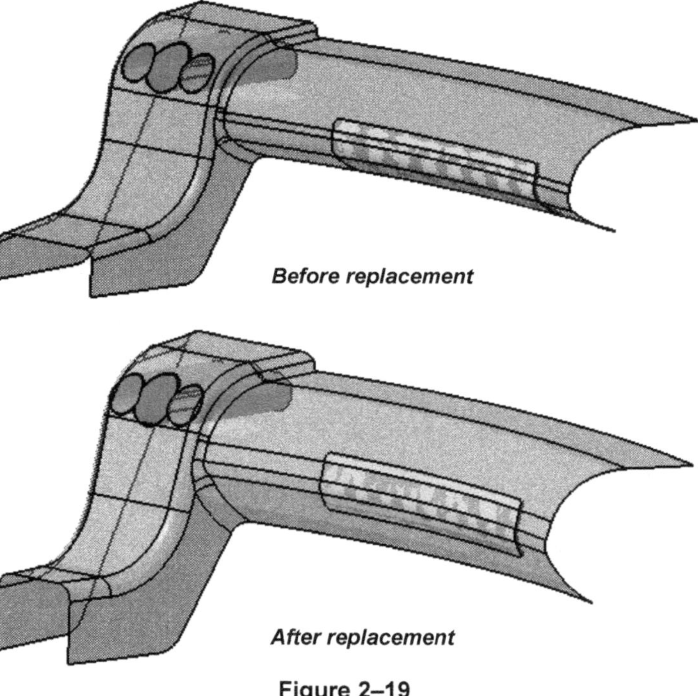

Figure 2–19

2.4 Parameters

In addition to wireframe and surface geometry, a skeleton model can also contain a variety of parameters and formula information that can be shared between the components of an assembly.

For example, a parameter that controls the default wall thickness is created in the **ML_REF** skeleton model shown in Figure 2–20. When this parameter is published, it can be used to control the thickness of the Shell feature in each of the six frame components of the assembly. This enables a design change to modify the wall thickness to be performed in one location.

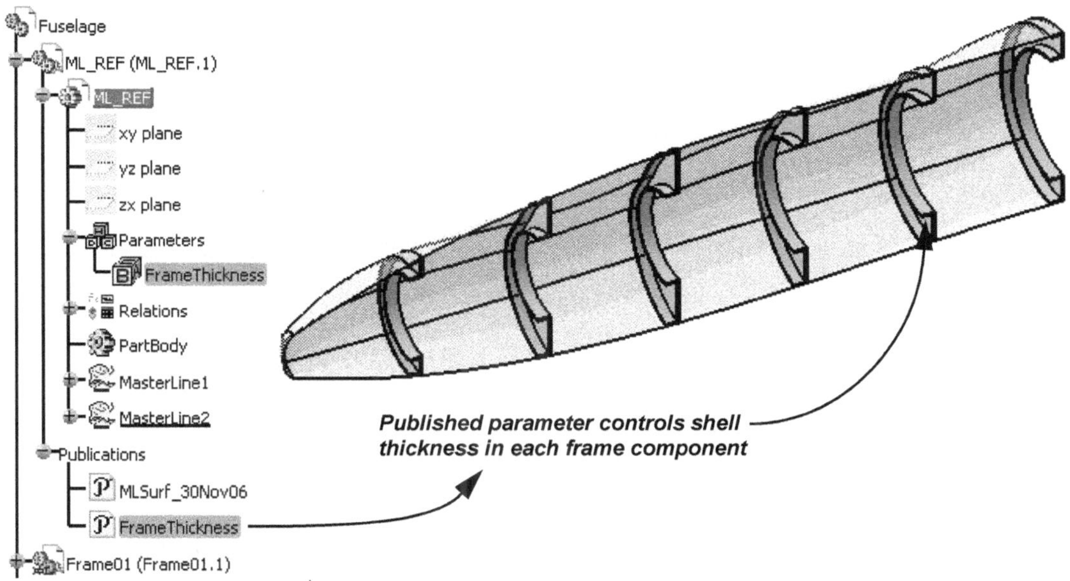

Figure 2–20

Parameter Display

By default, parameters and formulas are not displayed in the specification tree. To enable their display, select **Tools>Options>Infrastructure>Part Infrastructure>***Display* tab and enable the **Parameters** and **Relations** options.

Publishing a Parameter

To externally reference a parameter, it should be published in the skeleton model. This is done by clicking **Parameter** in the Publications dialog box. The Choose the parameter dialog box opens, listing all of the parameters currently stored in the model so that they can be selected for publication, as shown in Figure 2–21.

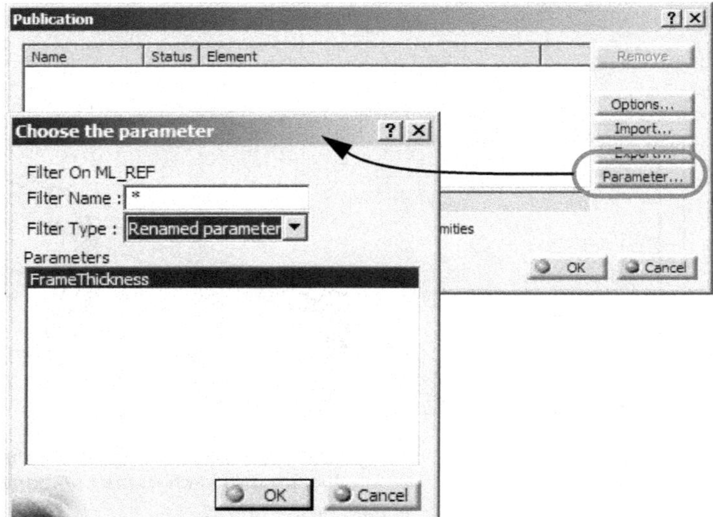

Figure 2–21

Use the *Filter* fields in the dialog box to locate the parameter to be published. For example, the **Renamed parameter** filter type can be selected to display all of the renamed and user-defined parameters.

When the parameter has been published, it is added to the Publications branch in the specification tree for external reference selection.

2.5 Creating a Skeleton

A skeleton model is created using the same techniques as a part, except that it cannot contain any solid geometry. A skeleton model is the first component placed in a Product file. All other components are constrained to or created from it.

Consider the following tips when creating a skeleton model:

- A skeleton model should not contain any solid elements.
- A skeleton model should contain referencing elements, such as surfaces, planes, lines, and points. This helps place the solid geometry from other parts into the assembly.

General Steps

Use the following general steps to create a skeleton model:

1. Create a new part file.
2. Create the skeleton geometry.
3. Publish geometry for external reference selection.
4. Assemble parts into the Product.
5. Reference parts to the skeleton.

Step 1 - Create a new part file.

Select **File>New** and select the **Part** option in the New dialog box. Enter a name that indicates that this file is being used as a skeleton model (e.g., **EngineSkeleton.CATPart**).

Step 2 - Create the skeleton geometry.

A skeleton model can be created using the options in the Surfacing workbenches, such as Wireframe and Surface Design or Generative Shape Design. The skeleton model for a remote control is shown in Figure 2–22. The entire model consists of surfaces and reference geometry.

To ensure that the size of the upper and lower sections are always the same, the skeleton is created as two surfaces; one for the upper section of the remote and one for the lower section. The model can now be added to a product and the top and bottom parts created.

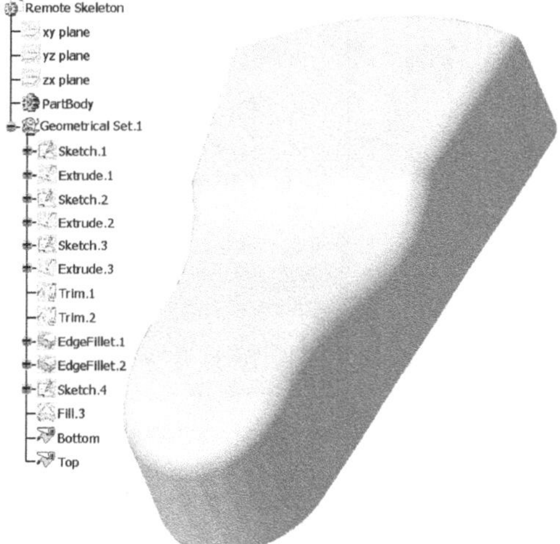

Figure 2–22

Step 3 - Publish geometry for external reference selection.

Once the skeleton geometry has been developed, it should be published before it is used as a reference to create geometry in other components. In this example, the top and bottom surfaces are published, as shown in Figure 2–23.

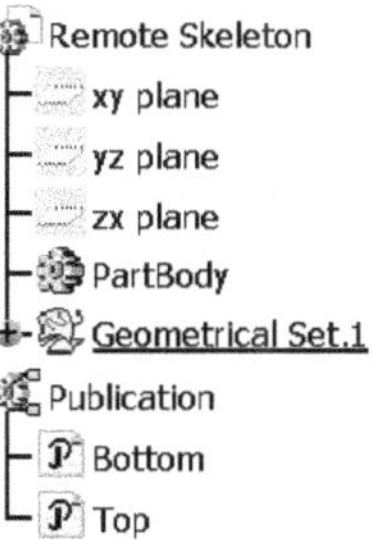

Figure 2–23

Step 4 - Assemble parts into the Product.

The skeleton model is always the first part brought into a product. All other parts are then constrained to or created from it. Two empty part files (top cover and bottom cover) are then added to the Product file (**Remote Skeleton.CATPart**), as shown in Figure 2–24.

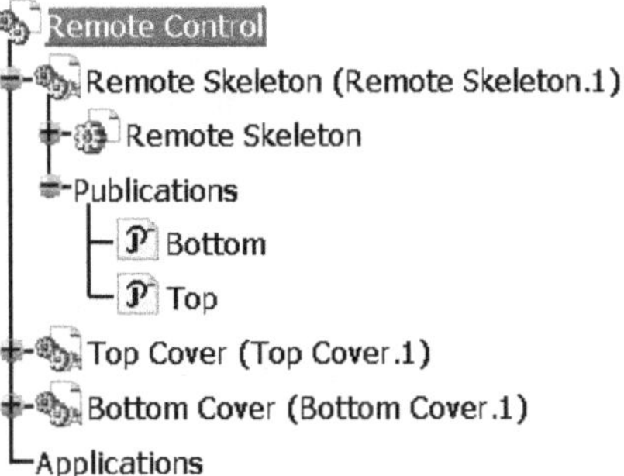

Figure 2–24

Step 5 - Reference parts to the skeleton.

To ensure that the remote maintains the design intent, the solid geometry used to create the top and bottom covers should reference the skeleton model. This way, if a change to the remote is required, only the skeleton model needs to be adjusted.

Any changes to the skeleton model are not reflected in the top or bottom parts if ***Keep link with selected object*** *is not selected.*

Before creating the top and bottom covers, you must create an external link between two part files. Select **Tools>Options** to open the Options dialog box. Select **Infrastructure>Part Infrastructure** in the Options dialog box. Select the *General* tab and select **Keep link with selected object**, as shown in Figure 2–25.

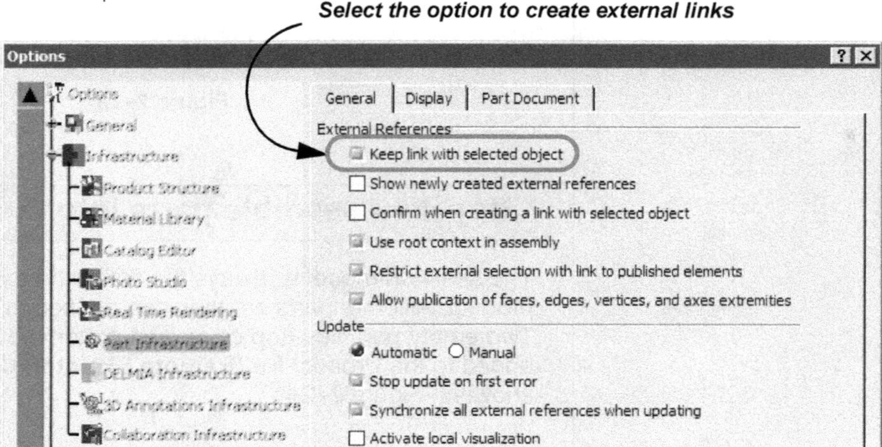

Figure 2–25

The top of the remote control is created by applying a thickness to the **Top** surface in the skeleton model, as shown in Figure 2–26.

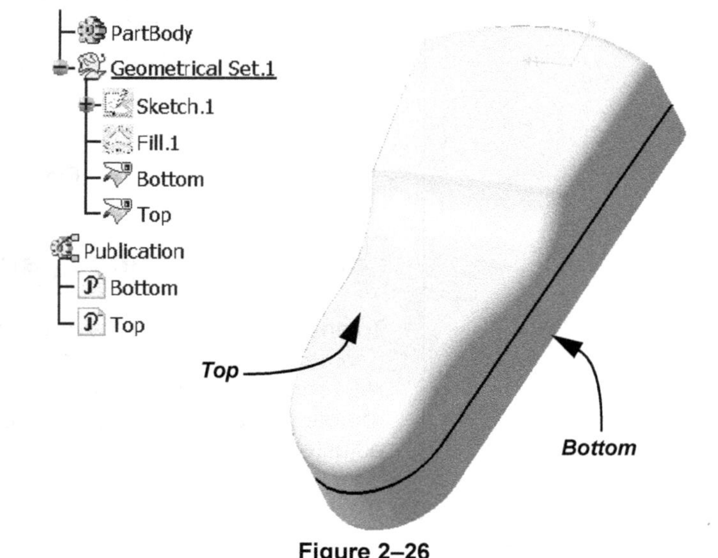

Figure 2–26

Once the top part has been created, CATIA creates another geometrical set in the top cover part called **External References**. This geometrical set contains an external link to the **Top** surface, as shown in Figure 2–27.

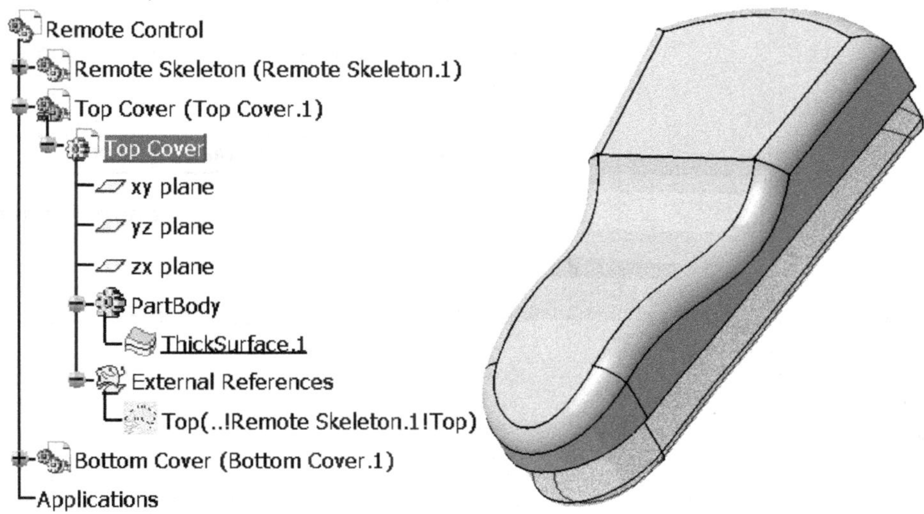

Figure 2–27

Once the external link has been created, the icon representing the top cover changes, as shown in Figure 2–28. The new icon indicates that the part file now contains an external reference.

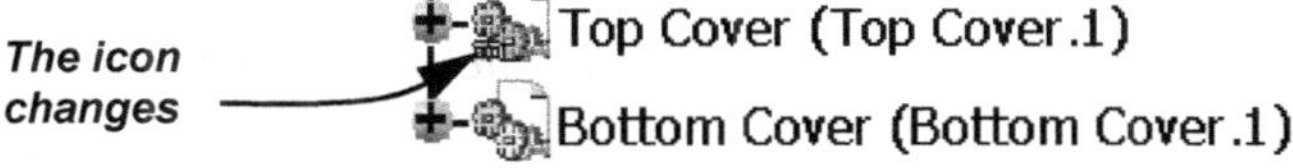

Figure 2–28

The bottom cover is created using the same technique as the top cover. Once completed, any required changes to the size of the remote can be made from the skeleton model. The part files display the changes once they have been updated.

Practice 2a

Skeleton Model I

Practice Objective

- Create a skeleton model.

In this practice, you will create reference features to create a skeleton model.

Task 1 - Set Part Number to Manual Input.

By setting this option, the system prompts you for a part name when you create a new part or product file.

1. Select **Tools>Options>Infrastructure>Product Structure**.
2. Select the *Product Structure* tab.
3. Select **Manual input**, as shown in Figure 2–29.

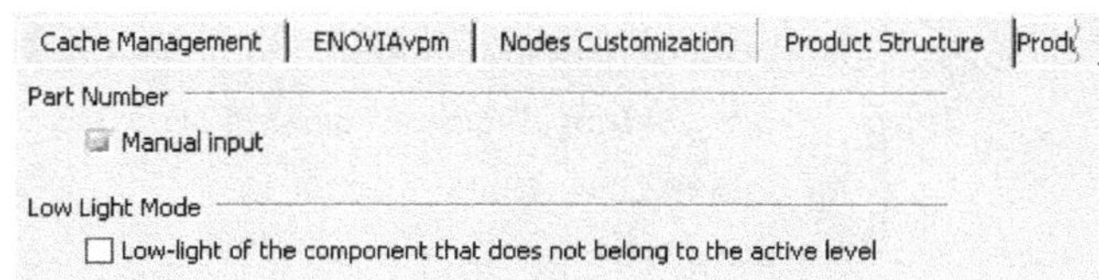

Figure 2–29

4. Click **OK**.

Task 2 - Create a new part file.

1. Create a new part file.
2. In the New Part dialog box, for the part name, enter **Skeleton** and clear the **Enable hybrid design** option.
3. Rename the yz plane as **CenterLine**. The specification tree displays as shown in Figure 2–30.

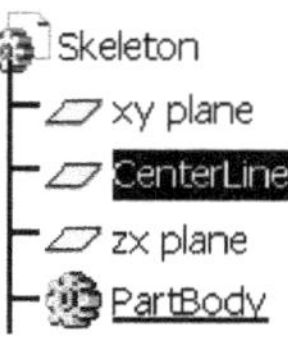

Figure 2–30

Task 3 - Create reference geometry.

1. Create a reference point at the **0,0,0** location, as shown in Figure 2–31.

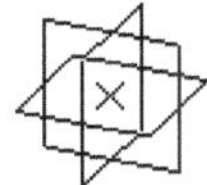

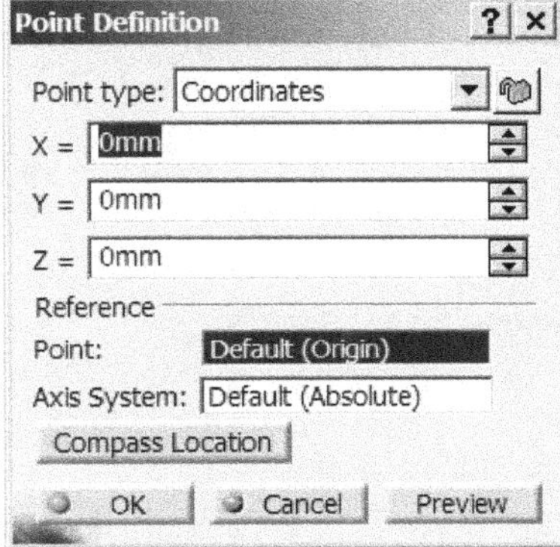

Figure 2–31

2. Create a reference line by selecting the references and entering the value, as shown in Figure 2–32.
   - *Line type:* **Point-Direction**
   - *Point:* **Point.2**
   - *Direction:* **CenterLine**
   - *End:* **12.5**
   - *Length Type:* **Length**
   - Select **Mirrored extent**.

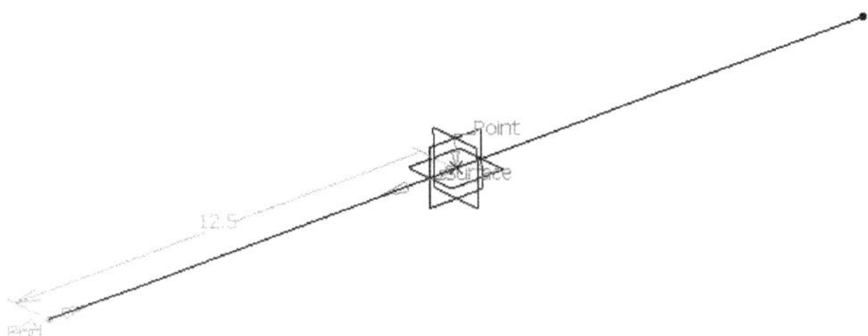

Figure 2–32

3. Create a reference line by entering the information shown in Figure 2–33. If required, click **Reverse Direction** to create the line in the orientation shown in Figure 2–33.

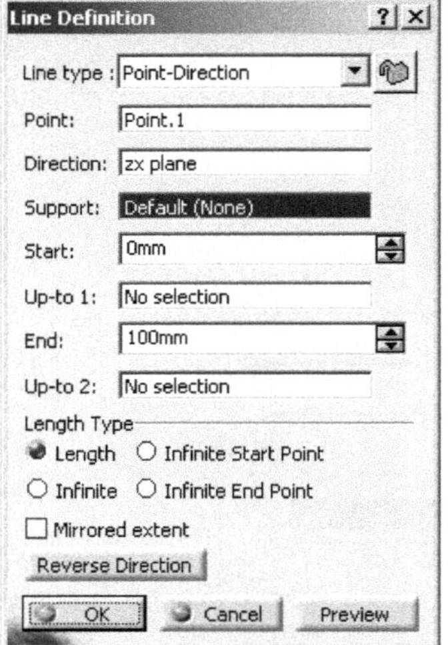

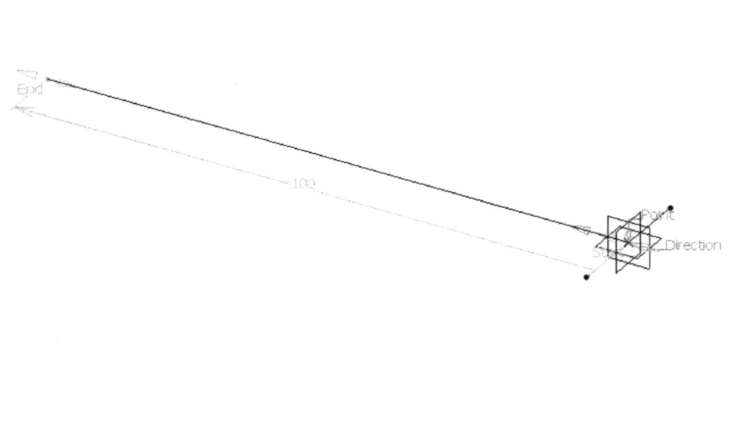

Figure 2–33

4. Create a reference plane, as shown in Figure 2–34. The Angle is a negative value.

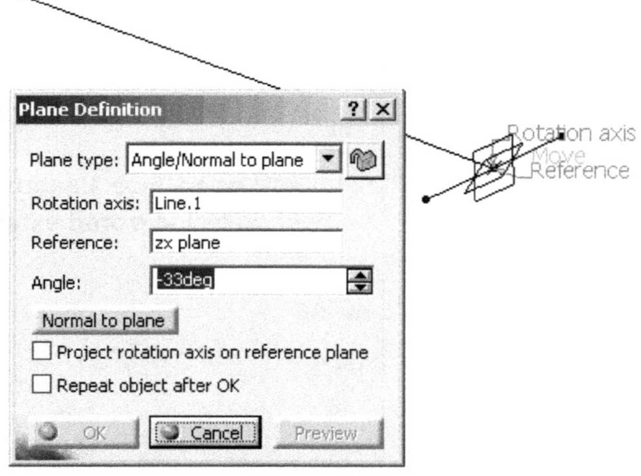

Figure 2–34

5. Create a third reference line, as shown in Figure 2–35.

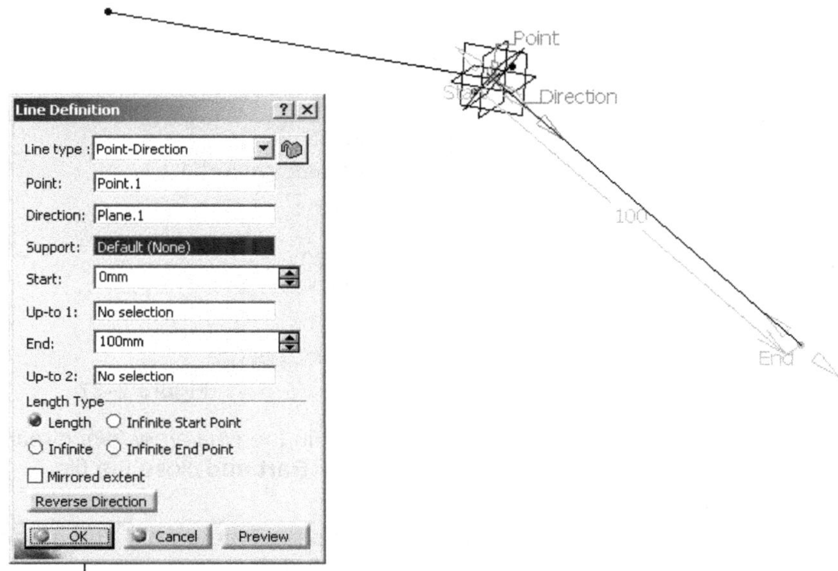

Figure 2–35

6. Rename *Line.2* as **OutputCenterLine** and *Line.3* as **InputCenterLine**, as shown in Figure 2–36.

Keyboard shortcut: Press <Alt>+<Enter> to open the Properties dialog box for a selected feature.

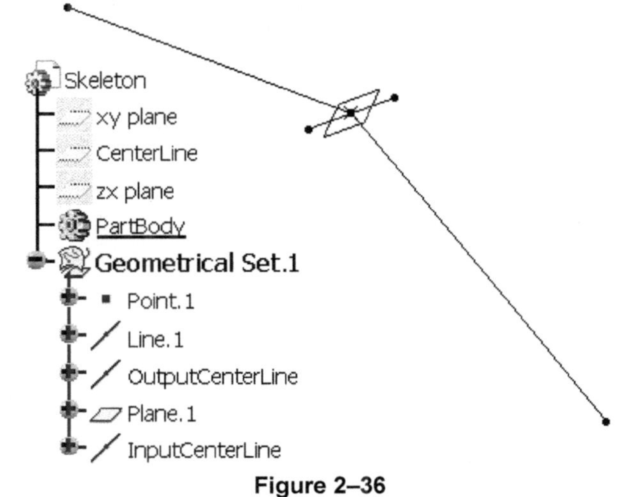

Figure 2–36

7. Hide the four reference planes and **Line.1**, as shown in Figure 2–37.

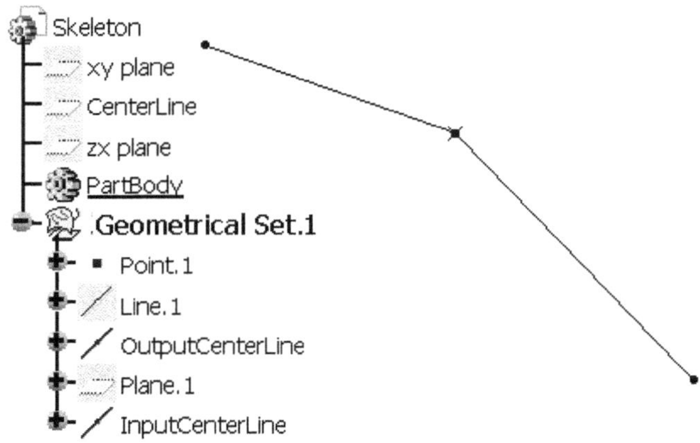

Figure 2–37

8. Save the part in the *UniversalJoint* directory as **Skeleton.CATPart** and close the file.

Task 4 - Create a new assembly and assemble components to the skeleton.

1. Create a new product. For the part number, enter **UniversalJoint**.
2. Assemble **Skeleton.CATPart** as the base component and apply a Fix constraint. The model displays as shown in Figure 2–38.

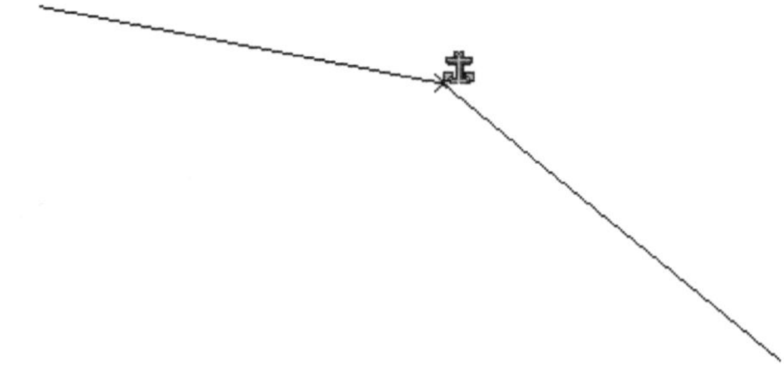

Figure 2–38

3. Assemble **OutputShaft.CATPart**. Use the compass to reposition the part, as shown in Figure 2–39.

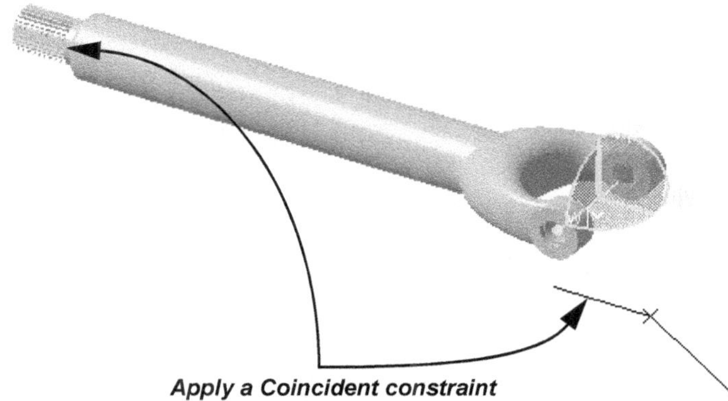

Figure 2–39

4. Apply a Coincident constraint between:

   - *Skeleton:* **OutputCenterLine**
   - *OutputShaft:* (implicit axis)

   Ensure that you zoom in on the area shown in Figure 2–40 to be able to select the implicit axis.

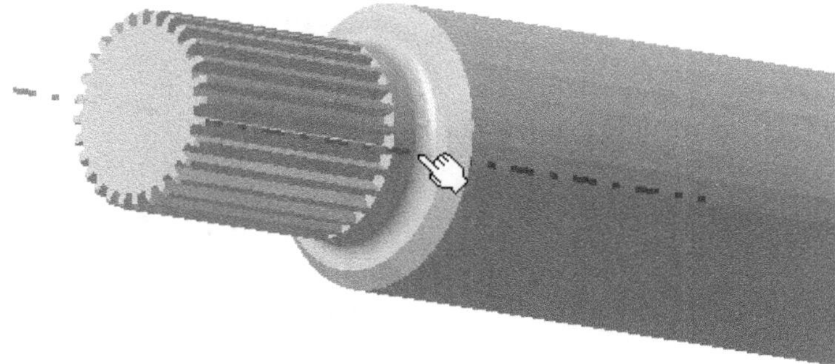

Figure 2–40

5. Assemble **Spider.CATPart**.

6. In the specification tree, expand **Skeleton** and **1652** (Spider), as shown in Figure 2–41.

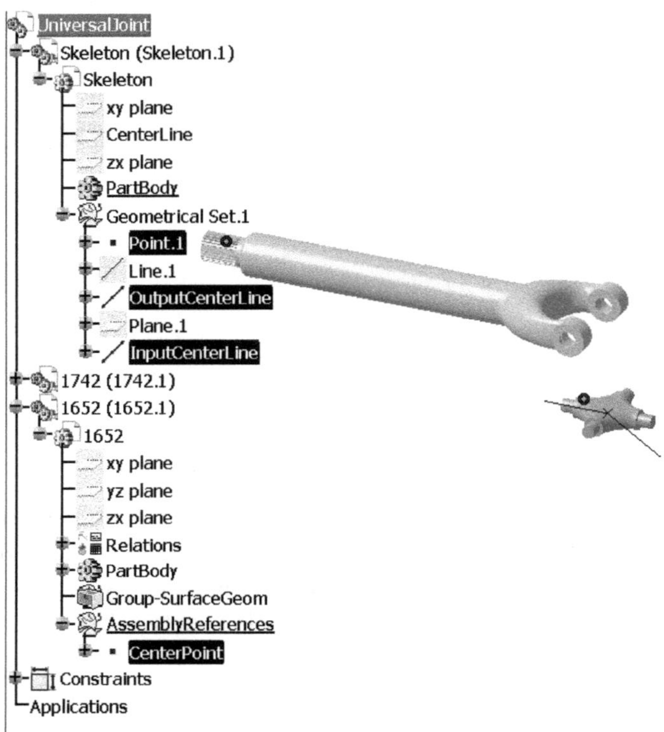

Figure 2–41

7. Apply a Coincident constraint between:

   - *Skeleton:* **Point.1**
   - *1652:* **CenterPoint**

   Select these references in the specification tree.

8. Apply a Coincident constraint between:

    - *Spider:* (implicit axis)
    - *OutputShaft:* (implicit axis)

    Refer to Figure 2–42.

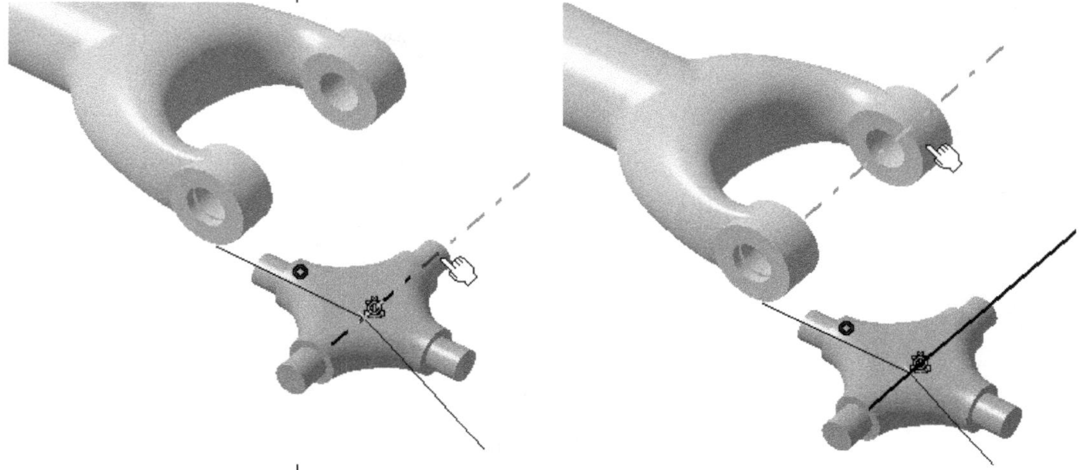

Figure 2–42

9. Update the assembly. It displays as shown in Figure 2–43.

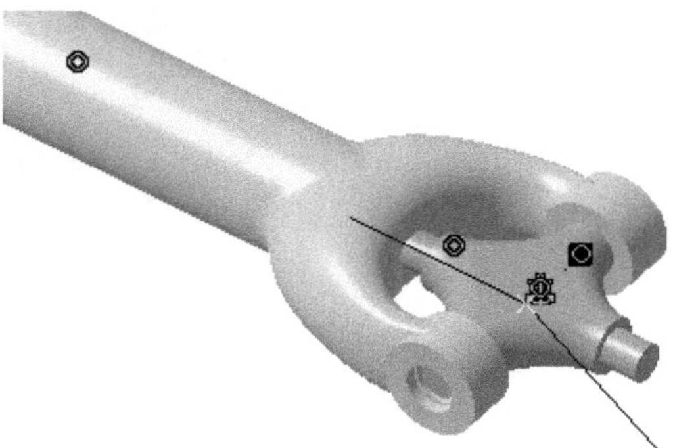

Figure 2–43

10. Assemble **InputShaft.CATPart**. Position the part as shown in Figure 2–44.

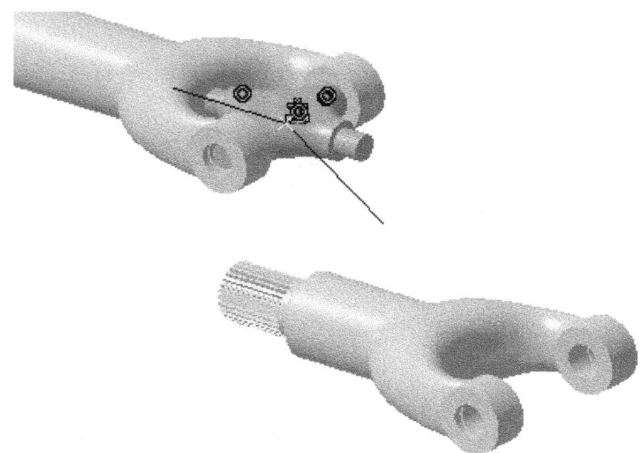

Figure 2–44

11. Apply a Coincident constraint between:

    - InputShaft: (implicit axis)
    - Spider: (implicit axis)

    Select the implicit axis shown in Figure 2–45.

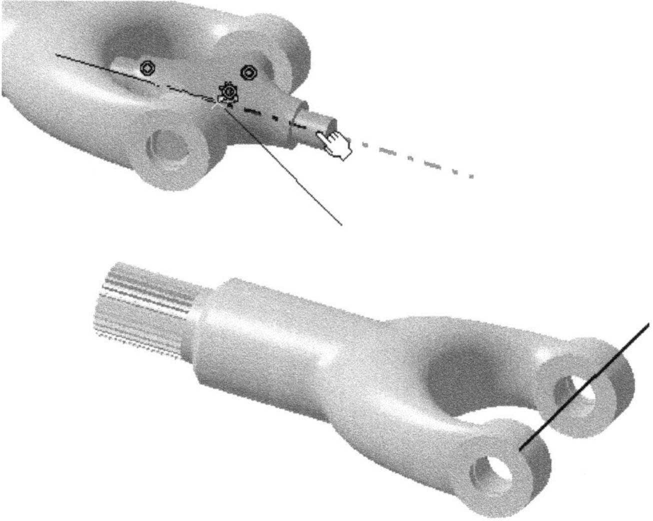

Figure 2–45

12. Apply a Coincident constraint between:

- Skeleton: **InputCenterLine**
- InputShaft: (implicit axis)

Select the implicit axis shown in Figure 2–46.

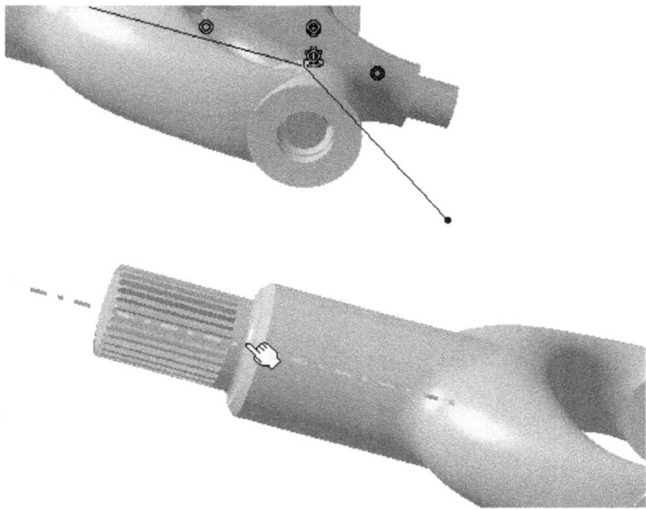

Figure 2–46

Task 5 - Manipulate the assembly.

1. After updating the assembly, the result displays as shown in Figure 2–47.

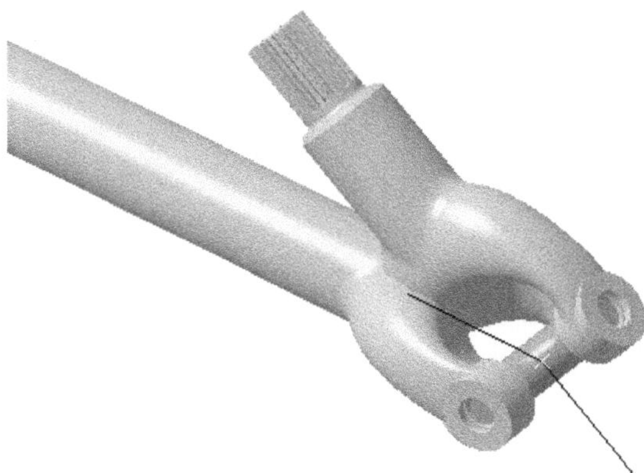

Figure 2–47

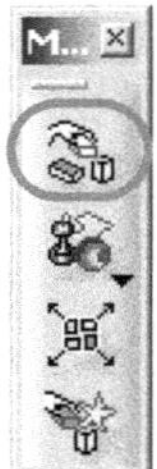

2. Click (Manipulation). The Manipulation Parameters dialog box opens as shown in Figure 2–48.

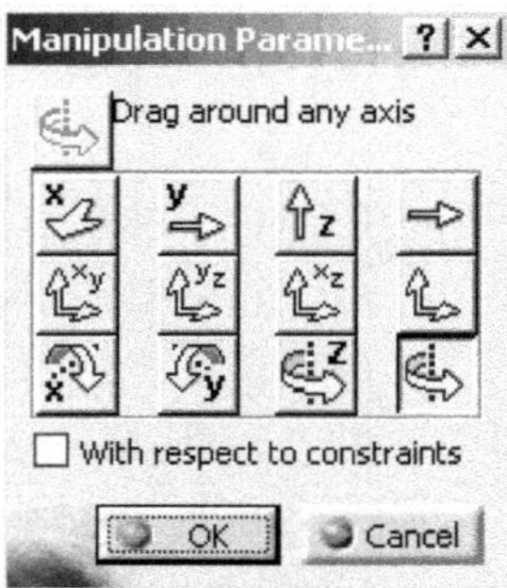

Figure 2–48

3. Click (Drag around any axis) and select the implicit axis, as shown in Figure 2–49.

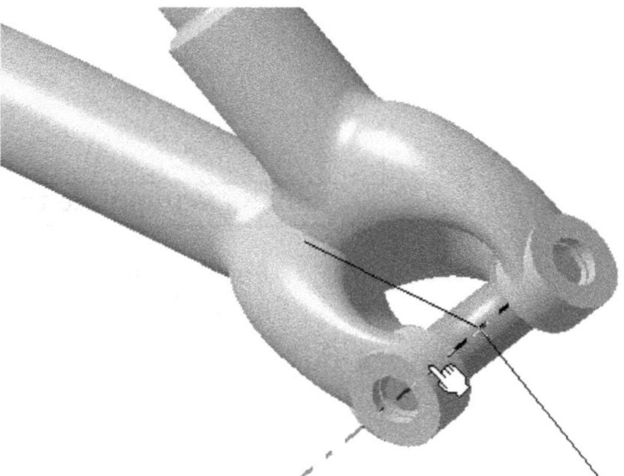

Figure 2–49

*Leave the **With respect to other constraints** option cleared.*

4. Select the **InputShaft**, hold the mouse button and drag the part to the location shown in Figure 2–50.

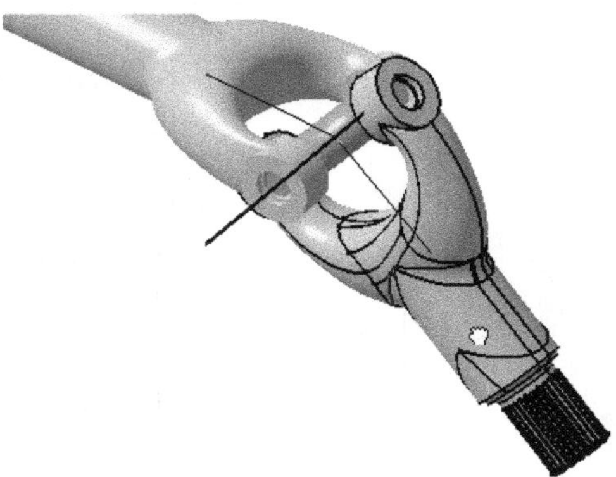

Figure 2–50

5. Click **OK**.

6. Update the assembly.

7. Another way to manipulate the assembly is to adjust the values of the reference elements in the Skeleton part file. In the specification tree, double-click on **Plane.1** twice as shown in Figure 2–51. This enables you to edit the feature.

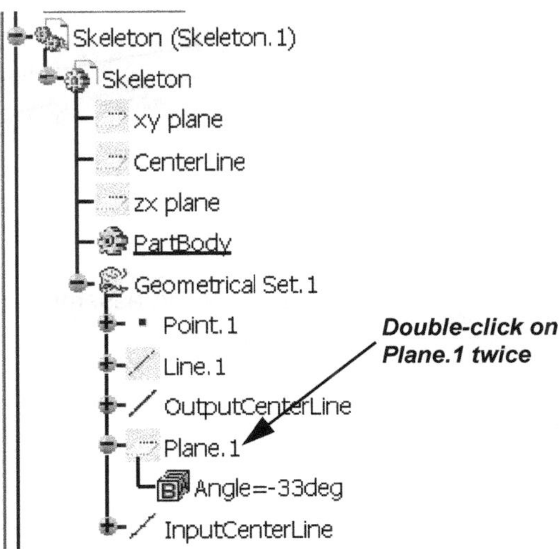

Figure 2–51

8. Set the *angle value* to **33 deg**.

9. Click **OK**.

10. In the specification tree, double-click on **UniversalJoint** as shown in Figure 2–52. By doing so, you are sent back to the Assembly Design workbench.

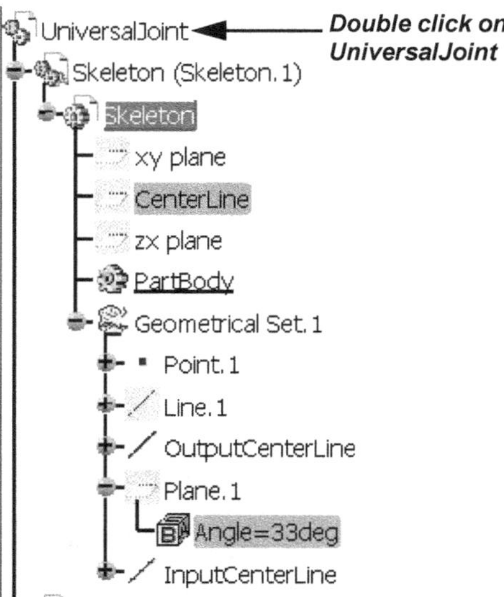

Figure 2–52

11. Update the assembly. It displays as shown in Figure 2–53. The parts update based on the **Plane.1** new angle.

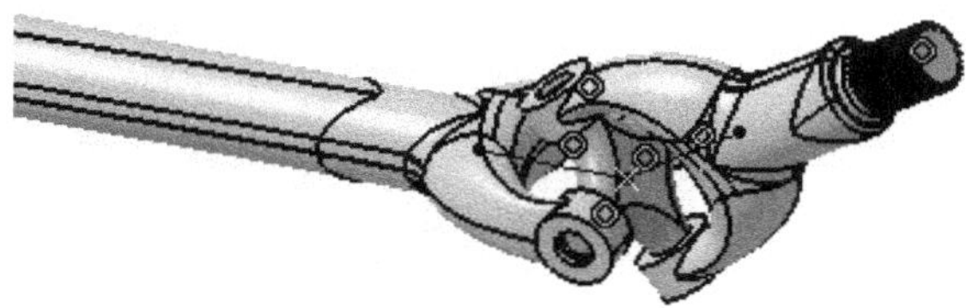

Figure 2–53

12. Save the assembly in the *UniversalJoint* folder and close the file.

Practice 2b Designing with Publications

Practice Objectives

- Publish a surface.
- Publish a parameter.
- Replace a publication with an updated feature.

In this practice, you will develop a frame component for the fuselage of an aircraft. The exterior skin of the aircraft has been defined by the Analysis team and will be used to control the shape of the frame component. This skin has been placed in a skeleton model along with some parameter information. To externally reference this information, the surface and a parameter will be published.

These publications will be used to develop a split and Shell feature in the frame component. When the frame geometry has been defined, the published surface will be updated with a new exterior skin surface. The completed component displays as shown in Figure 2–54.

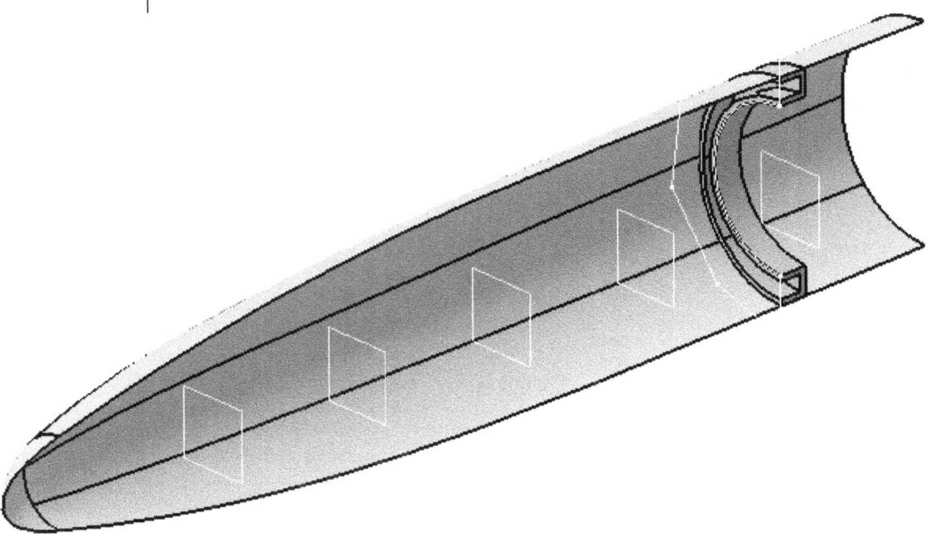

Figure 2–54

Task 1 - Open ML_REF.CATPart.

In this task, you will open the skeleton model and investigate the wireframe, sketched and surface geometry, and parameter that have been developed.

1. Open **ML_REF.CATPart** in the *Fuselage* folder. The skeleton part displays as shown in Figure 2–55.

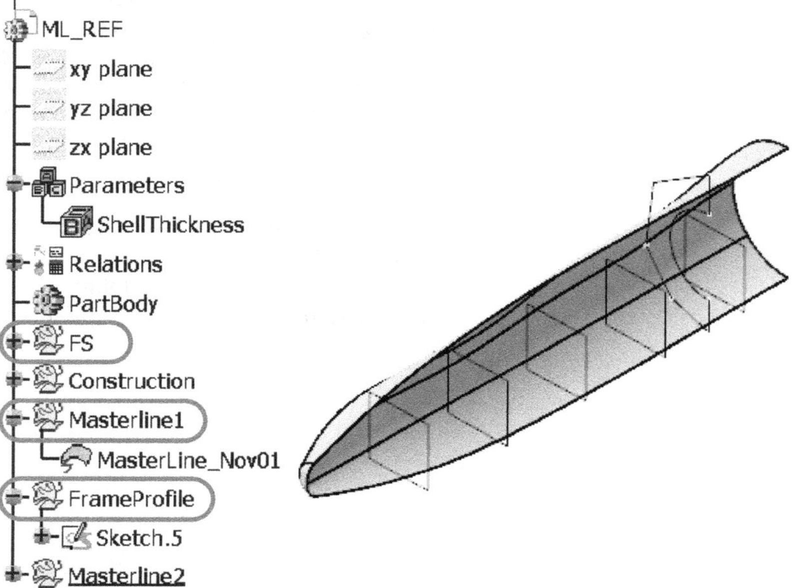

Figure 2–55

2. Investigate the geometry that resides in the skeleton part. This geometry is described as follows:

Object	Description
Parameters	A **ShellThickness** parameter has been defined to control the thickness of each Frame component.
FS	The geometrical set contains a reference plane to locate each of the frame components in the assembly.
Masterline1	The geometrical set contains the exterior skin surface that is used to trim the frame components.
FrameProfile	The geometrical set contains the profile for the frame component.

Task 2 - Publish the Masterline surface.

In this task, you will publish the masterline surface. This surface will be used to trim the frame components in the assembly to ensure that they always conform to the interior skin of the fuselage.

1. Select **Tools>Publication**. The Publication dialog box opens as shown in Figure 2–56.

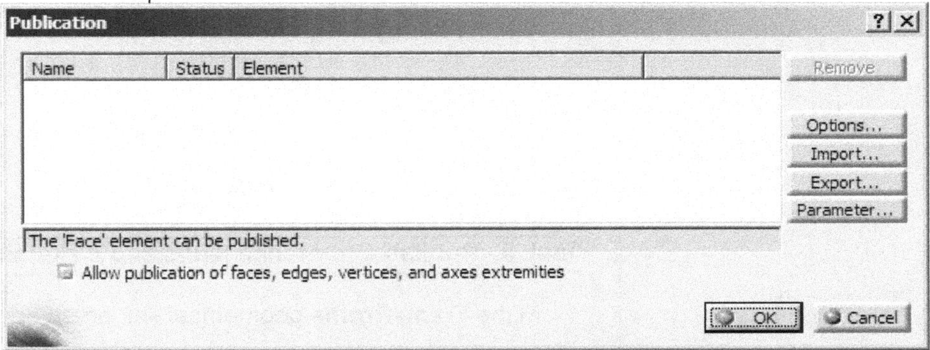

Figure 2–56

2. Select the **Masterline_Nov01** datum surface in the **Masterline1** geometrical set. The surface is published, as shown in Figure 2–57.

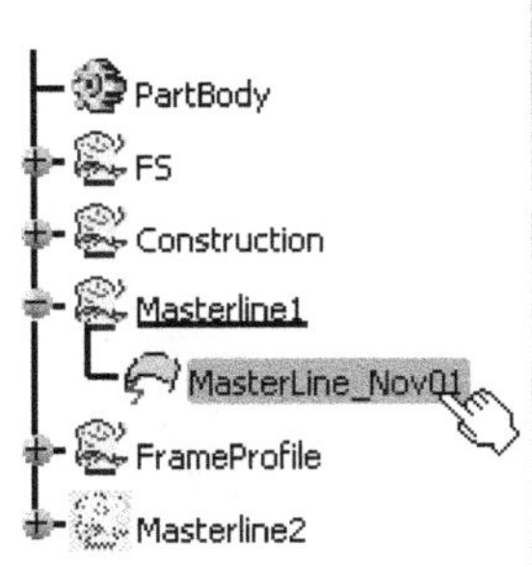

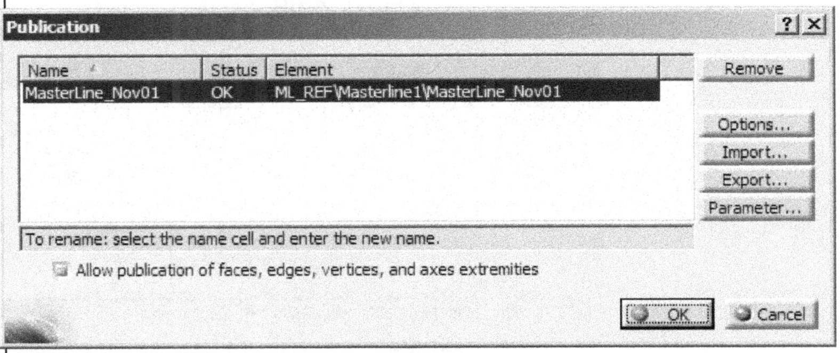

Figure 2–57

3. To rename the publication, select **MasterLine_Nov01** in the dialog box and then select **MasterLine_Nov01** again to change the name to **MasterLineSurf**.

4. Click **OK**. The published element displays in a new Publication branch in the specification tree, as shown in Figure 2–58.

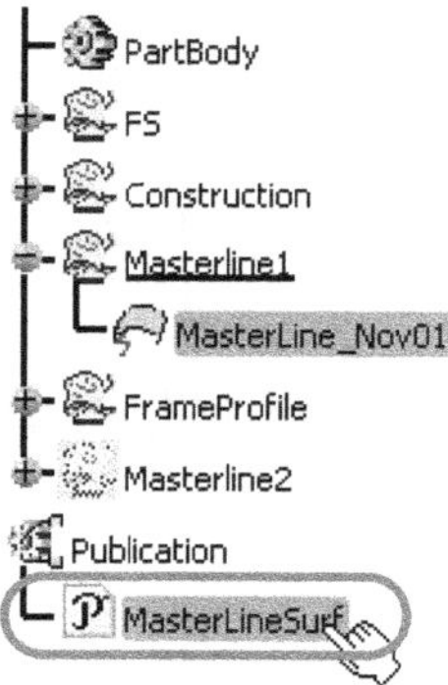

Figure 2–58

Task 3 - Publish a reference plane and a sketch.

1. In the **FrameProfile** geometrical set, preselect **Sketch.5**.
2. Select **Tools>Publication**. With the sketch preselected, the system prompts you to publish the selected element.
3. Click **Yes**. The sketch is added to the Publication dialog box.
4. Rename the sketch as **FrameProfile**, as shown in Figure 2–59.

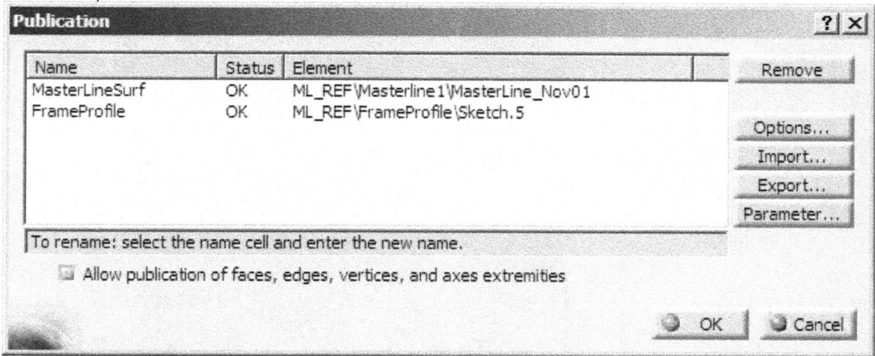

Figure 2–59

5. Publish the **Frame5** reference plane in the **FS** geometrical set. Do not rename the published element. The Publications dialog box opens as shown in Figure 2–60. Keep the Publication dialog box open for the next task.

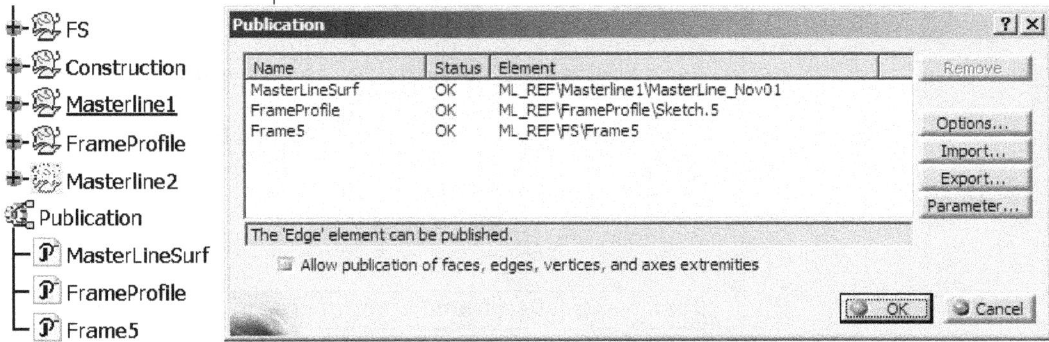

Figure 2–60

Task 4 - Publish a parameter.

1. Click **Parameter** in the Publication dialog box. The Choose the parameter dialog box opens as shown in Figure 2–61.

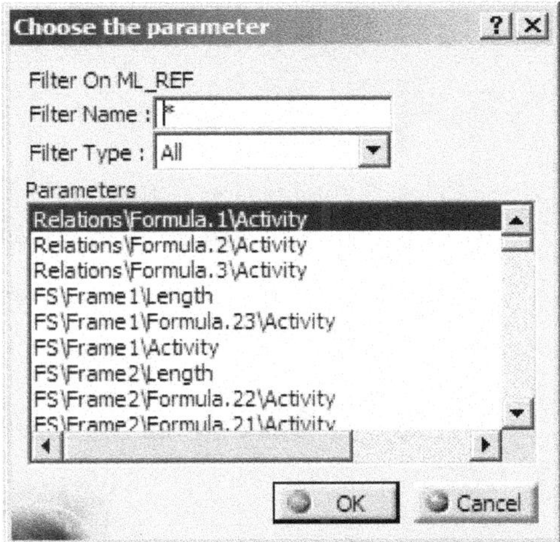

Figure 2–61

2. In the Filter Type drop-down list, select **Renamed parameters**. The only parameter listed is **ShellThickness**.
3. Click **OK** to publish the **ShellThickness** parameter.
4. Save the model and close the window.

Task 5 - Create a new product and assemble the skeleton.

1. Create a new CATProduct file named **Fuselage**.
2. Ensure that you are in the Assembly Design workbench.
3. Insert **ML_REF.CATPart**.

Task 6 - Create a frame component.

1. Right-click on **Fuselage** and select **Components>New Part**.
2. For the part number, enter **Frame5**.
3. Click **No** so that the new part is assembled at the origin of the assembly. The specification tree displays as shown in Figure 2–62.

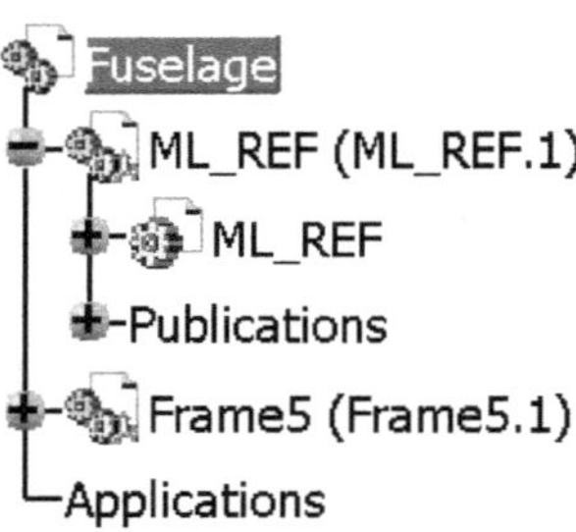

Figure 2–62

Task 7 - Set options for contextual design.

1. Select **Tools>Options>Infrastructure>Part Infrastructure**.
2. Select the *General* tab.

3. Enable the following options as shown in Figure 2–63:
    - **Keep link with selected object**
    - **Restrict external selection with link to published elements**

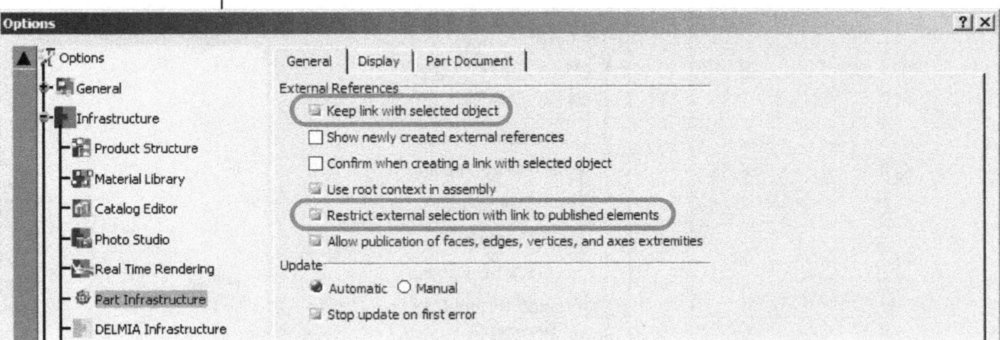

Figure 2–63

4. Click **OK**.

Task 8 - Perform contextual design.

In this task, you will develop the geometry for the **Frame5** component. The part will be developed by creating a Pad that references the published sketch. Next, the part will be trimmed to the published surface. Finally a Shell feature will be used to complete the geometry.

1. In the specification tree, expand **Frame5** and activate the part, as shown in Figure 2–64.

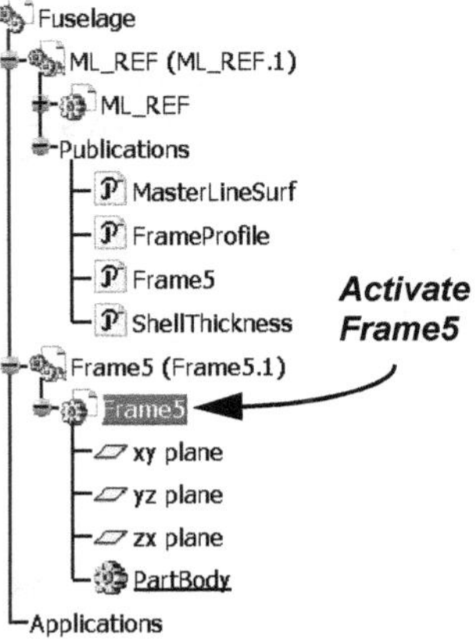

Figure 2–64

2. Ensure that you are in the Part Design workbench.

3. Create a Pad feature. To define the profile of the Pad, select the **FrameProfile** element in the **Publications** branch in the **ML_REF** part, as shown in Figure 2–65.

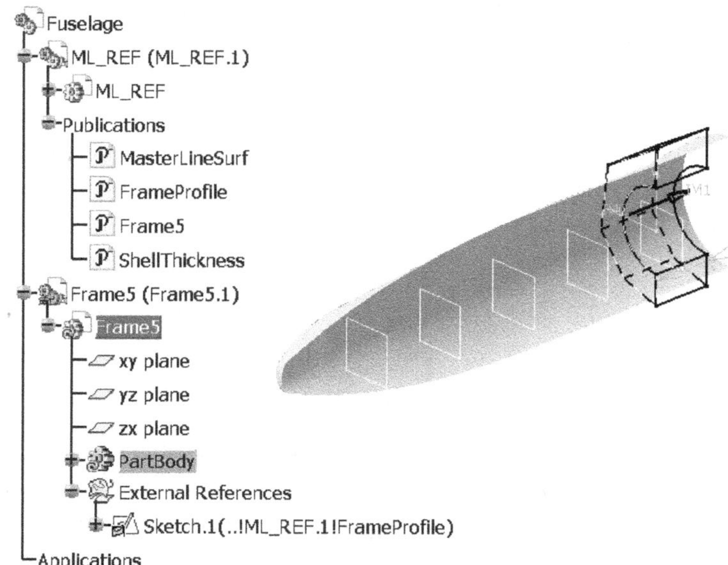

Figure 2–65

Design Considerations

When selecting an element from another model, the system will add an External References branch to the specification tree that contains the link to the referenced element. In this case, the system has locally named the element Sketch.1. This sketch is an associative link to the FrameProfile publication.

4. Enter a *depth* of **5mm** and complete the feature. The model displays as shown in Figure 2–66.

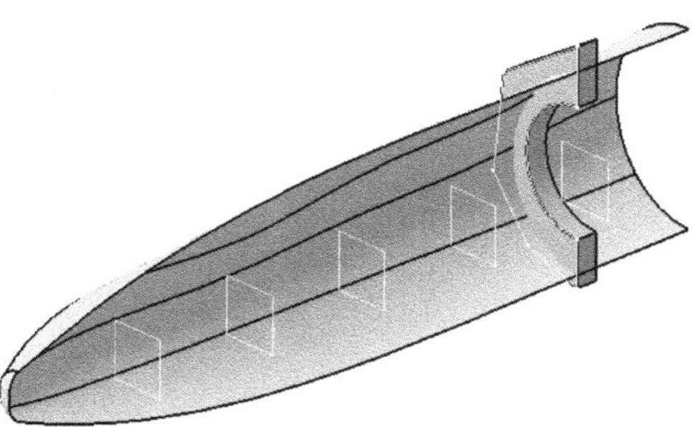

Figure 2–66

5. In the Surface-Based Features toolbar, click (Split). This feature will use the Masterline surface to trim away geometry from **Frame5**. The Split Definition dialog box opens as shown in Figure 2–67.

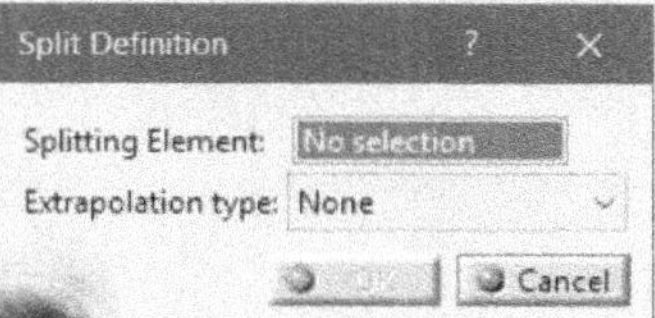

Figure 2–67

6. Select the **MasterlineSurf** publication.

7. Arrows display on the model, indicating the direction of material to keep. Ensure that the arrows point toward the center of the model, as shown in Figure 2–68.

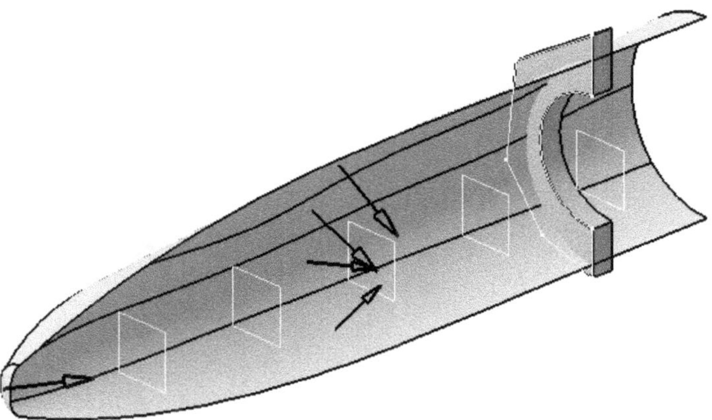

Figure 2–68

8. Click **OK** to complete the operation. The assembly displays as shown in Figure 2–69.

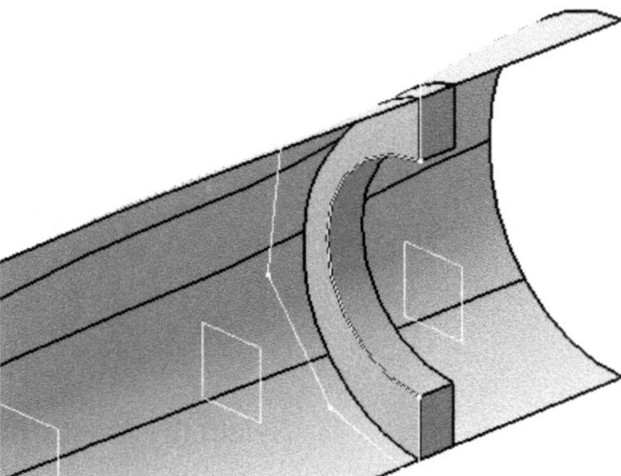

Figure 2–69

9. Create a Shell feature with an inside thickness of 1mm that removes three faces to create the geometry shown in Figure 2–70.

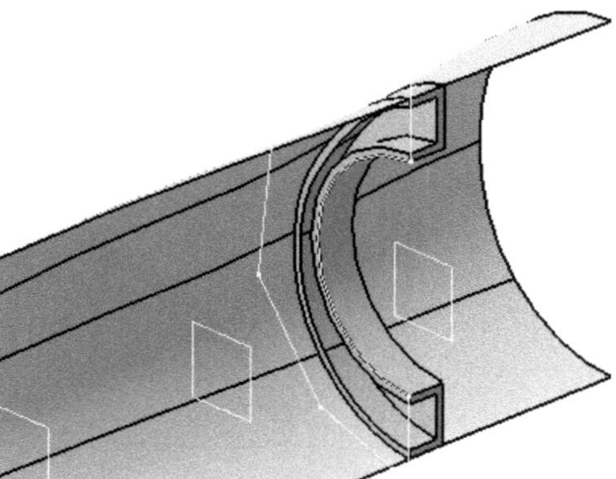

Figure 2–70

10. Save the **Frame5** part model in the *Fuselage* folder.

Task 9 - Modify a publication.

In this task, you will modify the MasterLineSurf publication to reference an updated version of the surface from the design team.

1. Activate the **ML_REF** component.
2. Show the **Masterline2** geometrical set. It contains a second datum surface, as shown in Figure 2–71. This new surface must be used to create the frame components in the Fuselage assembly.

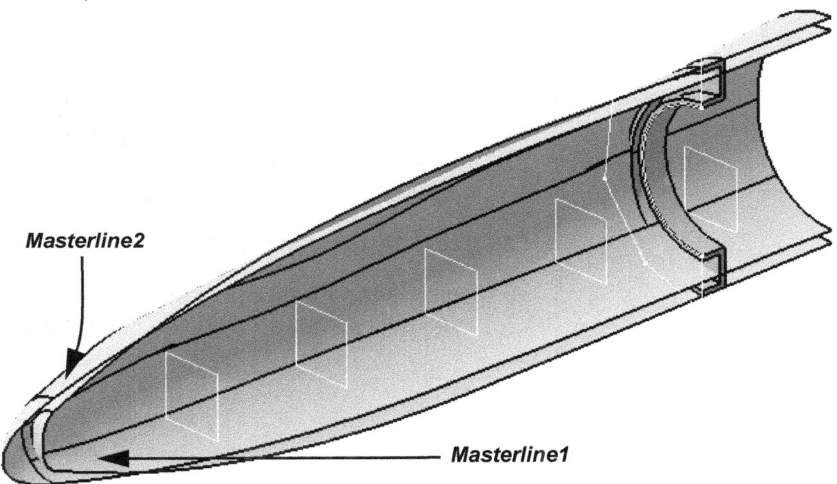

Figure 2–71

3. In the **Masterline01** geometrical set, hide the **MasterLine_Nov01** surface.
4. Select **Tools>Publication**.
5. In the dialog box, select the **MasterLineSurf** element.

6. In the **Masterline2** geometrical set, select the **Masterline_Nov23** datum surface. The system prompts you to confirm the replacement of the published element, as shown in Figure 2–72.

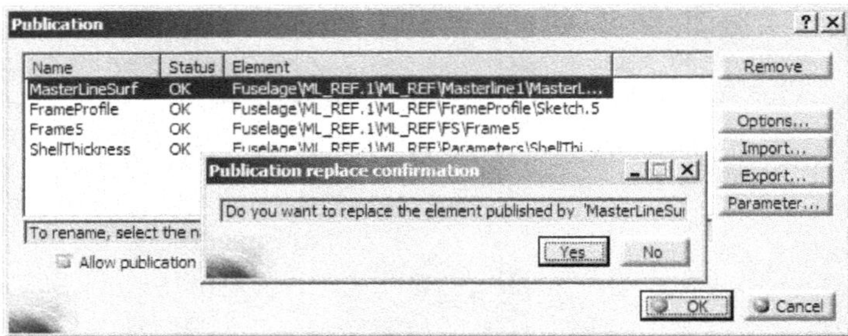

Figure 2–72

7. Click **Yes**. The publication used to develop the **Frame5** component now references the latest master line surface. The **Frame5** component displays in red indicating that it requires an update due to the change.

8. Click **OK** to close the Publications dialog box.

9. Activate the **Fuselage** assembly and update the model. The assembly displays as shown in Figure 2–73.

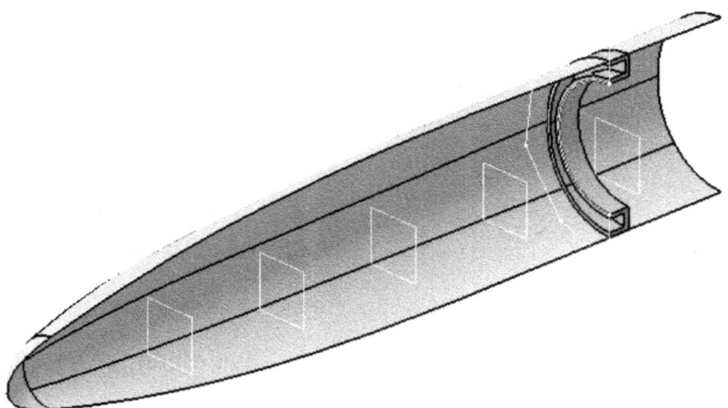

Figure 2–73

10. Use **Save Management** to save the assembly in the *Fuselage* folder.

11. Close the window.

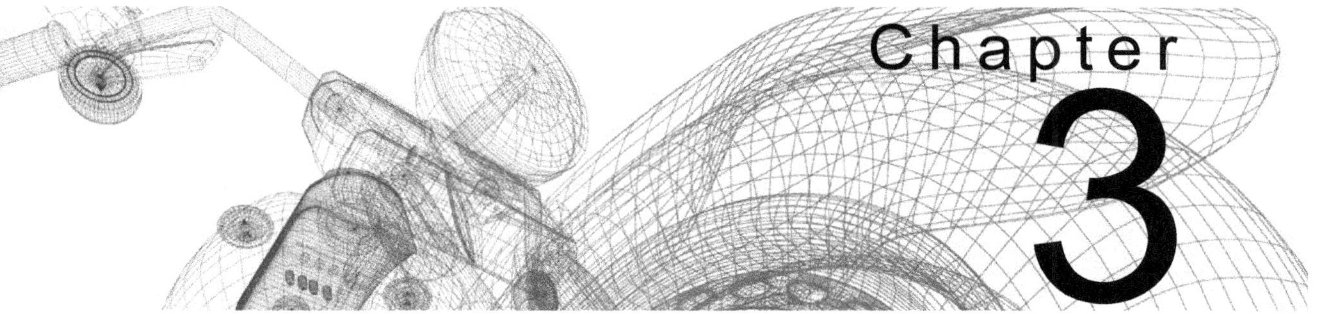

Link Management

This chapter introduces the methods used to create, investigate, maintain, and remove links between assembly components.

Learning Objectives in this Chapter

- Understand how to manage links between components that are established when existing geometry from one component is used to help build another.
- Review the symbols used in the Specification Tree to indicate referenced geometry.
- Learn how to manage external links.
- Understand how to work in a collaborative design environment.
- Understand how a Work in Progress (WIP) assembly is used as a temporary product file that only houses components relevant to what the designer must accomplish.
- Review several collaborative design best practices.
- Convert a product to a part.
- Convert a product to a part while maintaining an associative link.

3.1 Link Management

Links between components are established when existing geometry from one component is used to help build another. Referencing geometry in one model to build new features in another can be an effective way of ensuring that geometry in several models is correct when changes are made. Preserving links between the original geometry and the copy enables multiple parts to be updated by only modifying one part.

An external reference can be created when referencing geometry in another component for the following reasons:

- Selecting a sketch support.
- Creating geometrical and dimensional constraints.
- Specifying a depth option that requires a selection.
- Projecting and intersecting 3D or silhouette edges.
- Copying geometry using the **Paste Special** and **As Result With Link** options.

When an external reference is established, it creates an additional branch in the specification tree, as shown in Figure 3–1. If the external reference is pasted into an existing geometrical set, the **External References** branch is not created and the reference is placed in the geometrical set.

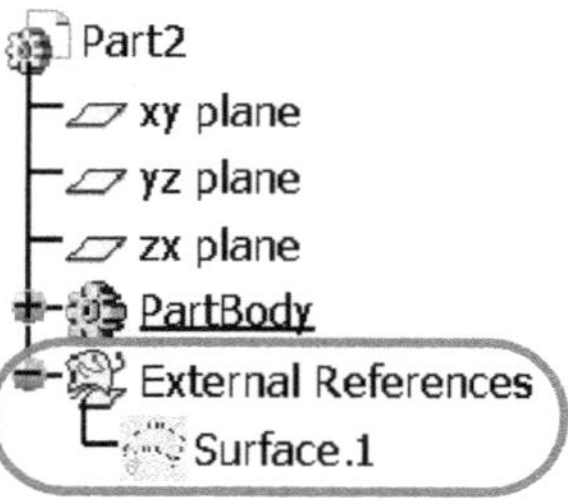

Figure 3–1

Carefully consider the use of external links. Links can create large file sizes and references to external documents. To modify linked geometry, the referenced file must be available and loaded into CATIA.

When creating external references, two types of links can be created: **Reference-Reference** and **Reference-Instance**.

Reference-Reference Links

A Reference-Reference link is created when geometry is copied from one part to another without the use of a product file. The geometry is pasted into the new part based on part origins and the instance positioning is lost. This method is convenient when instance positioning is not important or when a model has been designed using body coordinates, because these parts overlay with the same origin.

When pasting a published reference between parts in separate windows, the resulting feature name contains an exclamation mark, as shown in Figure 3–2. This can be used to determine that a Reference-Reference link has been defined.

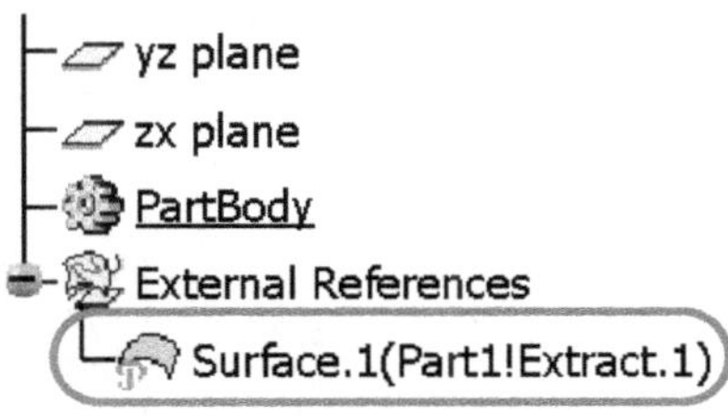

Figure 3–2

Reference-Instance Links

A Reference-Instance link is created when geometry is copied from one part to another in the context of an assembly. When copying geometry in an assembly, the instance positioning is maintained.

When pasting a published reference between parts in an assembly, the resulting feature name does not contain an exclamation mark.

3.2 Referenced Geometry Symbols

When using external references, CATIA reports the current status of the link with referenced geometry symbols in the specification tree of the target part. The symbols are shown next to each referenced element under **External References** in the specification tree.

Referenced geometry symbols are described as follows:

Symbol	Description
	Reference is up to date.
	Source geometry is modified. Geometry must be synchronized to incorporate source geometry changes in the target part.
	Source geometry file is deleted or cannot be found.
	External link is deactivated. Synchronization is not possible even if **Synchronize all external references for update** is activated.
	External reference is isolated or broken.

3.3 Managing External Links

Creating references to other documents helps ensure consistent designs. As the number of documents increases, it might be difficult to remember where information in a document is being read from. The Links dialog box enables you to manage external links in documents.

*To access one body in the document, select the body before selecting **Edit>Links**.*

The Links dialog box enables you to review the external references of an entire document or just one body in the document. Select **Edit>Links** to open the Links dialog box. The dialog box contains two tabs: *Links* and *Pointed Documents*.

Links Tab

The *Links* tab lists all of the external references in the selected element. Select a link in the window to display its full path at the bottom of the dialog box, as shown in Figure 3–3.

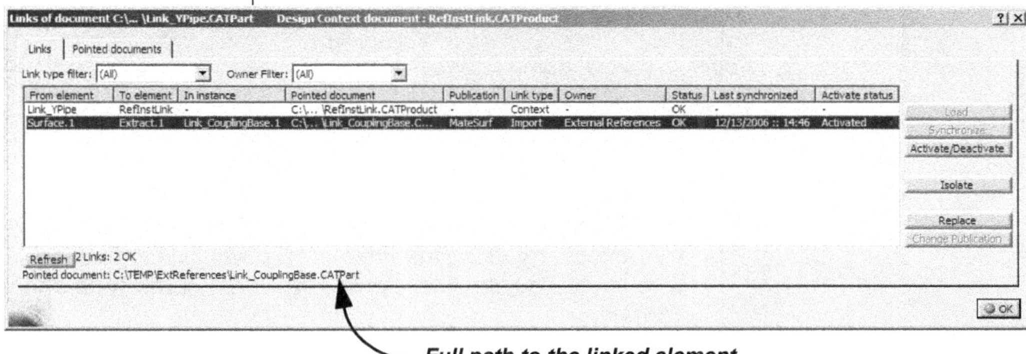

Figure 3–3

The various columns provide information on the selected link. They are described as follows:

Column	Description
From Element	Referenced element.
To Element	Referencing element.
Pointed Document	Document containing referenced element.
Link Type	Type of reference (e.g., Import, CCP, etc.).
Owner	Body that link belongs to in current body.
Status	Can be shown as: • **OK** • **Not Synchronized** • **Reference Not Found** • **Document Not Found** • **Document Not Loaded** • **Isolated**
Last Synchronized	Time and date link was updated to original copied element.
Active Status	Status of link (activated or deactivated).

If the document you are reviewing contains a number of external references, try using the Filter drop-down lists to find the reference. You can filter the information by **Link type** and/or **Owner**.

Use the following icons on the right side of the tab to help manage links:

- Load
- Synchronize
- Activate/Deactivate
- Isolate
- Replace
- Change Publication

Clicking **Load** opens a document that contains an external linked element in the session. The **Load** function only loads body information; it does not actually open the body. A document that is **not loaded**, as shown in Figure 3–4, means that the reference body is not in session and CATIA is displaying the last known configuration of that body. If changes are made to the linked element, they are not displayed in the body until the referenced document is loaded.

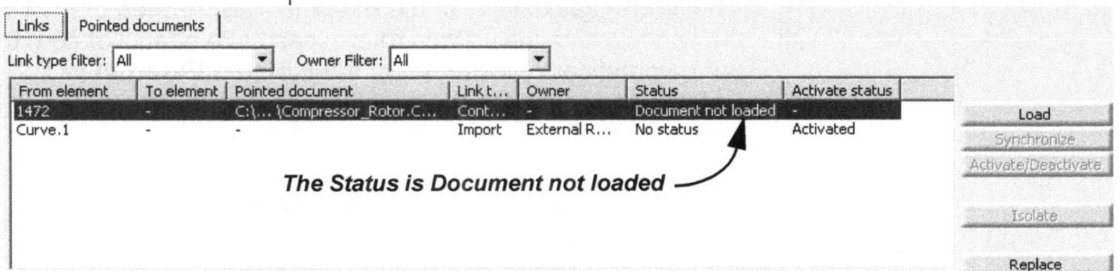

Figure 3–4

A link also synchronizes when the body is updated, as long as the linked documents are loaded and the link is active.

Clicking **Synchronize** updates a link. If a change is made in the linked element, the copied element in the current document needs to be synchronized to the referencing document to reflect the changes. This icon is only available if the highlighted link needs to be updated. If a link requires synchronization, the link type denotes **not Synchronized**, as shown in Figure 3–5. The Link Type changes to **OK** once a link is synchronized.

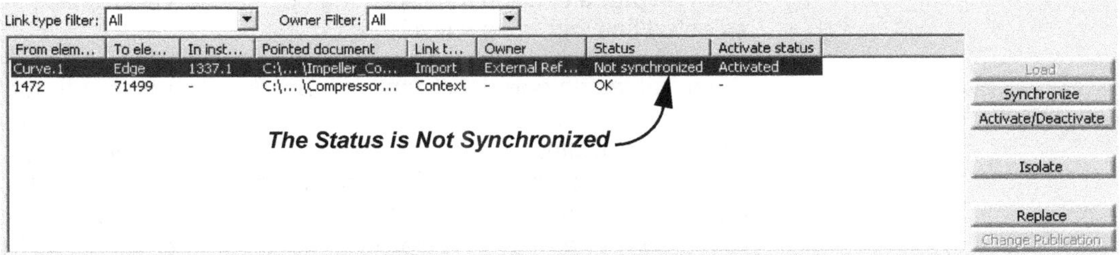

Figure 3–5

Clicking **Activate/Deactivate** activates or deactivates the status of a link. Deactivating a link temporarily breaks the association between the copied element and its reference. This prevents the element from synchronizing with the reference document while the body is being updated. To reactivate a link, click **Activate/Deactivate** again.

If changes are made to the reference document while the link was deactivated, **Synchronize** displays.

Clicking **Isolate** removes the link between the referenced document and the current document. An isolated link is no longer displayed in the dialog box and cannot be re-linked. To recreate a link, you need to copy the referenced element again and delete the element that was isolated.

Link references display in the **External References** branch in the specification tree. Once references have been isolated, they are automatically moved under the **Isolated External References** branch in the specification tree, as shown in Figure 3–6.

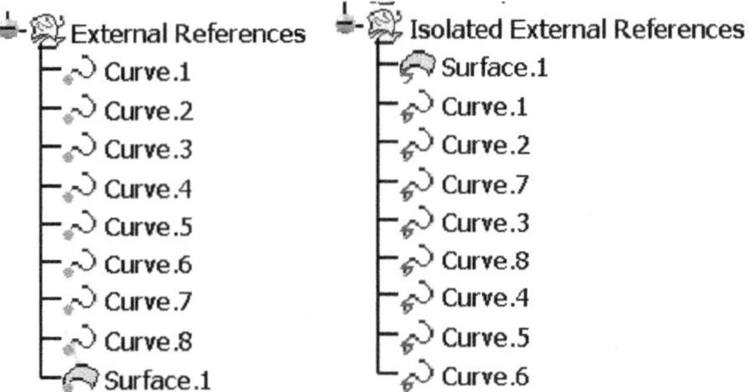

Figure 3–6

Click **Replace** to open the replacing document. This replaces the selected link with a new link.

When replacing one document with another, remember that the replacing elements must be compatible with the original (e.g., you cannot replace a circular element with a linear element). Additionally, you cannot replace a document with a document of the same name. It is recommended that you replace a document with a copy of a body that was created using **File>Save As**. This ensures that the references in the old document update correctly to the new document.

Click **Change Publication** to replace the selected publication with a new one. To use this option, the link must be part to part and not in the context of an assembly. Only one link can be changed at a time using this option.

Pointed Documents Tab

The *Pointed Documents* tab displays additional information on the document that contains the referenced elements. Select a reference in the *Pointed document* column to display a preview image of the referenced document, as shown in Figure 3–7.

When investigating external links with Product files, the *Pointed Documents* tab lists the file path to the directly referenced component, and the file path to the Product file.

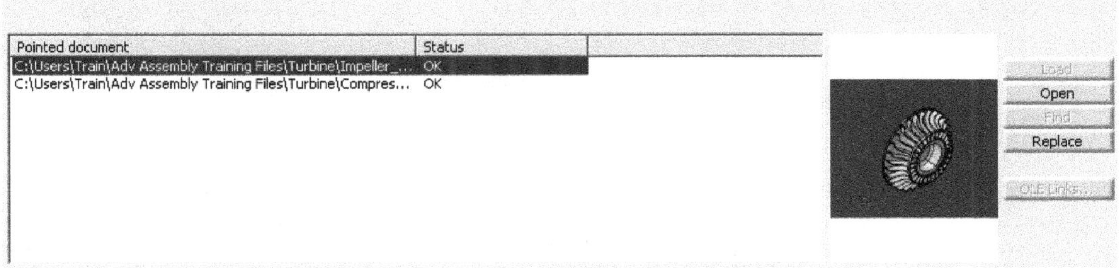

Figure 3–7

Use the following icons on the right side of the tab to help manage the documents that contain the referenced elements:

- Load
- Open
- Find
- Replace

Clicking **Load** opens the selected document in the session. Loading a document this way is the same as loading it from the *Links* tab. If changes have been made to any elements in the reference document, those elements need to be synchronized in the *Links* tab.

Clicking **Open** opens the selected document and makes it the active document in the session. This option is useful for quickly locating the original file if changes need to be made.

Clicking **Find** locates broken links. The File Selection dialog box opens and you can browse to any missing documents. Documents often go missing if they have been moved from the folder from which CATIA last opened them or have been renamed. For example, a document could display a status of **Document not found**.

Use **Find** to browse to the new location of the document and update the link. Once updated, the status changes to **OK**, as shown in Figure 3–8.

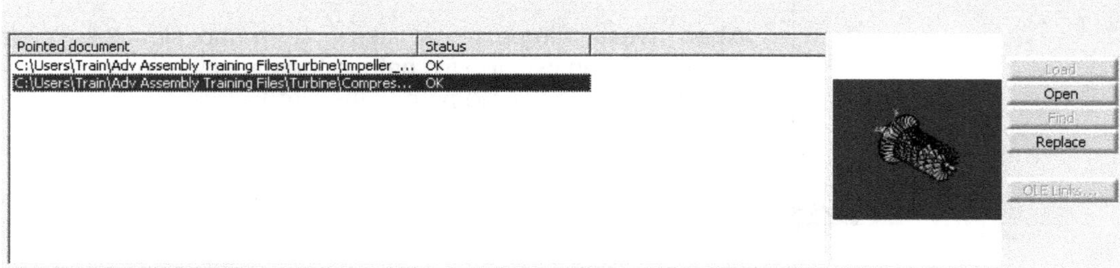

Figure 3–8

Replace is similar to the option in the *Links* tab, except that it reroutes all of the referenced elements from the original file to the new file. **Replace** in the *Links* tab only reroutes the selected link to the new document.

3.4 Collaborative Design

In a collaborative design environment, many designers work concurrently to design various components of an overall assembly.

Typically, a Project Manager is responsible for the overall project as shown in Figure 3–9. They create the overall assembly structure and determine which components need to be designed by which designers based on their expertise. The Project Manager must also facilitate communication between all members of the team.

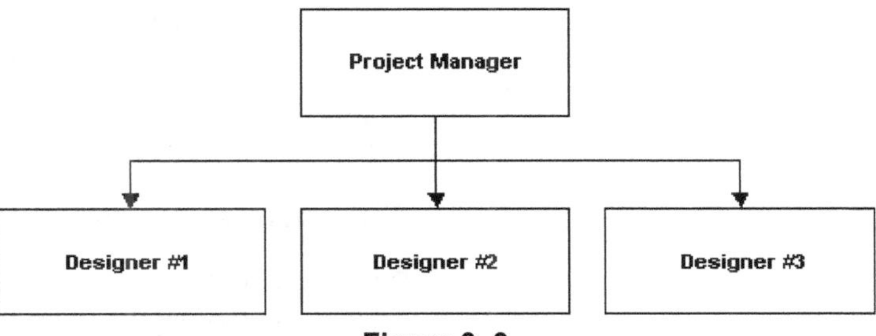

Figure 3–9

Consider the assembly shown in Figure 3–10. It requires the expertise of many team members.

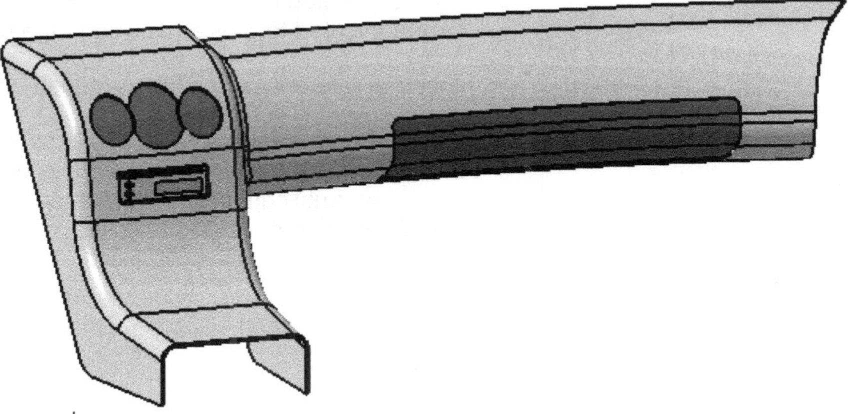

Figure 3–10

The Project Manager develops an overall product structure, as shown in Figure 3–11, and must ensure that the overall design considerations are propagated to the components in the assembly for designers to use.

Figure 3–11

While this environment has many benefits, it is important to consider the issues that can cause difficulties, such as:

- Files can be accidentally overwritten or deleted.
- Computational resources can be taxed, because a collaborative design environment is often used when working with very large, complex assemblies.
- There can be difficulties in ensuring that everyone is working with the latest revisions of the assembly. Files might not be correctly stored or design changes not correctly communicated to those involved in the project.
- External references can be created to unrelated components.

You have already seen some solutions to these issues. Skeleton models can help ensure that everyone is working with the latest revisions and publications can help ensure that unnecessary relationships are not created.

3.5 Work in Progress Assembly

A collaborative design environment is often used when working with large, complex assemblies that require a large amount of computational resources. However, a designer is typically only working with some of the components making up the overall assembly and often does not need to open the entire assembly.

A Work in Progress (WIP) assembly is a temporary product file that only houses components relevant to what the designer must accomplish. A WIP assembly helps alleviate some of the system resource issues associated with working on large assemblies.

Another benefit of using a WIP assembly is to help ensure that changes are not accidentally made to models (ideally, a PDM system is used and reference models can be checked out of the system as read-only). While the WIP assembly method is typically used in conjunction with a PDM system, it can still be applied when not using one.

General Steps

Use the following general steps to create a WIP assembly:

1. Create an empty assembly file.
2. Insert the reference data.
3. Insert the design data.
4. Create geometry.
5. Save the design data.

Step 1 - Create an empty assembly file.

A WIP assembly is a temporary product file that only houses files from the overall assembly that the designer needs to complete their portion of the project. Select **File>New>Product** to create an empty assembly, as shown in Figure 3–12.

Figure 3–12

Reference data consists of existing components that aid in the design of the required components. Reference components help you design in the context of the top-level assembly without needing the top-level assembly to be open. This data should never be modified inside the WIP assembly.

Carefully consider the reference data required for completion of the design components. By only inserting the minimum number of reference components required to create the design components, you can keep computer resources to a minimum. For example, the assembly shown in Figure 3–13 is required.

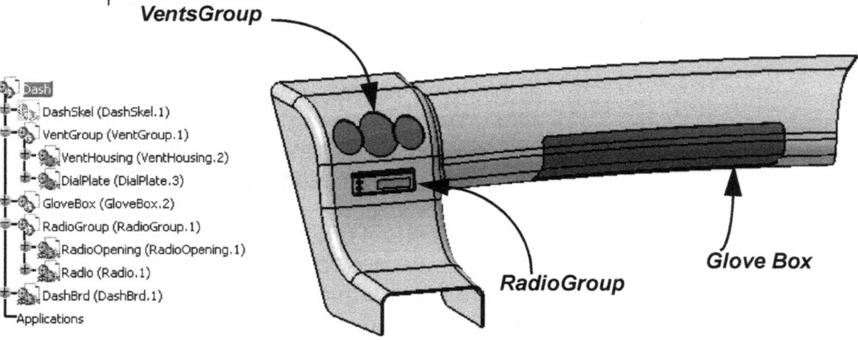

Figure 3–13

The designer must create the **RadioOpening** component in the RadioGroup subassembly. To create this component, the skeleton model and **VentGroup** components from the top-level assembly are required as reference data as shown in Figure 3–14. The rest of the assembly is not required, so only the two essential components are inserted into the WIP.

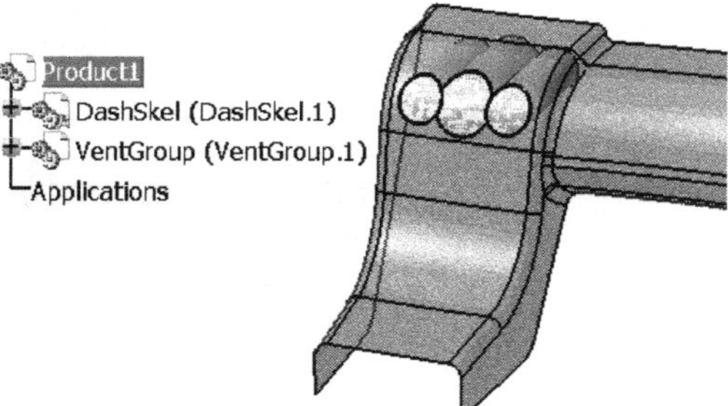

Figure 3–14

Step 2 - Insert the design data.

Design data is the geometry that you are going to modify or create. When working in a collaborative design environment, empty components have often already been created at the top level to define the structure for the assembly. These empty components can be inserted into the WIP assembly so that geometry can be added to them.

To continue with the same example, the Project Manager has already created an empty component in the top-level assembly for the **Radio Opening** component. The empty component is inserted into the WIP assembly, as shown in Figure 3–15, and the geometry is added to it.

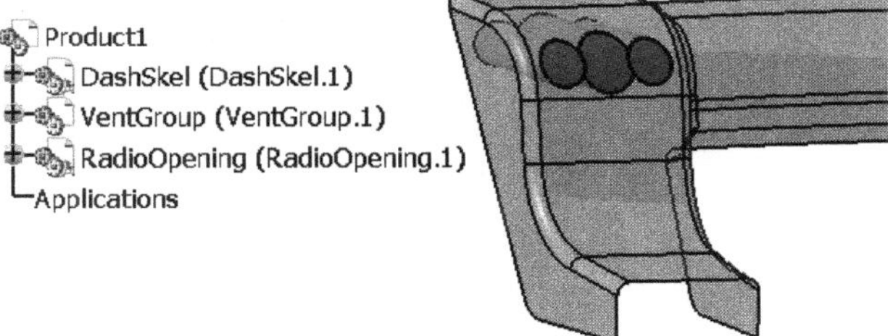

Figure 3–15

Step 3 - Create geometry.

Once the reference and design data have been inserted into the WIP assembly, geometry can be constructed, as shown in Figure 3–16.

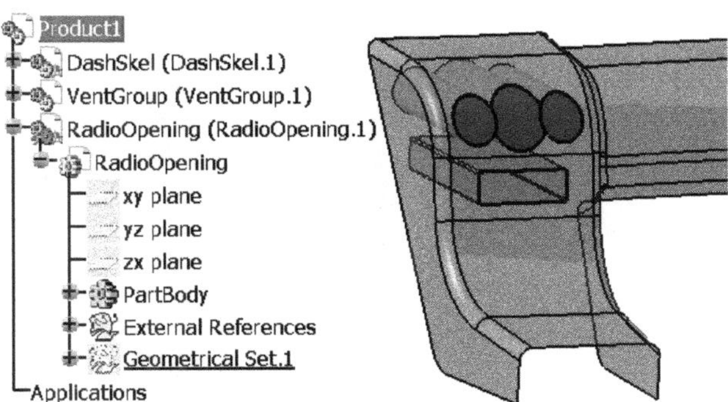

Figure 3–16

By using publications and referencing a skeleton model, you can maintain correct parent/child relationships. Remember to give careful consideration when referencing geometry in another component to build the design data. Logical external references are essential for flexible, robust design work.

Step 4 - Save the design data.

Save the design data at least once a day to the central location for the entire project. This ensures that others using your design data as their reference data have the most up-to-date geometry. Because reference geometry should not be changed inside the WIP assembly, this data should not be saved to the central location. This avoids overwriting someone else's work.

3.6 Collaborative Design: Best Practices

While each company develops their own standards on how they want their collaborative design environment to operate based on company standards, existing data, file management, etc., there are some best practices that should be considered:

- Ensure that there is good communication in the group.

  One of the key benefits of collaborative design is that projects can be quickly and accurately completed. If communication is not maintained between the designers, incorrect information can set back a project's completion date considerably. It is important to carefully consider the references that are being established and to ensure that unnecessary references are not being created. Skeleton models and publications can be a key tool in keeping all models accurate and up to date.
- Keep the WIP assembly as light as possible.

  Using a WIP assembly can help keep computer resources to a minimum. However, inserting unnecessary reference components into the WIP assembly can defeat its purpose. Always consider which components need to be referenced to design the required models, and only copy the necessary components.
- Use a PDM system.

  Many PDM systems are available and using one can be key to keeping an organized project. PDM systems help avoid some of the pitfalls associated with collaborative work. They can ensure revision control, that files are not accidentally overwritten or deleted, and that reference data is maintained as read-only in the WIP assembly. While a PDM system is not essential to collaborative design work, it is recommended.
- Keep the reference components as read-only.

  Keeping reference data as read-only helps designers avoid accidentally making changes to them in the WIP assembly. Using a PDM system can help in this practice. By ensuring that reference components used in the WIP assembly are set to a read-only status, you can be sure that changes are not accidentally made to the models.

- Links should always go from top downward.

  Ensuring that external links always go from the top-level downward helps avoid circular references.
- Avoid unnecessary external links.

  External references help create robust models that can be quickly modified when necessary. However, creating unnecessary or illogical references can make design changes difficult. Always consider the external reference being created and ask whether creating the reference helps maintain the design intent of the model. If it does not, do not create the reference.

*To create a new component, select **Insert>New Component**.*

- Create empty components for the reference and design data.

  Consider creating empty components for the reference and design data in the WIP assembly. These components help organize the Product structure. However, do not create a physical CATProduct file that needs to be maintained.

3.7 Converting a Product to a Part

The **Generate CATPart from Product** tool enables you to convert an entire product, including all of the associated subassemblies and parts, into a single CATPart model. This can be useful in the following situations:

- To simplify a complex assembly.
- To send a featureless version of an assembly to another CATIA user.
- To manage the bill of materials. (For example, to a manufacturer, a spark plug is an assembly. However, an automotive company would consider this a single part.)

When converting an assembly to a part model, consider the following:

- Elements that are hidden are not converted.
- Components that are deactivated are not converted.
- For large assemblies, the use of cache management reduces conversion time. Each component is temporarily switched to design mode and converted.
- Each component is converted to an isolated solid feature. By stripping away feature information, the conversion ensures that proprietary or confidential part information is removed from the resulting CATPart model.

General Steps

Use the following general steps to generate a part file from a product:

1. Open the assembly.
2. Start the **Generate CATPart from Product** tool.
3. Select the Product.
4. Complete the operation.

Step 1 - Open the assembly.

Open the CATProduct that is going to be converted. A **Spark Plug** assembly consisting of seven components is shown in Figure 3–17.

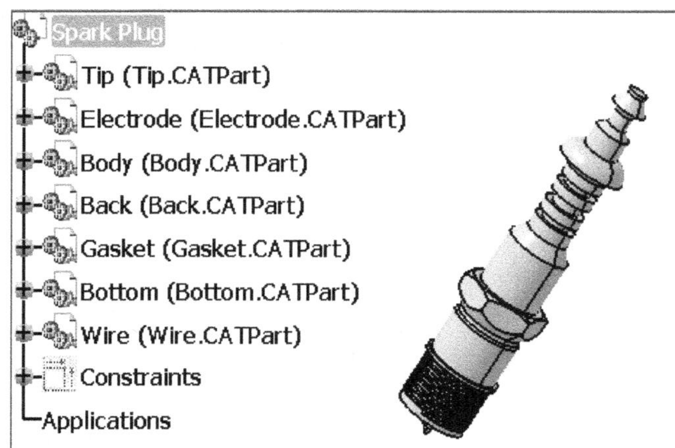

Figure 3–17

Hide any components that should not be included in the final CATPart model. Hidden and deactivated components are excluded from the conversion.

Step 2 - Start the Generate CATPart from Product tool.

When the required product has been opened, select **Tools>Generate CATPart from Product** to begin the conversion. The Generate CATPart from Product dialog box opens as shown in Figure 3–18.

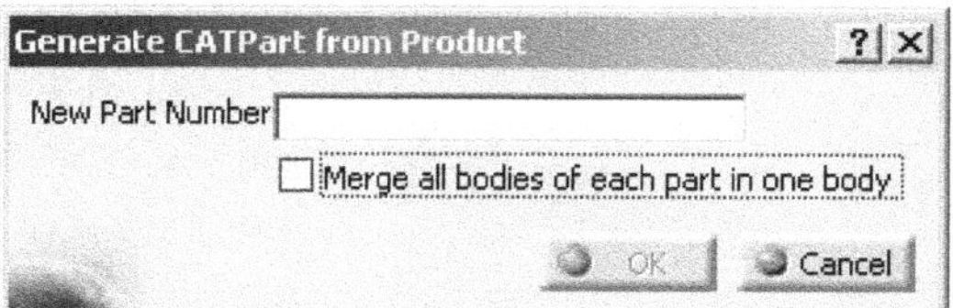

Figure 3–18

In the specification tree, select the assembly to be converted. For example, the top-level assembly **Spark Plug** is selected. A part number for the new part model automatically displays in the dialog box, as shown in Figure 3–19. The part number consists of the assembly name followed by **_AllCATPart**, and can be edited manually.

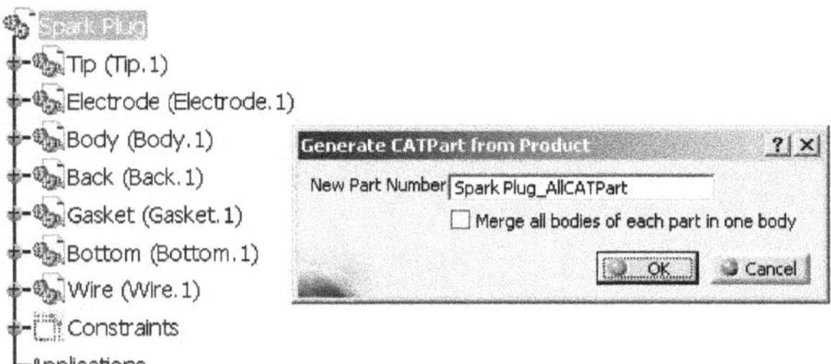

Figure 3–19

Step 3 - Complete the operation.

To create the merged CATPart model, click **OK**. The system creates the model and opens it in a new CATIA window. The specification tree for the merged part created with default options is shown in Figure 3–20.

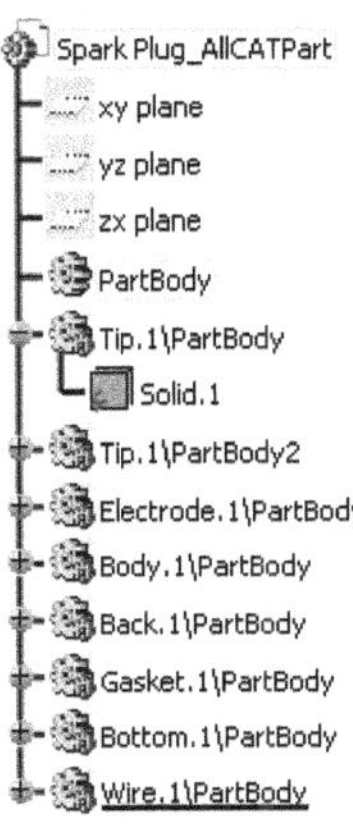

Figure 3–20

Each body contains an isolated solid feature that represents the original part geometry.

Each body is named after the component that was merged. With default options, the system creates a new body for each body in a component (e.g., **Tip.1\PartBody** and **Tip.1\PartBody2**). Options in the Part to Product dialog box enable you to control how the system handles multi-body parts.

Body Options

The **Merge all bodies of each part in one body** option affects the resulting CATPart when there are multiple bodies in one or more of the parts that make up the original assembly. For example, the **Tip** component has two bodies, as shown in Figure 3–21.

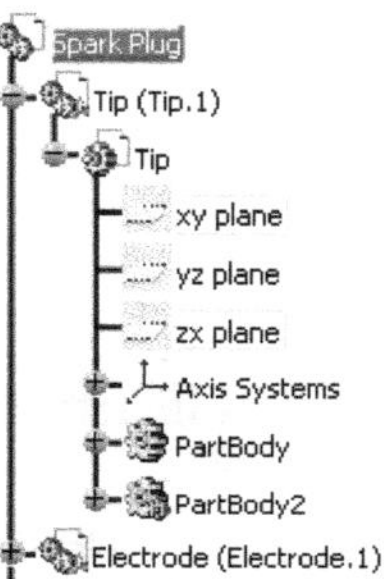

Figure 3–21

When the **Merge all bodies of each part in one body** option is selected, the system places the geometry from all of the bodies in a single body. The first feature in the body is an isolated solid representing the geometry of the first body. All other bodies are assembled using a boolean operation, as shown in Figure 3–22

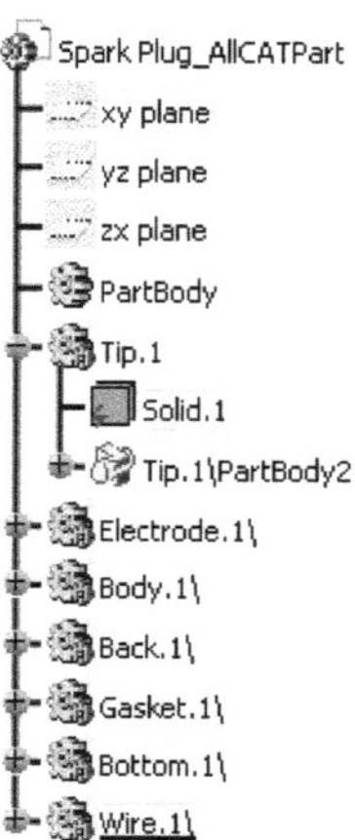

Figure 3–22

3.8 Associativity Function

The **Associativity** feature is similar to the **Generate CATPart from Product** tool. The only difference is that a link is established between the assembly components and the part model. The associative part is also instantiated into the assembly. The single part version of the assembly can be kept updated using this link.

General Steps

Use the following general steps to create an associative part:

1. Open the assembly.
2. Create the associative part.
3. Complete the operation.

Step 1 - Open the assembly.

Open the CATProduct that has the associative model. A **Spark Plug** assembly, consisting of seven components is shown in Figure 3–23.

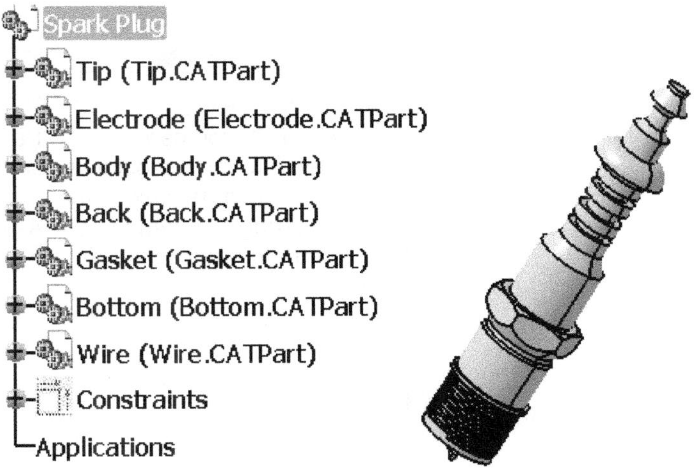

Figure 3–23

Step 2 - Create the associative part.

When the required product has been opened, click (Associativity). The Assembly Part Association dialog box opens as shown in Figure 3–24.

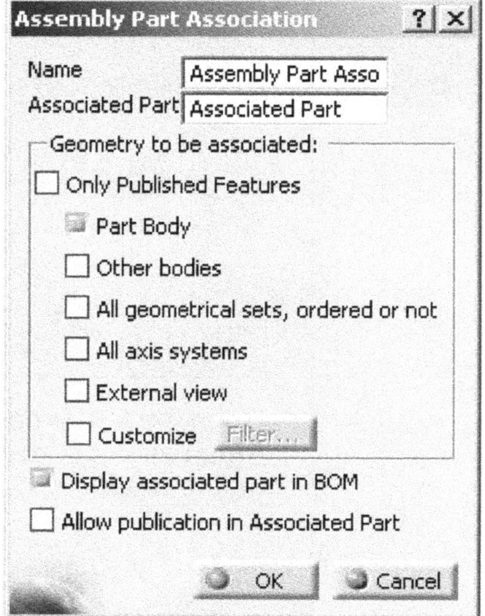

Figure 3–24

If required, you can specify the different geometry types to be copied into the associative part by selecting the options in the *Geometry to be associated* area. You can also rename the part by entering the name in the *Associated Part* area. If you want to rename the assembly feature name, you can use the *Name* area.

Step 3 - Complete the operation.

When all of the required selections are finished, click **OK** to complete the feature. The model displays in the specification tree as shown in Figure 3–25. Every single body in the model represents one of the components of the assembly.

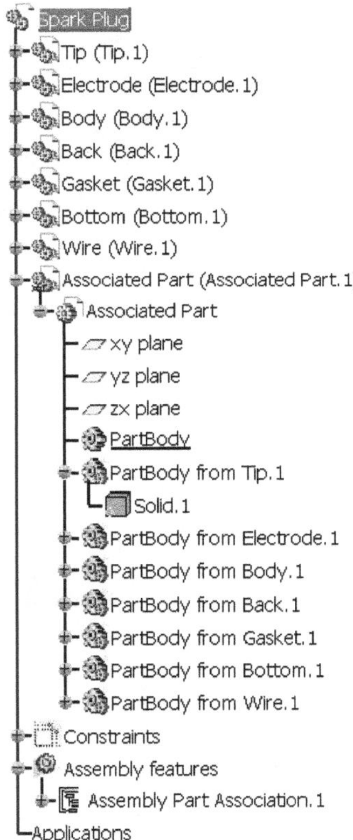

Figure 3–25

Practice 3a Link Types

Practice Objectives

- Develop a reference-reference link.
- Develop a reference-instance link.

In this practice, you will investigate two methods of creating linked geometry. The first method involves a **Copy** and **Paste** operation between two part models that have been opened in separate windows. You will then compare this to a **Copy** and **Paste** operation between the same two parts that have been positioned in an assembly.

The linked geometry you develop will be used to define the interface between the coupling base and y-pipe components. The face from the completed coupling model will be used to develop a Pad in the y-pipe. The completed geometry displays as shown in Figure 3–26.

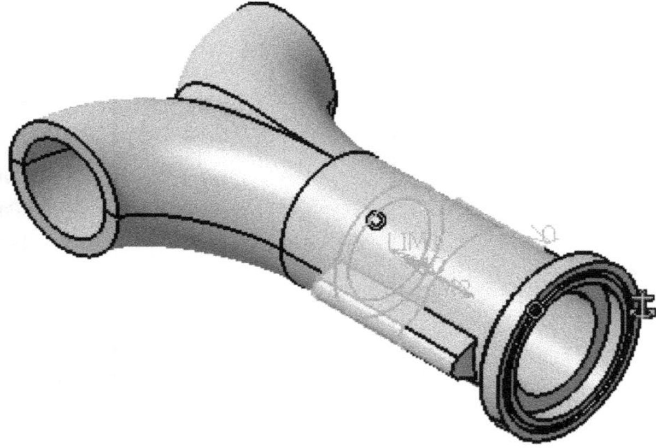

Figure 3–26

Task 1 - Publish geometry.

1. Open **Link_CouplingBase.CATPart** from the *Link* folder.
2. Expand and show **Geometrical Set.1**. It contains an extract of the top face of the part, as shown in Figure 3–27. This surface will be used to develop geometry in the y-pipe mating part.

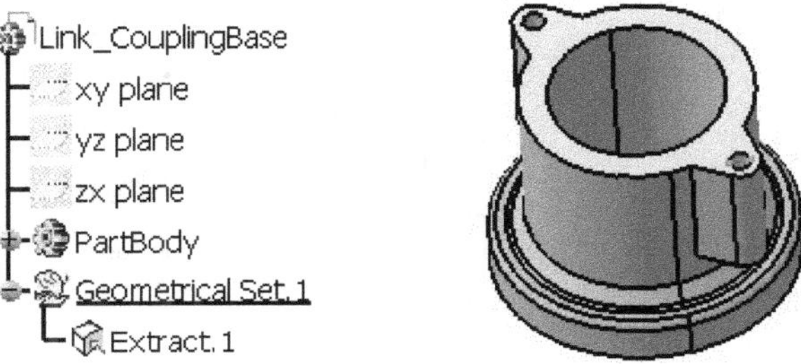

Figure 3–27

3. Publish **Extract.1** and rename the publication as **MateSurf**. The specification tree displays as shown in Figure 3–28.

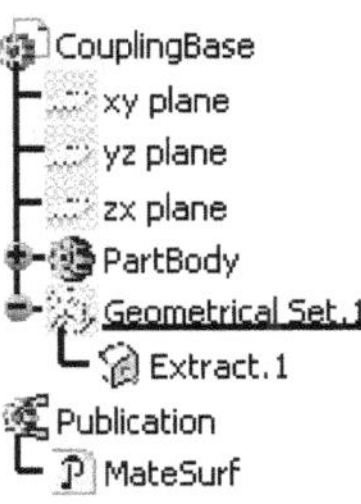

Figure 3–28

4. Save the model and keep **Link_CouplingBase.CATPart** open for the next task.

Task 2 - Open the ypipe model and manage the windows.

1. Open **Link_YPipe.CATPart** in a new window.
2. Select **Window>Tile Vertically** to display both parts in CATIA at the same time.

Task 3 - Create a Reference-Reference link.

A Reference-Reference link is generated between two models that are open in separate windows. In this task, a **Copy** and **Paste** operation will be performed to create the link.

1. Activate the **Link_CouplingBase** window and copy the **MateSurf** publication in the specification tree.
2. Activate the **Link_YPipe** window and select **Edit>Paste Special**. The Paste Special dialog box opens as shown in Figure 3–29.

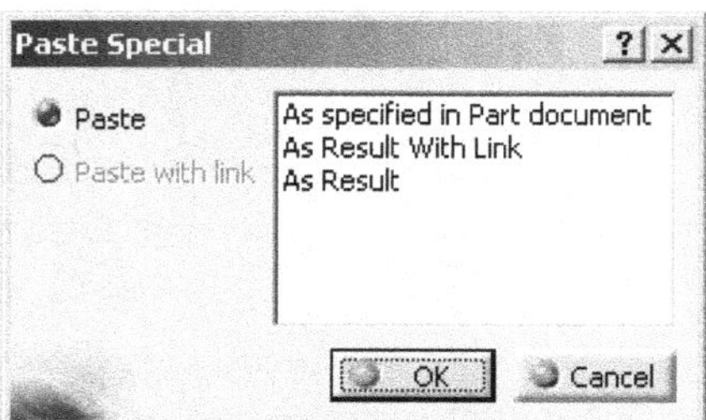

Figure 3–29

3. Select **As Result With Link** and click **OK**. The copied surface is added to the y-pipe model, as shown in Figure 3–30.

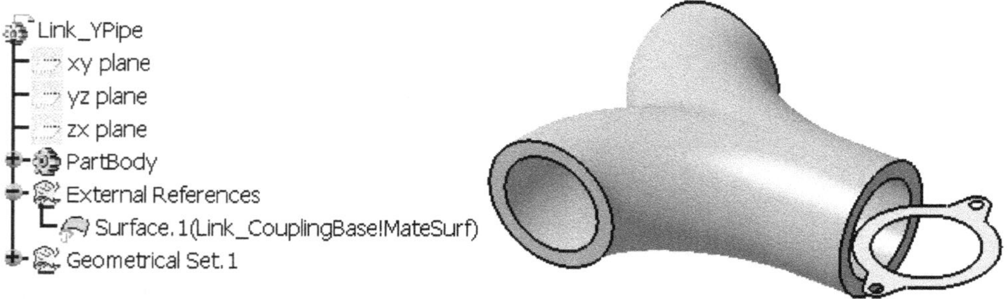

Figure 3–30

Design Considerations

A Reference-Reference link occurs when geometry is copied and pasted without the use of an assembly to define the positioning information. This results in the pasted data being placed at the same location with respect to the default axis system of the source model. This type of link is useful when positioning is not important (for example, when developing a linked parameter) or when the parts are to be developed using in-place modeling techniques.

The position of the copied geometry can be modified using transformation techniques from the Generative Shape Design workbench. A transformation operation, such as a rotation about the y-axis (as shown in the example in Figure 3–31) still maintains an associative link to the original publication. However, the end result is that all positioning is driven by the y-pipe part and will not change due to modifications to the coupling base.

This image is for demonstration purposes only. Do not perform this transformation.

Figure 3–31

4. Close all of the windows without saving.

Task 4 - Create an assembly.

1. Create a new product file with the name **RefInstLink**.
2. Insert **Link_CouplingBase.CATPart** and fix the component in the assembly.
3. Insert **Link_YPipe.CATPart**. Do not constrain the component in the assembly, so that it displays in its default location, as shown in Figure 3–32.

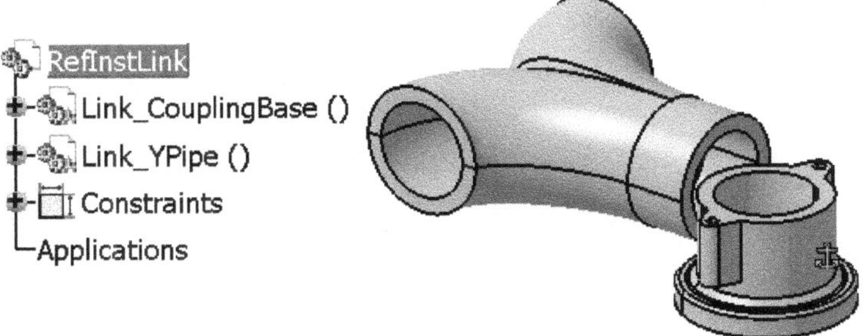

Figure 3–32

Task 5 - Develop a Reference-Instance link.

1. Activate the **Link_YPipe** component in the Part Design workbench.
2. In the tree, expand the **Link_CouplingBase** component to display the **Publications** branch.
3. Copy the **MateSurf** publication and paste it into **Link_YPipe** using the **Paste Special** and **As Result With Link** options. The copied surface displays as shown in Figure 3–33.

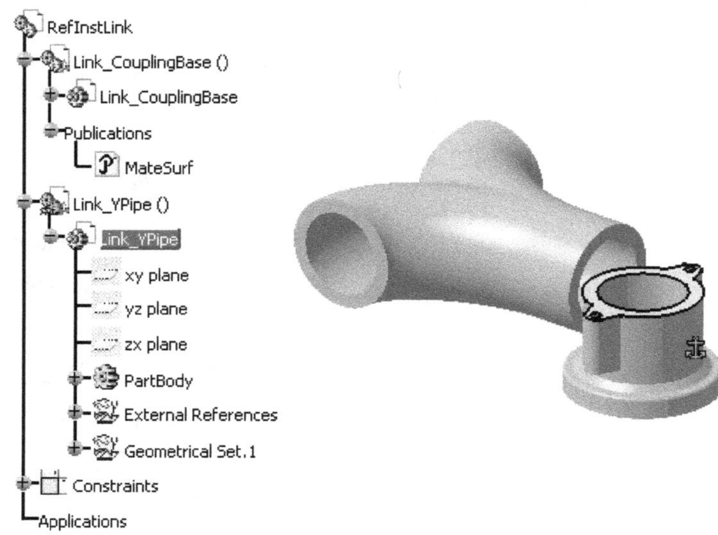

Figure 3–33

Design Considerations

When generating a Reference-Instance link between two components in an assembly, the position of the linked geometry is driven by the position of the source component in the assembly. Therefore, moving the **Link_YPipe** component into its assembled location will reposition the copied surface in the **Link_YPipe** part. This is because its position relative to the **Link_CouplingBase** component has changed.

To demonstrate this, you will reposition the **Link_YPipe** component. You will open the **Link_YPipe** model in a separate window first so that you can see the direct impact of the reposition operation on the copied surface.

Task 6 - Reposition Link_YPipe.

1. Activate the **RefInstLink** assembly.
2. In the specification tree, right-click on **Link_YPipe** and select **Link_YPipe object>Open in New Window**.
3. Hide the **External References** geometrical set.
4. Select **Window>Tile Vertically** to display the assembly and part simultaneously.
5. Activate the assembly window and add two assembly constraints (coincidence between axes and 30mm offset between faces) so that the updated assembly displays as shown in Figure 3–34.

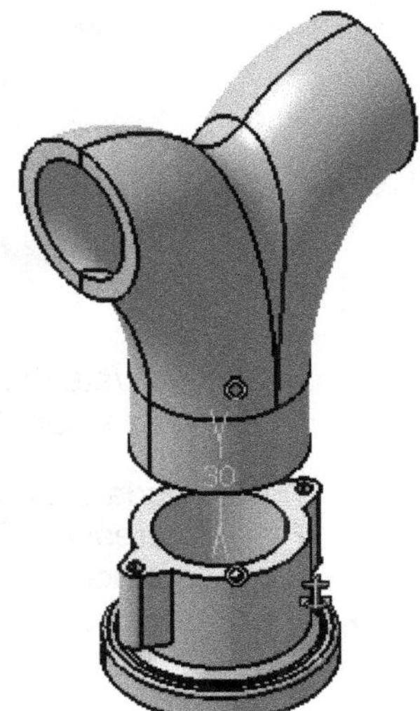

Figure 3–34

6. Activate the **Link_YPipe** window. If required, show the **External References** geometrical set and note that the relative position of the copied surface has changed.

Task 7 - Create a pad and modify the assembly positioning.

1. With the **Link_YPipe.CATPart** window active, create a Pad feature using the following parameters:
   - *Profile:* **MateSurf copied surface**
   - *Direction:* **yz plane**
   - *First Limit Type:* **Up to plane**
   - *Limit:* **Select the face shown in Figure 3–35**

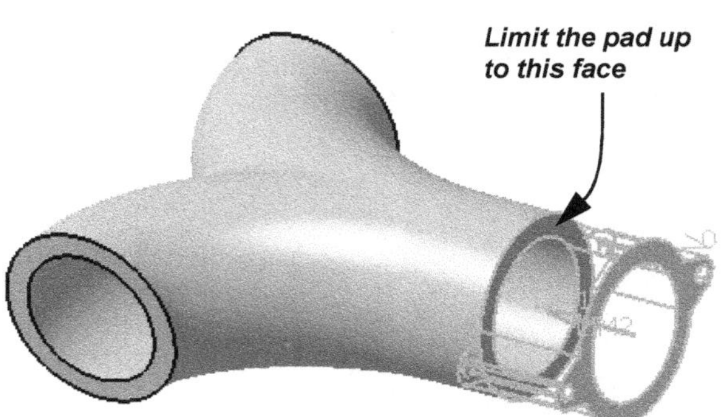

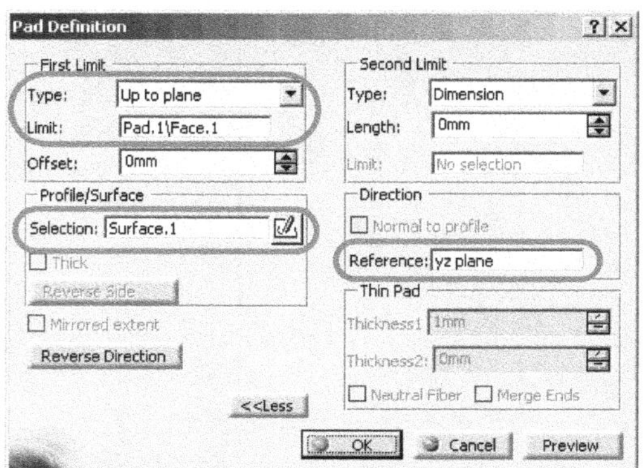

Figure 3–35

2. Activate the assembly window and modify the value of the *Offset constraint* to **40mm**.
3. Update the assembly. The length of the Pad has now increased. This is due to the position change of the copied surface in **YPipe**, based on the relative position change of the two components in the assembly.
4. Save the assembly and close the window.

Practice 3b

Creating a WIP

Practice Objectives

- Create an empty product.
- Add reference data.
- Add design data.

In this practice, you will create a work in progress (WIP) assembly. A WIP assembly is a tool used in contextual design to help alleviate the computer resource issues associated with large assembly work. A WIP is a temporary assembly that only houses the data necessary to complete the required components. In this practice, you will create a WIP that can be used to create the hoses that run from the intake manifold to the left and right heads of the engine, as shown in Figure 3–36.

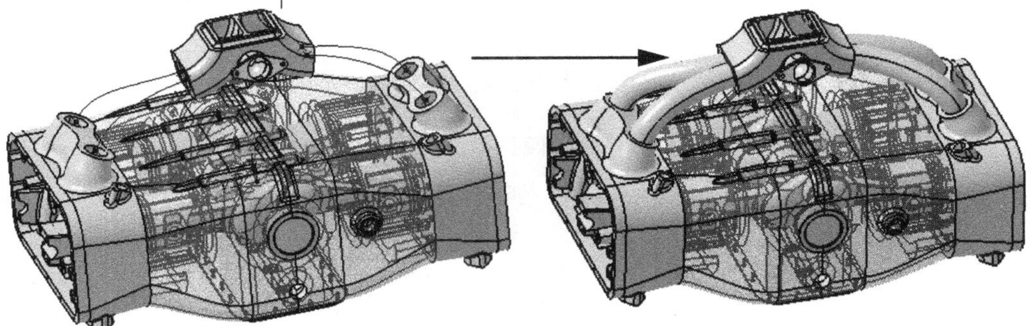

Figure 3–36

Task 1 - Open the top-level assembly.

In this task, you will open the top level assembly to review the geometry and determine the reference data required to create the hoses.

1. Open **Engine.CATProduct** in the *Engine_WIP* directory.

2. The **HoseRight** and **HoseLeft** components have already been created, as shown in Figure 3–37. These components do not currently contain any geometry.

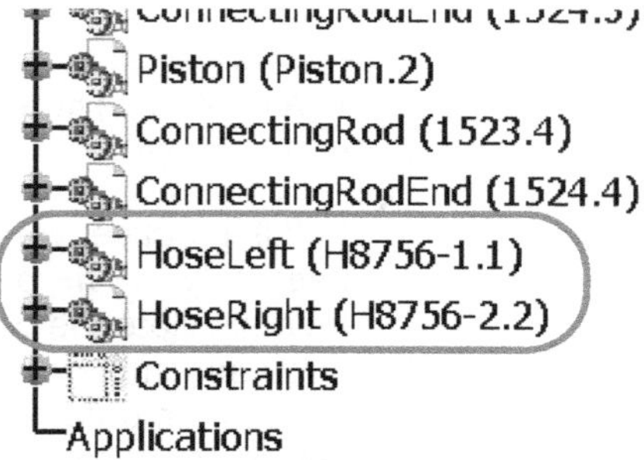

Figure 3–37

3. The splines have also been created, as shown in Figure 3–38. They were created and published in the skeleton model and will be used as center curves when creating the hoses. All of the geometry required for the creation of the hoses is found in the skeleton. Although the hoses could be created in the top-level assembly, it is not necessary to have the rest of this assembly open.

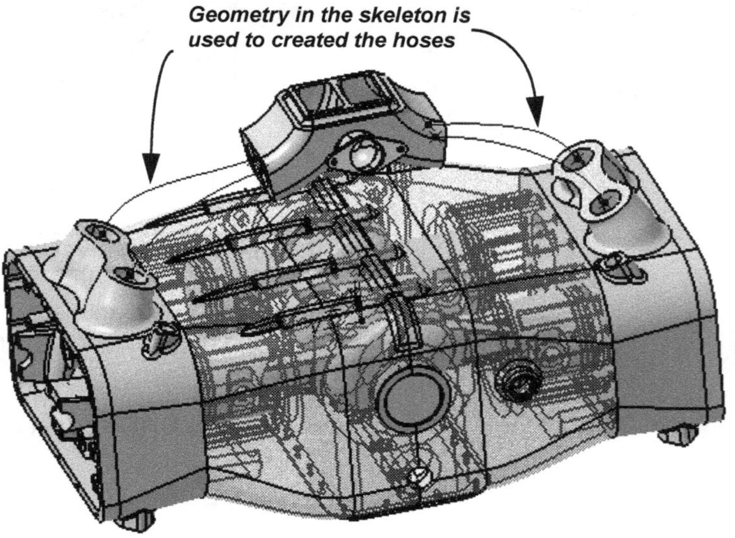

Figure 3–38

4. Close the assembly.

Task 2 - Create a Product file.

1. Create an empty Product with the name **WIP_Hoses** as shown in Figure 3–39 and save in the *Engine_WIP* folder.

Figure 3–39

Task 3 - Add the reference data.

Design Considerations

Reference data is existing geometry that will be used to create the design data. In this case, the only component necessary to create the hose is the skeleton model. It is good practice to only copy the reference data that is necessary for your component. Inserting additional reference data will unnecessarily tax the computer resources.

1. In the specification tree, right-click on the top-level assembly and select **Components>Existing Component**.
2. Insert **Skeleton.CATPart** from the *Engine_WIP* folder into the assembly, as shown in Figure 3–40.

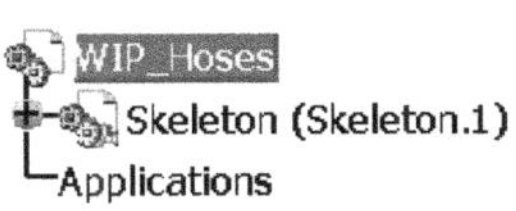

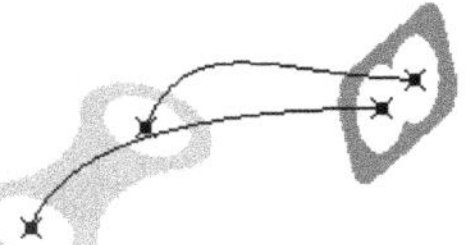

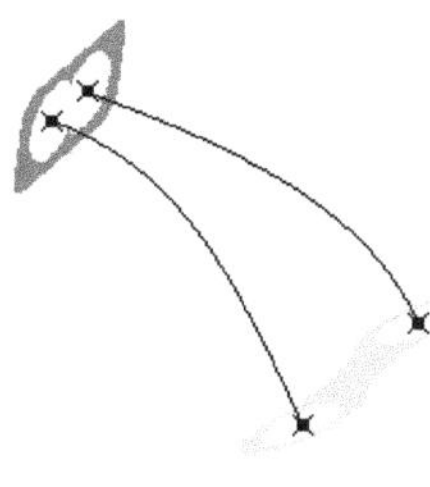

Figure 3–40

Task 4 - Add the design data.

Design Considerations

Design data is the geometry that you will be modifying or creating. To help keep the specification tree organized, you will create an empty component in which to insert the left and right hose components. By creating a new component (instead of a new Product), no new physical file is created that will need to be maintained.

1. In the specification tree, right-click on the top-level assembly and select **Components>New Component**.
2. Name the new component **DesignData**.
3. In the specification tree, right-click on the DesignData component and select **Components>Existing Component**.
4. Insert **HoseRight.CATPart**.
5. Insert **HoseLeft.CATPart** into the **DesignData** component. The specification tree displays as shown in Figure 3–41.

Figure 3–41

6. Save and close the WIP assembly.

Practice 3c

Contextual Design

Practice Objective

- Use a WIP assembly to create in context geometry.

In this practice, you will create geometry in the context of an assembly. Because opening all of the components in the assembly can be taxing on computer resources, a WIP assembly has been created. You will create hoses that extend from the intake manifold to the left and right heads of the engine, as shown in Figure 3–42.

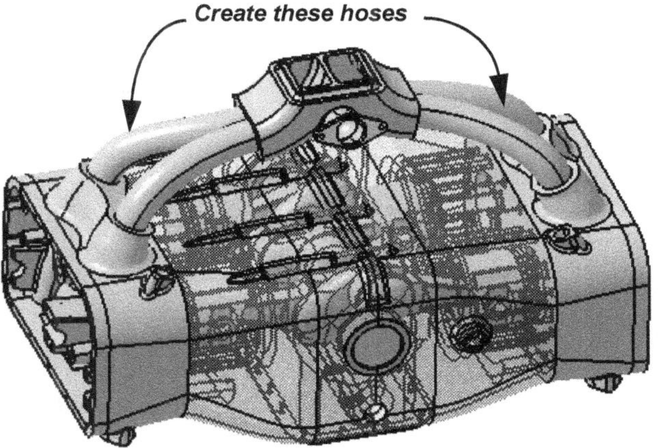

Figure 3–42

Task 1 - Open the WIP assembly.

1. Open **WIP_Hosesb.CATproduct**.

   You can also continue to use the WIP assembly that you created in the previous practice.

Design Considerations

The WIP assembly includes all of the reference data required to create the hoses. A component has been created that houses the design data as shown in Figure 3–43 (in this case, the **HoseLeft** and **HoseRight** components). Currently, these components do not contain any geometry. You will create the geometry.

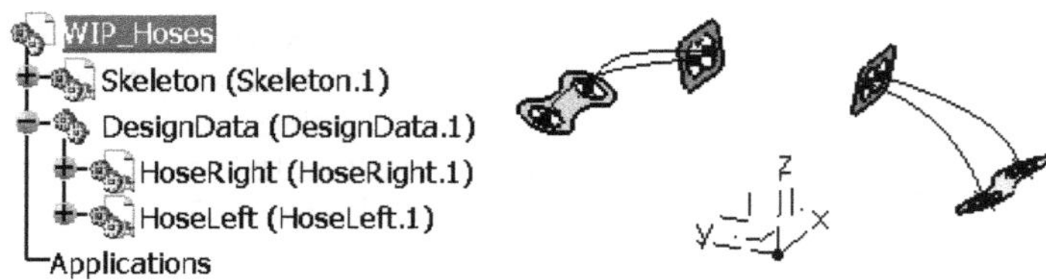

Figure 3–43

Task 2 - Create the right hose.

Design Considerations

In the next two tasks, you will create the hoses. Because the purpose of this practice is to demonstrate how to use a WIP assembly for contextual design, you will create the hoses using a Rib feature from the Part Design workbench. To obtain more precise geometry for the hose component, surface features should be considered.

1. Activate the **HoseRight** component.
2. Ensure that the Part Design workbench is active.
3. Click (Rib).
4. Select the **Right_HoseProfile1** published element in the skeleton model as the profile.
5. Select the **RightHose_CenterCurve1** published element in the skeleton model as the center curve as shown in Figure 3–44.

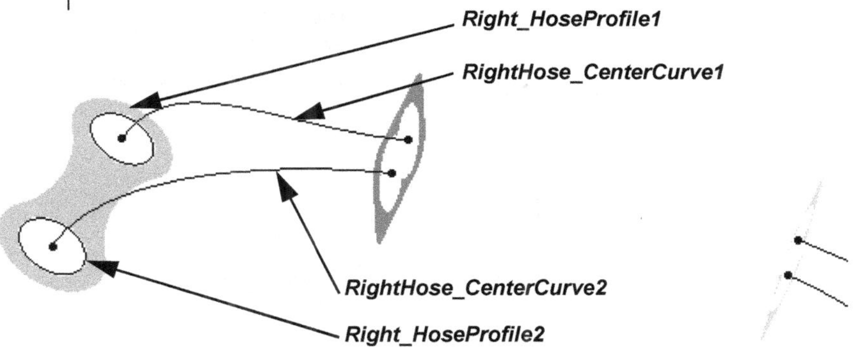

Figure 3–44

6. Click **OK** to complete the Rib feature.
7. Create a second Rib using the **Right_HoseProfile2** published element in the skeleton model as the profile, and the **RightHose_CenterCurve2** published element as the center curve. The model displays as shown in Figure 3–45.

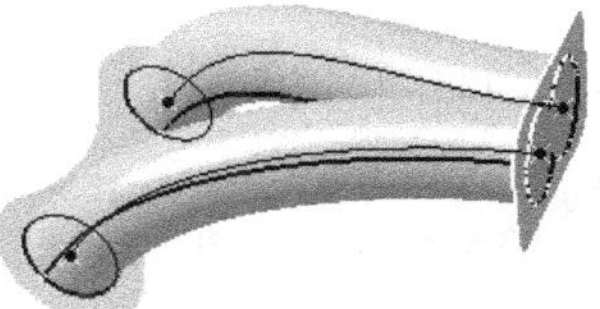

Figure 3–45

8. Click (Shell).
9. Select the end surfaces of both Ribs, as shown in Figure 3–46, as the faces to remove.

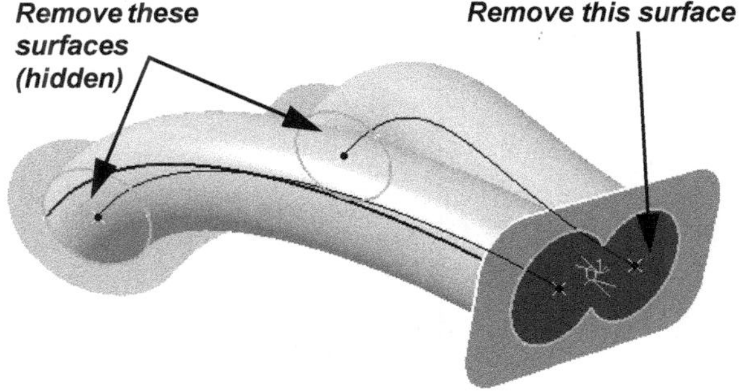

Figure 3–46

10. Enter a *default outside thickness* of **2** and a *default inside thickness* of **0** and complete the operation. The model displays as shown in Figure 3–47.

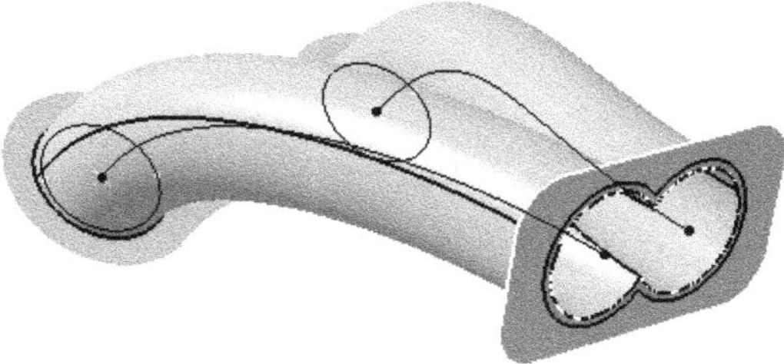

Figure 3–47

Task 3 - Create the left hose.

1. Activate the **HoseLeft** component.
2. Ensure that the Part Design workbench is active.
3. Click (Rib).
4. Select the **Left_HoseProfile1** published element in the skeleton model as the profile.
5. Select the **LeftHose_CenterCurve1** published element in the skeleton model as the center curve as shown in Figure 3–48.

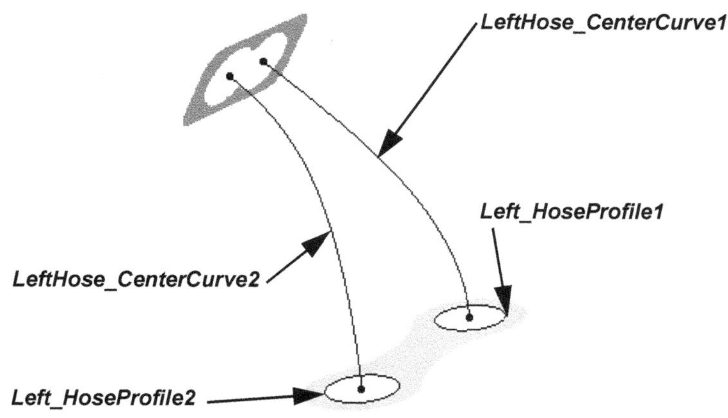

Figure 3–48

6. Click **OK** to complete the Rib feature.
7. Create a second Rib using the **Left_HoseProfile2** published element in the skeleton model as the profile and the **LeftHose_CenterCurve2** published element as the center curve. The model displays as shown in Figure 3–49.

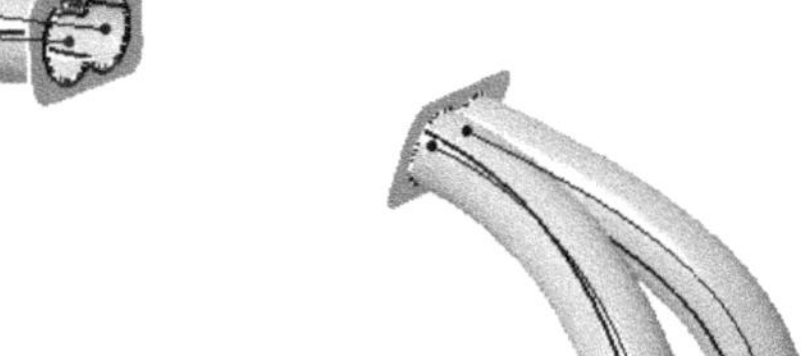

Figure 3–49

8. Click (Shell).
9. For the faces to remove, select the end surfaces of both Ribs as shown in Figure 3–50.

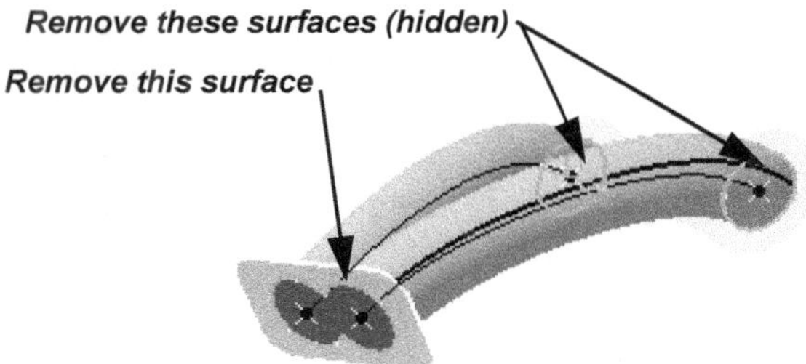

Figure 3–50

10. Enter a *default outside thickness* of **2** and a *default inside thickness* of **0** and complete the operation. The model displays as shown in Figure 3–51.

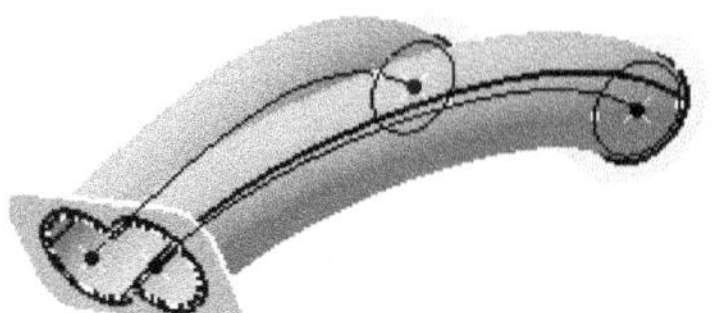

Figure 3–51

11. Use the **Save Management** tool to save the **WIP_Hoses**b assembly.

Task 4 - Review the top-level assembly.

1. Open **Engine.CATProduct**.
2. For clarity, hide the **Skeleton** component. The **HoseLeft** and **HoseRight** components are now up to date in the top-level assembly, as shown in Figure 3–52.

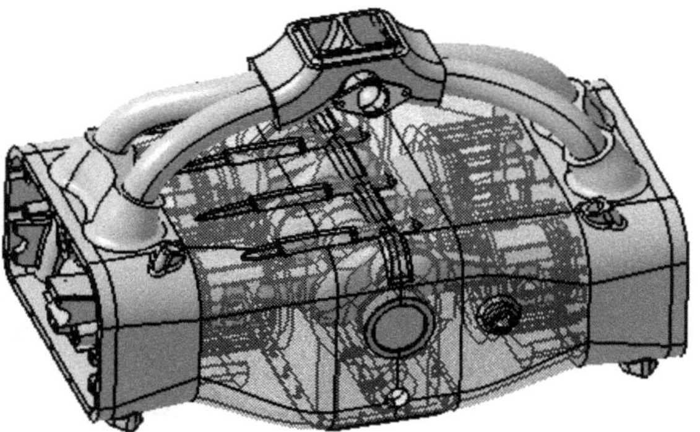

Figure 3–52

Design Considerations

If additional changes to the hoses are not required, the WIP assembly can be deleted. The WIP assembly is a temporary assembly used to help reduce computer resources when working with large assemblies. If additional changes to the hoses are required after the WIP assembly has been deleted, another WIP assembly could be created in which to make the modifications.

Practice 3d

Creating a CATPart from CATProduct

Practice Objective

- Create a CATPart from a CATProduct.

In this practice, you will create a CATPart file from a product using the **Generate CATPart from Product** tool.

Task 1 - Open a Product file.

1. Open **SparkPlug.CATProduct** from the *SparkPlug* folder. The assembly displays as shown in Figure 3–53.

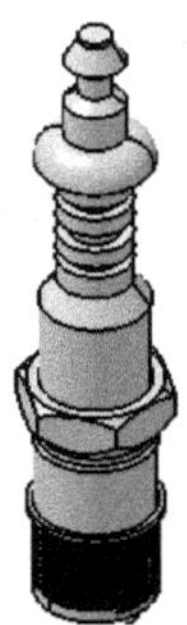

Figure 3–53

2. In the specification tree, expand the **Tip** branch. Two part bodies are present.

Task 2 - Generate a CATPart from the Product.

1. Select **Tools>Generate CATPart from Product**. The dialog box opens as shown in Figure 3–54.

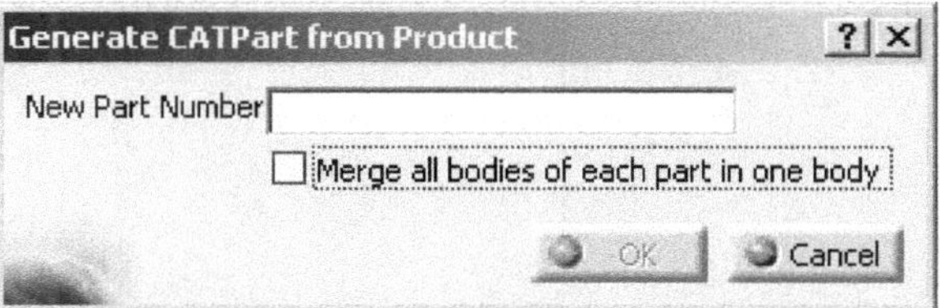

Figure 3–54

2. In the specification tree, select the product as shown in Figure 3–55.

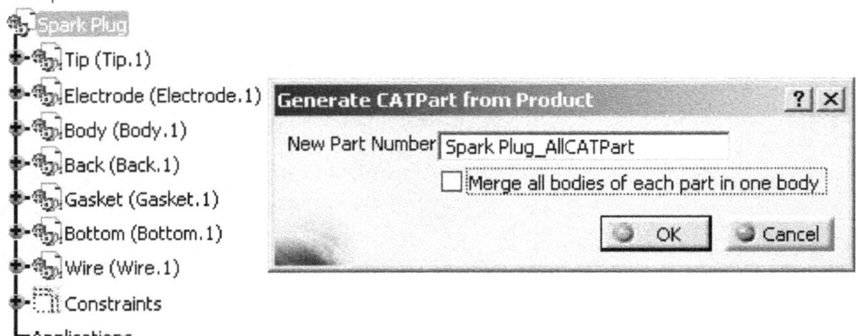

Figure 3–55

3. Click **OK**. The CATPart is generated as shown in Figure 3–56. Two part bodies start with the name **Tip.1**. This is because there were two part bodies under the part **Tip** in the original assembly.

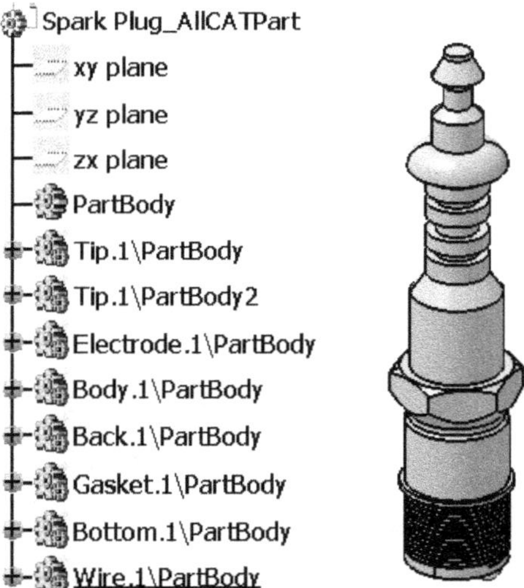

Figure 3–56

Task 3 - Generate a CATPart with merged bodies.

1. Ensure that the **SparkPlug.CATProduct** window is active.
2. Click **Tools>Generate CATPart from Product** and select the product in the specification tree.
3. In the *New Part Number* field, enter **_Merge**. In the dialog box, select **Merge all bodies of each part in one body**, as shown in Figure 3–57.

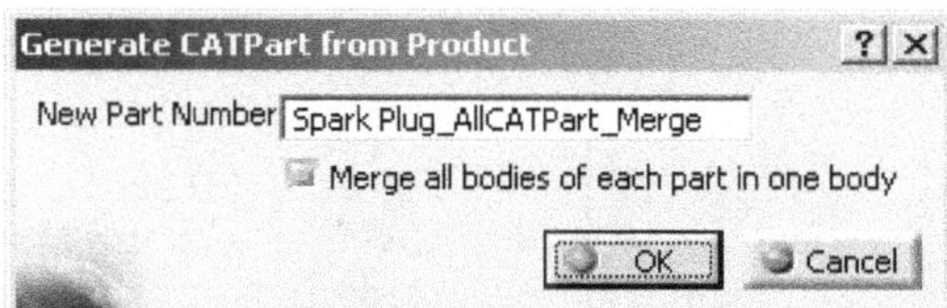

Figure 3–57

4. Click **OK**. The CATPart is generated, as shown in Figure 3–58. There is only one part body with the name **Tip.1**. The two bodies in the original **Tip.CATPart** are now placed under the **Tip.1** branch instead of being created as two separate bodies.

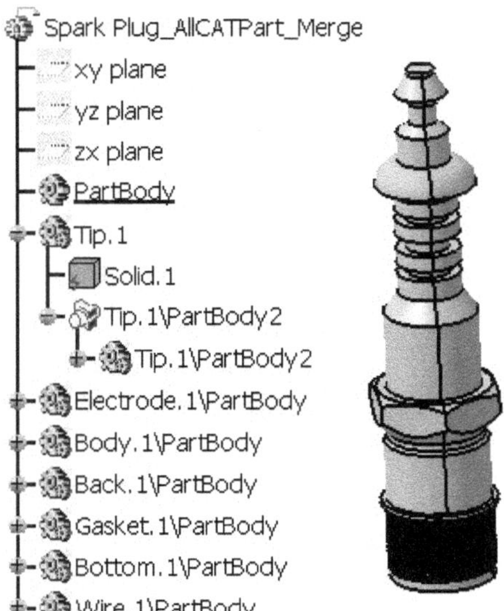

Figure 3–58

5. Explore the specification trees of both CATParts generated from the product and note any differences.

   Figure 3–59 shows the specification tree of the generated CATPart with the **Merge all bodies of each part in one body** option not selected.

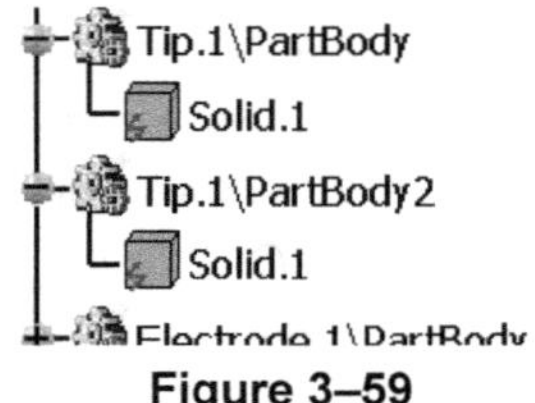

Figure 3–59

   Figure 3–60 shows the specification tree of the generated CATPart with the **Merge all bodies of each part in one body** option selected.

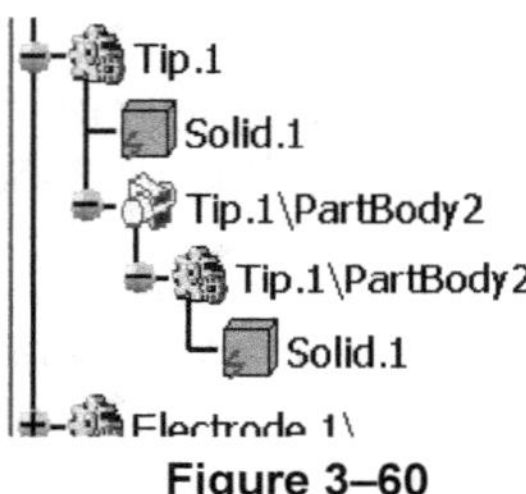

Figure 3–60

Task 4 - Create an associative CATPart.

In this task, you will create an associative part that will be used for exporting the latest version of the assembly.

1. Ensure that the **SparkPlug.CATProduct** window is active.
2. Select **Tools>Options>Infrastructure>Part Infrastructure**. In the *General* tab, disable the **Restrict external selection with link to published elements** option.

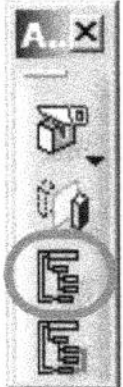

3. Click (Associativity). The Assembly Part Association dialog box opens as shown in Figure 3–61.

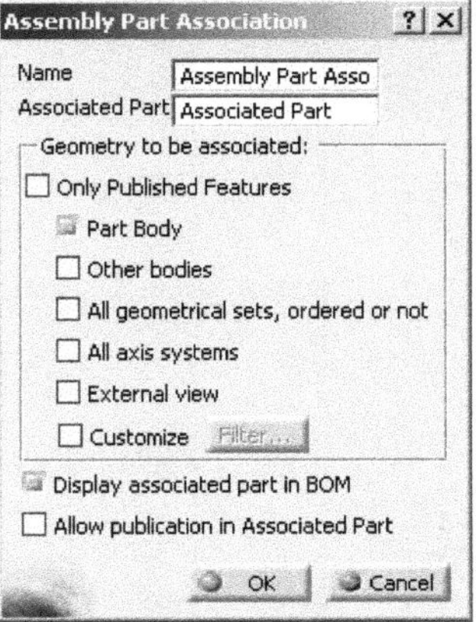

Figure 3–61

4. Click **OK**. The model displays in the specification tree as shown in Figure 3–62. Every single body in the model represents one of the components of the assembly.

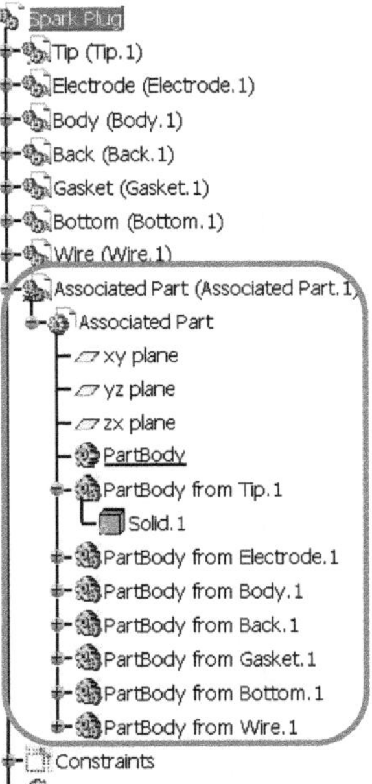

Figure 3–62

5. Save and close the files.

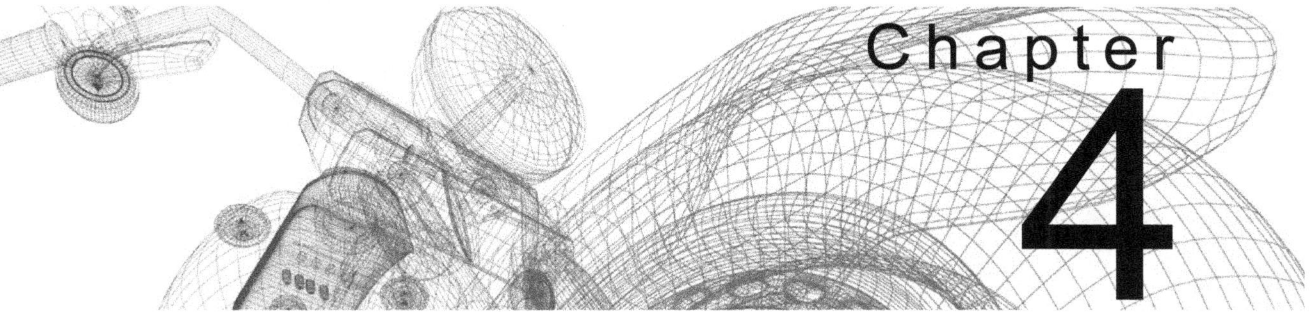

Product Analysis

Analysis tools in the Assembly Design workbench provide access to information about your assembly model. The analyses present this information to you in a structured, easy-to-read format. These tools report information about the components, constraints, degrees of freedom and dependencies. They help maintain the product design intent.

Learning Objectives in this Chapter

- Understand how to control Degrees of Freedom in an assembly.
- Learn how to analyze constraints.
- Understand component dependencies that arise when components are constrained together.

4.1 Degrees of Freedom

When a component is inserted into an assembly, the unconstrained model is positioned in a default location and orientation with respect to the rest of the assembly. This component can translate to any position or rotate to any orientation. The ability to translate or rotate is known as *degrees of freedom*. An unconstrained component has six degrees of freedom: three translation and three rotation with respect to a coordinate reference framework, as shown in Figure 4–1.

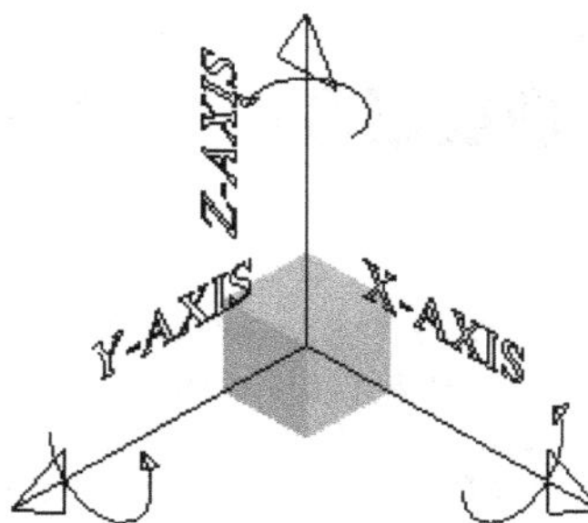

Figure 4–1

As constraints are added to a component they restrict degrees of freedom (DOF). Some examples of constraints are shown as follows:

Constraint	Constrained DOF	Unconstrained DOF
(Axial Coincidence)	4	2 Rotation about the axis Translation along the axis

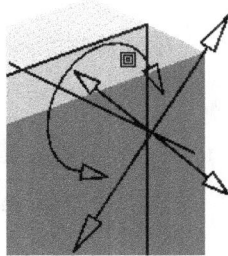

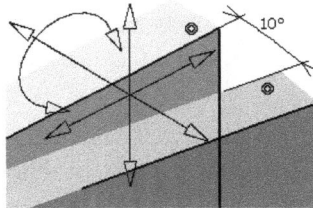

(Offset) and (Contact)	3	3 Translation in plane Rotation normal to plane
(Angle)	2	4 Translation in all directions Rotation normal to plane
(Fix) and (Fix Together)	6	0 Completely constrained

Analyze Degrees of Freedom

When constraining a component to complete a design, ensure that it does not have any unconstrained degrees of freedom. You can check the degrees of freedom of a component by activating the component and selecting **Analyze>Degrees of Freedom**. Three possible results can occur:

- The component is unconstrained.
- The component is fully constrained.
- The component is constrained but has degrees of freedom.

Component is unconstrained

If the component does not have any constraints defined, the message box shown in Figure 4–2 opens.

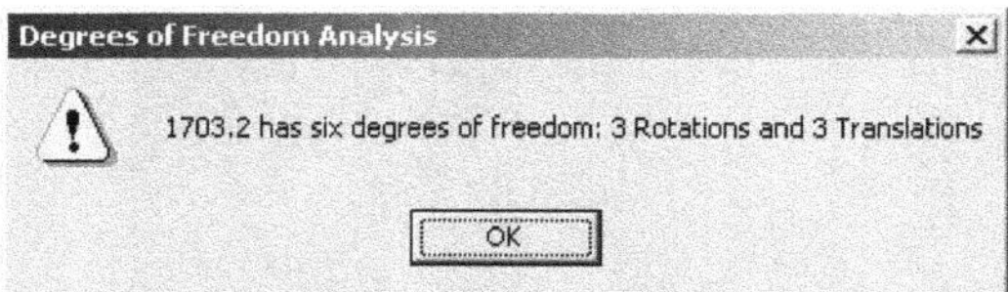

Figure 4–2

Component is fully constrained

If the component is constrained in all six degrees of freedom, the message box shown in Figure 4–3 opens.

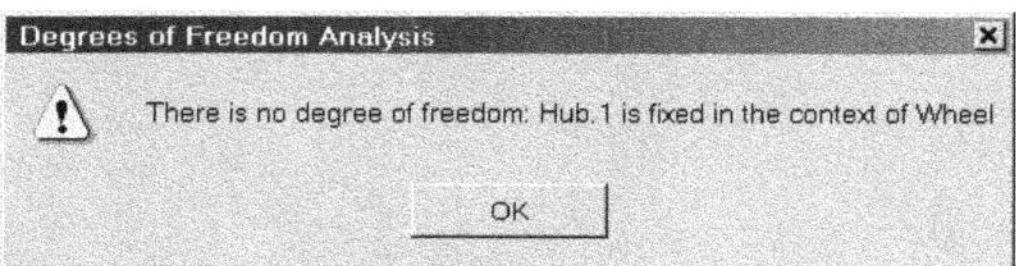

Figure 4–3

Component is constrained but has degrees of freedom

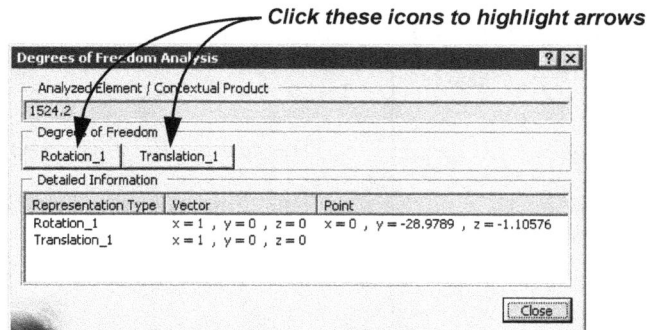

If the model has between one and five degrees of freedom, the Degrees of Freedom Analysis dialog box opens as shown in Figure 4–4.

The degrees of freedom in the top-level assembly can also be analyzed in the Constraints Analysis dialog box.

Click these icons to highlight arrows

Figure 4–4

The dialog box lists the degrees of freedom of the component and enables you to display vector arrows on the model to see its direction.

4.2 Constraints Analysis

A constraints analysis provides information about the constraints and degrees of freedom for the entire product. To perform a constraints analysis, activate the top-level assembly and select **Analyze>Constraints**. The Constraint Analysis dialog box always contains the *Constraints* and *Degrees of Freedom* tabs for the top-level assembly, as shown in Figure 4–5. The drop-down list at the top of the dialog box enables you to set the active model.

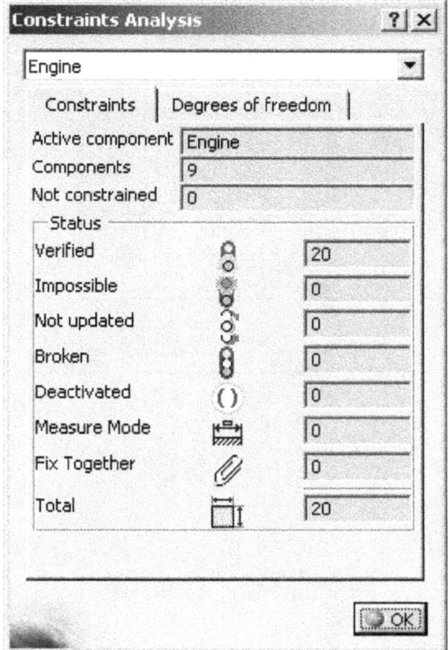

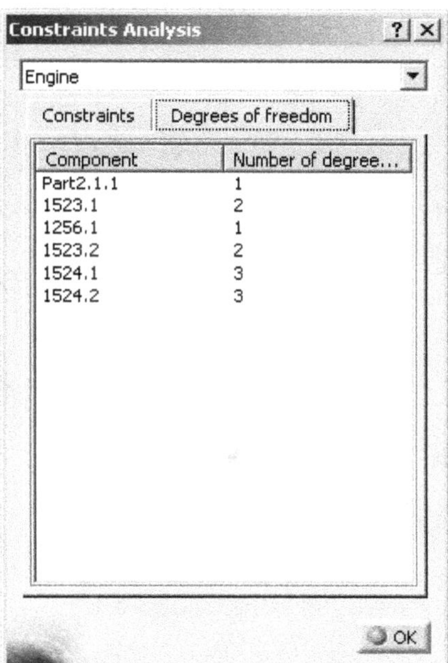

Figure 4–5

The *Constraints* tab displays a variety of information about the active model. The total number of components and the number of unconstrained components (six degrees of freedom) display at the top. The *Status* area displays specific constraint information, including the number of verified constraints and the total number of constraints. Verified constraints indicate constraints that are successfully updated in the model.

If any of the other status indicators have values greater than zero, additional tabs display in the dialog box listing the specific constraints with that status. An example is shown in Figure 4–6.

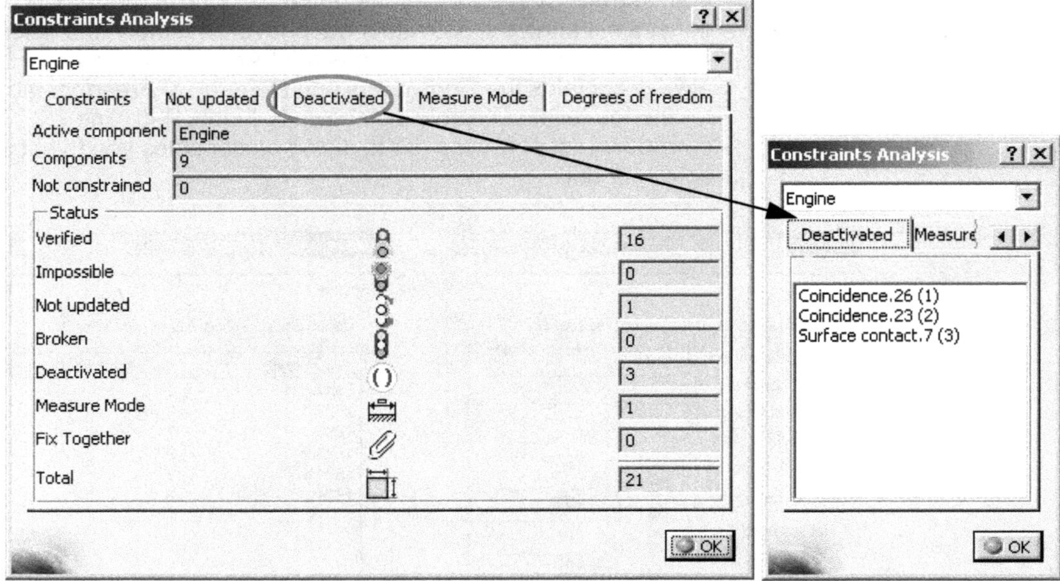

Figure 4–6

4.3 Component Dependencies

When a constraint is created, a dependency occurs between the two selected models, known as a parent/child relationship. The assembly reference is the parent and the component reference is the child.

For example, a bolt is placed into the assembly shown in Figure 4–7. A Coincidence constraint is applied between the axis of the bolt and the hole in the block. As a result, the block becomes a parent to the bolt. Without the block or the hole reference in the block, the constraint cannot be updated and the bolt (the child component) is under-constrained.

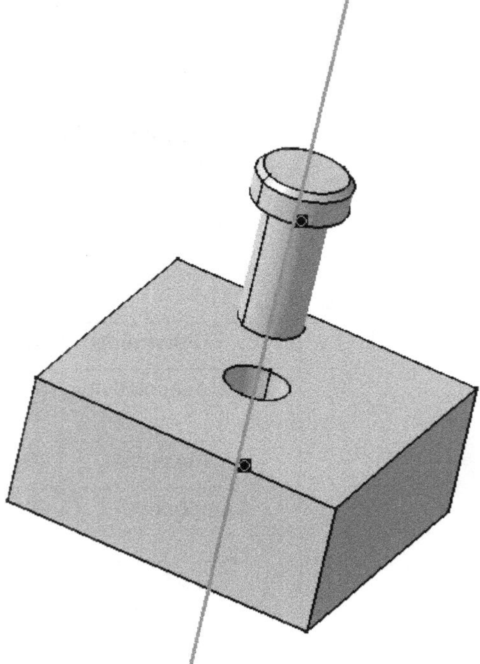

Figure 4–7

To check for component dependencies, select **Analyze>Dependencies**. The Assembly Dependencies Tree dialog box opens, displaying the name of the active model, as shown in Figure 4–8.

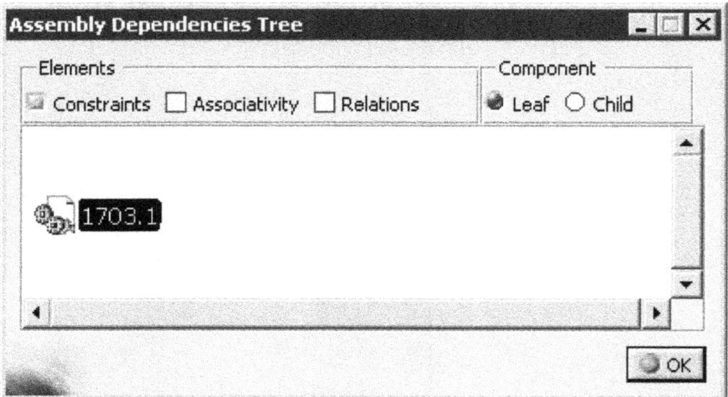

Figure 4–8

The options in the Assembly Dependencies Tree dialog box are described as follows:

Option		Description
Elements		Determines the information that displays in the Analysis dialog box using one of the following options:
	Constraints	Displays the constraints belonging to the active model.
	Associativity	Displays components that have been edited in the context of the assembly.
	Relations	Displays any formulas in the active element.
Component		Filters the components displayed in the Analysis dialog box using one of the following options:
	Leaf	Hides the children of a component.
	Child	Displays the children of a component.

The constraints of a component can be displayed by double-clicking on the component name, as shown in Figure 4–9.

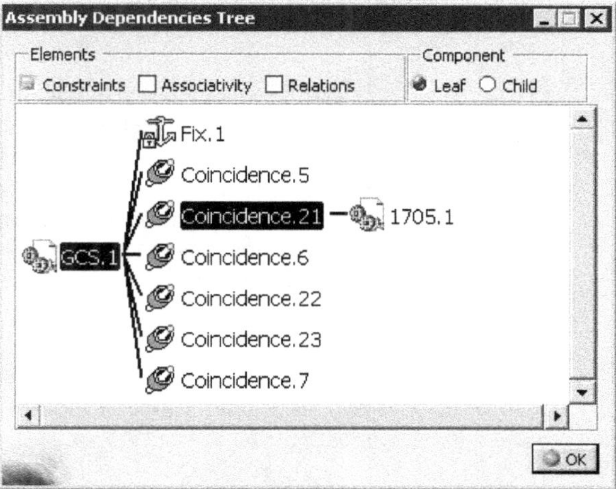

Figure 4–9

To access additional options, right-click on a component or constraint in the Assembly Dependencies Tree dialog box and select an option. The available options are described as follows:

Options	Description
Expand all	Expands the entire tree to display all relationships.
Set as new root	Sets the selected component or constraint as the current element being analyzed.
Change activation	Toggles the activation status of a constraint.

Practice 4a Degrees of Freedom

Practice Objective

- Analyze degrees of freedom.

In this practice, you will create a Product file and assemble the **Hub** part as the base component. The **WheelRim** part is assembled to the **Hub** part. The resulting configuration displays as shown in Figure 4–10. You will analyze the degrees of freedom throughout the assembly process to demonstrate how applying assembly constraints affects the degrees of freedom of a component.

Figure 4–10

Task 1 - Create a Product file.

1. Create a product file.
2. For the part number, enter **Wheel** as shown in Figure 4–11.

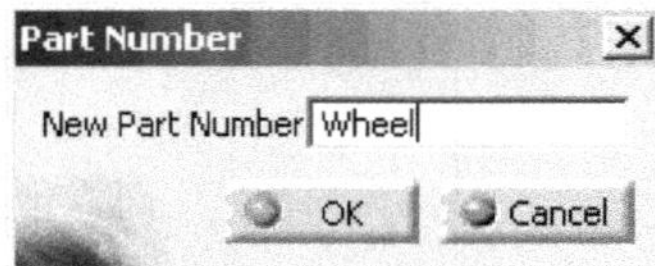

Figure 4–11

Task 2 - Assemble the base component.

1. Assemble **Hub.CATPart** from the *Wheel* directory and apply a Fix constraint. The assembly displays as shown in Figure 4–12.

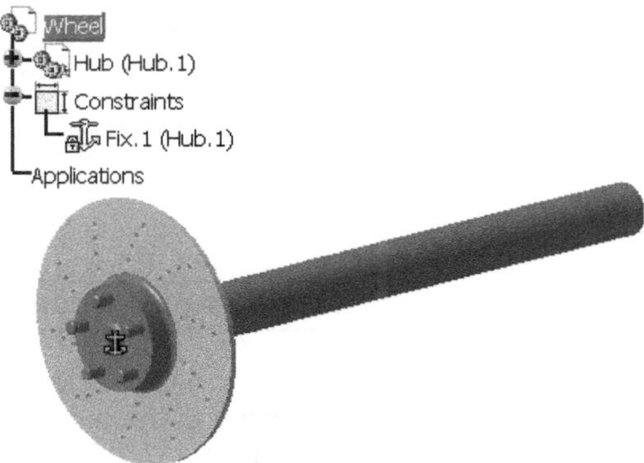

Figure 4–12

Task 3 - Analyze component degrees of freedom.

1. In the specification tree, right-click on the **Hub** part and select **Hub.1 object>Component Degrees Of Freedom**.

   The Degrees of Freedom Analysis dialog box opens, indicating that there is no degree of freedom for **Hub.1**, as shown in Figure 4–13. This is because the Fix constraint has been applied.

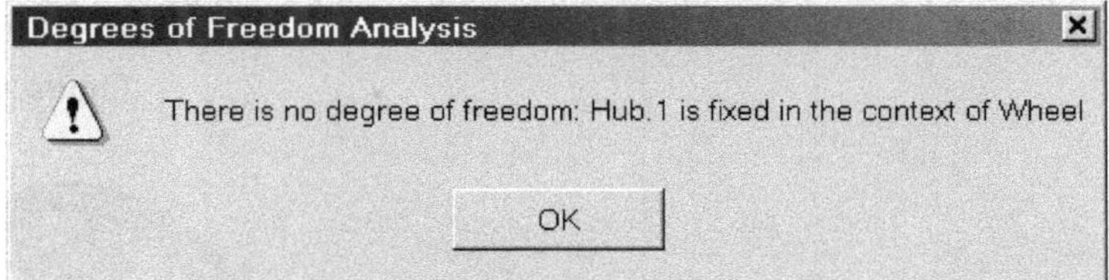

Figure 4–13

2. Click **OK** to close the dialog box.

Task 4 - Assemble the second component.

1. Insert an existing component named **WheelRim** into the *Wheel* assembly.

2. In the specification tree, right-click on the **WheelRim** part and select **WheelRim.1 object>Component Degrees Of Freedom** to analyze its degrees of freedom.

   The system reports that **WheelRim** has six degrees of freedom, as shown in Figure 4–14.

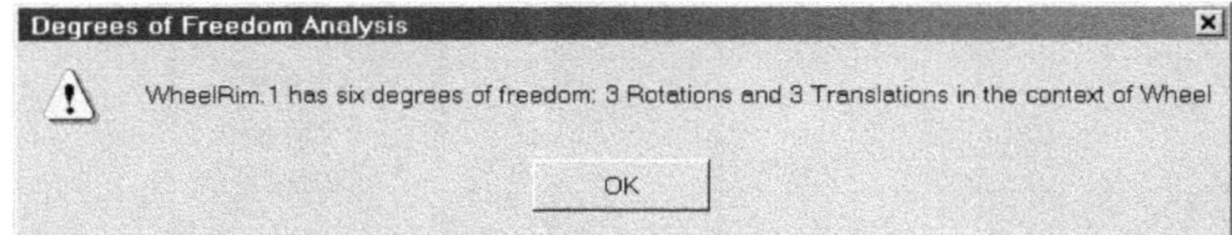
Degrees of Freedom Analysis
WheelRim.1 has six degrees of freedom: 3 Rotations and 3 Translations in the context of Wheel
OK

Figure 4–14

Task 5 - Apply a constraint to the WheelRim.

1. Apply a Coincident constraint between the axis of the **Hub** part and the axis of the **WheelRim** part, as shown in Figure 4–15 and Figure 4–16.

Figure 4–15

Figure 4–16

2. Update the assembly.

3. Analyze the degrees of freedom for the **WheelRim** part. The Degrees of Freedom Analysis dialog box opens as shown in Figure 4–17, indicating two degrees of freedom. The **WheelRim** currently has a rotational and a translational degree of freedom.

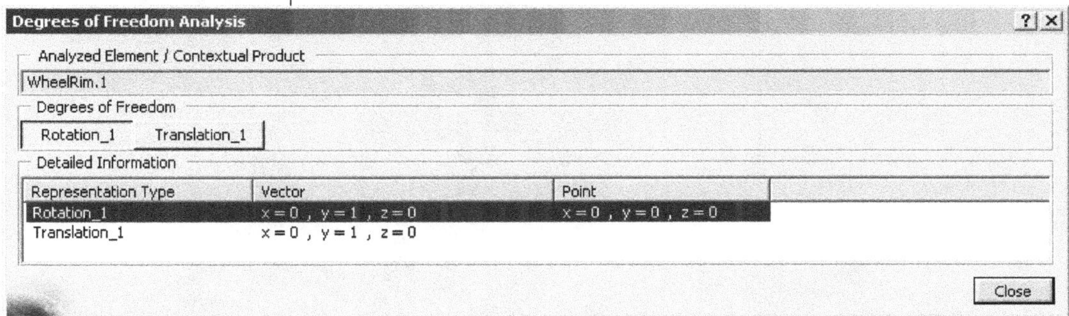

Figure 4–17

4. Click **Close**.

5. Reposition the **WheelRim** part, as shown in Figure 4–18, using the compass.

Figure 4–18

6. Apply a Coincident constraint between the surfaces, as shown in Figure 4–19.

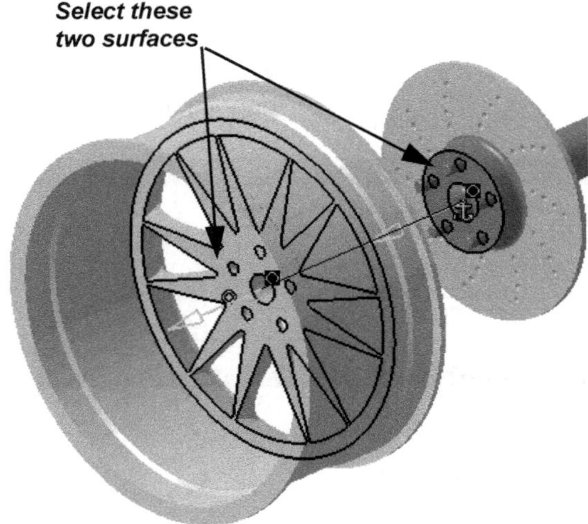

Figure 4–19

7. Ensure that the *Orientation* is set to **Opposite**, as shown in Figure 4–20.

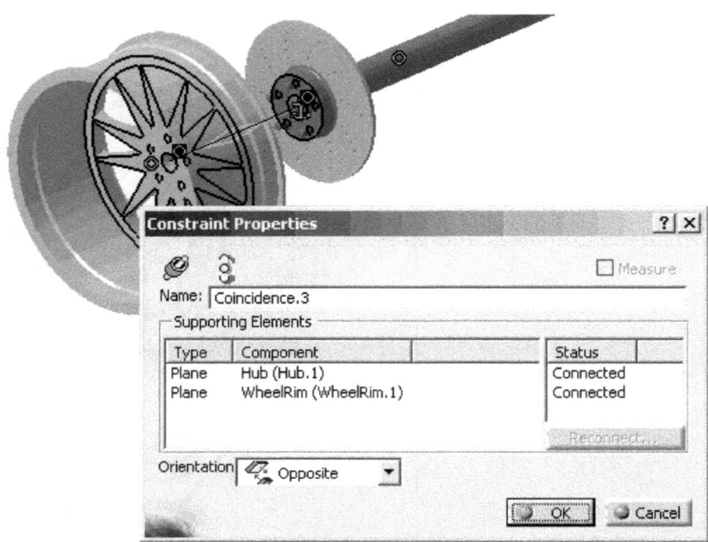

Figure 4–20

8. Update the assembly.

9. Analyze the degrees of freedom for the **WheelRim** part. This part should only have one (Rotational) degree of freedom as shown in Figure 4–21.

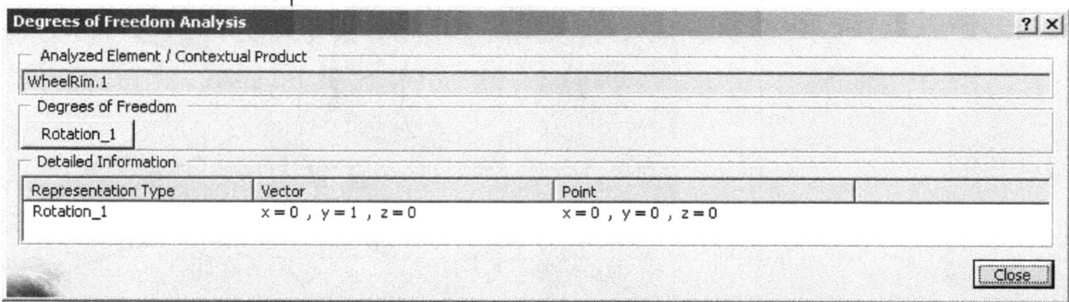

Figure 4–21

10. Use the compass to drag the **WheelRim** to a location, as shown in Figure 4–22.

Figure 4–22

11. Apply a Coincident constraint between one stud of the **Hub** part and one of the mounting holes of the **WheelRim**, as shown in Figure 4–22 and Figure 4–23.

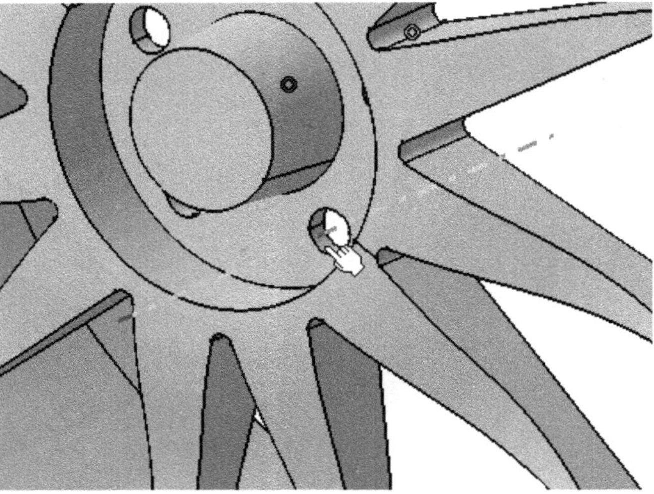

Figure 4–23

12. Update the assembly.

13. Perform a Component Degrees of Freedom analysis for the **WheelRim** part. It should not have any degrees of freedom, as shown in Figure 4–24.

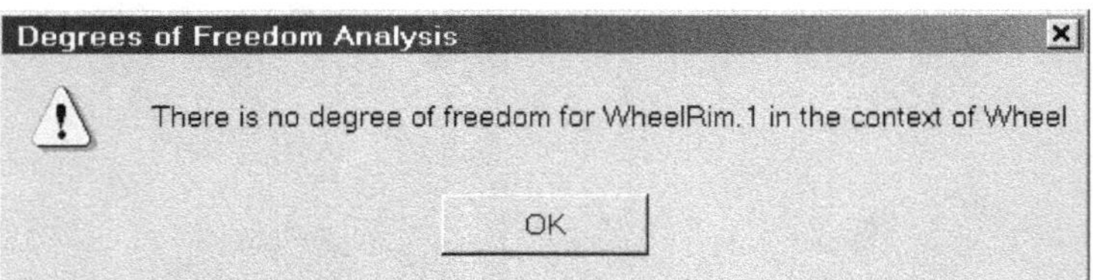

Degrees of Freedom Analysis
There is no degree of freedom for WheelRim.1 in the context of Wheel
OK

Figure 4–24

14. Save the model and close the file.

Practice 4b

Product Analysis

Practice Objectives

- Analyze degrees of freedom.
- Analyze constraints.
- Snap components.

In this practice, you will create the top-level assembly product for the Axial Centrifugal Compressor. You will start by assembling components with and without constraints. Unconstrained components are placed into the assembly to provide a three-dimensional layout of the assembly. You will also analyze assembly constraints and degrees of freedom.

Task 1 - Create a Product file for the top-level assembly.

1. Create a Product file.
2. For the part number, enter **251-D21** and save it as **AxialCentrifugalCompressor** in the *Turbine* directory.

Task 2 - Assemble the skeleton component.

Remember that a skeleton model should always be the first component added to an assembly.

1. Assemble **CompressorSkeleton** from the *Turbine* directory and apply a Fix constraint as shown in Figure 4–25.

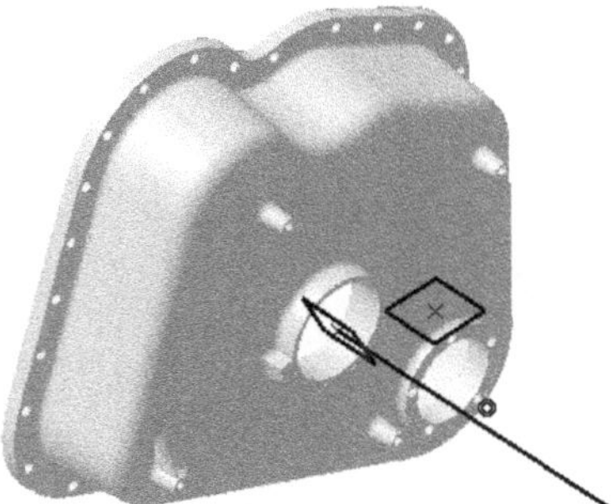

Figure 4–25

Task 3 - Assemble AftCover to the skeleton.

1. Assemble **AftCover** from the *Turbine* directory and drag the model to the location shown in Figure 4–26.

2. Create a Coincidence constraint between the RotationalAxis of **CompressorSkeleton** and the axis of **AftCover**, as shown in Figure 4–26.

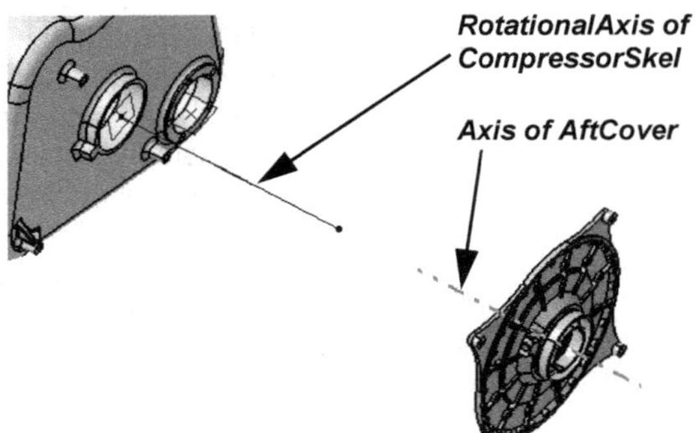

Figure 4–26

3. Create a Coincidence constraint between the planar face of **AftCover**, as shown in Figure 4–27, and the MountingPlane of **CompressorSkeleton**.

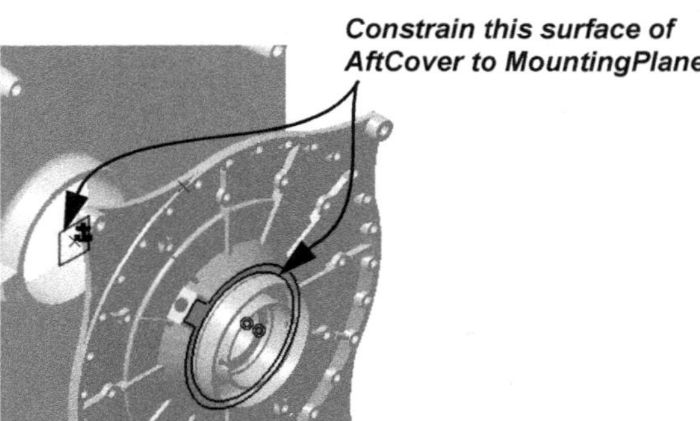

Figure 4–27

4. In the Constraint Properties dialog box, set the *Orientation* to **Opposite** as shown in Figure 4–28.

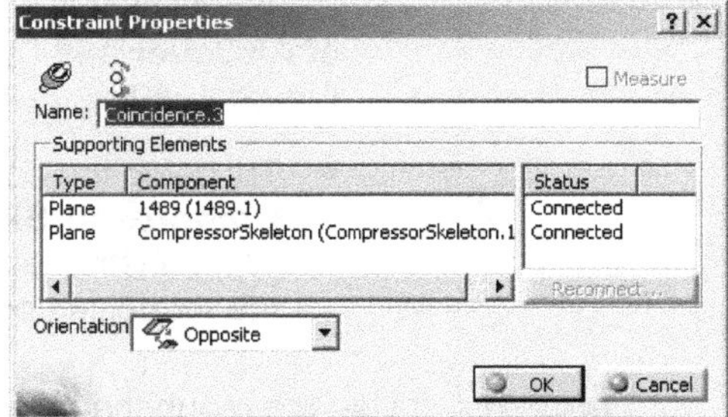

Figure 4–28

5. Update the assembly.

Task 4 - Investigate the degrees of freedom of AftCover.

1. Right-click on **1489 (1489.1)** and select **1489.1 object> Component Degrees Of Freedom**. The Degrees of Freedom Analysis dialog box opens as shown in Figure 4–29.

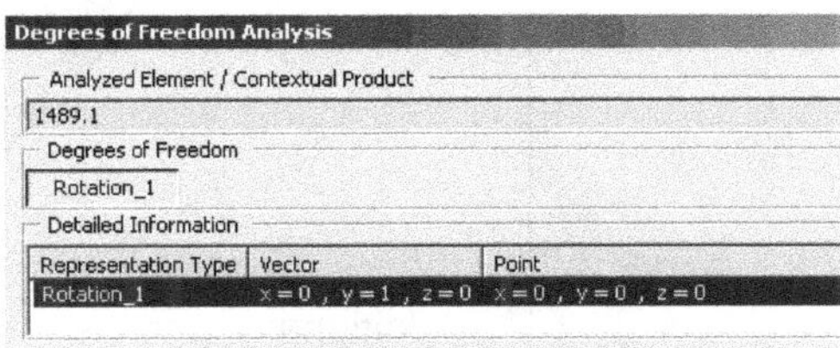

Figure 4–29

2. Click **Rotation_1** to highlight the rotational arrow in the display window.

   The model contains the following degrees of freedom:

   - The Coincidence constraint between the implicit axis removes four degrees of freedom. The two remaining degrees of freedom are rotation about the axis and translation along the axis.
   - The Coincidence constraint between the faces of **AftCover** and the **MountingPlane** removes the remaining translational degree of freedom.
   - The model is left with one degree of freedom: rotation about the RotationalAxis of **CompressorSkeleton**. To remove this degree of freedom, a Coincidence constraint must be created between the mounting holes of the two models.

3. Click **Close**.

4. Create a Coincidence constraint between the mounting holes of **AftCover** and **CompressorSkeleton** as shown in Figure 4–30.

    - Try using the compass and dragging **AftCover** away from **CompressorSkeleton** to see the cylindrical surfaces. The constrained position of **AftCover** is restored when the model is updated.

Design Considerations

Use the mounting hole of the **GearBoxInterface** that has the stiffeners, as shown in Figure 4–30.

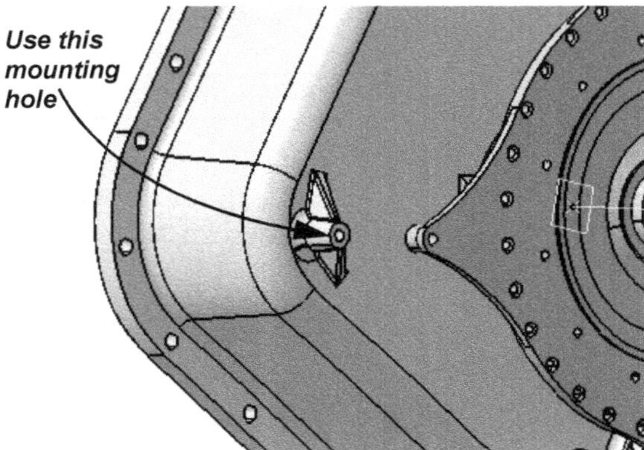

Figure 4–30

Additionally, use the mounting hole of **AftCover** that is closest to the port, as shown in Figure 4–31

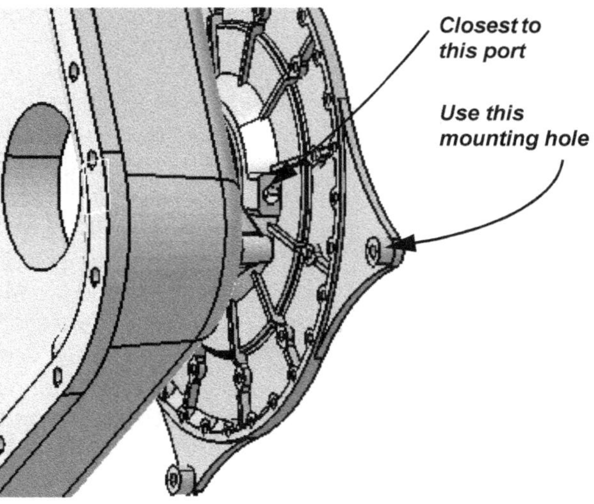

Figure 4–31

5. Click [icon]. The assembly displays as shown in Figure 4–32.

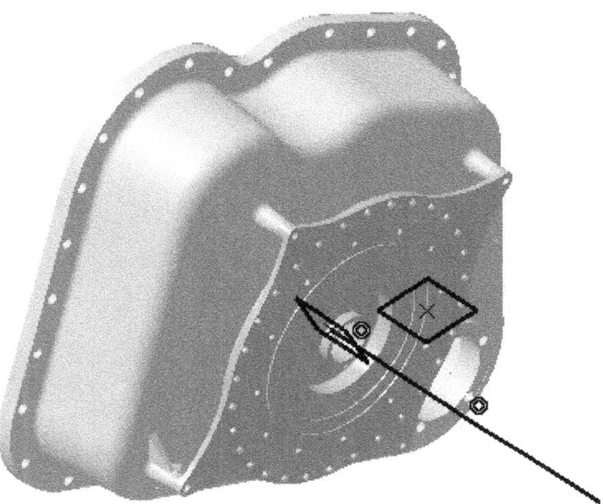

Figure 4–32

6. Check the Component Degrees of Freedom for part 1489. A message window opens as shown in Figure 4–33, indicating that the component is fully constrained.

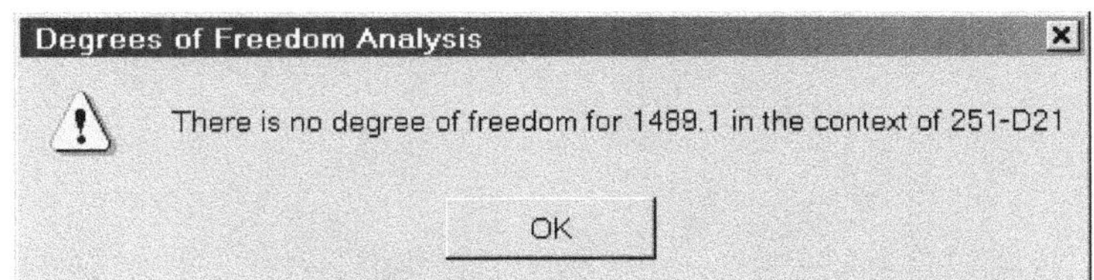
Degrees of Freedom Analysis
There is no degree of freedom for 1489.1 in the context of 251-D21
OK

Figure 4–33

Task 5 - Assemble CompressorRotor.CATProduct.

If **CompressorRotor.CATProduct** was not completed in the previous practice, it can be opened from the *Completed\Rotor* folder.

1. Assemble **CompressorRotor.CATProduct** into the top-level assembly and drag it to a position similar to that shown in Figure 4–34.

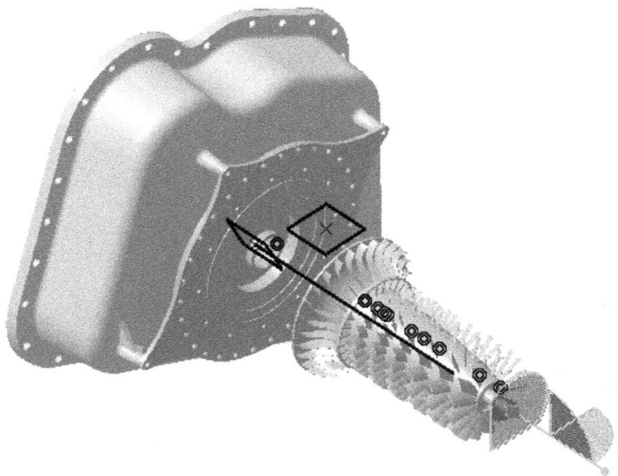

Figure 4–34

2. Click (Coincidence Constraint) and apply the constraint to the implicit axis of the CompressorRotor (part number **71499**) and the RotationalAxis of the **CompressorSkeleton**, as shown in Figure 4–35.

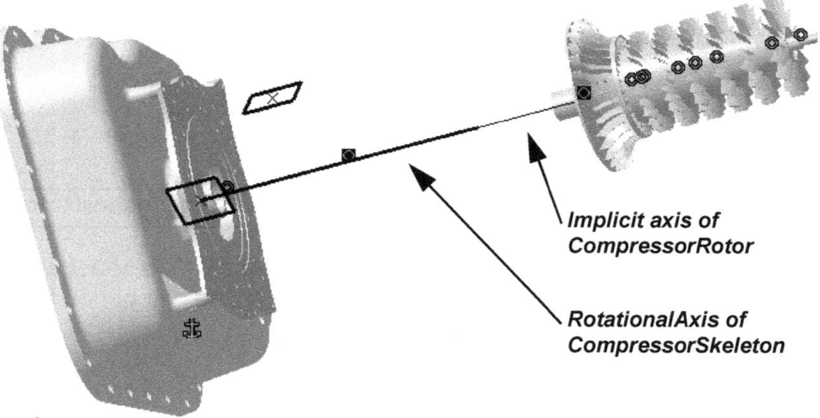

Figure 4–35

3. Constrain the face of CompressorRotor (part number **71499**) with the face of the AftCover (part number **1489**), as shown in Figure 4–36. Use (Offset Constraint) with an **Opposite** orientation. For the *offset value,* enter **2.8**.

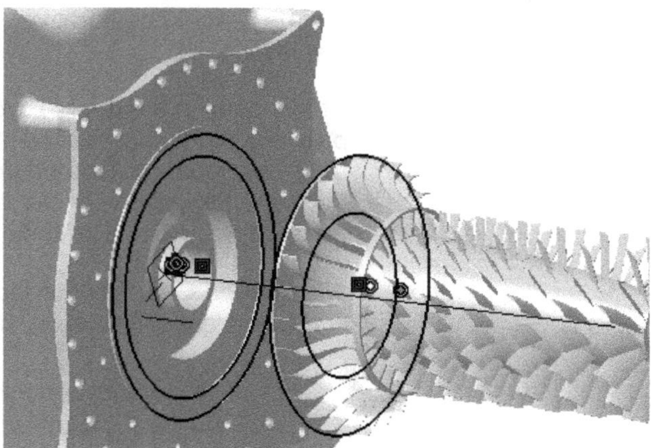

Figure 4–36

4. Click . The assembly displays as shown in Figure 4–37.

Figure 4–37

5. Analyze the degrees of freedom for the CompressorRotor product (part number **71499**). The remaining degree of freedom is rotational. This degree of freedom is intentional. It enables you to simulate the motion of the rotor product rotating in the compressor.

Task 6 - Bring additional model information into the assembly.

Design Considerations

When working with a top-down design technique, include as much information at the top-level assembly as possible. This process should be iterative, with information being added as it displays.

At this point in the design cycle, additional components from a previous model are reused in the design. The exact location of these components is not currently known. The components are added to the assembly, but left unconstrained until enough information is available to fully constrain them.

1. Hide the GearBoxInterface Geometrical Set of the **CompressorSkeleton**, as shown in Figure 4–38.

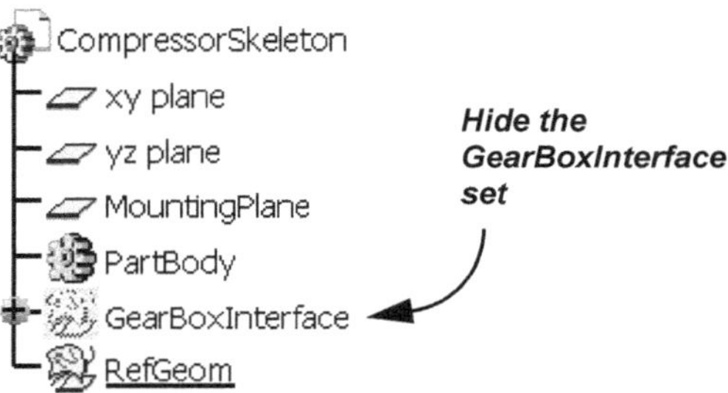

Figure 4–38

2. Assemble **ImpellerCover.CATPart** from the *Turbine* directory.

3. Drag the ImpellerCover (0811) forward toward **1st_Stage**, as shown in Figure 4–39.

Figure 4–39

Task 7 - Snap the component into position.

1. In the Move toolbar, click  (Snap).
2. Select the axis of the ImpellerCover (part number **0811**). You need to zoom in and select a cylindrical surface on the part. When the axis is highlighted, the cursor indicates a cylindrical surface with .
3. In **CompressorSkeleton**, select the **RotationalAxis** reference line as shown in Figure 4–40.

When snapping components, select references from the unconstrained component first. The first component selected moves to snap to the second component.

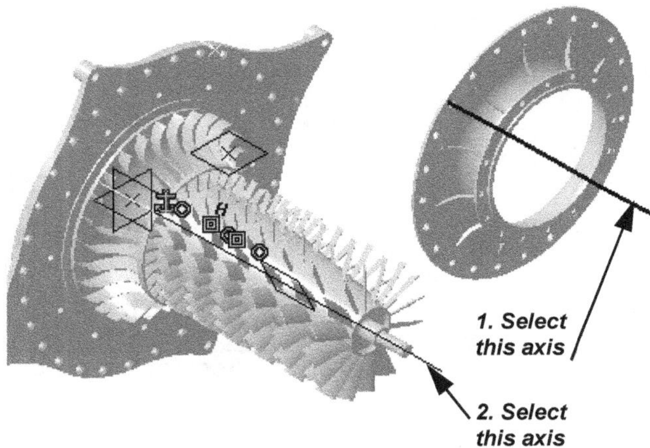

Figure 4–40

4. Directional arrows display as shown in Figure 4–41. Select anywhere in the display to accept the position.

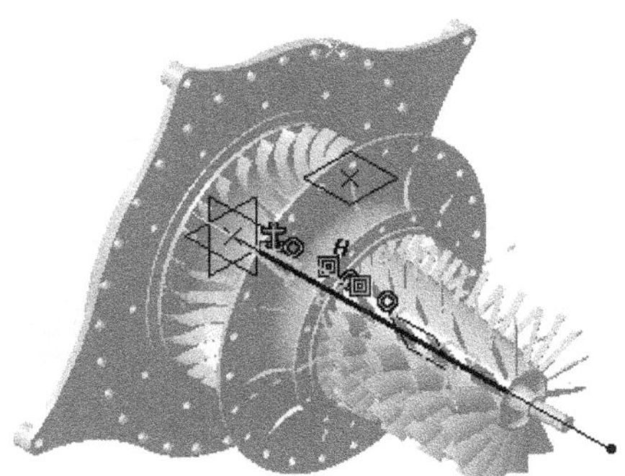

Figure 4–41

5. In the specification tree, expand the **Constraints** branch as shown in Figure 4–42. The snap functionality positioned the component but did not apply a constraint.

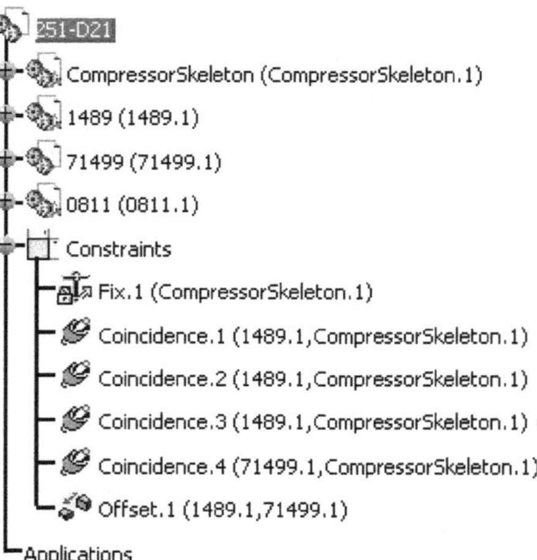

Figure 4–42

6. Create a Coincident constraint between the axis of the ImpellerCover (part number **0811**) and the RotationalAxis reference line of the **CompressorSkeleton**.

Task 8 - Assemble a product.

1. Assemble **AirEntry.CATProduct**.
2. Drag the model to the approximate position shown in Figure 4–43.

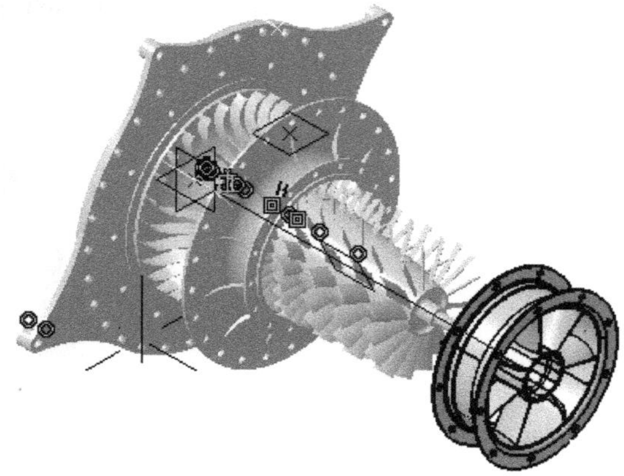

Figure 4–43

3. Click (Snap) and select the two surfaces shown in Figure 4–44. Remember to select references from the unconstrained component first.

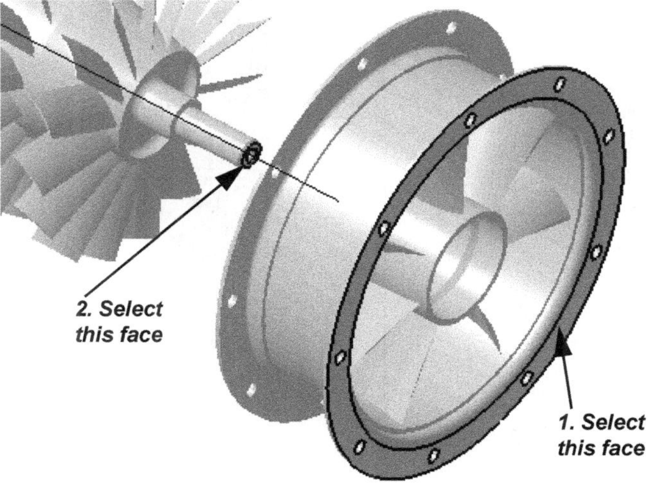

Figure 4–44

4. Select the arrow to reverse the direction, as shown in Figure 4–45.

*The **Air entry** component might not yet align though the axis of the assembly.*

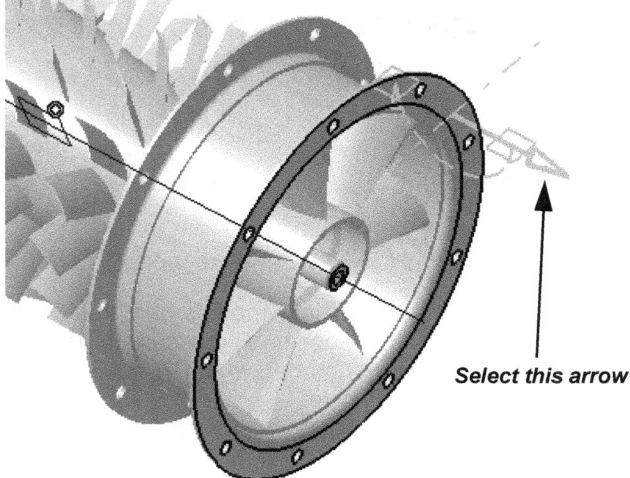

Figure 4–45

5. Snap the axis of the **AirEntry** (72320) to the RotationalAxis of the **CompressorSkeleton**. The model displays as shown in Figure 4–46.

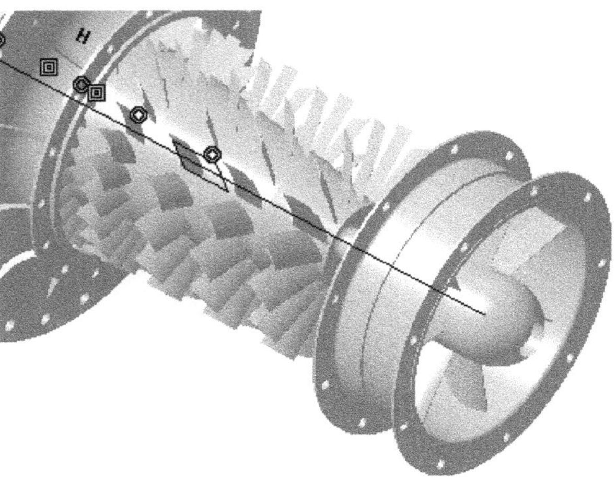

Figure 4–46

6. Check the Component Degrees Of Freedom for part **72320**. The message window indicates that the air entry product still has six degrees of freedom, as shown in Figure 4–47. Snapping components repositions the model, but does not add any constraints.

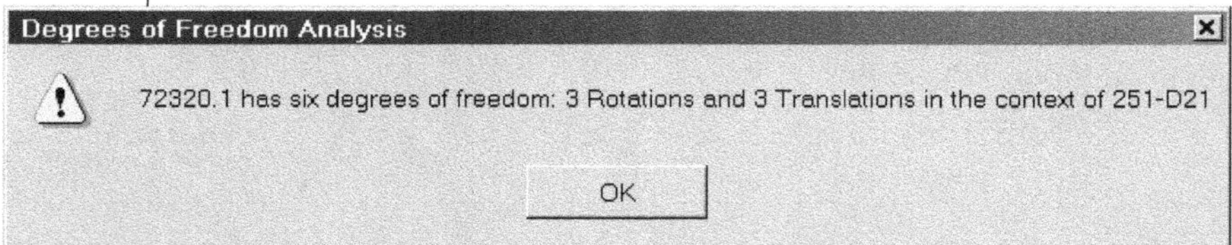
Degrees of Freedom Analysis
72320.1 has six degrees of freedom: 3 Rotations and 3 Translations in the context of 251-D21
OK

Figure 4–47

7. Save the model.

If any models from the *Completed* folder were used to build the assembly, be sure to use **Save Management** to save all of the models in the *Turbine* folder.

Task 9 - Analyze the constraints.

1. Select **Analyze>Constraints**. The Constraints Analysis dialog box opens as shown in Figure 4–48.

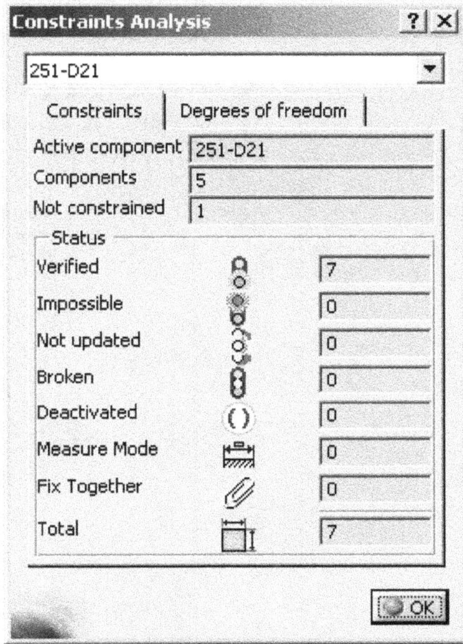

Figure 4–48

The current model is the top-level assembly **251-D21**. The analysis displays five assembled components, one of which is unconstrained. The *Status* area identifies a total of seven constraints without any errors.

2. Select the *Degrees of Freedom* tab. The models with unconstrained degrees of freedom are listed, as shown in Figure 4–49.

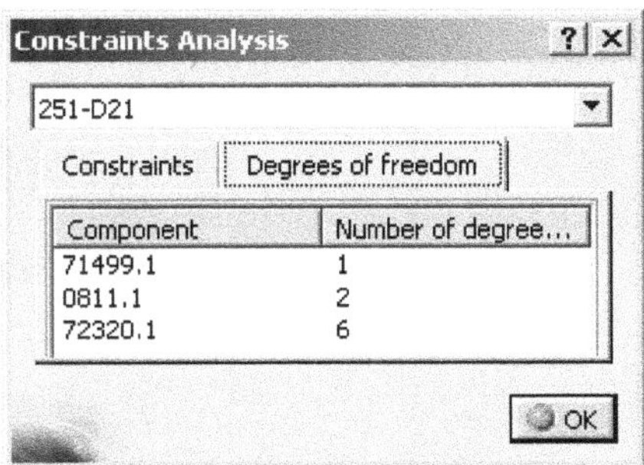

Figure 4–49

3. Select each model to highlight it in the specification tree and main window. Model **72320** (AirEntry) has six degrees of freedom. This is the model that was snapped into position in Task 8. It has been placed in an effort to include as much information as possible, despite the fact that final references are not available at this point in the design cycle. This component is fully constrained later.

4. Analyze the constraints for one of the subassemblies. Set the current model to **71499** by selecting it in the drop-down list, as shown in Figure 4–50.

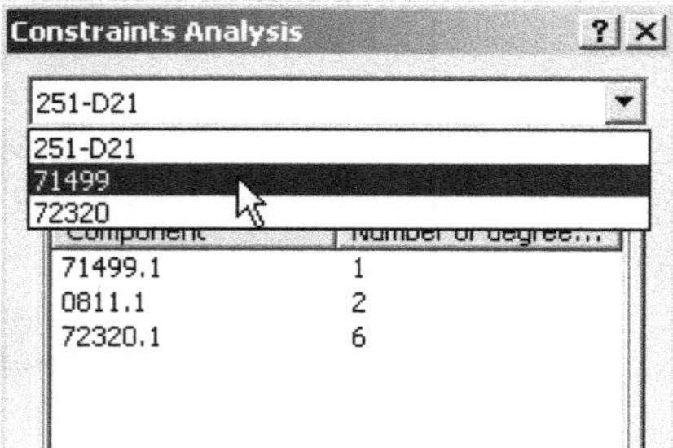

Figure 4–50

The Constraints Analysis dialog box updates to report the information, as shown in Figure 4–51.

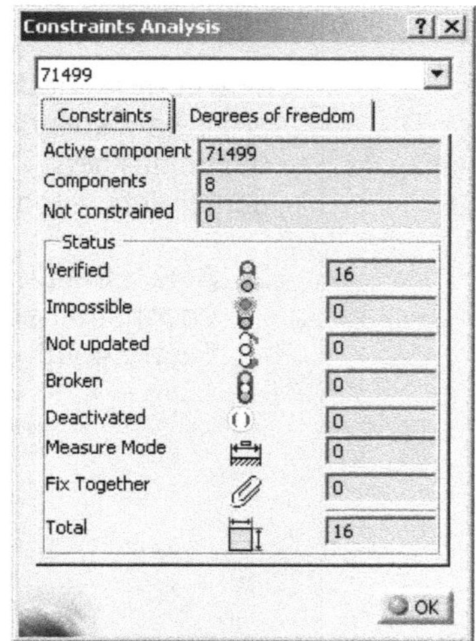

Figure 4–51

5. Click **OK**.

6. Select **Analyze>Dependencies**.

Design Considerations

This analysis creates a tree structure displaying each constraint and referenced model in the top-level assembly. Assembly constraints create parent/child relationships between components in a Product file. This analysis is a valuable tool for determining the parent/child relationships between assembly components. The dialog box opens as shown in Figure 4–52.

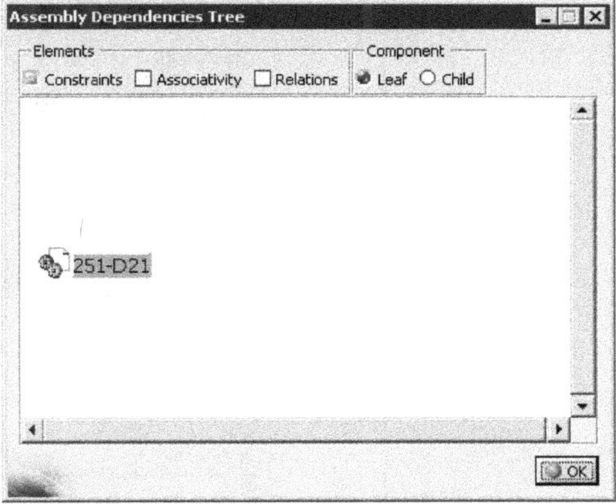

Figure 4–52

7. In the dialog box, double-click on **251-D21**. Six constraints are listed.

8. Double-click on each constraint to highlight the models that are referenced by that constraint. The Assembly Dependencies Tree dialog box opens as shown in Figure 4–53.

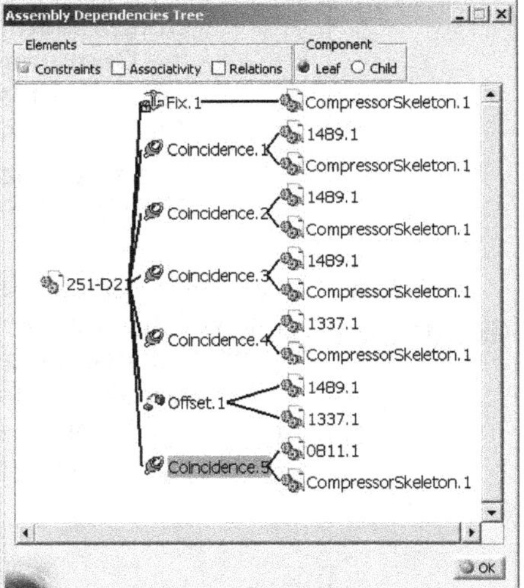

Figure 4–53

9. Right-click on **CompressorSkeleton.1** and select **Set as new root** to display its constraints.

10. Double-click on each constraint to display the referenced model. The Assembly Dependencies Tree dialog box opens as shown in Figure 4–54.

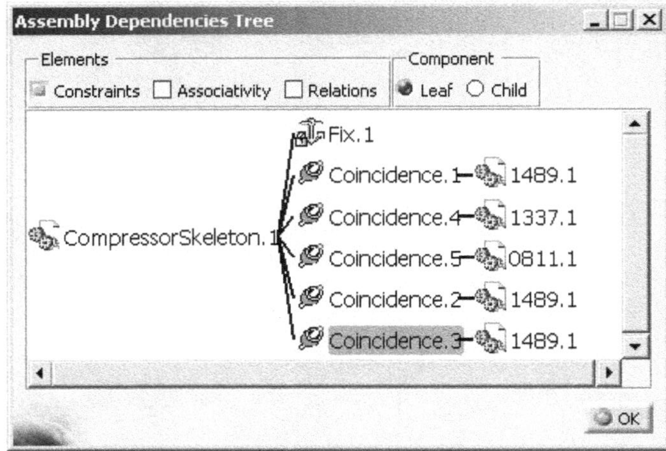

Figure 4–54

Note the following relationships:

- Part **1489** (AftCover) has three constraints directly to the **CompressorSkeleton**. It is fully constrained to only the **CompressorSkeleton**, therefore **1489** only has one father, **CompressorSkeleton**.
- Part **1337** (Impeller) is the base component of the **CompressorRotor** assembly. It has a single reference to the **CompressorSkeleton** (RotationalAxis). You might remember that it also has an Offset constraint to the **AftCover** part.
- The axis of part **0811** (ImpellerCover) is constrained to the RotationalAxis of **CompressorSkeleton**.

Design Considerations

Remember to carefully consider the type of constraints to use and which components to reference. This is how you capture the design intent of an assembly. Using a skeleton model is an effective way of constraining components to a common reference. In this case, the Rotational Axis of the skeleton acts as the common reference.

11. Clear the **Constraints** option to return to the top-level view (the root is reset to the top-level).

12. Select **Constraints**.

13. Right-click on the Offset constraint and select **Change Activation**. The constraint is deactivated in the dialog box and specification tree, as shown in Figure 4–55.

References for a constraint must be displayed again when the activity of a constraint is changed.

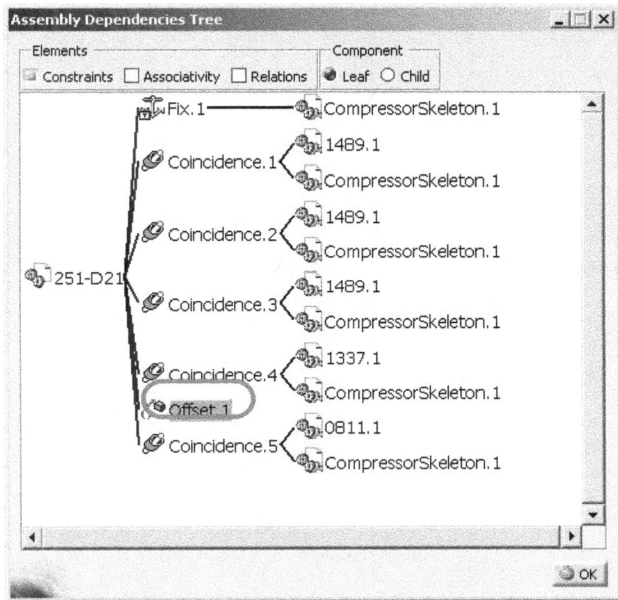

Figure 4–55

14. Repeat Step 13 to activate the Offset constraint.

15. Click **OK**.

16. Save the assembly and close the file.

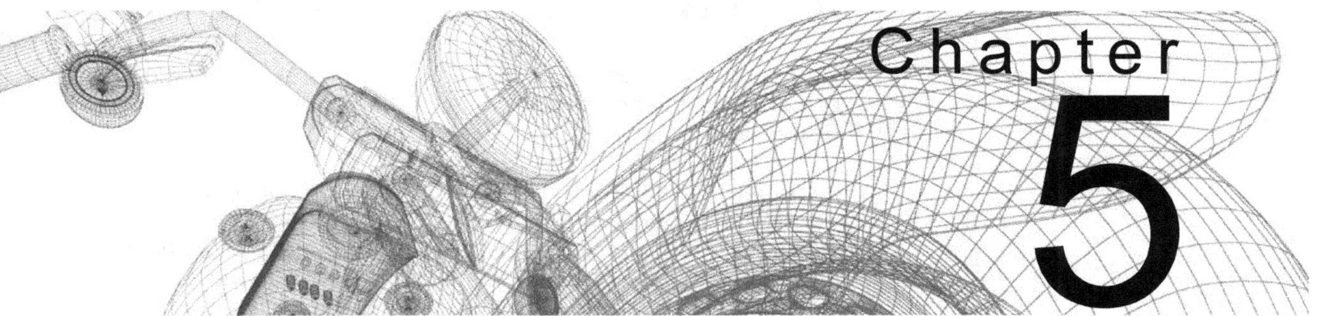

Component Duplication

Component duplication saves modeling time. As with feature duplication, component duplication techniques enable you to reuse data and control its placement.

Learning Objectives in this Chapter

- Understand the advanced Paste options.
- Learn how to reuse an existing pattern.
- Learn how to Instantiate multiple instances of a component.
- Understand how to create Symmetry features to transform an existing component.

5.1 Advanced Paste Options

Copy and **Paste** techniques speed up the process of bringing components into an assembly (e.g., **Edit >Copy** and **Edit>Paste**).

By default, constraints of the source model are not pasted with the new component and the model must be manually constrained in the assembly. Advanced Copy and Paste options enable you to paste the constraints of the source model with the new model. Select **Tools>Options>Mechanical Design> Assembly Design** and select the *Constraints* tab to display the advanced Paste commands. The Paste component options are shown in Figure 5–1.

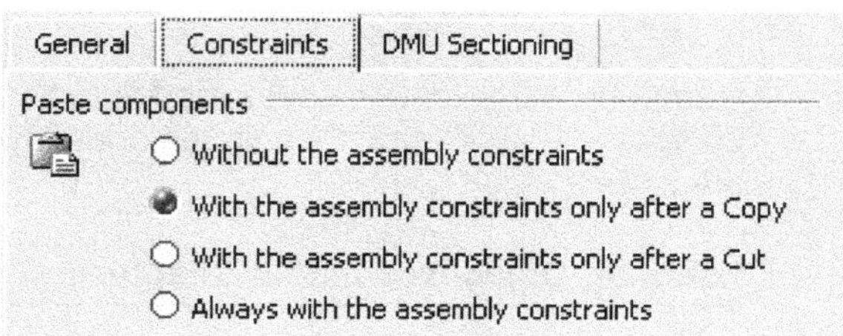

Figure 5–1

5.2 Reuse Pattern

If a component is assembled by referencing the leading (or first) feature of a pattern, that pattern can be reused to quickly assemble more components. To reuse a pattern, click (Reuse Pattern) in the Constraints toolbar. The Instantiation on a pattern dialog box opens as shown in Figure 5–2.

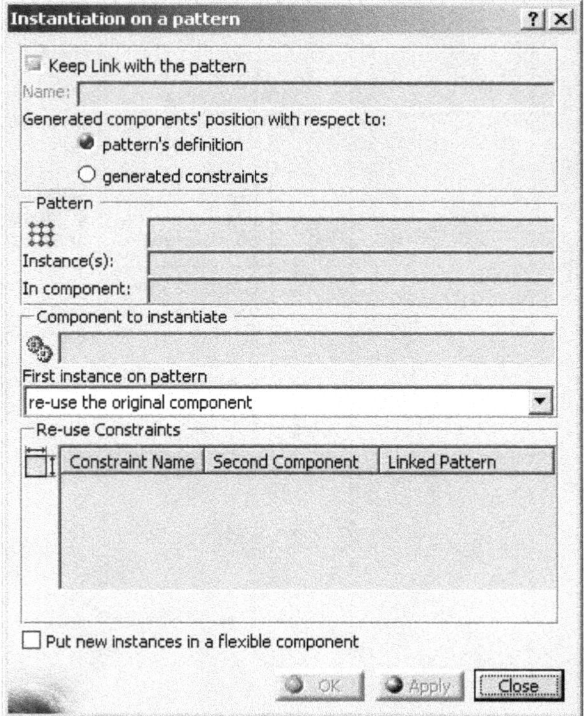

Figure 5–2

Select the model to pattern and the pattern to reuse.

The required options in the Instantiation on a Pattern dialog box are described as follows:

Option	Description
Keep link with the pattern	Associates the position of the instantiated components to the selected pattern.
Pattern's definition	Initially generates the position of the instantiated components with respect to the pattern.
Generated constraints	Initially generates the position of the instantiated components with respect to the constraints of the original component.
First instance on pattern	Controls the component that is used for the first instance of the pattern using one of the following options:
Reuse the original component	Uses the original component in the pattern. The component stays in its current location in the specification tree.
Create a new instance	Uses a new instance of the component in the pattern. The original component is left in its current location in the specification tree.
Cut and paste the original component	Relocates the original component in the specification tree and places it as the first instance in the pattern.

5.3 Instantiating Multiple Instances

Multi-instantiation duplicates components in an assembly. The placement of the new component in the assembly is determined using translational dimensions with respect to the original component. The direction of the translation is defined by selecting a reference axis (X, Y, or Z), or selecting geometry on the model. Multiple instances of the component can be created. These instances are positioned in increments of placement dimensions.

The constraints of the instantiated component are not copied. Therefore, the location of each new component is independent to the original component. They must be individually constrained in the assembly and can be deleted independent of the other instances. However, the geometry of new components is dependent on the original component.

General Steps

Use the following general steps to instantiate multiple instances of a component:

1. Start the **Multi-instantiation** operation.
2. Select the component to instantiate.
3. Define multi-instantiation parameters.
4. Specify a reference direction.
5. Constrain the instantiated components.

Step 1 - Start the Multi-instantiation operation.

Click (Define Multi Instantiation) in the Product Structure Tools toolbar. The Multi-Instantiation dialog box opens as shown in Figure 5–3.

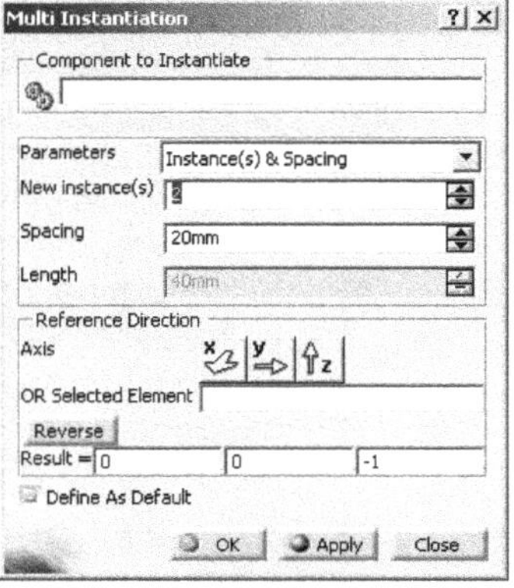

Figure 5–3

Step 2 - Select the component to instantiate.

Alternatively, you can select the component first and then click .

Select the component that you want to have multiplied in the model or specification tree. Any component can be selected to multiply, including skeleton models.

Step 3 - Define multi-instantiation parameters.

Define the parameters for a multi-instantiation operation by selecting one of the following combinations:

- Instance(s) & Spacing
- Instance(s) & Length
- Spacing & Length

Once you define the parameters, the dialog box updates accordingly. The selected parameter scheme establishes the driving dimensions.

Step 4 - Specify a reference direction.

Specify the reference direction by selecting an **Axis** icon in the dialog box. If the direction of instantiation does not lie along one of these axes, a geometry element can be selected from the model. The direction of instantiation can be reversed by clicking **Reverse**.

The *Result* field displays the X-, Y-, and Z-components of the direction of instantiation. Once you have selected a direction, a preview of the new instances displays on the model, enabling you to confirm your selection, as shown in Figure 5–4.

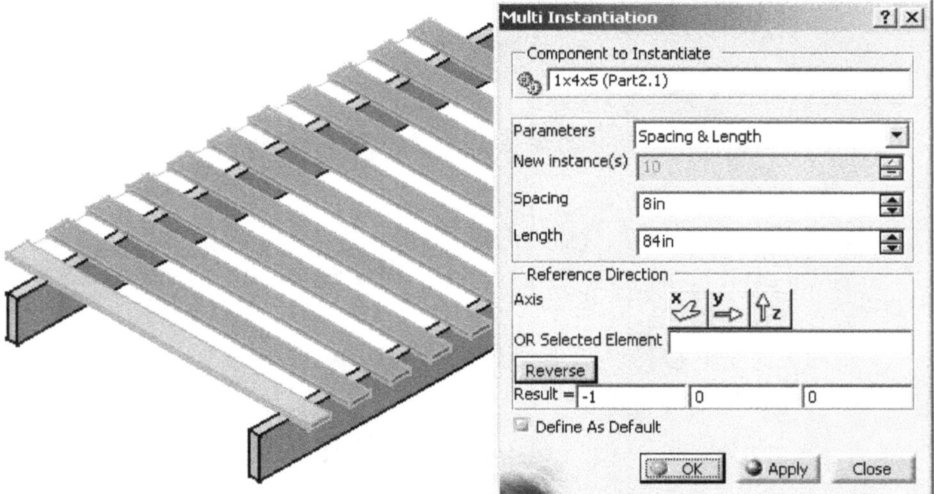

Figure 5–4

Step 5 - Constrain the instantiated components.

Once the instantiated components have been placed in the assembly, constraints must be added to each new component.

Fast Multi-Instantiation

Fast multi-instantiation uses the parameters and direction from the last multi-instantiation operation to instantiate the selected component. To perform a fast multi-instantiation operation, click (Fast Multi-Instantiation) and select the component to multiply.

5.4 Creating Symmetry Features

Symmetry features transform an existing component in an assembly with respect to a symmetry plane. Depending on the settings of the symmetry feature, a new model is created or the source model is transformed. If a new model is created, it can be opened as a separate model and used in other assemblies.

General Steps

Use the following general steps to transform an existing component in an assembly:

1. Start the **Symmetry** operation.
2. Select the symmetry plane.
3. Select the model to transform.
4. Define the symmetry conditions.

Step 1 - Start the Symmetry operation.

Click (Symmetry) in the Assembly Features toolbar. The Assembly Symmetry Wizard dialog box opens as shown in Figure 5–5.

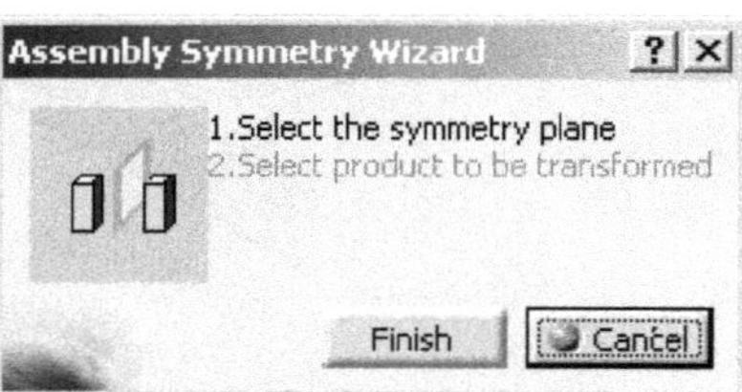

Figure 5–5

Step 2 - Select the symmetry plane.

Select a planar reference on the model to define the symmetry plane. This reference can be a model face, planar surface feature, or reference plane. Remember to consider parent/child relationships when selecting a symmetry plane.

Once the symmetry plane has been selected, the Assembly Symmetry Wizard dialog box updates as shown in Figure 5–6.

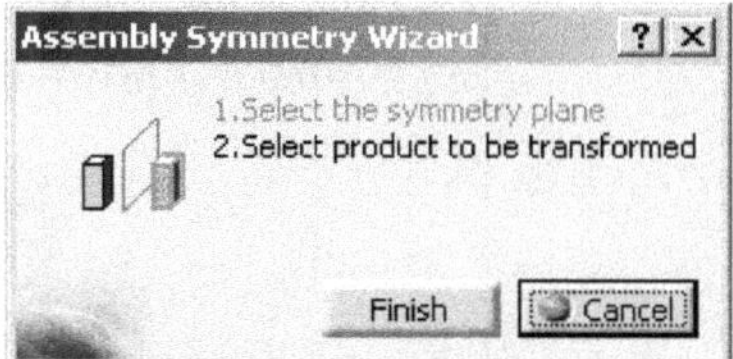

Figure 5–6

Step 3 - Select the model to transform.

The model to be transformed can be a part model or subassembly. However, only one component can be selected per symmetry operation. Once the model has been selected, a preview of the transformed component displays and the Assembly Symmetry Wizard dialog box expands to display additional options, as shown in Figure 5–7.

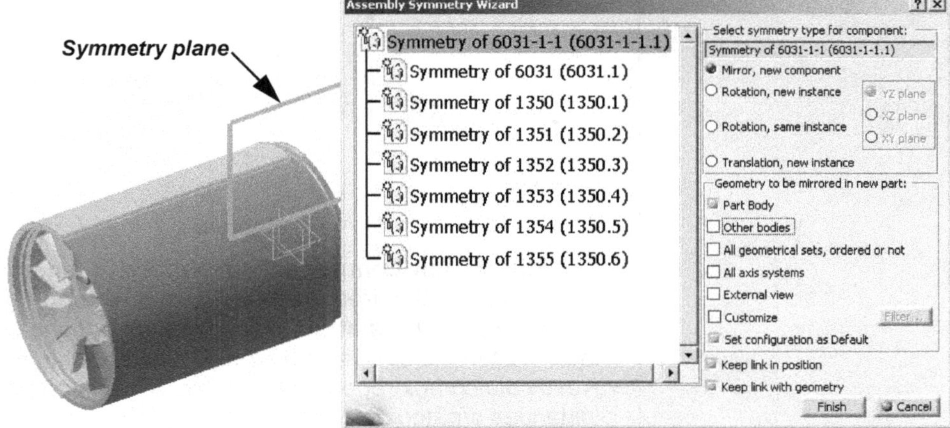

Figure 5–7

Step 4 - Define the symmetry conditions.

Define the symmetry conditions by selecting one of the options shown in Figure 5–8.

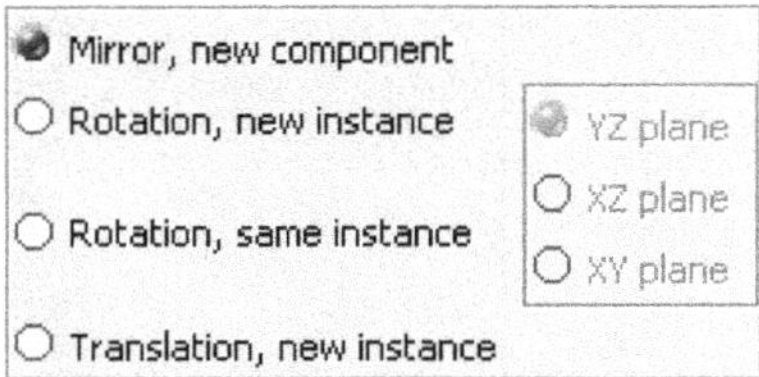

Figure 5–8

Mirror, New Component

This option creates a new model that contains a mirror image of the source component. An example of a left wing created using this option is shown in Figure 5–9.

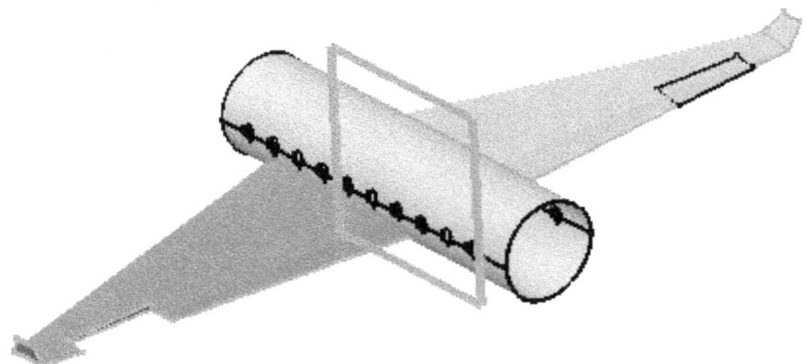

Figure 5–9

The **Mirror, new component** option creates a new component in the specification tree. Additionally, the **Rotation, new instance** and **Translation, new instance** options create new instances in the specification tree. The Assembly Symmetry Result dialog box reports the number of new components or instances created as a result of the symmetry operation as shown in Figure 5–10.

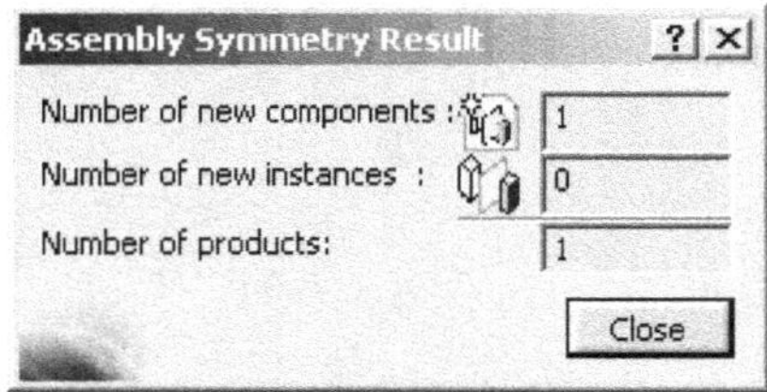

Figure 5–10

Rotation, new instance

This option creates a rotated symmetrical component. The left wing (shown in Figure 5–11), is mirrored and rotated about an axis. The axis is defined where the symmetry plane and selected reference plane (in this case XZ plane) intersect.

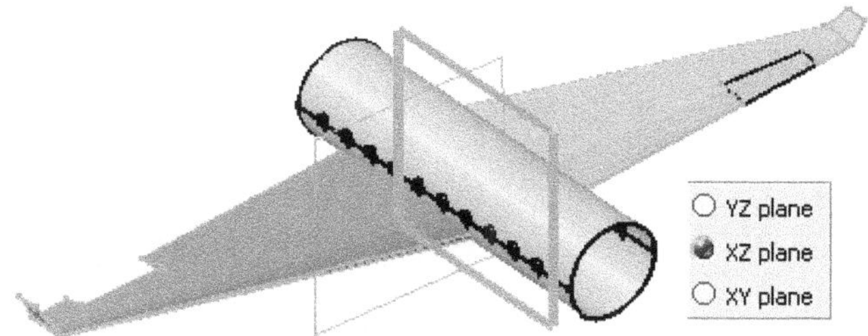

Figure 5–11

The XY plane (shown in Figure 5–12) defines the rotational axis.

The flap is rotated from its original location.

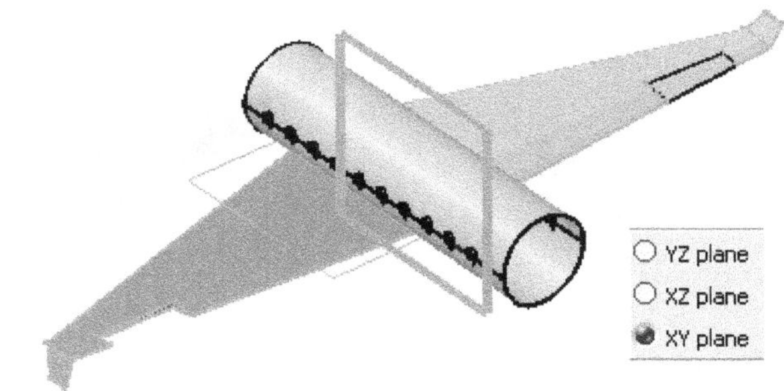

Figure 5–12

Rotation, same instance

This option mirrors and rotates the selected component, as shown in Figure 5–13.

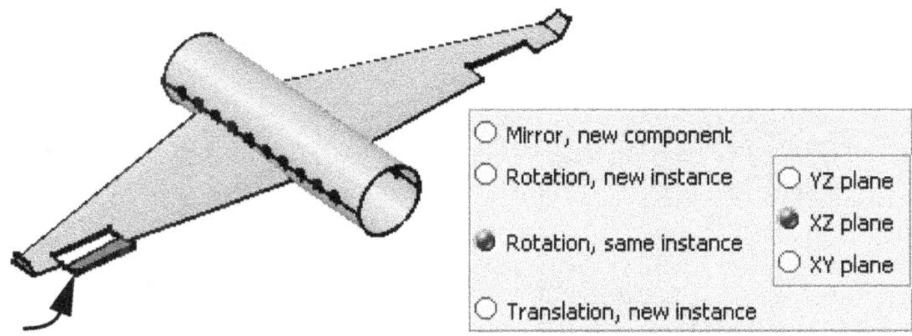

Figure 5–13

The Assembly Symmetry Result reports that no new components or instances have been created, as shown in Figure 5–14.

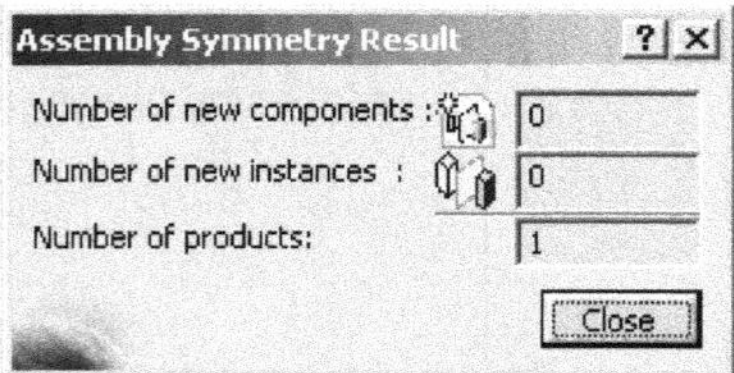

Figure 5–14

Translation, new instance

This option changes the orientation of components, as shown in Figure 5–15.

Dimensions cannot be specified for the translation operation.

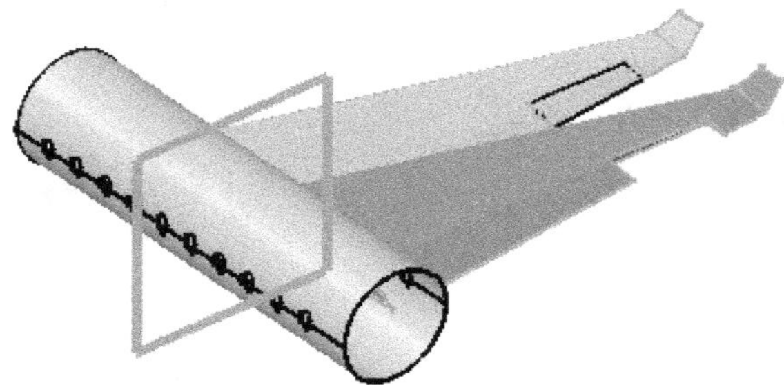

Figure 5–15

The **Keep link in position** option updates the symmetry result with positional changes to the source model.

The **Keep link with geometry** option updates the symmetry result with geometrical changes made to the source model, as shown in Figure 5–16. This link can be isolated.

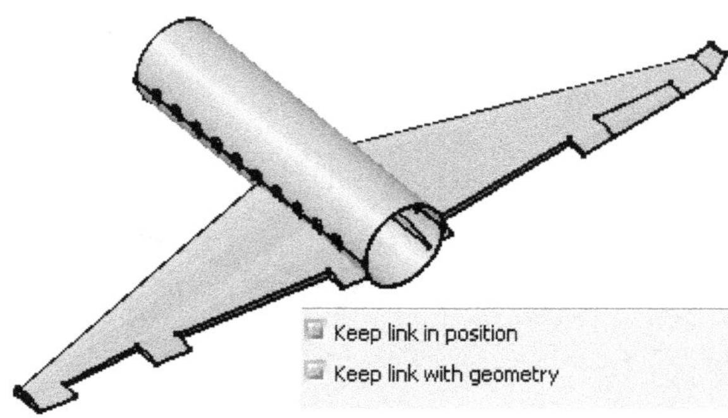

Figure 5–16

Technique Tip

Consider creating a temporary Product file and assembling one side of a symmetrical model. This enables the other side to be created quickly. Once completed, the temporary Product file can be deleted. The mirrored component can be a part or product model.

Practice 5a

Mirroring a Component

Practice Objective

- Create a new component by mirroring an existing component about a plane.

In this practice, you will create an opposite hand part. The model is the driver's side mirror from a car. You will use the **Create Symmetry** operation to create a passenger side mirror.

Task 1 - Create a new Product file and assemble a component.

1. Create a Product file named **Temp**.
2. Assemble **DriverSideMirror.CATPart** from the *Mirror* folder. The model displays as shown in Figure 5–17.

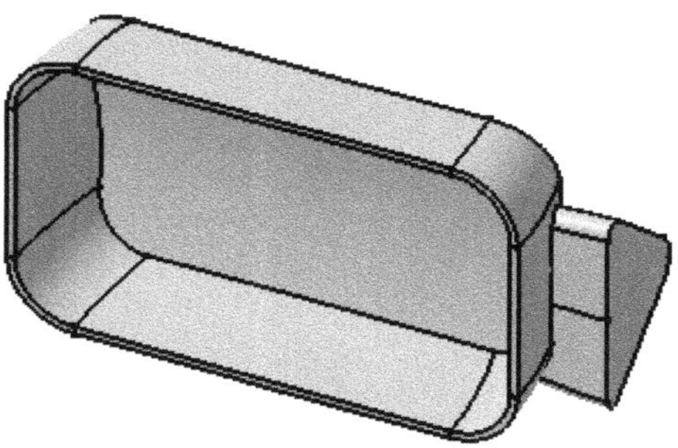

Figure 5–17

Task 2 - Create a symmetry component.

1. In the Assembly Features toolbar, click (Symmetry). The Assembly Symmetry Wizard dialog box opens as shown in Figure 5–18.

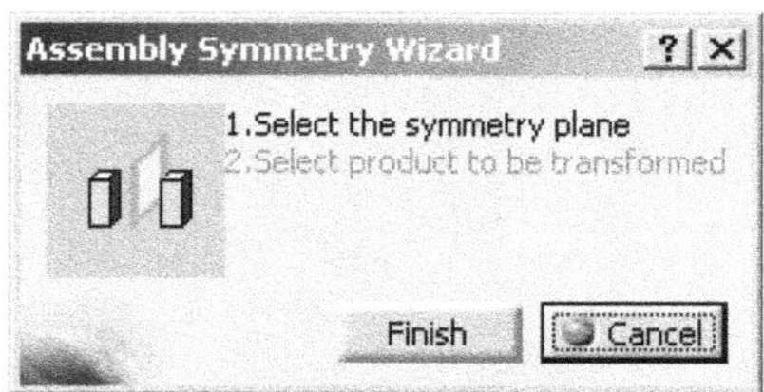

Figure 5–18

2. Select the face of the side mirror model to define the symmetry plane, as shown in Figure 5–19.

Figure 5–19

3. To define the product to be transformed, select the **DriverSideMirror** in the specification tree. Once selected, the Assembly Symmetry Wizard dialog box updates with the available transformation options. A preview of the mirrored model displays as shown in Figure 5–20.

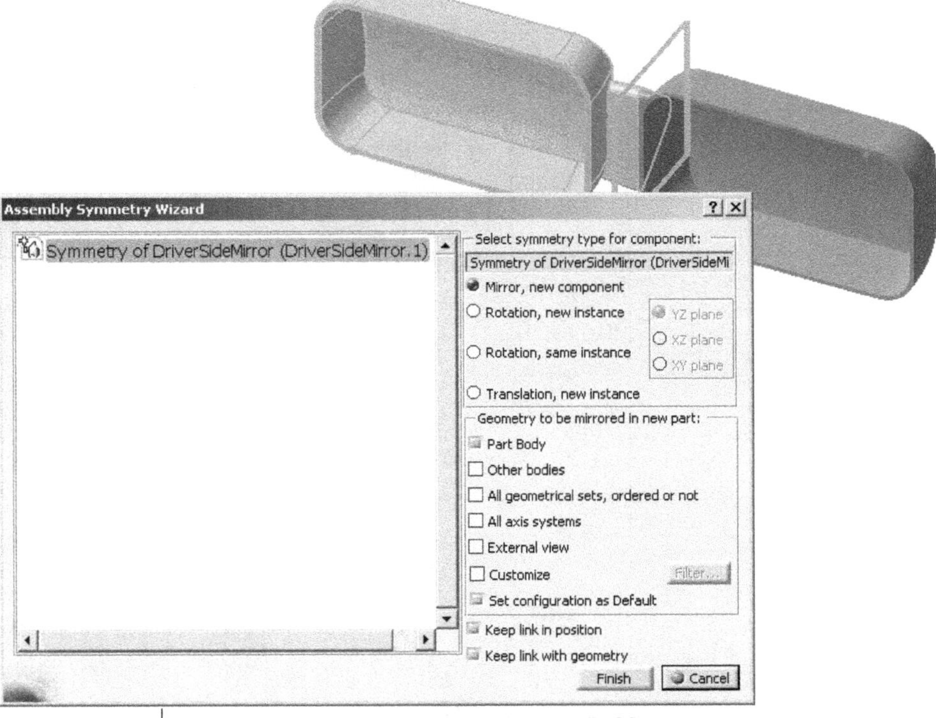

Figure 5–20

4. The default settings will create a new mirrored component, which is linked to the original component with respect to position and geometry. Accept the default options and click **Finish**. The model displays as shown in Figure 5–21.

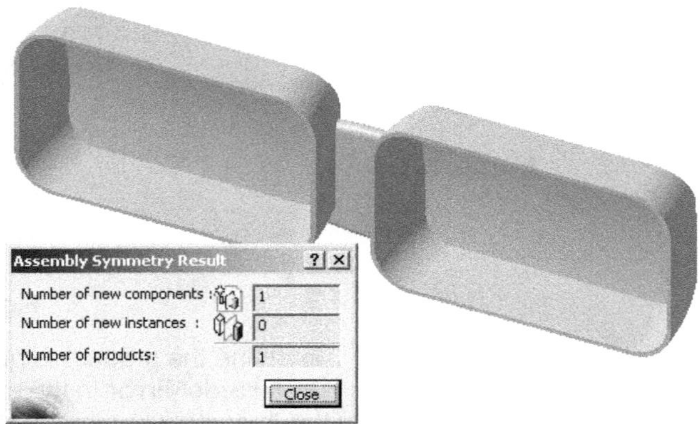

Figure 5–21

5. Click **Close**.

6. The **Assembly Symmetry.1** feature is added under the Assembly features branch in the specification tree as shown in Figure 5–22.

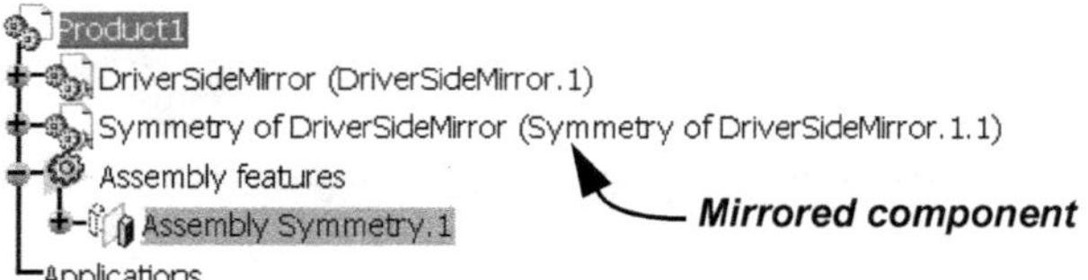

Figure 5–22

7. Rename the part number of the mirrored component as **PassengerSideMirror**, as shown in Figure 5–23.

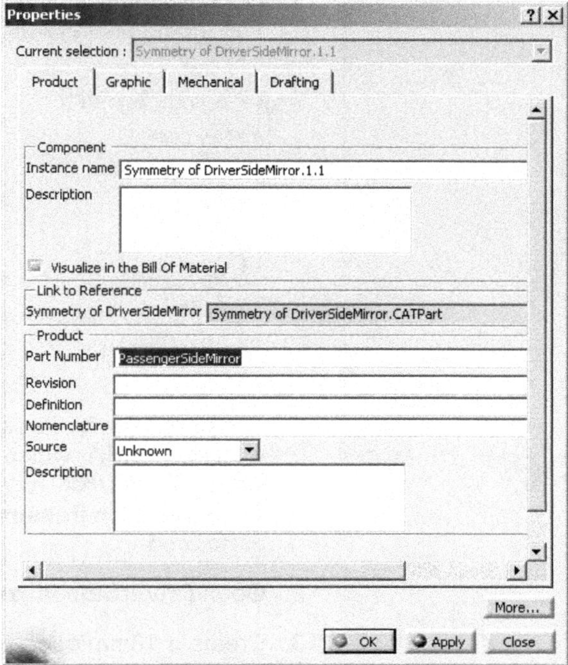

Figure 5–23

8. Double-click on the mirrored component in the specification tree to make it active and click (Save).

9. Enter **PassengerSideMirror.CATPart** as the name for the new component and save the file in the *Mirror* folder. The message window opens as shown in Figure 5–24.

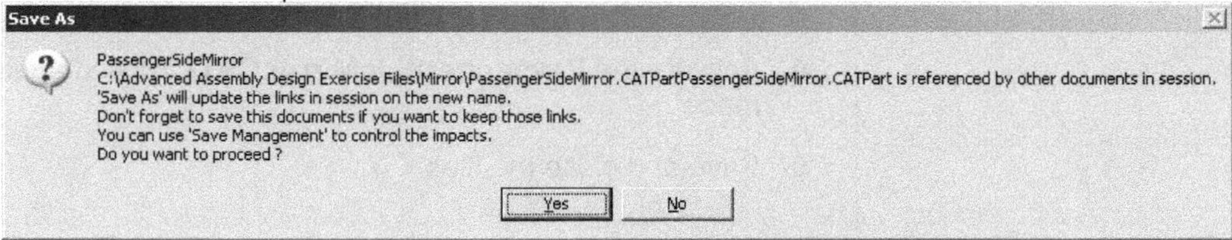

Figure 5–24

10. Click **Yes** to continue.

11. Close the assembly without saving.

Task 3 - Open the new component.

1. Open **PassengerSideMirror.CATPart** in the *Mirror* folder. The model displays as shown in Figure 5–25.

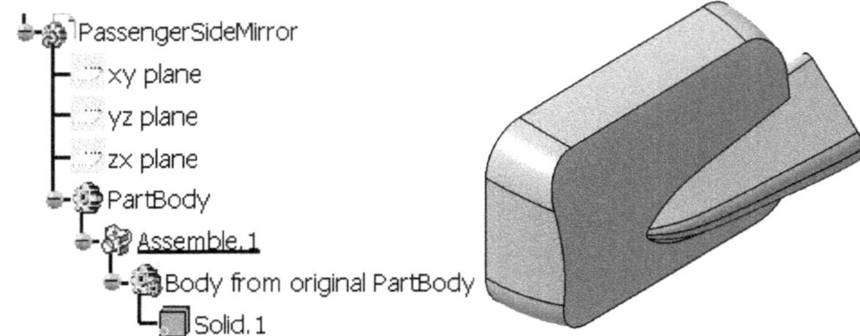

Figure 5–25

The geometry for **PassengerSideMirror** consists of a single feature, **Solid.1**, which is linked to the geometry of **DriverSideMirror**. Any changes made to **DriverSideMirror** are reflected in **PassengerSideMirror** when an update is performed.

2. Open **DriverSideMirror.CATPart** from the *Mirror* folder.
3. Create a 13mm edge fillet as shown in Figure 5–26.

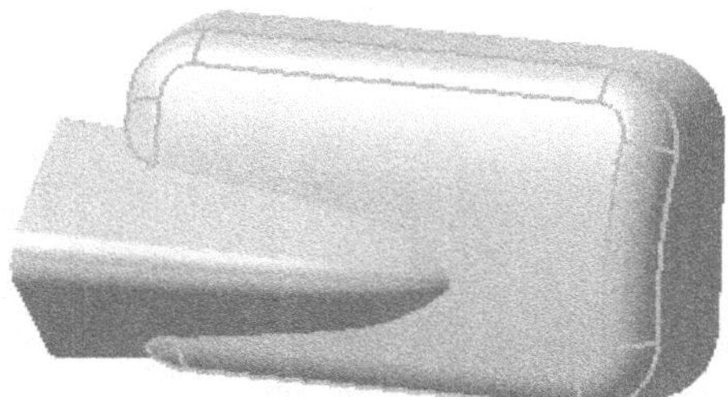

Figure 5–26

4. Activate the **PassengerSideMirror.CATPart** and update the model.
5. Save and close the files.

Practice 5b Duplication with Patterns

Practice Objective

- Reference a Part level pattern to instantiate a component.

In this practice, you will use a part pattern to instantiate a component.

Task 1 - Create a new Product file.

1. Create a Product file.
2. For the part number, enter **6851-1**.
3. Save the Product file as **DiffuserHousing** in the *Turbine* directory.

Task 2 - Assemble DiffuserHousing.CATPart.

1. Assemble **DiffuserHousing.CATPart** from the *Turbine* directory. The component displays as shown in Figure 5–27.

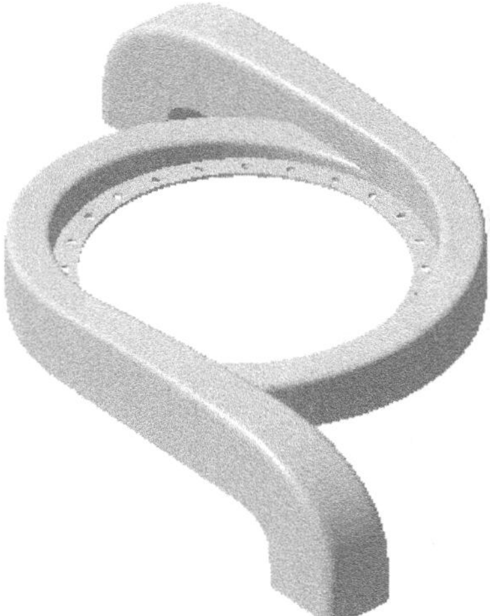

Figure 5–27

2. Apply a Fix constraint.

Task 3 - Locate the lead pattern feature.

In this task, you will assemble a stud to a Hole. The Hole is part of a pattern of Holes in the diffuser housing. The pattern can then be used to instantiate the stud part relative to the Hole pattern.

1. Expand the specification tree to display the features in the PartBody of **6851** (diffuser housing).

2. There are two Hole features with circular patterns in the specification tree. Select the Hole feature that belongs to the outer pattern of holes, as shown in Figure 5–28.

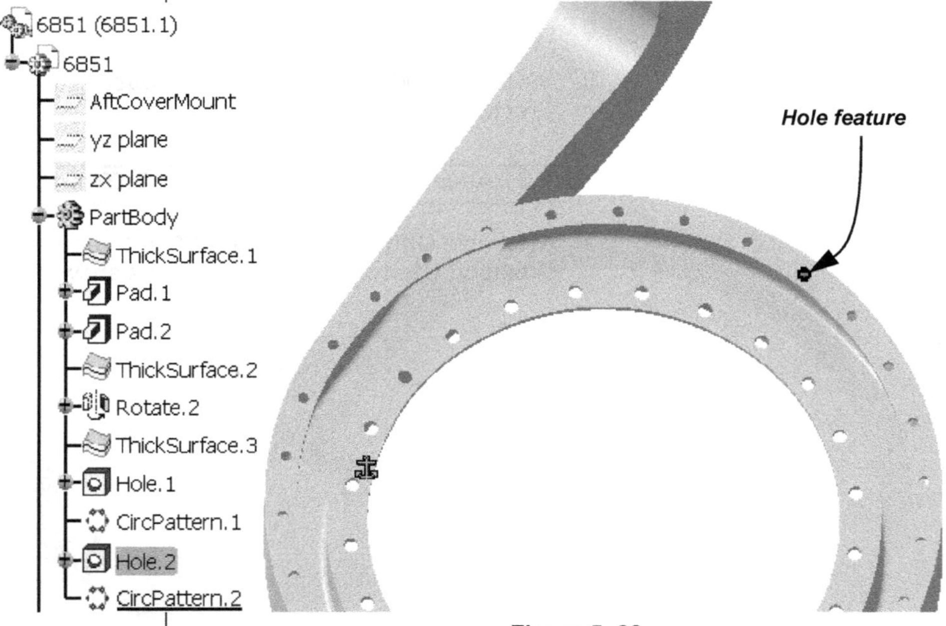

Figure 5–28

Task 4 - Assemble 10-32Stud.CATPart.

1. Assemble **10-32Stud.CATPart**.

2. Move the stud to a position next to the Hole from the outer pattern of Holes identified in Step 2 of the previous task, as shown in Figure 5–29.

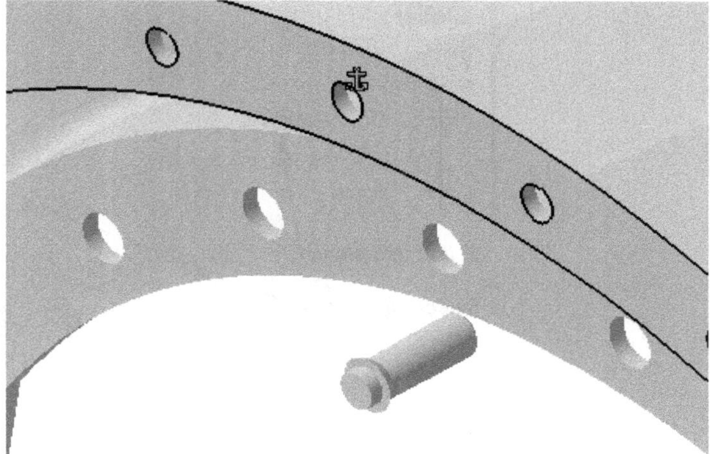

Figure 5–29

3. Add a Coincidence constraint between the axes of the bolt and any of the outer diameter Holes in the DiffuserHousing (part number **6851**), as shown in Figure 5–30.

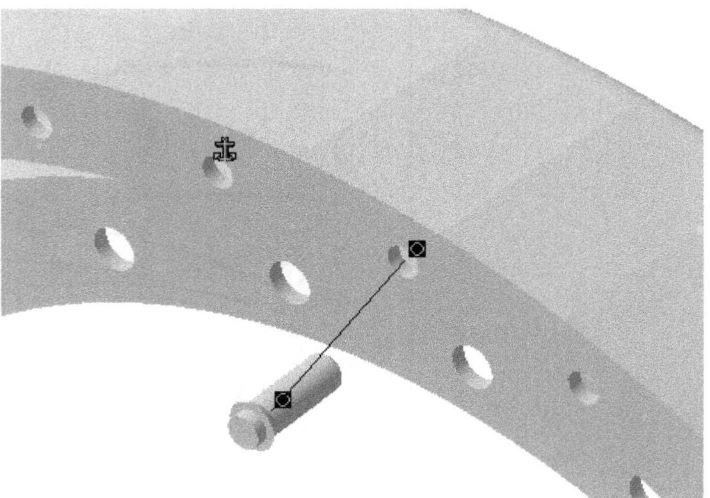

Figure 5–30

4. Add a Coincidence constraint between the face shown in Figure 5–31 and the **AftCoverMount** plane. Set the *Orientation* to **Same**. The **AftCoverMount** plane is hidden. Select it in the specification tree.

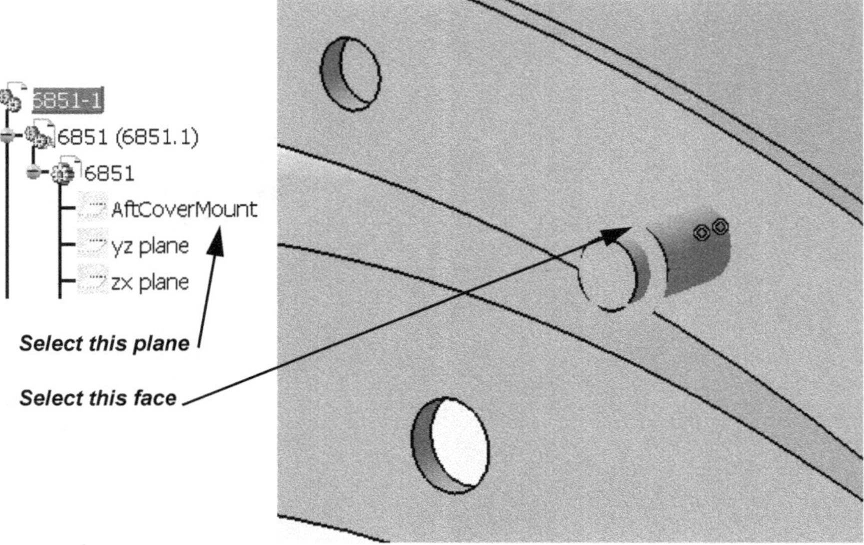

Figure 5–31

5. Click (Update All). The assembly displays as shown in Figure 5–32.

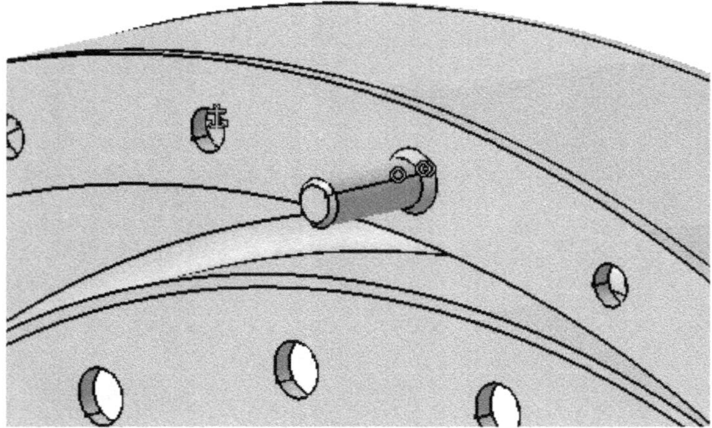

Figure 5–32

Task 5 - Reuse a part pattern to pattern a component.

1. Click (Reuse Pattern). The Instantiation on a pattern dialog box opens.
2. Select **10-32Stud** (**10-24 x 0.5** in the specification tree) as the component to instantiate.
3. Select **CircPattern.2** of the **6851** part as the pattern to reuse.
4. Click **OK** to complete the component pattern. The assembly updates as shown in Figure 5–33.

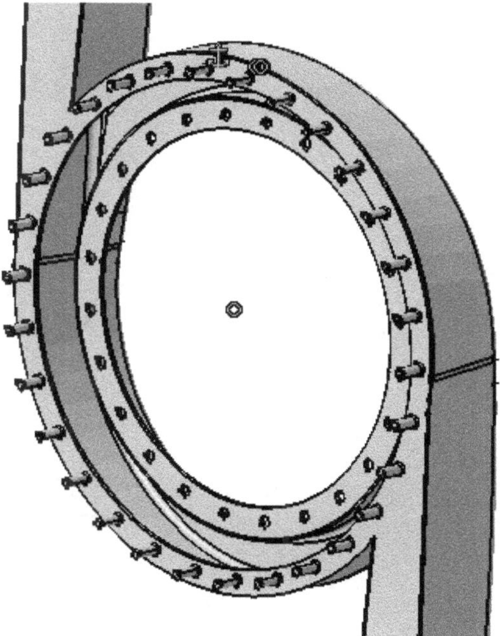

Figure 5–33

5. Save the assembly and close the file.

Task 6 - Open DiffuserVane.CATProduct and add an assembly annotation.

1. Open **DiffuserVane.CATProduct** from the *Turbine* folder. The assembly displays as shown in Figure 5–34.

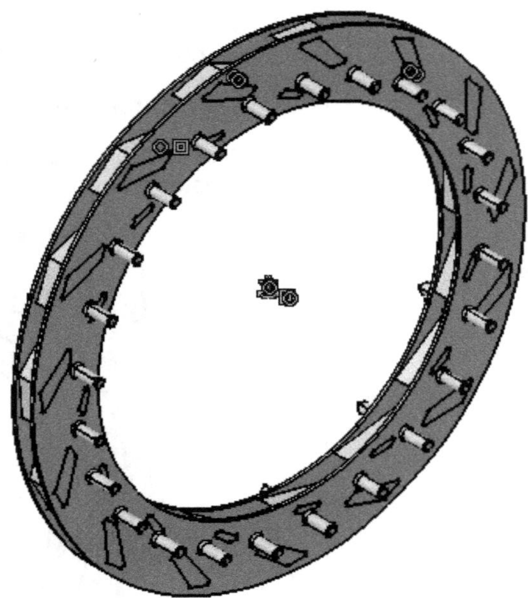

Figure 5–34

Design Considerations

Text with a leader must be added to the assembly so that when assembling this product into a higher level assembly, orientation and reference selection is more efficient.

2. In the specification tree, select **2412-1 (2412-1.1)**. There are 12 studs in this subassembly (you might need to rotate the model).
3. Select the background display so that the component is not selected.
4. In the Annotations toolbar, click [ABC icon] (Text with Leader).

5. Select the cylindrical face from one of the **10-24 Stud** parts assembled to **2412-1**. In the Text Editor dialog box, enter **12 Studs** as shown in Figure 5–35.

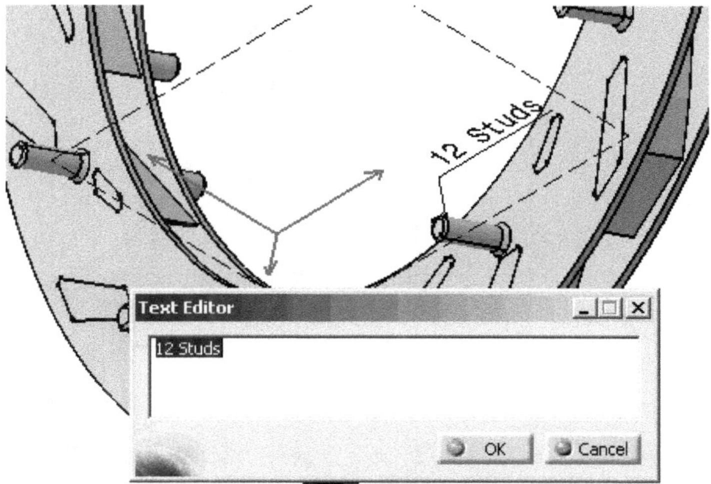

Figure 5–35

6. Click **OK** to complete the note.
7. Select the background display.
8. The text with leader is added to the specification tree. Expand **Annotation Set.1** and hide **Views** to toggle off the display of the view frame.
9. Expand **Notes** and change the properties of the *Display* tab of **Text.1** so that the 3D display is always **Parallel To Screen**, as shown in Figure 5–36.

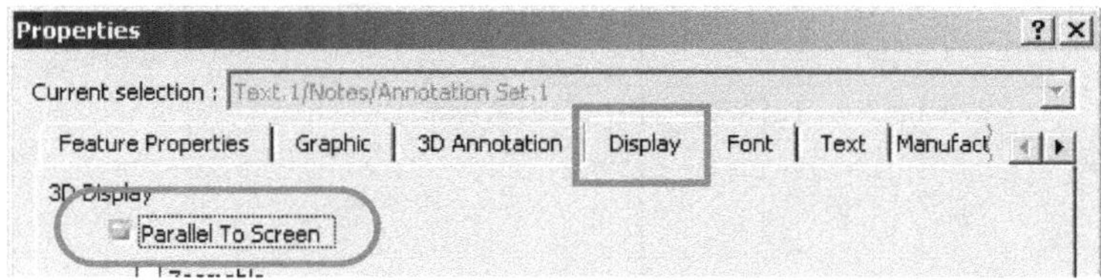

Figure 5–36

10. Spin the model to show how the text is always parallel to the screen regardless of model orientation. The annotation displays as shown in Figure 5–37.

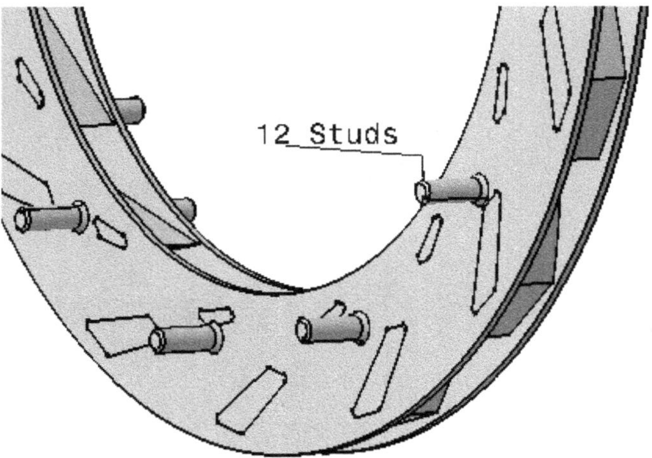

Figure 5–37

11. Save the assembly and close the file.

Practice 5c

Multi-Instantiation

Practice Objectives

- Multi-Instantiate a component.
- Replace a component.

In this practice, you will multi-instantiate the **Stator Band** part, fully constrain the instances, and replace the components. The completed assembly is shown in Figure 5–38.

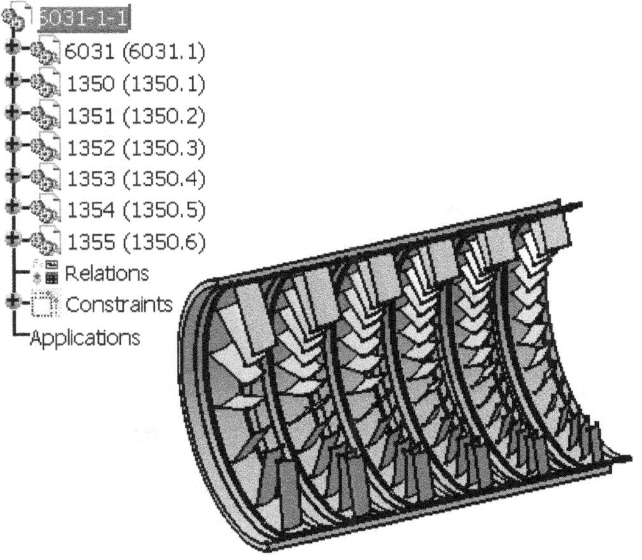

Figure 5–38

Task 1 - Create a Product file.

1. Create a Product file.
2. For the part number for this product, enter **6031-1-1**.
3. Save the file as **CompressorCase** in the *Turbine* directory.
4. Ensure that *units* are set to **millimeters**.

Task 2 - Assemble the first two components of the assembly.

1. Assemble **CompressorBody.CATPart** from the *Turbine* directory.
2. Apply a Fix constraint. The model displays as shown in Figure 5–39.

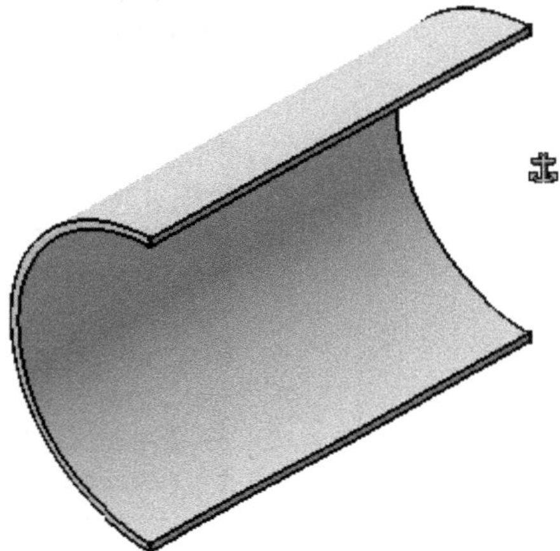

Figure 5–39

3. Assemble **StatorBand.CATPart** into the assembly.
4. Apply coincidence between the axes and update the assembly, as shown in Figure 5–40.

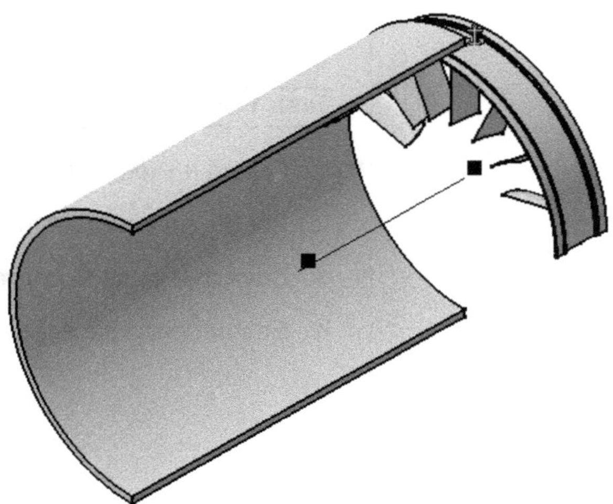

Figure 5–40

5. Use the compass to drag the part to the approximate location shown in Figure 5–41.

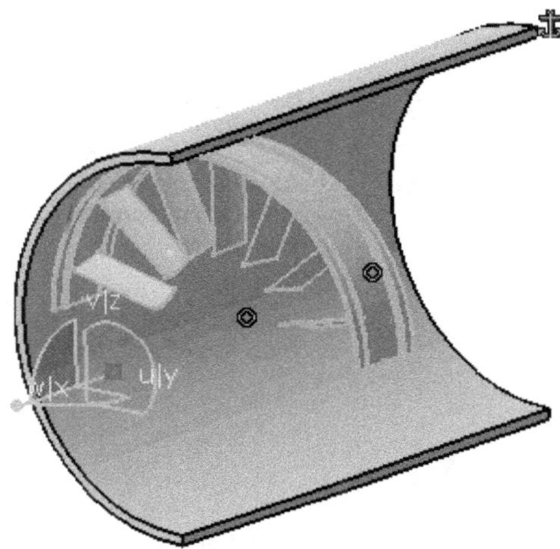

Figure 5–41

6. Apply an Offset constraint between the surfaces shown in Figure 5–42. For the offset value, enter **6.35**.

Use [icon] to apply an Offset constraint.

You might need to enter a negative value to achieve the same result.

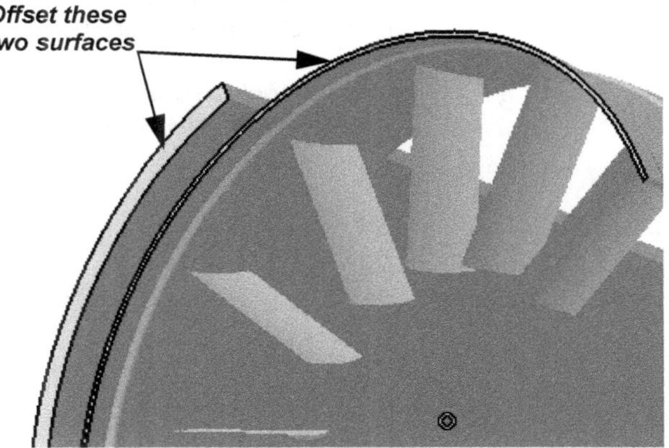

Figure 5–42

7. Ensure that the leading edge of the stator blade is near the end of the **CompressorCaseBody**, as shown in Figure 5–43. If it is not, redefine the Offset constraint and change the orientation.

You might also need to change the selected surface on the stator band to achieve the correct orientation.

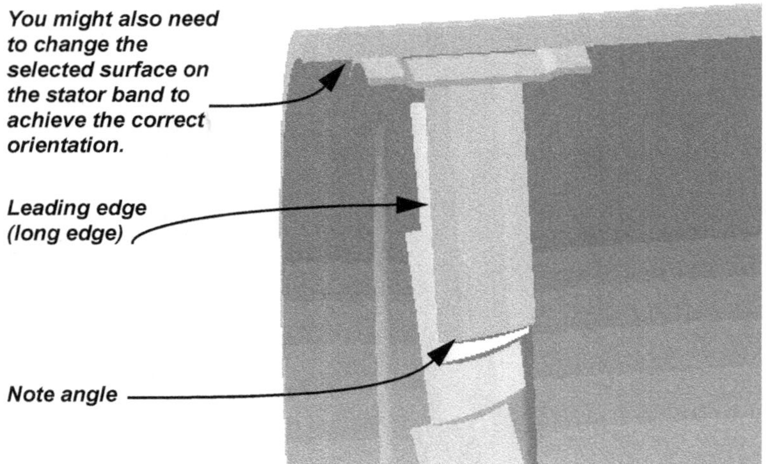

Figure 5–43

8. Apply a Parallel Angle constraint between the two surfaces shown in Figure 5–44.

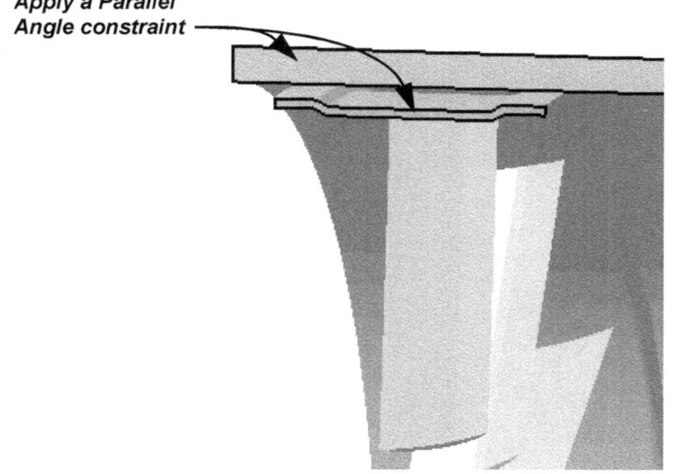

Figure 5–44

9. Update the assembly. The model displays as shown in Figure 5–45.

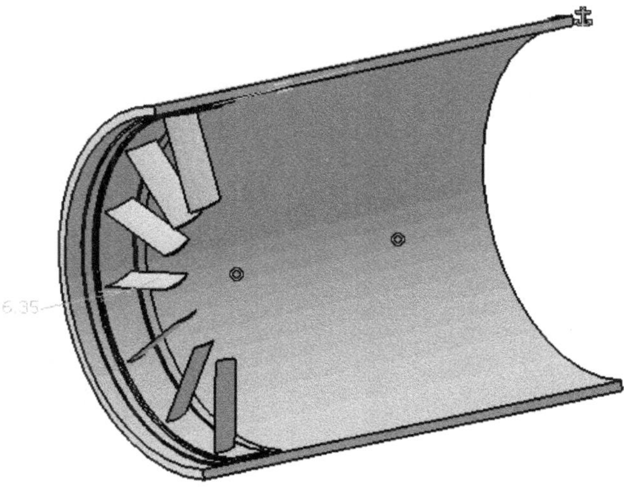

Figure 5–45

10. Save the model.

Task 3 - Multi-Instantiate a component.

1. Click (Define Multi Instantiation).
2. For the component to instantiate, select the **StatorBand (1350)**.
3. Enter the following parameters:
   - *Parameters:* **Instance(s) & Spacing**
   - *New instance(s):* **5**
   - *Spacing:* **25**
   - *Reference Direction:*
   - Click **Reverse**.

The Multi Instantiation dialog box opens as shown in Figure 5–46. The *Results* area displays the values **-1,0,0**.

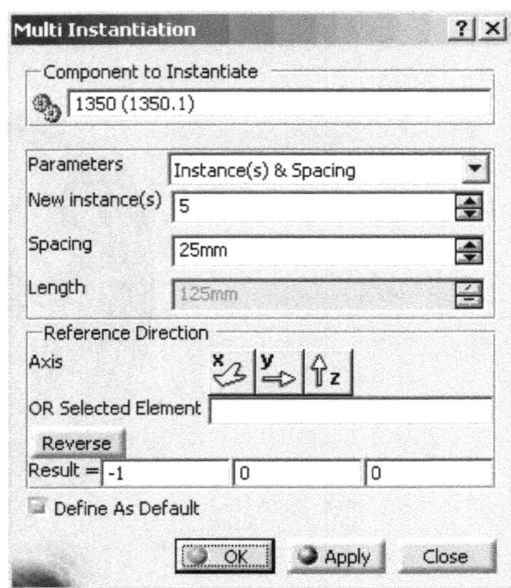

Figure 5–46

4. Click **OK**. The instantiated components display as shown in Figure 5–47.

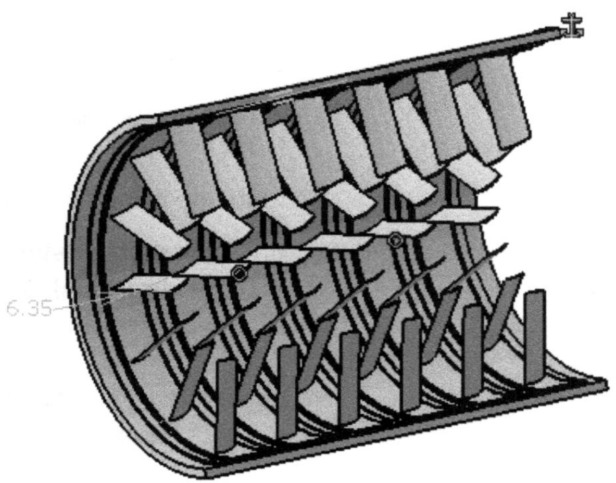

Figure 5–47

The multiple instances of part **1350** display in the specification tree, as shown in Figure 5–48. Constraints have not been created for the new components.

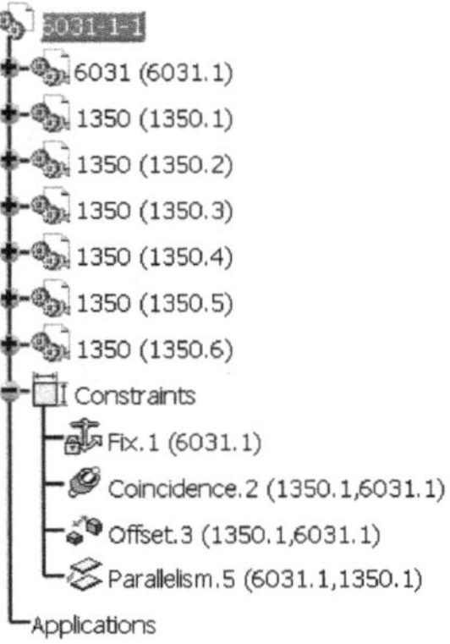

Figure 5–48

Task 4 - Fully constrain the instances.

1. Click to change the *Constraint Creation mode* to **Stack mode**.

2. Double-click on (Coincidence Constraint) and select the axis of part **6031**. Select the axes of the five instances in part **1351**. The five Coincidence constraints display as shown in Figure 5–49.

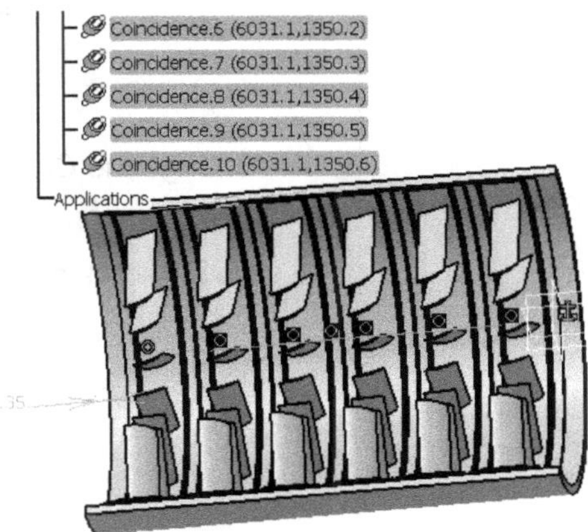

Figure 5–49

3. Maintain the Stack mode and constrain the surfaces shown in Figure 5–50 using a Coincidence constraint.

Double-click on .

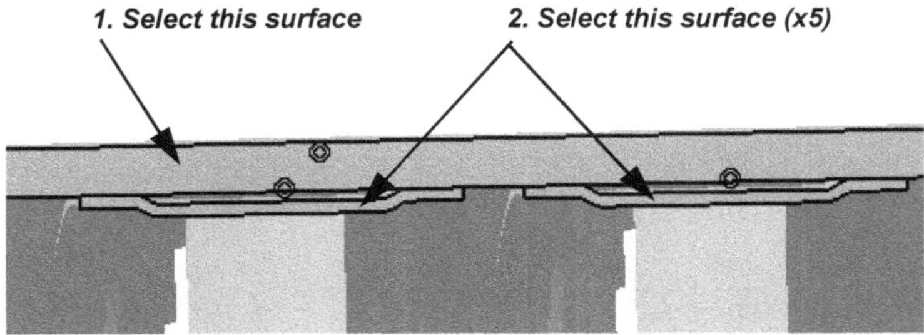

Figure 5–50

The constraints display as shown in Figure 5–51.

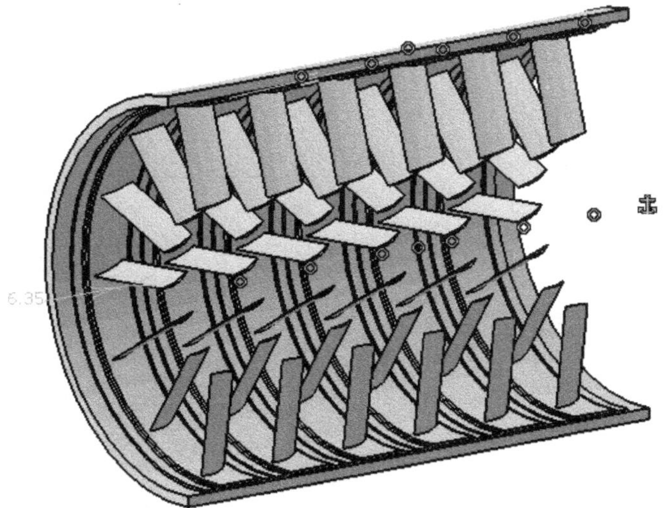

Figure 5–51

4. Change the Constraint Creation to (Chain mode).

5. Double-click on (Offset Constraint).

6. Apply an Offset constraint between the surfaces shown in Figure 5–52.

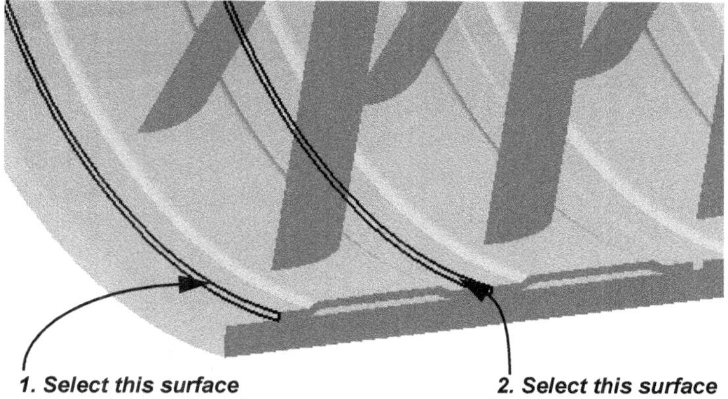

Figure 5–52

7. Enter **-30.5** for the *Offset* value, as shown in Figure 5–53.

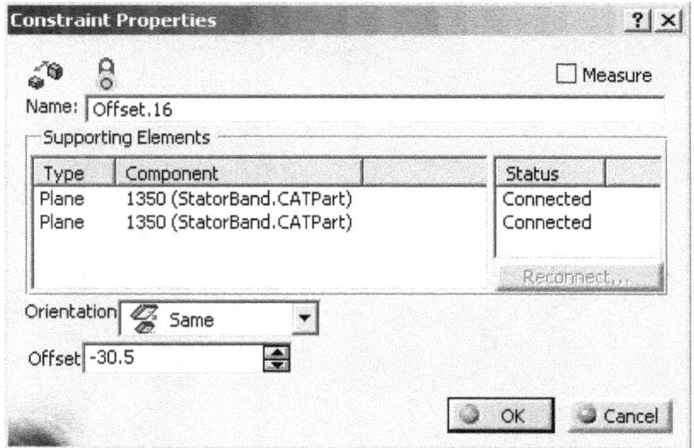

Figure 5–53

8. Select the surface shown in Figure 5–54. Enter **-30.2** for the *Offset* value.

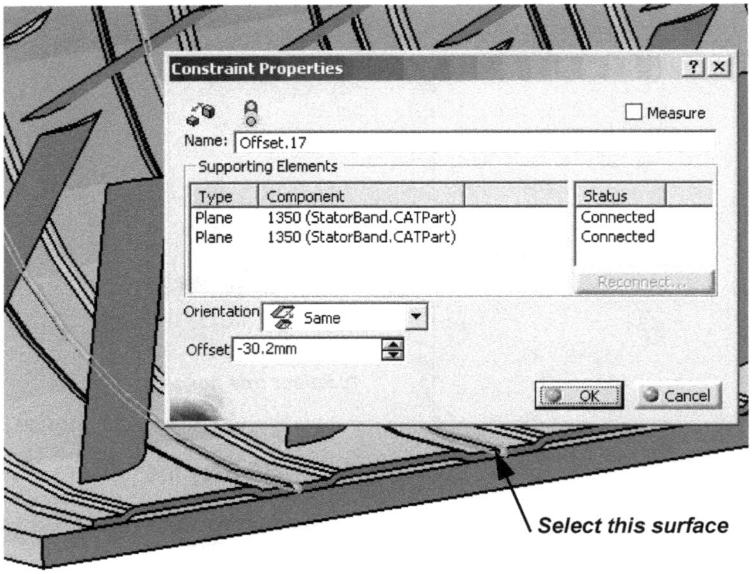

Figure 5–54

9. Continue adding Offset constraints between the StatorBands in the same manner using the values listed.

Between Components	Offset
1350.3 - 1350.4	-27.9
1350.4 - 1350.5	-27.0
1350.5 - 1350.6	-26.2

10. Click . The model displays as shown in Figure 5–55 and Figure 5–56.

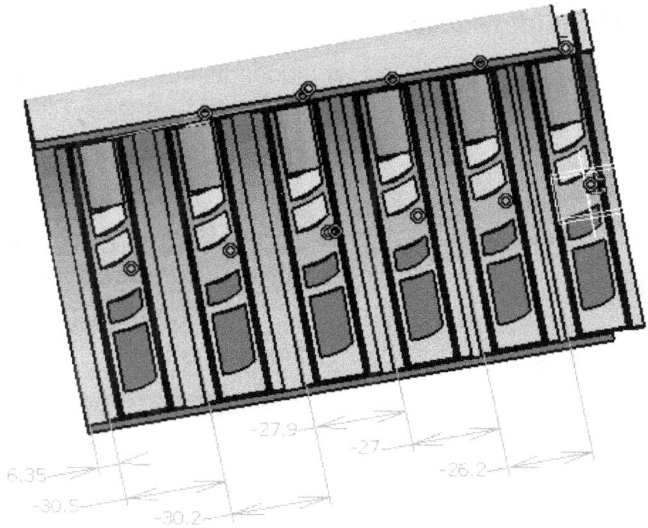

Figure 5–55

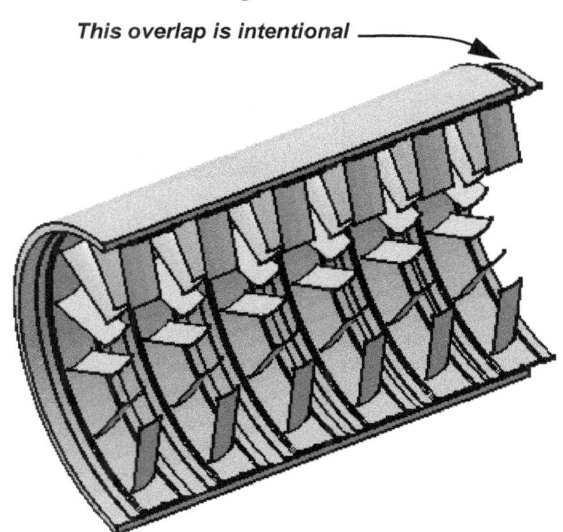

Figure 5–56

11. Save the model. Do not close the file.

Task 5 - Create a Product file.

Design Considerations

In this task, a Product file is created and propagated with all of the configurations of the **StatorBand** (**1350**) part, which are used in the **CompressorCase** product. This technique brings the components *in session* and enables you to use the **Replace Component In Session** option.

1. Create a Product file but do not save it.

2. Click (Catalog Browser) and open **Compressor.catalog** in the *Turbine* directory.

   The Catalog Browser dialog box opens as shown in Figure 5–57.

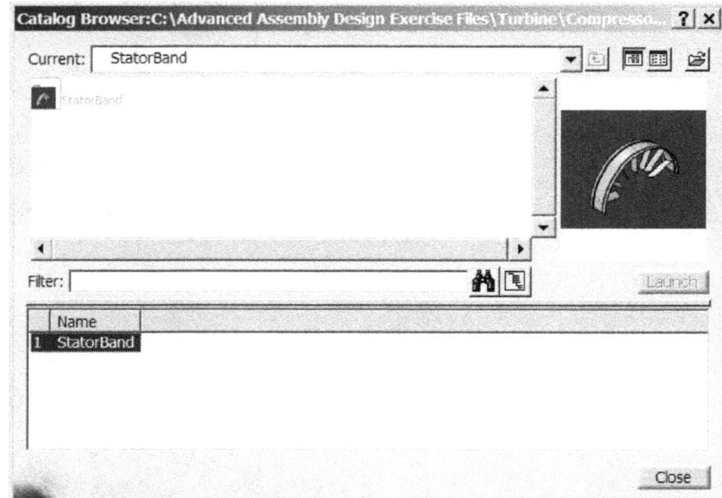

Figure 5–57

3. Double-click on **StatorBand>1351**, as shown in Figure 5–58.

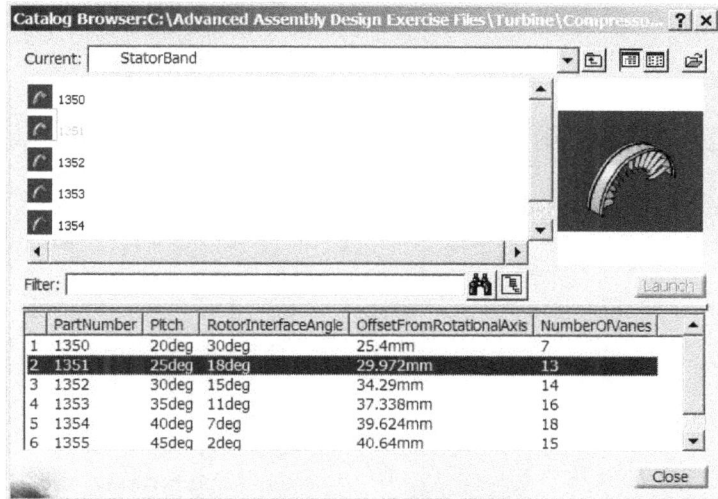

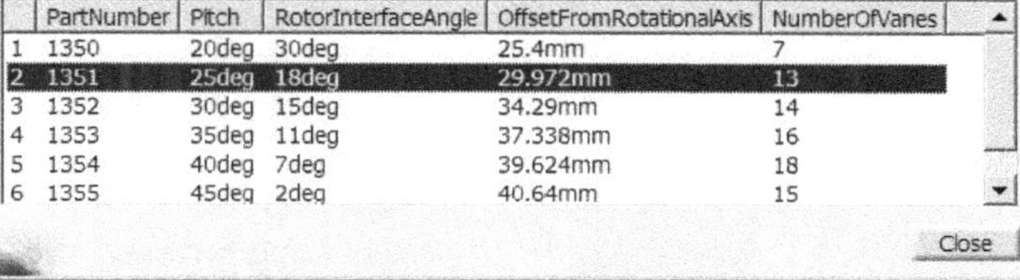

Catalog Browser:C:\Advanced Assembly Design Exercise Files\Turbine\Compresso...
Current: StatorBand
1350
1351
1352
1353
1354
Filter:
Launch
PartNumber | Pitch | RotorInterfaceAngle | OffsetFromRotationalAxis | NumberOfVanes
1 1350 20deg 30deg 25.4mm 7
2 1351 25deg 18deg 29.972mm 13
3 1352 30deg 15deg 34.29mm 14
4 1353 35deg 11deg 37.338mm 16
5 1354 40deg 7deg 39.624mm 18
6 1355 45deg 2deg 40.64mm 15
Close

Figure 5–58

The model displays as shown in Figure 5–59.

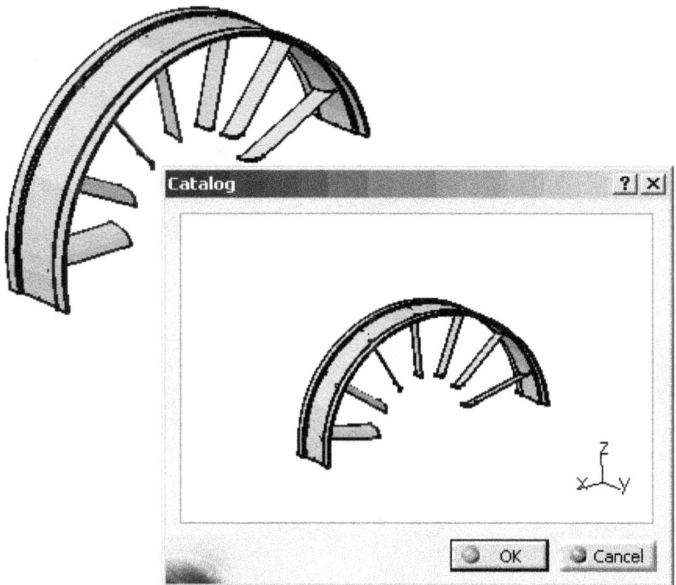

Figure 5–59

4. In the Catalog preview window, click **OK**.

5. Add part numbers **1352**, **1353**, **1354**, and **1355**. Do not constrain the components. The components and specification tree display as shown in Figure 5–60.

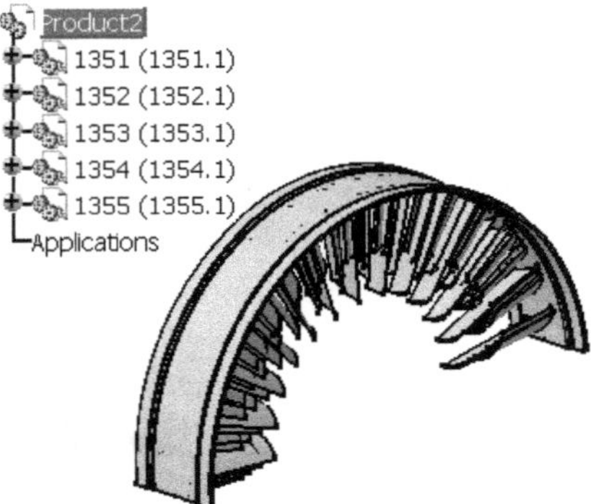

Figure 5–60

6. In the catalog browser, click **Close**.

Task 6 - Replace components.

1. Activate **CompressorCase.CATProduct**.
2. In the specification tree, right-click on **1350** (**1350.2**) and select **Components>Replace Component In Session**.
3. In the Select New Component dialog box, select **1351** as shown in Figure 5–61.

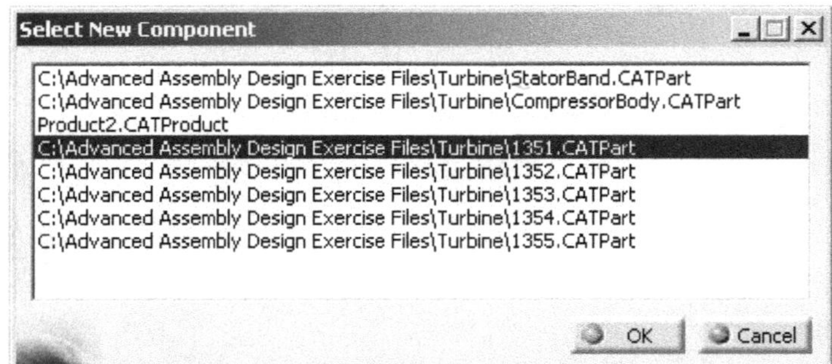

Figure 5–61

4. Click **OK**.

5. Select **No**, as shown in Figure 5–62.

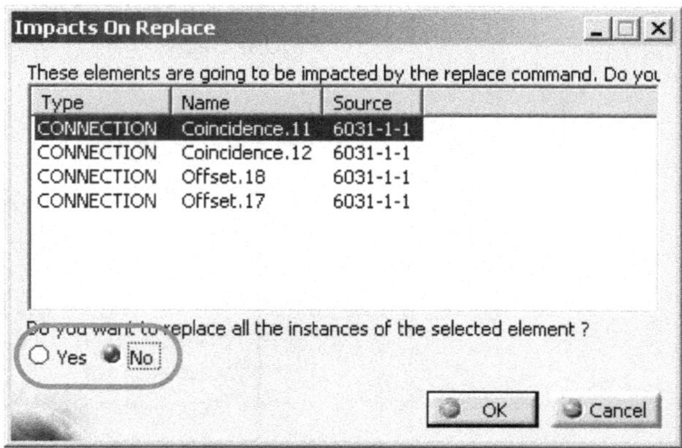

Figure 5–62

6. Click **OK**. The catalog instance displays as shown in Figure 5–63.

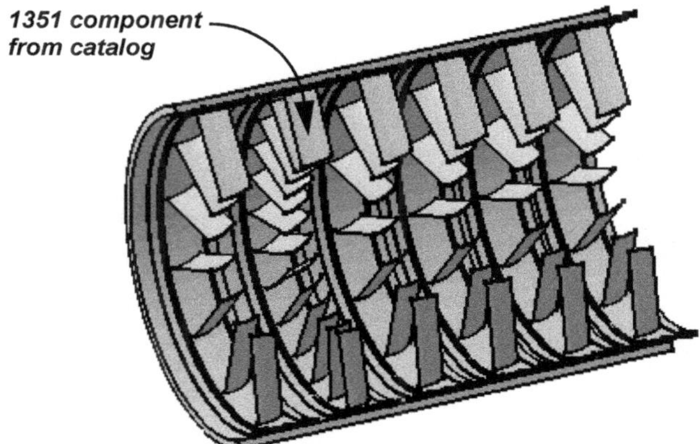

Figure 5–63

7. Repeat Steps 2 to 5 to replace the four remaining StatorBand models with the sequential part numbers in session, described as follows:

Replace	With
1350 (1350.3)	1352
1350 (1350.4)	1353
1350 (1350.5)	1354
1350 (1350.6)	1355

8. Hide the constraints.

   The model and specification tree display as shown in Figure 5–64.

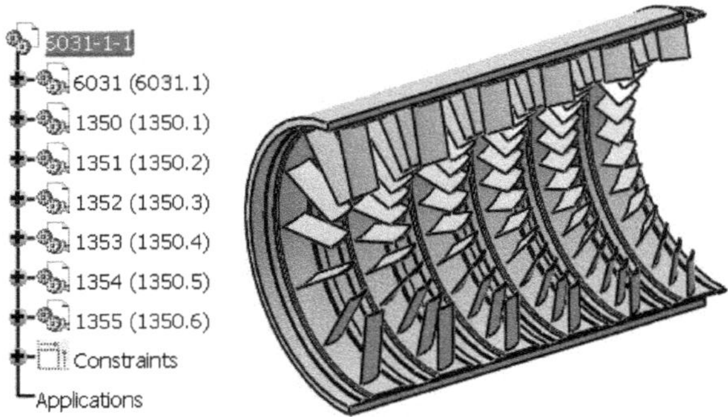

Figure 5–64

9. Save the model and close the window.

10. Close the temporary assembly without saving.

Assembly Performance Management

As product models become larger, visualizing and manipulating the model becomes more complex. CATIA provides a number of tools that help reduce the complexity of the product model and enable you to work more efficiently with large amounts of data.

Learning Objectives in this Chapter

- Create exploded views.
- Use assembly management techniques to increases your efficiency when working in the Assembly Design workbench.
- Create scenes.
- Use assembly variants to create variations of your assembly designs.

6.1 Creating Exploded Views

Exploded views enable you to visualize a group of constrained components separately in the context of the assembly. The component positions in the exploded view are temporary and return to their assembled locations when the model is updated.

General Steps

Use the following general steps to create an exploded view:

1. Access the **Explode** options.
2. Position exploded components.

Step 1 - Access the Explode options.

Click (Explode) in the Move toolbar to explode an assembly. The Explode dialog box opens as shown in Figure 6–1.

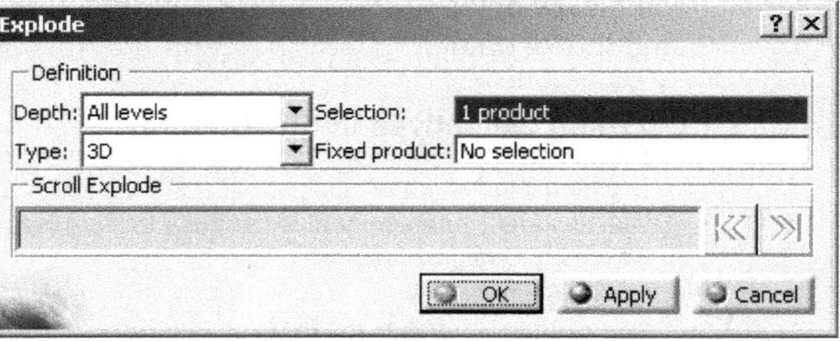

Figure 6–1

Options for the Explode dialog box are described as follows:

Options		Description
Depth		Determines which components in the assembly are exploded.
	All	Explodes all levels of the assembly.
	First	Explodes all first-level components of the assembly. In this case, subassembly components are not exploded.

Type		Determines the exploded placement of the components.
	3D	Places components in a 3D arrangement with respect to the position of the unexploded assembly.
	2D	Explodes components to positions in the 2D plane of the current view. Use named views to determine the 2D explode plane.
	Constrained	Explodes components with respect to the constraints used to place them contextually in the assembly.
Selection		Specifies the product to explode. The active assembly is automatically selected. If multiple levels of the assembly are selected, the assembly explodes in stages.
Fixed Product		Select one component to remain fixed during the explode. If the *depth* is set to **All**, you can select a part. If the *depth* is set to **First**, you can select a subassembly.

Step 2 - Position exploded components.

Position in 3D or 2D

The components in the 3D explode can be positioned anywhere in 3D space, while the components in the 2D explode can only move in a 2D plane. This plane is always parallel to the screen and is therefore specified by orienting the model. The difference between 3D and 2D explode types is shown in Figure 6–2.

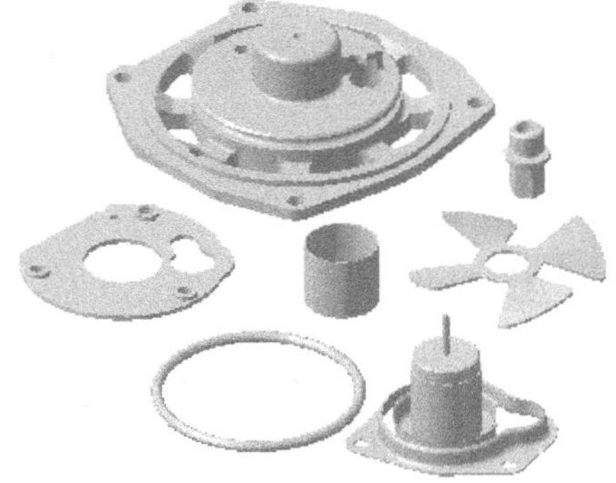

Type set to 3D

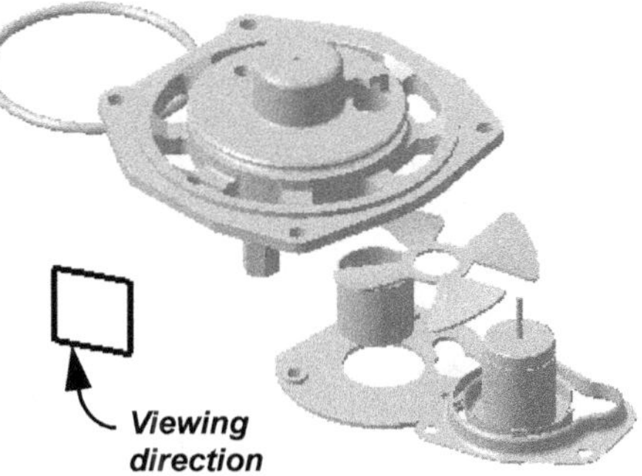

Type set to 2D

Figure 6–2

Position With Compass

When the model is exploded, the positions of individual components can be moved using the compass, as indicated by the Information Box shown in Figure 6–3.

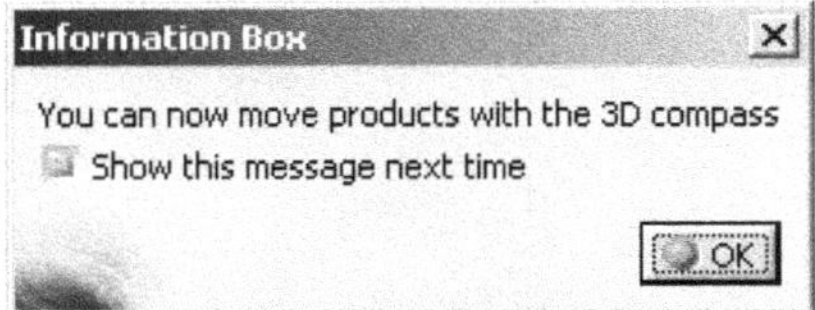

Figure 6–3

You can position the components to display how the assembly is put together. An example is shown in Figure 6–4.

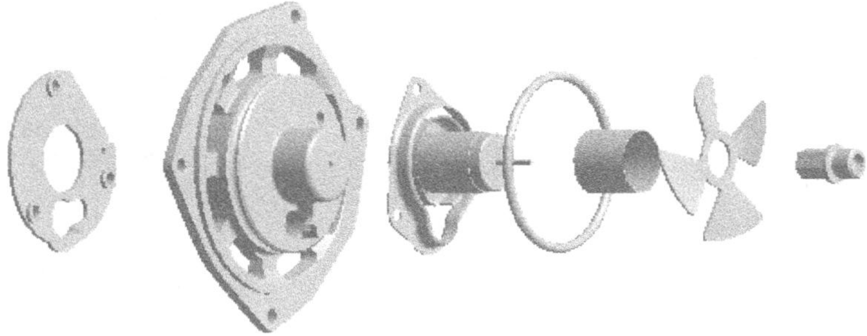

Figure 6–4

Position With Scroll Bar

Once an assembly has been exploded, the Scroll Explode bar shown in Figure 6–5 displays. It enables you to move the assembly components from their constrained positions to their exploded positions.

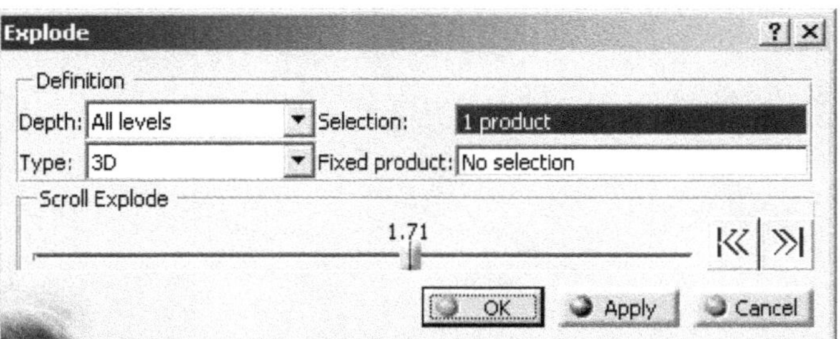

Figure 6–5

6.2 Assembly Management

Using assembly management techniques increases your efficiency when working in the Assembly Design workbench. The techniques enable you to control and simplify your display, which decreases retrieval and refresh times for the product.

Each technique can be performed independent of the parent/child relationships in the selected component.

Use the following techniques to reduce the update and retrieval times of your assembly and simplify your display:

- Hide/Show
- Activate/Deactivate
- Load/Unload

Hide/Show

The display of components in an assembly can be quickly toggled on and off by right-clicking on the component and selecting **Hide/Show**, or selecting **View>Hide/Show> Hide/Show**.

The **Hide/Show** operation simplifies your display. The settings for a **Hide/Show** operation are saved with the product model. The hidden or shown status of a component is indicated by the **Components** symbol in the specification tree, as shown in Figure 6–6.

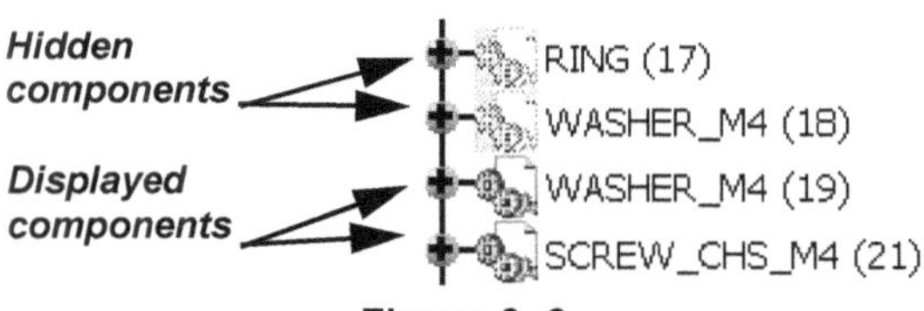

Figure 6–6

Activate/ Deactivate

Similar to **Hide/Show**, **Activate/Deactivate** simplifies the display of components in the product. If you deactivate a component, its geometry is also removed from consideration by the assembly. This means that the component is not calculated by the system during update, which decreases update time.

To toggle the activation status, right-click on a component and select **Representation**. Four available options are described as follows:

Option	Description
Activate Node	Activates the selected part model in the product.
Deactivate Node	Deactivates the selected part model in the product.
Activate Terminal Node	Activates the selected product model (subassembly or top-level assembly).
Deactivate Terminal	Deactivates the selected product model (subassembly or top-level assembly).

Although deactivation temporarily removes the model from the assembly, the model still displays in a drawing of the assembly. The system keeps a representation of the model in memory, which is used to create drawing views.

The settings for an **Activate/Deactivate** operation are not saved with the product model. Regardless of earlier settings, when a product is opened, all of the components are activated. The activated or deactivated status of a node or terminal node is indicated by the **Components** symbol in the specification tree, as shown in Figure 6–7.

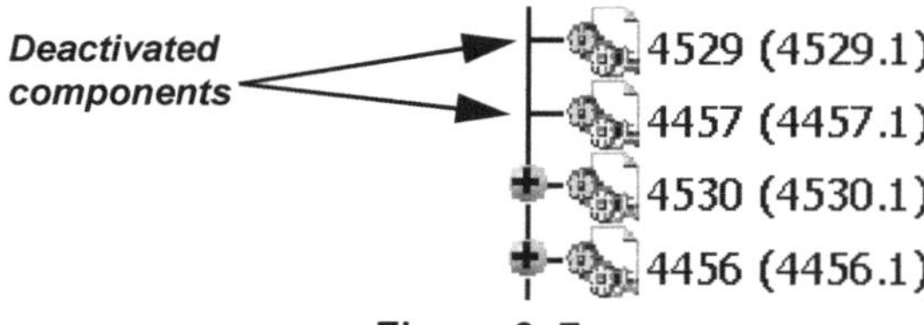

Figure 6–7

A method for handling complex assemblies on loading is to toggle on an option to avoid loading default shapes when opening a product. This enables you to select the components that you want to activate in the specification tree, after the file has been opened.

To set this option, select **Tools>Options>Infrastructure>Product Structure** and select the *Product Visualization* tab. Select **Do not activate default shapes on open**, as shown in Figure 6–8.

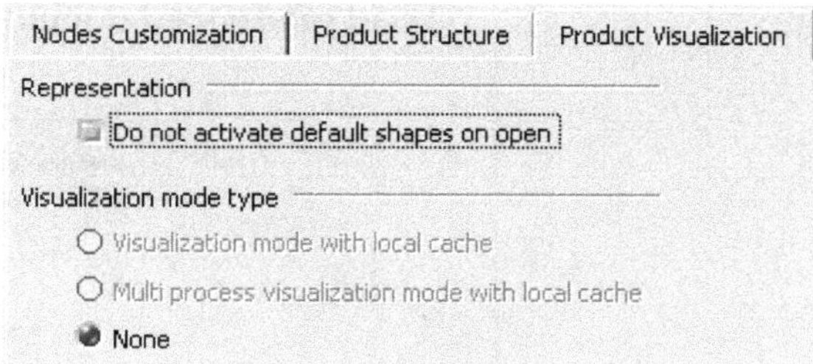

Figure 6–8

Load/Unload

Load/Unload enables you to remove or restore components from the product. Right-click on the component and select **Components>Unload** to remove a component or **Components>Load** to restore a component.

When unloading a component, it is completely removed from memory and the unloaded component is not displayed in either the assembly or assembly drawing. Additionally, if the component is assembled more than once, all instances of the component are unloaded from the assembly because the model is removed from memory.

Unloaded components display with a unique symbol in the specification tree, as shown in Figure 6–9.

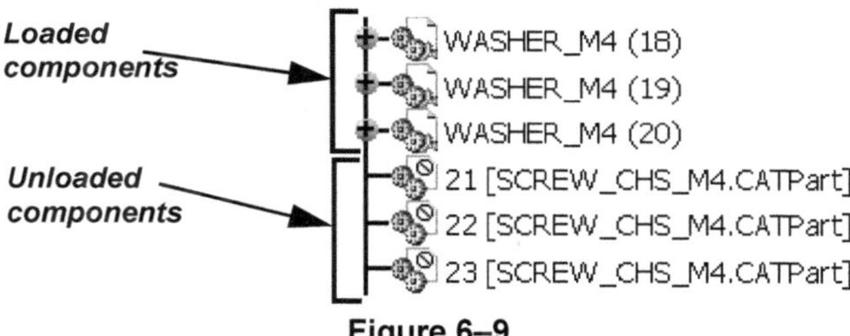

Figure 6–9

The settings for a **Load/Unload** operation are not saved with the product model. By default, all of the components are loaded when a product is opened. It is possible to configure the system to not load any of the components of an assembly. Select **Tools>Options>General** and select the *General* tab. Clear the **Load referenced documents** option, as shown in Figure 6–10.

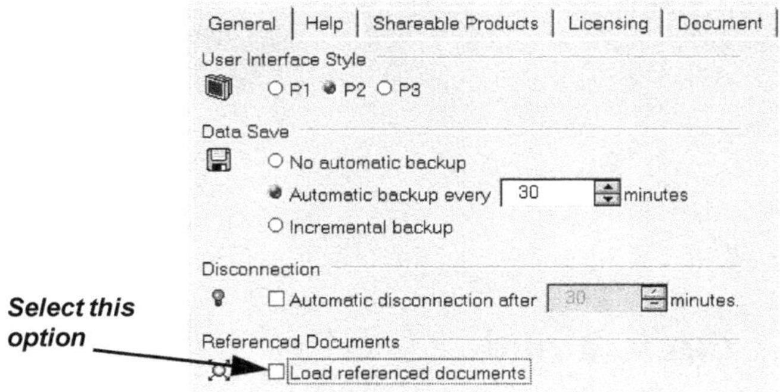

Figure 6–10

With this option disabled, the assembly model loads more quickly. No model geometry displays, but the specification tree lists all of the components in the assembly. You can then individually load only the components of the assembly that are required in the specification tree.

Product Load Management

Product Load Management automates multiple **Load/Show/Hide** operations and is accessed by clicking (Selective Load) in the Product Structure Tools toolbar. The Product Load Management dialog box opens as shown in Figure 6–11.

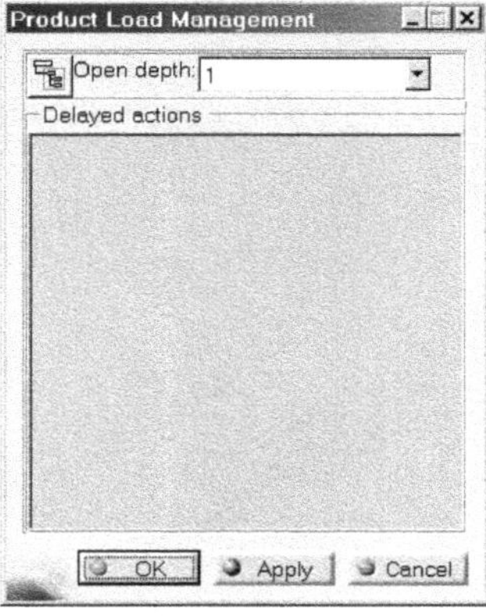

Figure 6–11

To perform an operation on a component, the component must be in an unloaded state. Select the component in the specification tree or main window and click [icon] to add the component to the delayed actions window.

The Open depth drop-down list sets the recursive level of the selected product. You can select **1**, **2**, or **all**.

The operation is then listed in the *Delayed actions* field, but is not updated in the model until **Apply** or **OK** is clicked. You can then specify several operations and apply them to the model simultaneously instead of performing several individual operations.

Summary

The **Load/Show/Hide** operations are summarized to help you decide which technique best suits your assembly.

Operation	Settings saved with model	Removed from memory
Hide/Show	Yes	No
Activate/Deactivate	No	No (displayed in the drawing)
Load/Unload	No	Yes (hidden in the assembly or the drawings)

6.3 Creating Scenes

Exploded views and the **Load/Show/Hide** operations enable you to work with a simplified version of your model. However, the operations must be performed on the fly. Scenes enable you to save the various view setting configurations of your product model for reuse. You can quickly switch between scenes and view settings without having to manually configure them each time they are required.

General Steps

Use the following general steps to configure and save a view:

1. Create a new scene.
2. Configure the scene.
3. Apply the scene to the product.

Step 1 - Create a new scene.

Click (Enhanced Scene) in the Scenes toolbar. The Enhanced Scene dialog box opens as shown in Figure 6–12.

Figure 6–12

By default, a name is automatically generated for each scene. The first scene is titled Scene.1, the second Scene.2, etc. To create a scene with a user-defined name, clear the **Automatic naming** option and enter a name for the scene.

Click **OK** to create the scene. When the scene is created, the background color changes to indicate that the **Scene** window is active. The name of the scene is added to the specification tree under **Applications>Scenes**.

Overload Mode

Overloaded component attributes are attributes in a scene that behave independent of the assembly. When the scene is applied, changes made to the assembly after the scenes creation do not affect overloaded components. You can overload component positions, graphical attributes, activation and hide/show states, and viewpoints. The overload mode options are described as follows:

Overload Mode	Description
Partial	The default mode. No attribute is considered overloaded until it has been modified in the scene or explicitly overloaded. Once the scene has been created, any attribute that has not been overloaded is impacted by changes in the assembly.
Full	All attributes are considered overloaded. Once the scene has been created, any changes to the assembly do not affect the scene.

Step 2 - Configure the scene.

You can configure the following component attributes using scenes:

- **Hide/Show** state
- **Activate/Deactivate** state
- Define explode positions
- Save viewpoints

In the Scene window, the Enhanced Scenes toolbar displays, as shown in Figure 6–13.

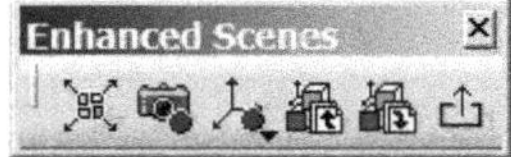

Figure 6–13

Click (Explode) and use the Explode dialog box to define the exploded view.

To define a new viewpoint, orient the model to the required viewpoint and click (Save Viewpoint).

Once the scene has been configured, click (Exit Scene). The model returns to the original view settings

Overloading Partial Scenes

In **Partial** mode, only attributes that have been modified in the scene remain unchanged when changes are made to the assembly. You can overload unchanged components using the DMUNavigatorSceneOverload toolbar, as shown in Figure 6–14. Select the component(s) and then select the appropriate icon based on the attribute you want to overload.

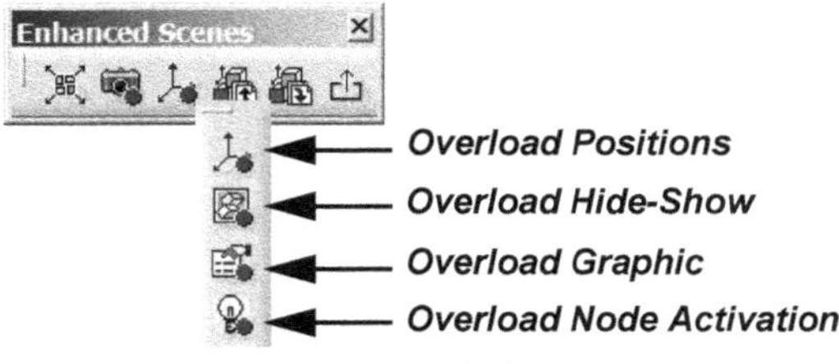

Figure 6–14

Resetting Attribute Values

You can reset attribute values using the **Apply Scene on Assembly** and **Apply Assembly on Scene** tools. To reset a component attribute that was modified in the scene back to its assembly value, use the **Apply Assembly on Scene** tool. Click (Apply Assembly on Scene) to open the Apply Assembly on Scene dialog box, as shown in Figure 6–15.

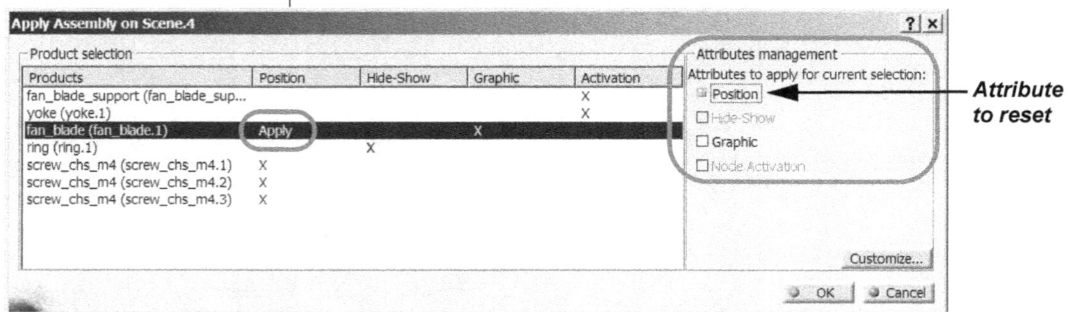

Figure 6–15

You can also reset the value of an assembly attribute back to the overloaded component value using (Apply Scene on Assembly).

Components whose attributes have been modified are listed in the dialog box. The type of attribute change is noted by an **X** in the corresponding column. To reset an overloaded attribute back to the current assembly value, select the component in the dialog box. In the *Attributes management* area in the dialog box, select the attribute option that you want to apply. Click **OK** to apply the changes.

Step 3 - Apply the scene to the product.

There are two ways of working with a scene of a product. You can edit the scene and work with the assembly configuration directly in the scene editor. Otherwise, you can apply the scene to the product.

To apply the scene to the assembly model, select the scene in **Applications** in the specification tree. Right-click and select ***object>Apply Scene on Assembly>Apply the Entire Scene**.

A default scene does not exist for an assembly. Once you have applied a scene with specific view settings, the only way to return to the original settings is to create an additional scene. Therefore, it is recommended that you create a scene without any configurations before creating any additional scenes. The scene can then be used as the default to restore the assembly to its original configuration.

6.4 Assembly Variant

Creating an Assembly Variant

An assembly variant enables you to quickly and easily create variations of your design rather than recreating similar assemblies multiple times. Assembly variants are created and stored in the assembly.

General Steps

Use the following general steps to create an assembly variant:

1. Create an assembly variant.
2. Apply the required configuration to the product.

Step 1 - Create an assembly variant.

To create different variations of the assembly, all of the required components should have been instantiated into the assembly.

Click (Define Variant Generic Product) in the Assembly Variant toolbar. The Variant Generic Product Definition dialog box opens as shown in Figure 6–16. There is one variant in the dialog box named **All Variants**, which includes all of the components of the assembly.

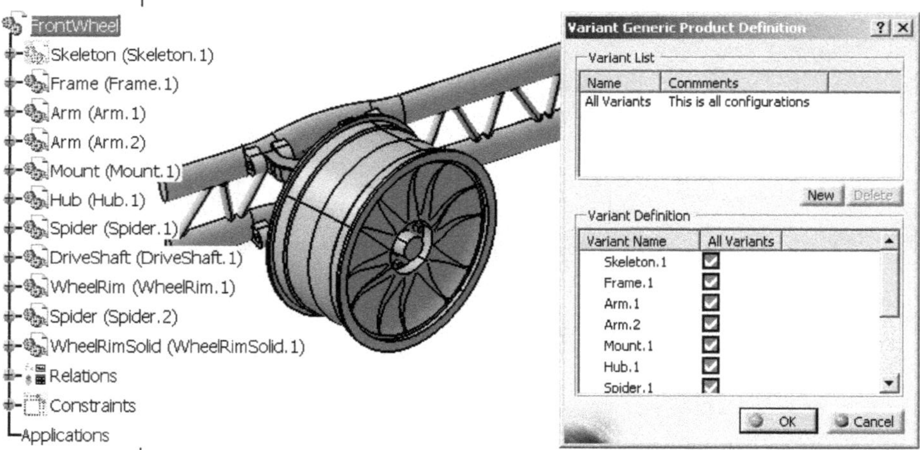

Figure 6–16

Click **New** to add a variant. It can be renamed by clicking on it in the *Name* area, and you can add a comment for the variant as required.

Clear the components from the *Variant Definition* area to exclude them from the variant, as shown in Figure 6–17. The preview of the variant can be seen from the model, as shown in Figure 6–18.

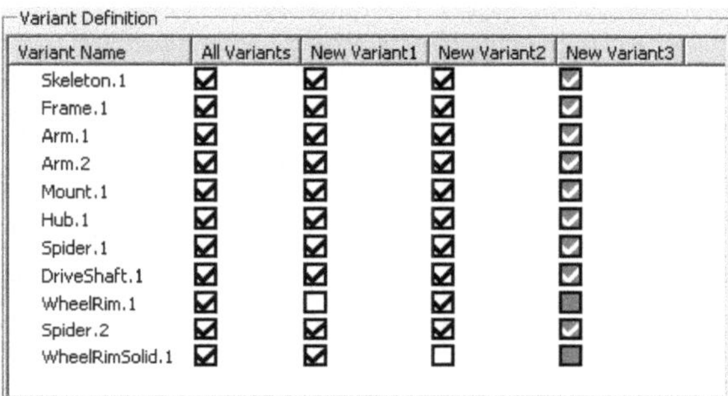

Figure 6–17

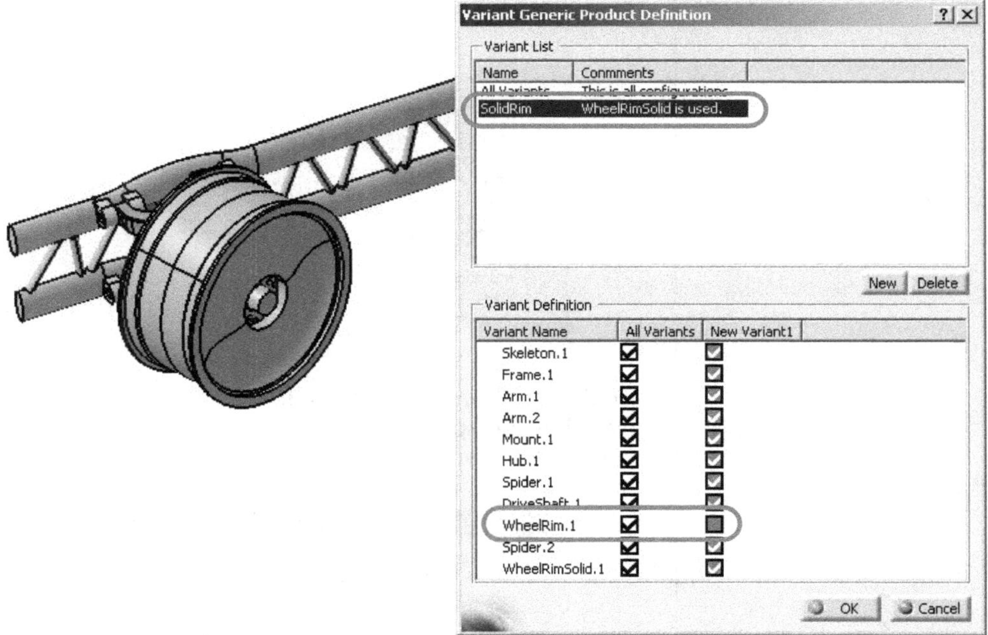

Figure 6–18

When all of the required variants have been created, click **OK**.

Step 2 - Apply the required configuration to the product.

When the configurations have been created, a design table for the variant displays in the Relations branch in the specification tree as shown in Figure 6–19. To enable the visibility of the Relations branch in the specification tree, select **Tools> Options>Infrastructure>Product Structure**.

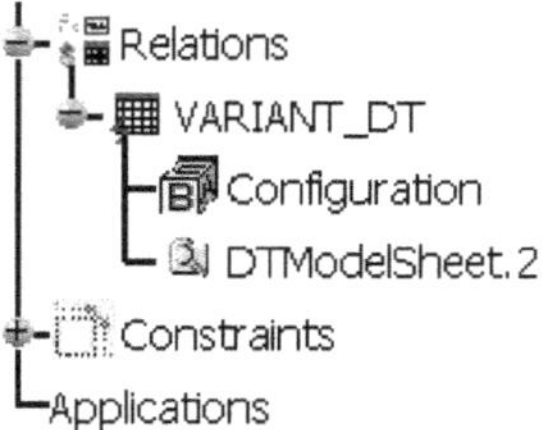

Figure 6–19

Select the *Tree Customization* tab, highlight **Relations** in the Specification Tree Order list, and click **Activate** as shown in Figure 6–20.

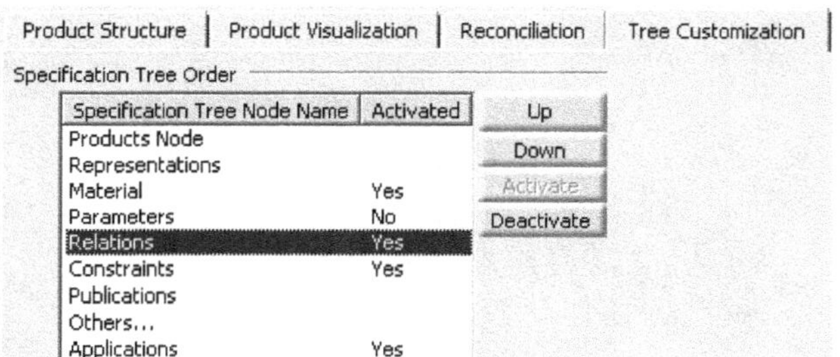

Figure 6–20

Double-click twice on **Configuration** under the **Relations** branch in the specification tree. The Edit Parameter dialog box opens as shown in Figure 6–21.

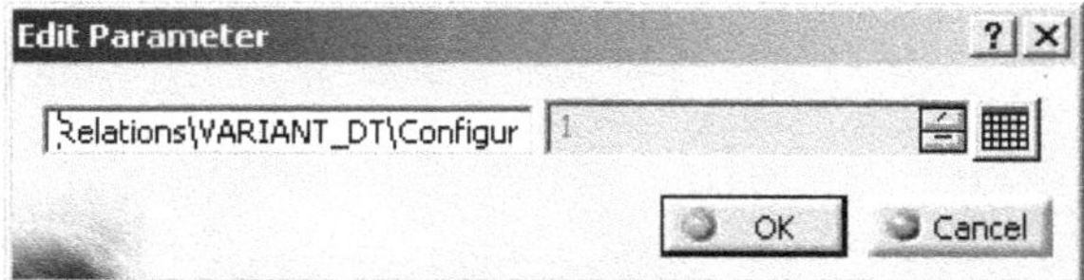

Figure 6–21

Click [icon] in the Edit Parameter dialog box. The VARIANT_DT ,configurations row : 1 dialog box opens as shown in Figure 6–22.

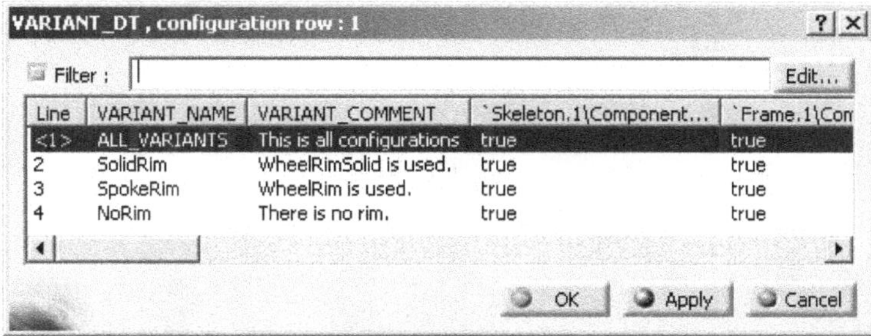

Figure 6–22

Highlight the required configuration in the list as shown in Figure 6–23 and click **Apply**. Click **OK** twice to close the dialog boxes.

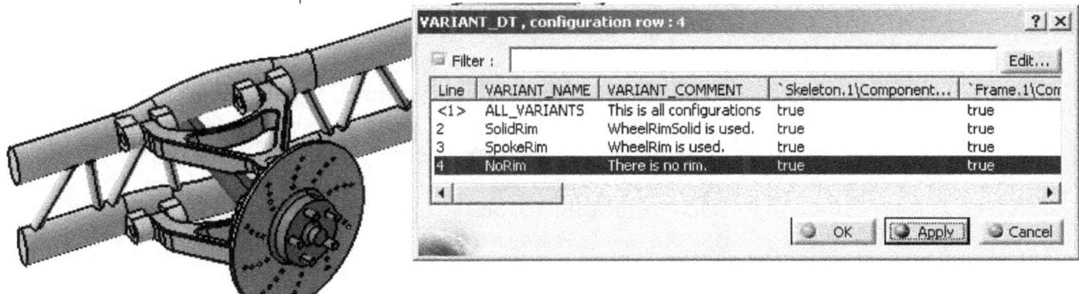

Figure 6–23

Instantiate a Variant

An assembly variant can be instantiated into an assembly using the **Instantiate Variant** feature. Activate the product in which you want to instantiate the configuration. Click [icon] (Instantiate Variant) in the Assembly Variant toolbar. The Variant Generic Product Instantiation dialog box opens.

Click **Select** and browse to the product file that contains the required assembly variant. All of the existing configurations display in the *Variant List* area as shown in Figure 6–24. Select the required configuration from the list and select **OK**.

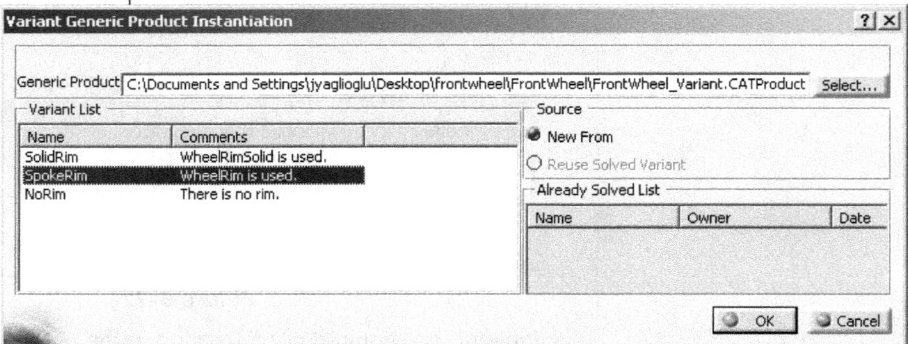

Figure 6–24

Replace a Variant

An instantiated assembly variant can be replaced using the **Replace Variant** feature. Click (Replace Variant) in the Assembly Variant toolbar and select a previously instantiated variant in the specification tree. The Variant Generic Product Instantiation dialog box opens.

Click **Select** and browse to the product file that contains the replacing assembly variant. All of the existing configurations display in the *Variant List* area as shown in Figure 6–25. Select the required configuration from the list and click **OK**.

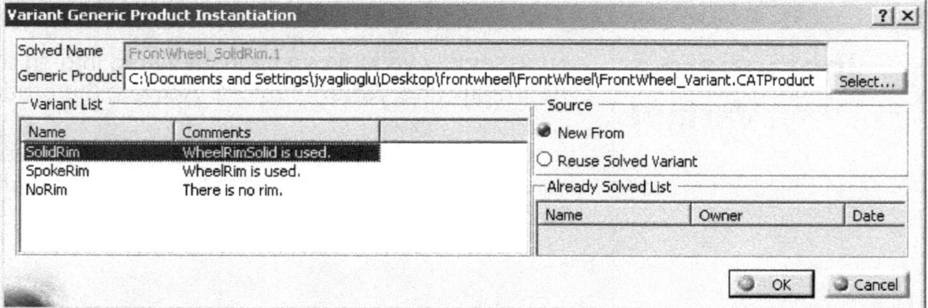

Figure 6–25

Practice 6a Creating Scenes I

Practice Objectives

- Create a scene.
- Apply a scene to an assembly.

In this practice, you will create various scenes and apply them to the assembly to facilitate the assembly of additional components.

Task 1 - Create a scene.

In this task, you will create a scene of the assembly as it is when it is first opened. This scene is being created so that you can quickly return the model to its original state. By default, scenes are created in **Partial** overload mode. This means components that have not be overloaded will not behave independent to the assembly. Since you do not want any changes to the model to affect the All Parts scene it will be created using the **Full** overload mode option. In this mode, all of the components in the scene will behave independent to the assembly.

1. Open **Fan.CATProduct** from the *Fan* directory. The assembly displays as shown in Figure 6–26.

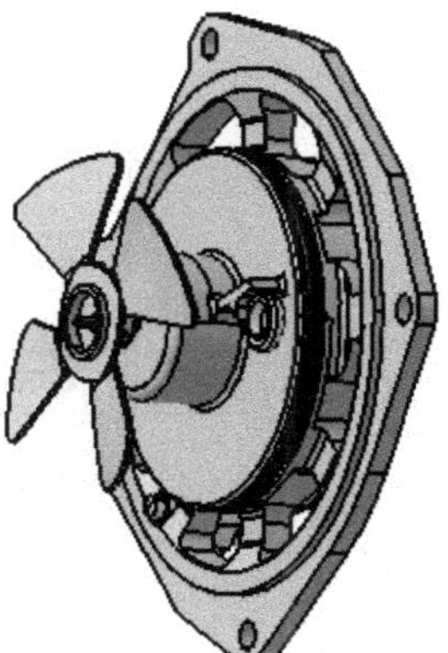

Figure 6–26

2. Click (Enhanced Scene).
3. Clear the **Automatic naming** option.

4. For the *Name*, enter **All Parts**.

5. Change the *Overload Mode* to **Full** as shown in Figure 6–27.

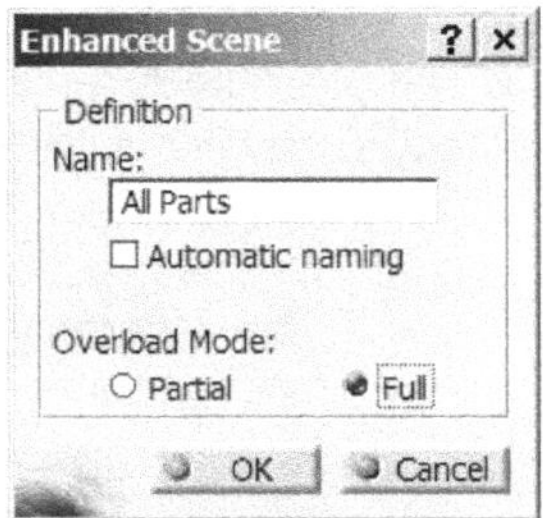

Figure 6–27

6. Click **OK**.

7. The system activates the **Scene** window. In the Warning box, select **Do not display this message again** and close the box.

8. Since this is a scene of all parts, no changes are required.

   Click (Exit Scene) to exit the **Scene** window. The scene name is added to the Scenes node under **Applications** in the specification tree, as shown in Figure 6–28.

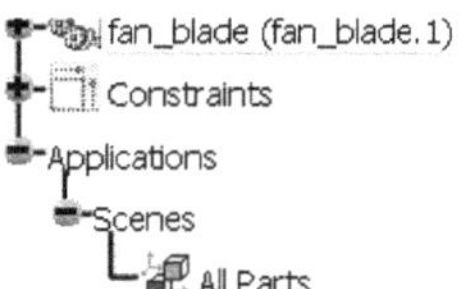

Figure 6–28

Task 2 - Create an exploded scene.

1. Create a scene named **Exploded**, as shown in Figure 6–29.

Figure 6–29

2. In the **Scene** window, click (Explode).

3. In the Depth drop-down list, select **First level** and in the Type drop-down list, select **Constrained**.

4. Select the *Fixed product* field. In the specification tree, select **Yoke**, as shown in Figure 6–30.

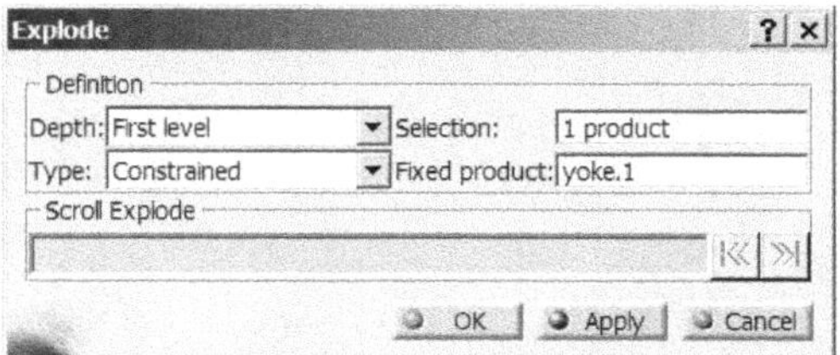

Figure 6–30

5. In the Explode dialog box, click **OK**.

You can move multiple components at the same time by selecting them in the specification tree while holding <Ctrl>.

6. Use the compass to modify the component positions, as shown in Figure 6–31.

Figure 6–31

7. Click (Exit Scene) to close the **Scene** window.

Task 3 - Apply a scene to the assembly.

1. Right-click on the Exploded scene and select **Exploded object>Apply Scene on Assembly>Apply the Entire Scene**.

2. Click to *unexplode* the assembly.

Task 4 - Create a scene.

1. Create a scene named **Yoke Removed**, as shown in Figure 6–32.

Figure 6–32

2. In the Scene window, right-click on the yoke component and select **Representations>Deactivate Node**.

3. Click (Exit Scene) to close the **Scene** window.

4. Apply the **Yoke Removed** scene to the assembly. The assembly displays as shown in Figure 6–33.

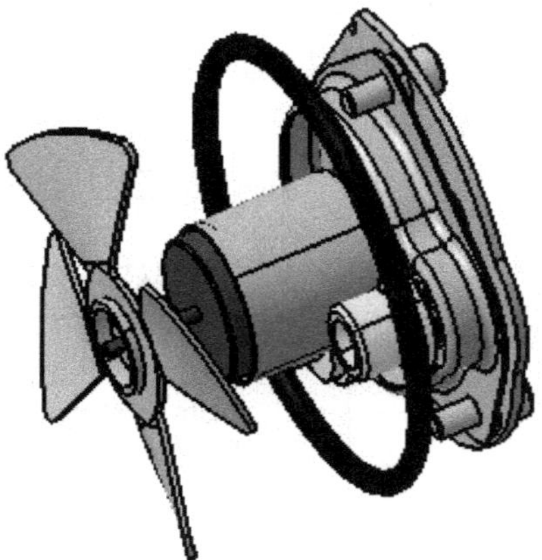

Figure 6–33

5. Apply the **All Parts** scene to the assembly.

Task 5 - Note the differences between Partial and Full overload mode.

In this task, you will gain a better understanding of the differences between **Partial** and **Full** overload mode.

1. Hide the **fan_blade** component.
2. Apply the **All Parts** scene. Note that the **fan_blade** component is redisplayed.
3. Hide the **fan_blade** component again.
4. Apply the **Yoke Removed** scene. Note that this time the **fan_blade** component is not redisplayed.
5. The **Yoke Removed** scene was created in **Partial** mode. Any changes to the assembly will affect components that were not overloaded. In the case of the **Yoke Removed** scene, the only component attribute that was overloaded was the activation state of the **Yoke**.
6. Show the **fan_blade** component.
7. Close the file without saving.

Practice 6b

Creating Scenes II

Practice Objectives

- Create a scene.
- Apply a scene to an assembly.
- Edit a scene.

In this practice, you will create various scenes and apply them to the assembly to facilitate the assembly of additional components.

Task 1 - Create a scene.

1. Open **AxialCentrifugalCompressor_Scenes.CATProduct** from the *Turbine>Scenes* directory.
2. Click (Enhanced Scene). The Enhanced Scene dialog box opens.
3. For the name of the scene, enter **Aft Cover**, as shown in Figure 6–34.

Figure 6–34

4. Click **OK**.

Task 2 - Deactivate components.

1. The system activates the **Scene** window. In the specification tree, select the four components shown in Figure 6–35.

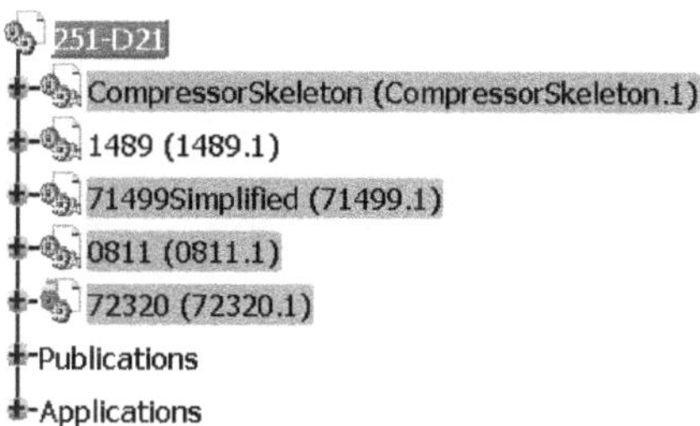

Figure 6–35

2. Right-click and select **Representations>Deactivate Node**. The assembly displays as shown in Figure 6–36.

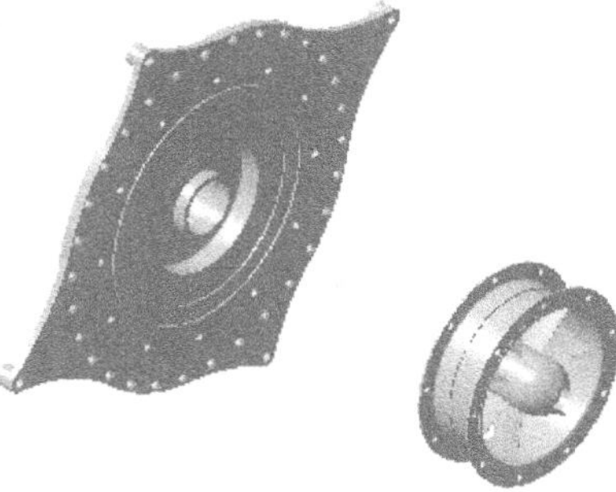

Figure 6–36

Design Considerations

The parts are deactivated but the subassembly remains displayed. Deactivate Node can only be applied to parts. The **Deactivate Terminal Node** option must be used to deactivate assemblies.

3. Right-click on **72320** and select **Representations> Deactivate Terminal Node** to deactivate the product.

   To ensure the **aft cover** remains displayed, overload its activation and hide/show states.

4. In the specification tree, select **1489**. Click (Overload Hide-Show).

5. In the specification tree, select **1489**. Click (Overload Node Activation).

6. Click (Exit Scene) to close the **Scene** window.

Task 3 - Apply a scene to an assembly.

1. In the specification tree, expand **Applications**. The scene is added to the specification tree, as shown in Figure 6–37. Select the **Aft Cover** scene.

Figure 6–37

2. Right-click and select **Aft Cover object>Apply Scene on Assembly>Apply the Entire Scene**. The model displays as shown in Figure 6–38.

Figure 6–38

Task 4 - Assemble a product.

1. Assemble **DiffuserVane.CATProduct** from the *Turbine* directory.

2. Drag the **DiffuserVane** (**70813**) to the position shown in Figure 6–39.

Figure 6–39

3. Apply a Coincidence constraint between the axis of **70813** and the **RotationalAxis** publication, as shown in Figure 6–40.

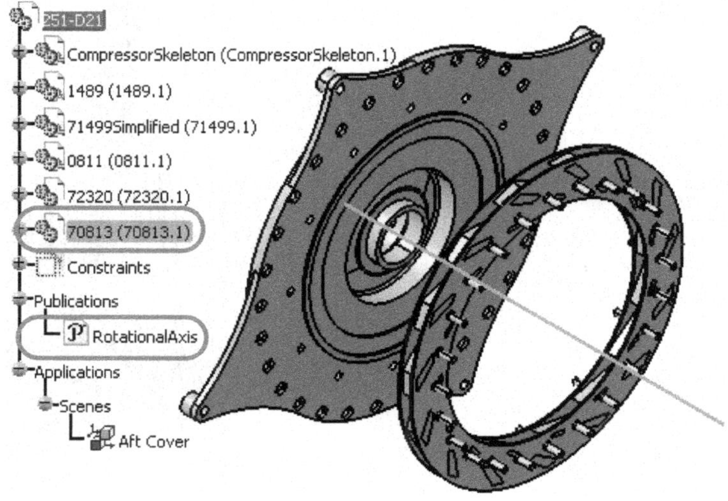

Figure 6–40

4. Apply a Coincidence constraint between any stud and any Hole in the smaller bolt circle, as shown in Figure 6–41.

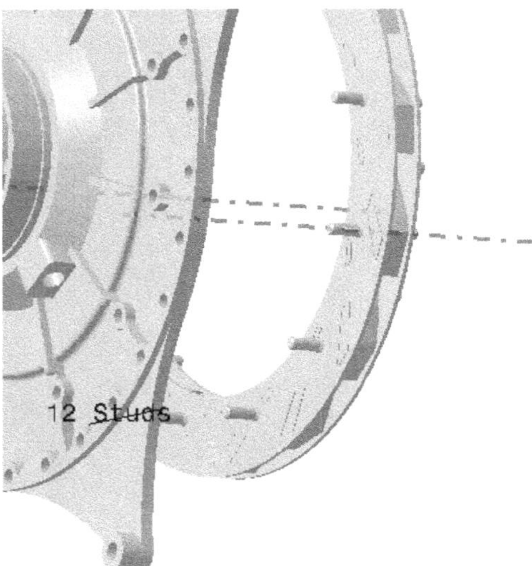

Figure 6–41

5. Apply a Contact constraint between the **12 Studs** side and the surface of the **AftCover**.

6. Click [icon]. The model displays as shown in Figure 6–42.

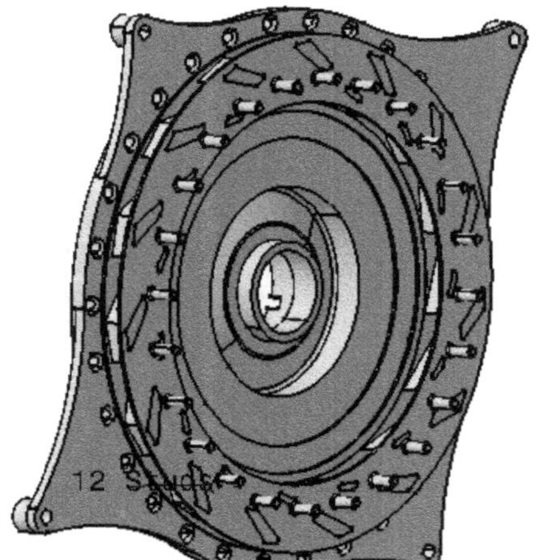

Figure 6–42

Task 5 - Create a scene.

1. Create a scene and enter **Impeller Cover** as the name, as shown in Figure 6–43.

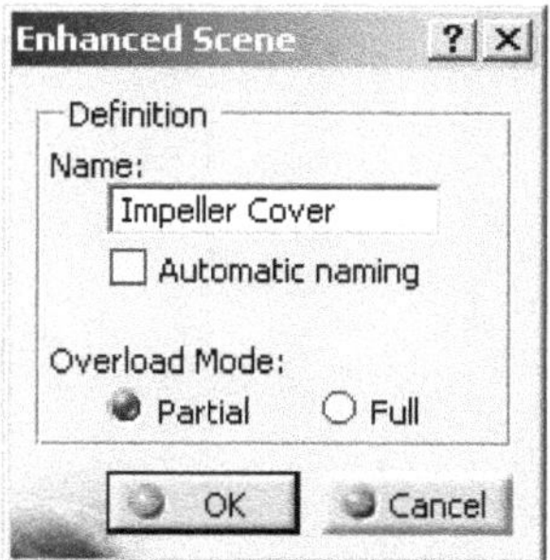

Figure 6–43

2. Select the two components in the specification tree shown in Figure 6–44. Use **Deactivate Terminal Node** to deactivate them.

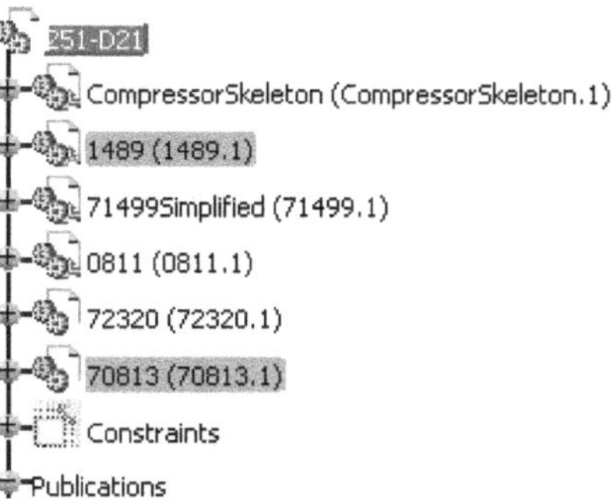

Figure 6–44

3. Use the **Activate Terminal Node** option to activate **ImpellerCover** (**0811**).

4. Click (Exit Scene).

5. In the specification tree, right-click on the **Impeller Cover** scene and select **Impeller Cover object>Apply Scene on Assembly>Apply the Entire Scene**.

6. Assemble **DiffuserHousing.CATProduct**.

7. If you did not complete the previous practice, open the **Turbine\Cache\DiffuserHousing.CATProduct** assembly.

8. Apply a Coincidence constraint between the axis of the **DiffuserHousing** and the **RotationalAxis** publication, as shown in Figure 6–45.

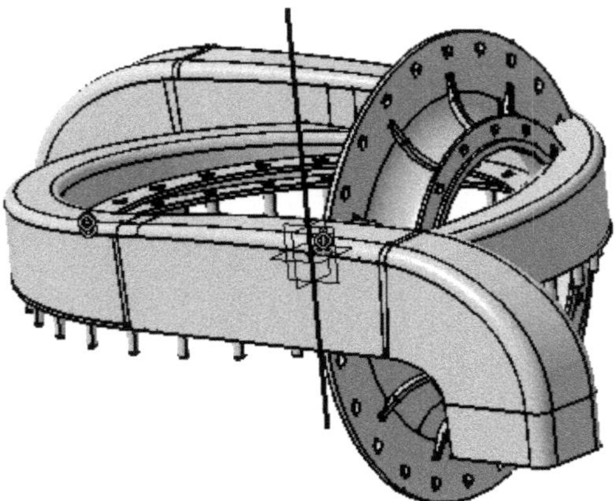

Figure 6–45

9. Click .

10. Apply a Coincidence constraint between any two holes, as shown in Figure 6–46.

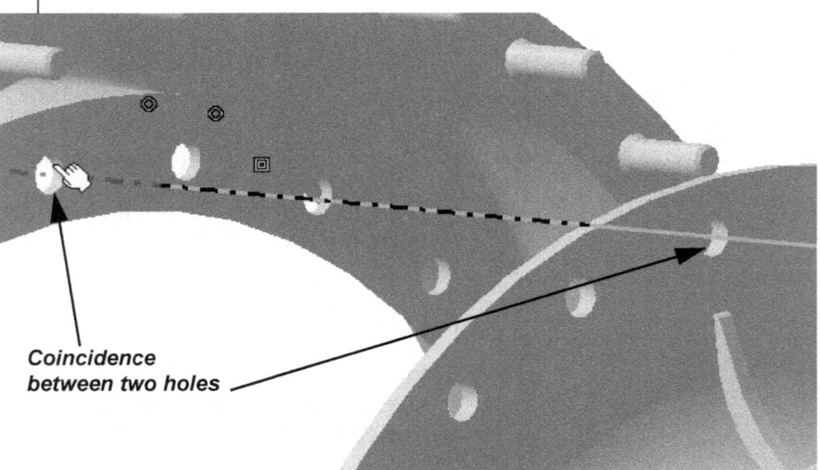

Figure 6–46

11. Apply a Contact constraint between the faces shown in Figure 6–47.

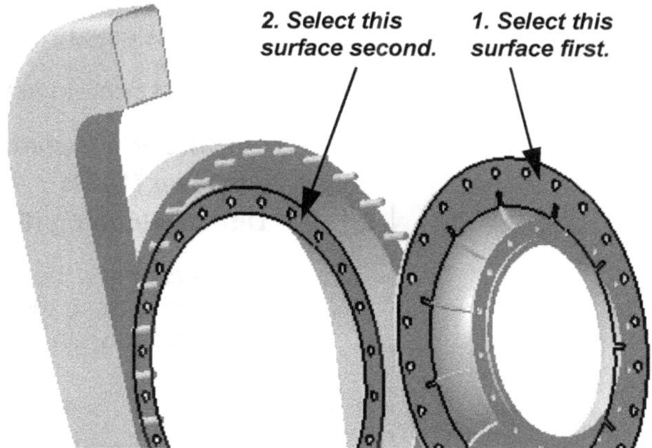
2. Select this surface second.
1. Select this surface first.

Figure 6–47

12. Update the assembly. The model displays as shown in Figure 6–48.

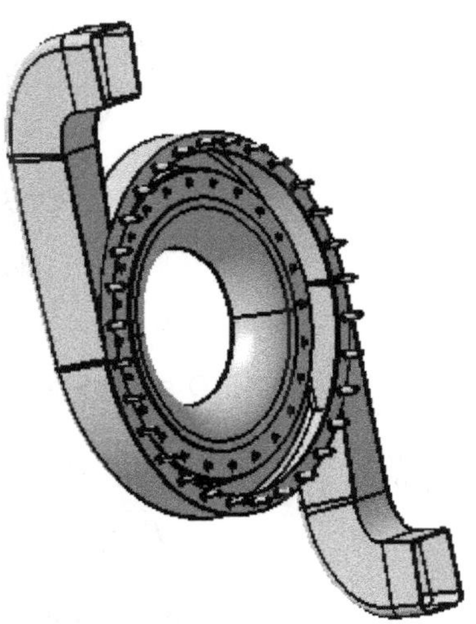

Figure 6–48

13. Save the model.

    If any models from the *Cache* folder were used to build the assembly, use **Save Management** to save all of the models to the *Turbine* folder.

Task 6 - Edit a scene.

1. In the specification tree, right-click on the **Impeller Cover** scene and select **Impeller Cover object>Definition**.
2. Use terminal node to activate the following geometry:
   - **CompressorSkeleton**
   - **AftCover (1489)**
   - **DiffuserHousing (6851-1)**
3. Apply the changes that were made in the scene to the assembly and close the **Scene** window. The assembly displays as shown in Figure 6–49.

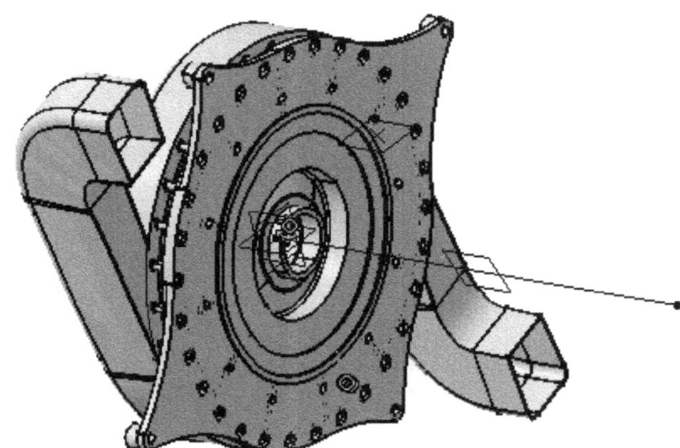

Figure 6–49

4. Drag **6851-1** and **0811** to the location shown in Figure 6–50.

*In the specification tree, preselect **6851-1** and **0811**.*

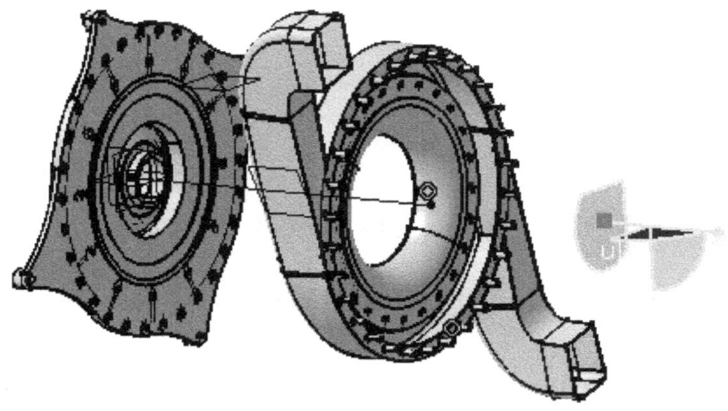

Figure 6–50

5. Apply a Coincidence constraint between:
   - YZ plane of **DiffuserHousing** (**6851**)
   - **DiffuserHousingReference** reference plane of **CompressorSkeleton**.
6. In the specification tree, select the references shown in Figure 6–51. Select the **Same** orientation.

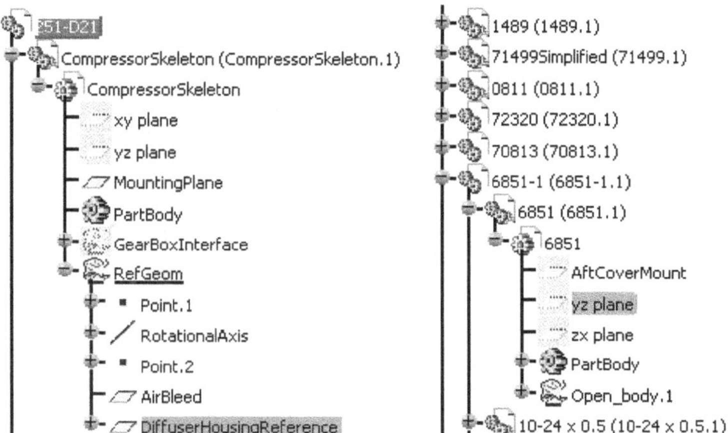

Figure 6–51

7. Click [icon]. The model displays as shown in Figure 6–52.

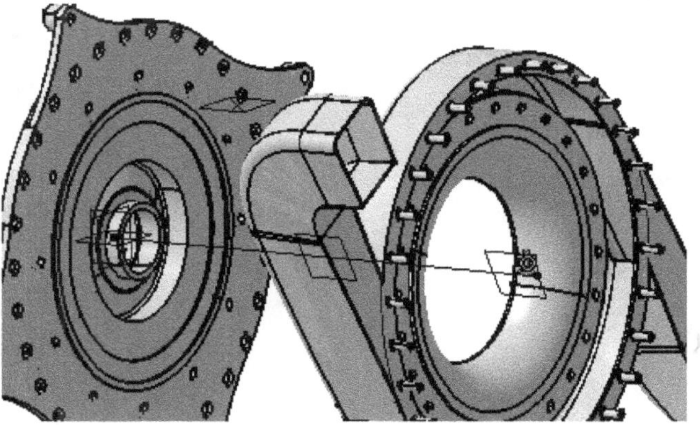

Figure 6–52

8. Apply a Coincidence constraint between:

   - **AftCoverMount** plane of **6851** (select the plane in the specification tree)
   - Surface of **AftCover** as shown in Figure 6–53
   - *Orientation:* **Same**

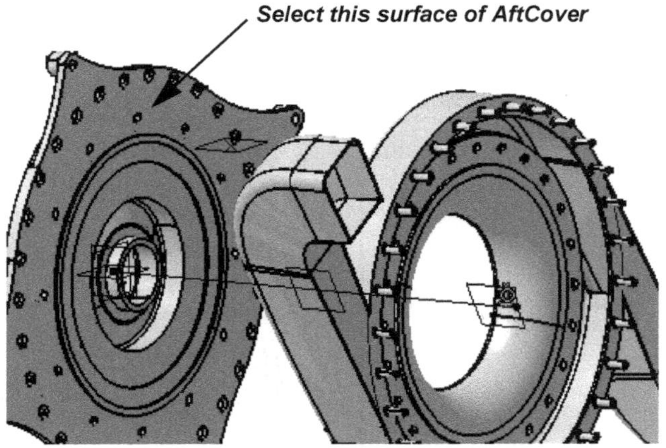

Figure 6–53

9. Click [icon]. The model displays as shown in Figure 6–54.

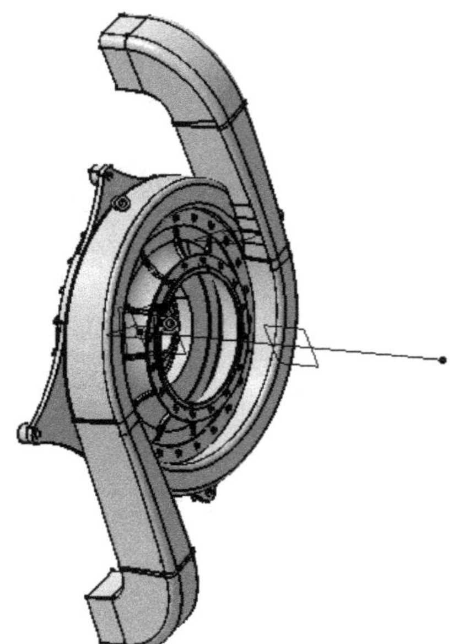

Figure 6–54

10. Show the **GearBoxInterface** geometrical set of the **CompressorSkeleton** to ensure that the **DiffuserHousing** is assembled correctly, as shown in Figure 6–55.

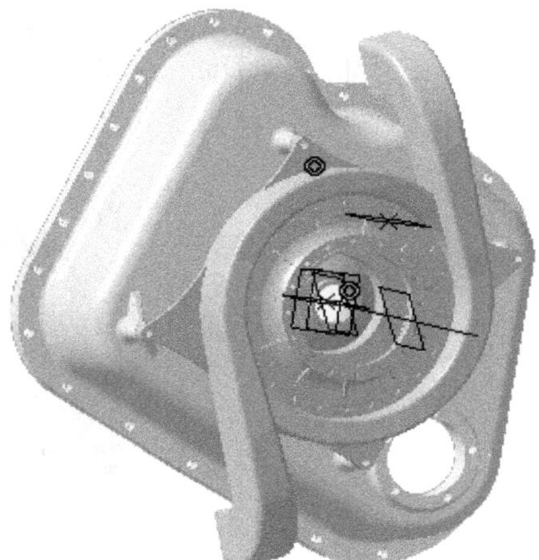

Figure 6–55

11. Hide the **GearBoxInterface**.

12. Save the model.

    If any models from the *Completed* folder were used to build the assembly, use **Save Management** to save all of the models in the *Turbine* folder.

Task 7 - Delete scenes.

Design Considerations

The two scenes created were useful for reducing update time and simplifying the screen display while components were being assembled. These scenes are no longer required and can be deleted.

1. Right-click on the **Aft Cover** and **Impeller Cover** scenes and select **Delete**.

   Although these scenes have been deleted, no change has occurred to the activation or deactivation of the components.

2. In the specification tree, select the top-level assembly (**251-D21**) and deactivate using terminal node.

Task 8 - Create a scene.

1. Create a scene called **Compressor Case**.
2. Activate **CompressorSkeleton**, **71499Simplified**, and **0811**. The model displays as shown in Figure 6–56.

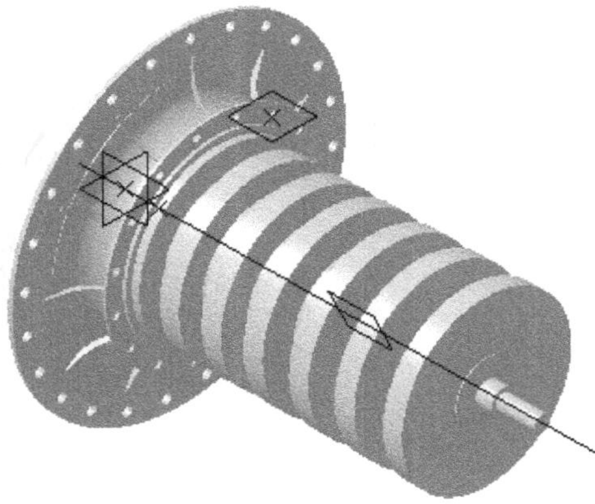

Figure 6–56

3. Exit the scene window.
4. Apply the **Compressor Case** scene.
5. Assemble **CompressorCase.CATProduct** as shown in Figure 6–57.

   If you did not complete the previous practice, open the assembly from the *Completed\Compressor Case* directory.

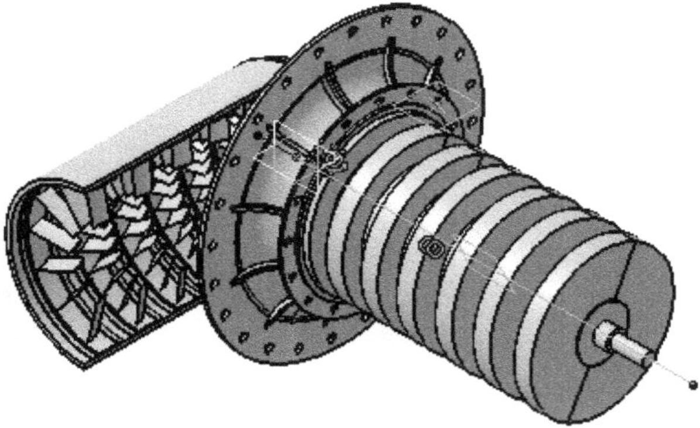

Figure 6–57

Remember to select the unconstrained component first.

6. Use (Snap) to snap the subassembly into position. Select the surfaces shown in Figure 6–58.

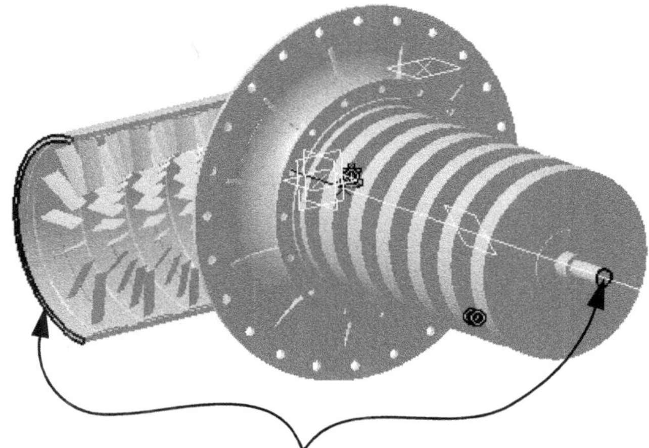

Figure 6–58

Note the orientation of the stator vanes in Figure 6–59.

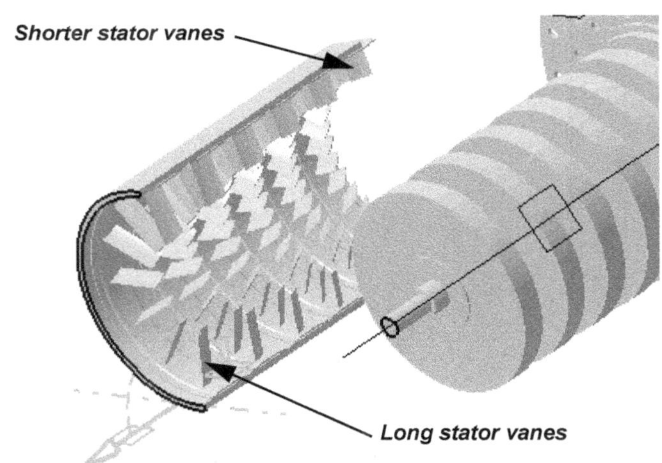

Figure 6–59

7. Select the background display to complete the snap.

8. Apply a Coincidence constraint between the axis of **CompressorCase** and the **RotationalAxis** publication, as shown in Figure 6–60.

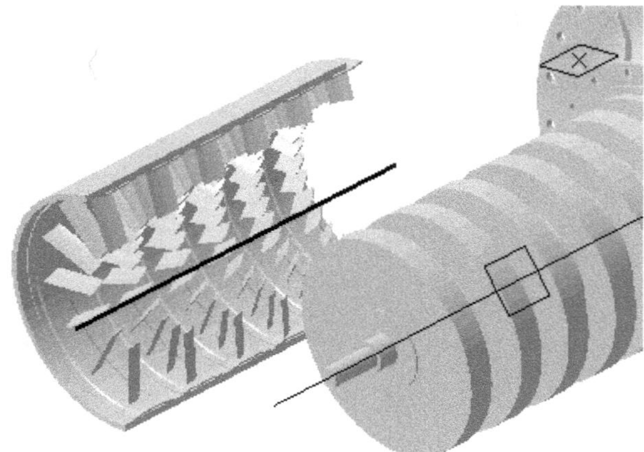

Figure 6–60

9. Click .

Task 9 - Manipulate the components.

1. Orient the model to (Back View), as shown in Figure 6–61.

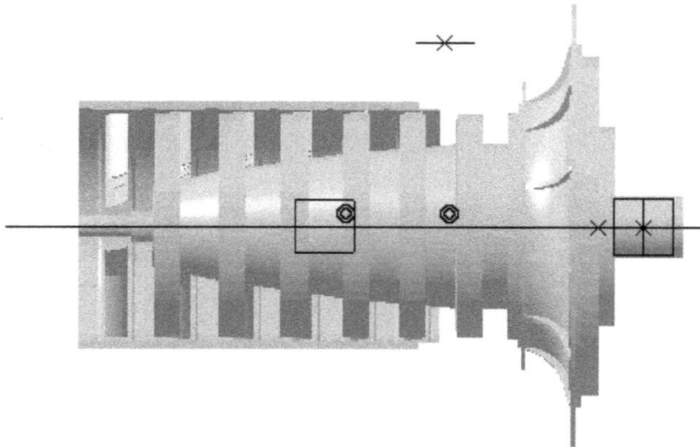

Figure 6–61

2. Click (Manipulation). The Manipulation dialog box opens as shown in Figure 6–62.

Figure 6–62

3. Click and select **With respect to constraints**, as shown in Figure 6–62.

4. Select the **CompressorCase** and drag it to a position so that the stator vanes are centered between the simplified turbine stages, as shown in Figure 6–63.

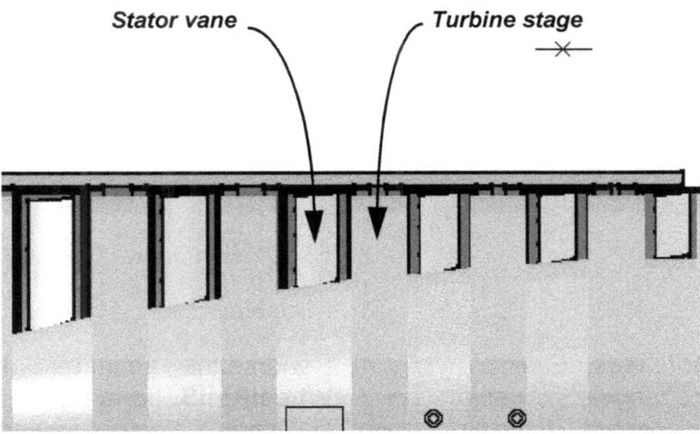

Figure 6–63

5. Save the model and close the file.

   If any models from the *Completed* folder were used to build the assembly, use Save Management to save all of the models in the *Turbine* folder.

Practice 6c Assembly Variant

Practice Objectives

- Create a variant.
- Apply a variant to an assembly.
- Instantiate a variant into an assembly.
- Replace an instantiated variant.

In this practice, you will create different configurations of an assembly and then apply them to the assembly. You will also instantiate a variant of the assembly to a different assembly.

Task 1 - Create a variant.

1. Open **FrontWheel_Variant.CATProduct** from the *FrontWheel* directory. The assembly displays as shown in Figure 6–64.

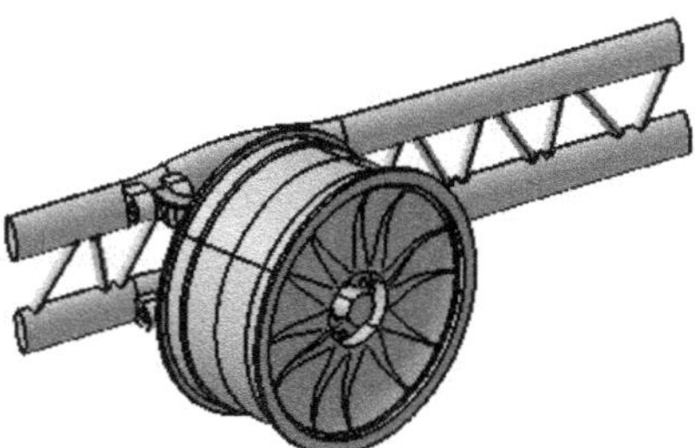

Figure 6–64

2. Click (Define Variant Generic Product).
3. Click **New**.

Do not press <Enter> after changing the name and comment. Doing so will close the dialog box. Instead, select anywhere in the graphics window to update the text.

4. Rename the variant as **SolidRim**. In *Comments* area, enter **WheelRimSolid is used.**. The Variant Generic Product Definition dialog box opens as shown in Figure 6–65.

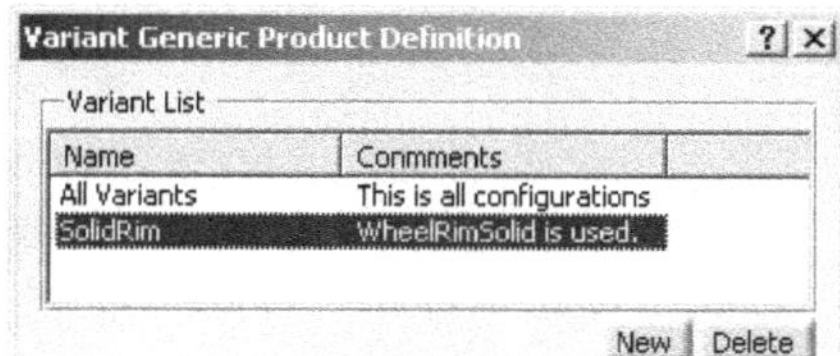

Figure 6–65

5. Clear **WheelRim.1** to exclude it from the assembly as shown in Figure 6–66.

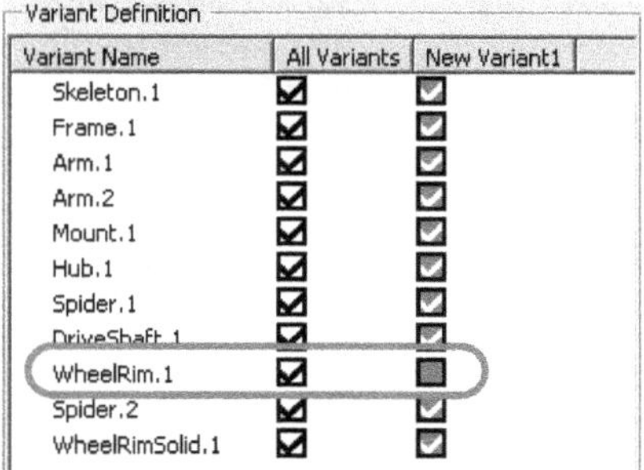

Figure 6–66

6. Create two more variants as shown in Figure 6–67.

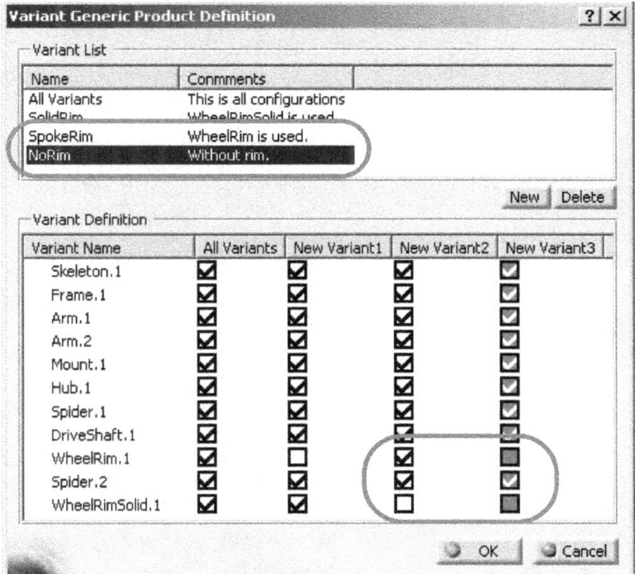

Figure 6–67

7. Click **OK**.

Task 2 - Change the settings.

When the configurations have been created, a design table for the variant displays in the **Relations** branch in the specification tree as shown in Figure 6–68.

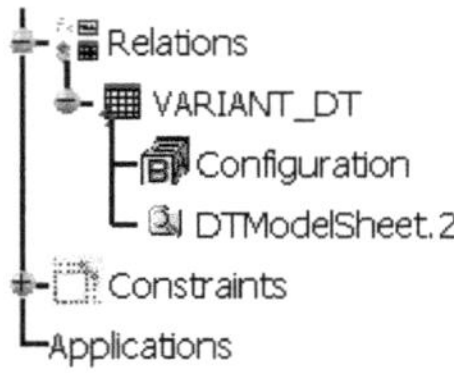

Figure 6–68

1. Select **Tools>Options>Infrastructure>Product Structure** to enable the visibility of **Relations** branch in the specification tree.
2. Select the *Tree Customization* tab. In the Specification Tree Order list, highlight **Relations**, and click **Activate** as shown in Figure 6–69.

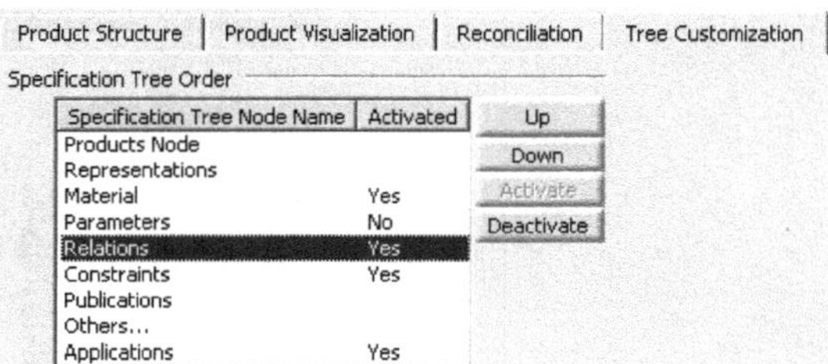

Figure 6–69

Task 3 - Apply a different variant.

In this task you will apply different configurations of the assembly.

1. In the specification tree, under the **Relations** branch, double-click twice on **Configuration**. The Edit Parameter dialog box opens as shown in Figure 6–70.

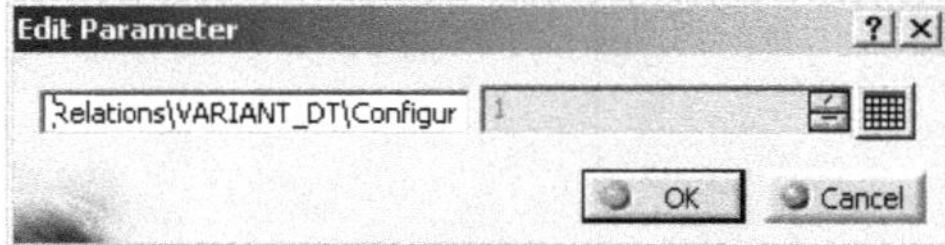

Figure 6–70

2. In the Edit Parameter dialog box, click [icon]. The VARIANT_DT ,configurations row : 1 dialog box opens as shown in Figure 6–71.

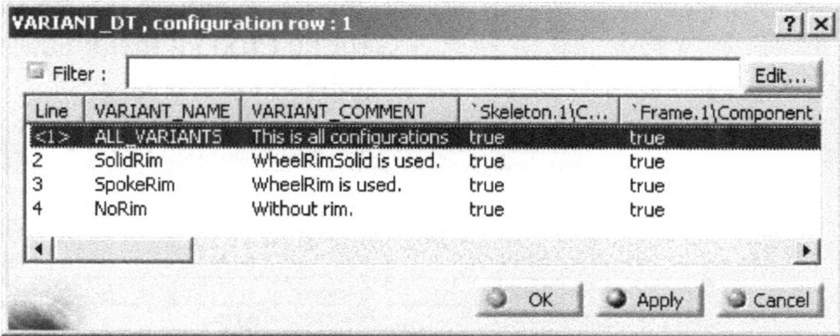

Figure 6–71

3. In the list, highlight **NoRim** configuration, and click **Apply**. Click **OK** twice to close the dialog boxes as shown in Figure 6–72.

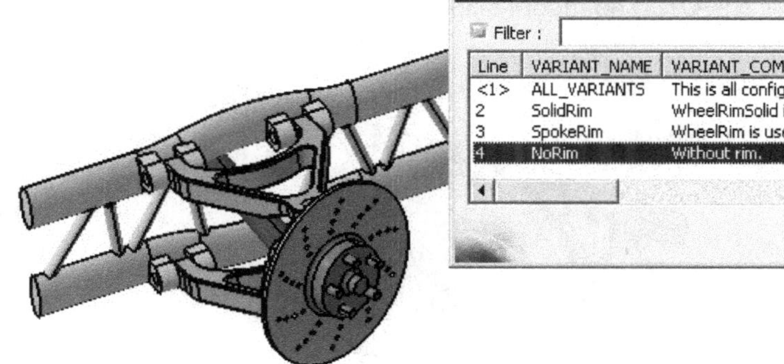

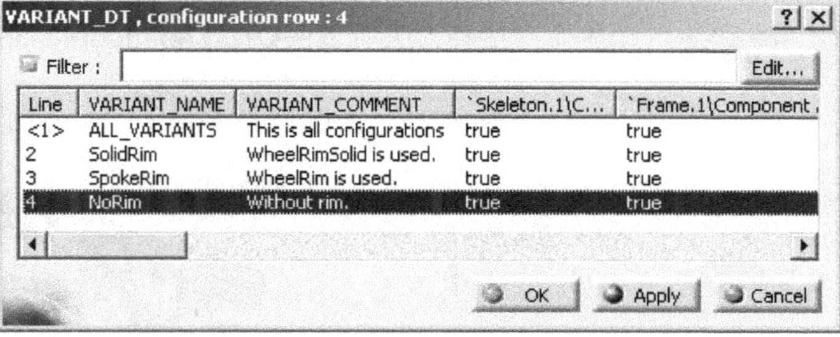

Figure 6–72

4. Save and close the file.

Task 4 - Instantiate a variant into an assembly.

In this task you will instantiate a variant into an assembly.

1. Create a new product.
2. Rename the product as **Variants**.
3. In the Assembly Variant toolbar, click [icon] (Instantiate Variant).

4. Click **Select** and browse to the *FrontWheel* directory.
5. Double-click on **FrontWheel_Variant.CATProduct**. All of the existing configurations display in the *Variant List* area.
6. In the list, highlight the **SpokeRim** configuration. The Variant Generic Product Instantiation dialog box opens as shown in Figure 6–73.

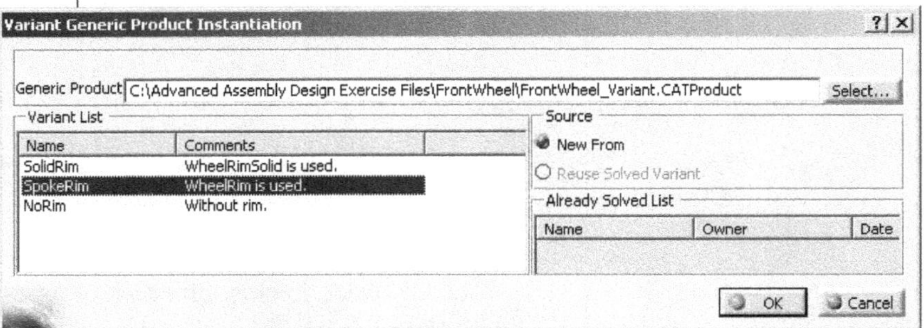

Figure 6–73

7. Click **OK**. The model displays as shown in Figure 6–74.

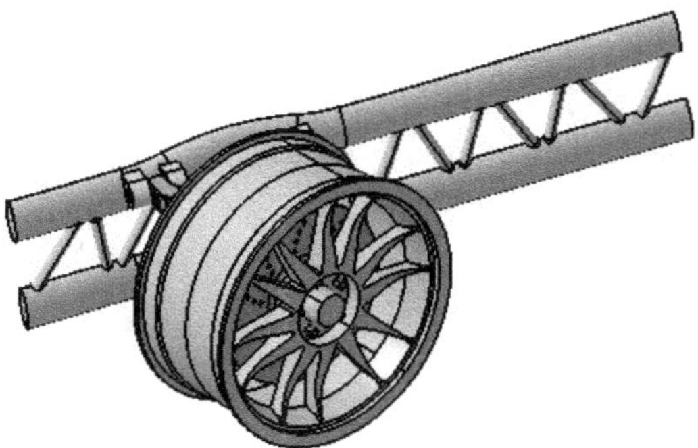

Figure 6–74

Task 5 - Replace an instantiated variant.

In this task you will replace an instantiated variant of an assembly.

1. In the Assembly Variant toolbar, click (Replace Variant) and then select the previously instantiated variant in the last task in the specification tree.
2. Click **Select** and browse to the *FrontWheel* directory.
3. Double-click on **FrontWheel_Variant.CATProduct**. All of the existing configurations display in the *Variant List* area.
4. Highlight the **SolidRim** configuration in the list and click **OK**. The model displays as shown in Figure 6–75.

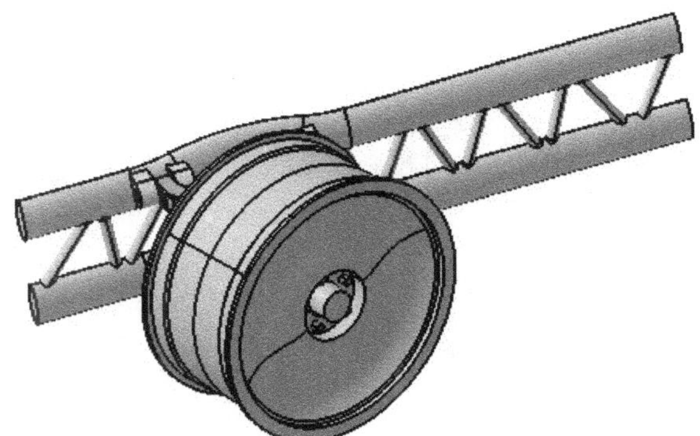

Figure 6–75

5. Save and close the model.

Space Analysis

This chapter focuses on the use of Space Analysis tools in the Assembly Design workbench. These tools are used to analyze engineering critical information, such as interference and section cuts.

Learning Objectives in this Chapter

- Learn to use the measurement tools.
- Learn how to check for clash between components.
- Understand how to section a model.
- Learn to conduct a distance analysis.

7.1 Measurements

CATIA provides tools to extract important information from your assembly model. The Measurements toolbar enables you to perform the following functions:

- Measure the distance between items on different parts.
- Measure the distance between items on a single part.
- Measure the mass properties of the assembly.

These functions can be accessed by using the Measure toolbar, as shown in or by using the Analyze menu in the menu bar.

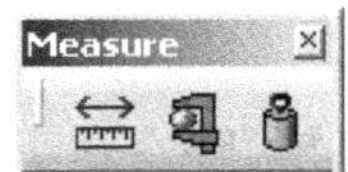

Figure 7–1

7.2 Check for Clash

Clash defines three main conditions that can exist between parts or assemblies, which describe how component positions relate to one another. These three conditions are:

Clearance

Clearance exists when two components have a space between them that is greater than zero but less than a distance that you specify. Typically, the clearance value is set to a minimum distance that should not be violated in your assembly. For example, you would typically set a clearance value for the offset parting distance of a mold or the distance a fuel line can be to a heat source.

Contact

Contact exists when two parts mate or touch each other. This condition means that neither clearance nor interference exists between the two parts. For example, the head of a bolt against a water pump or a gasket lying on a machined surface indicates contact.

Clash

Clash exists when two components collide or interfere with each other, such as when the geometry of one part lies inside geometry of the other. For example, a fastener whose diameter is too large for a hole, or a press-to-fit insert and a snap clip that display clash.

The **Clash** tool examines spacing conditions between components. Conducting a clash analysis enables you to do the following:

- Determine how many parts or subassemblies interfere with each other.
- Determine how many are in contact and how many violate a minimum distance criteria.
- Determine where the conditions exist.
- Determine whether or not the conditions are acceptable.
- Export the results.

General Steps

Use the following general steps to check for clash:

1. Set up the clash analysis.
2. Run the analysis.
3. Review the results.
4. Export the results.

Step 1 - Set up the clash analysis.

Click (Clash) in the Space Analysis toolbar to begin a clash analysis. The Check Clash dialog box opens as shown in Figure 7–2.

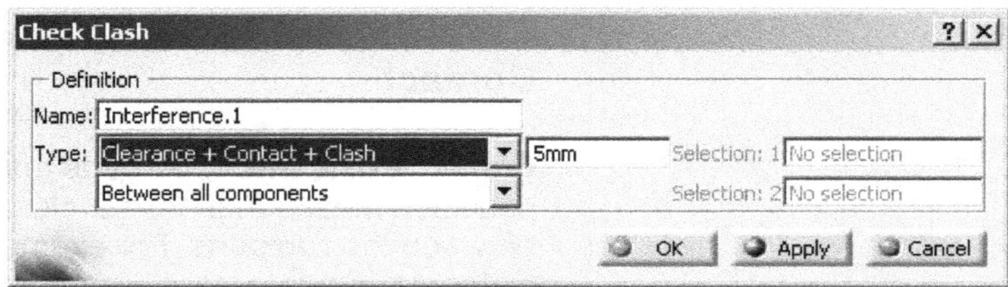

Figure 7–2

Select the type of computation in the Type drop-down list. The minimum clearance value can also be set if the type of computation includes clearance, as shown in Figure 7–3.

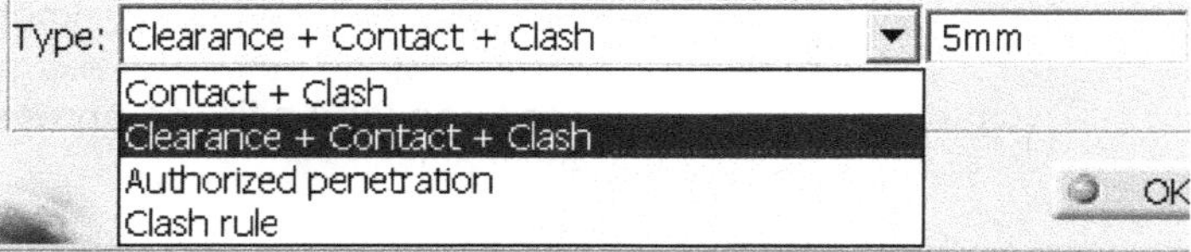

Figure 7–3

Four types of computation are available, as described as follows:

Computation Type	Description
Contact + Clash	Computes only contact and clash conditions of selected components.
Clearance + Contact + Clash	Same as Contact + Clash, but adds a clearance calculation to the selected components.
Authorized Penetration	Defines a range in which two parts can interfere, but not produce a clash result.
Clash Rule	Uses a Knowledge Rule to calculate clash results.

Select the method of selecting components in the drop-down list below the Type drop-down list, as shown in Figure 7–4.

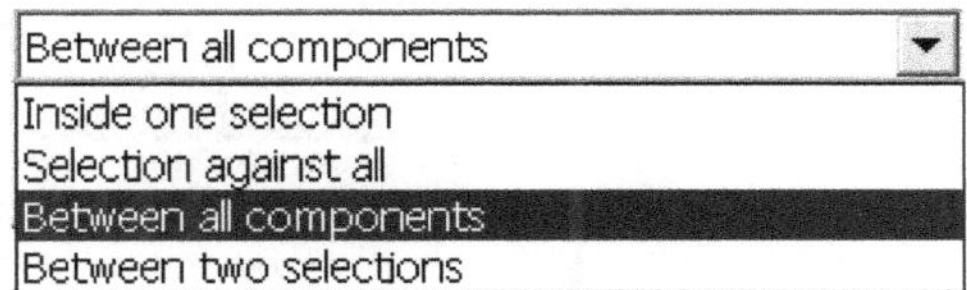

Figure 7–4

Four types of selections available are described as follows:

Selection Type	Description
Inside one selection	Calculates each part in a subassembly against all other parts in the same subassembly.
Selection against all	Calculates each subassembly against all other subassemblies in the current DMU session.
Between all components	Calculates each part against all other parts in the current DMU session. This is the default setting.
Between two selections	Selects a part or assembly to calculate against another part or assembly. The *Selection 1* and *Selection 2* fields become available when this option is selected.

Step 2 - Run the analysis.

After setting up the Clash analysis, you can run it by clicking **Apply**.

Step 3 - Review the results.

Once an analysis is run, the Check Clash dialog box expands to display all of the results. The top of the *Results* area displays the total number of interferences and the total number of each type of inference. The Filter drop-down lists can be used to specify which results display. The expanded Check Clash dialog box is shown in Figure 7–5.

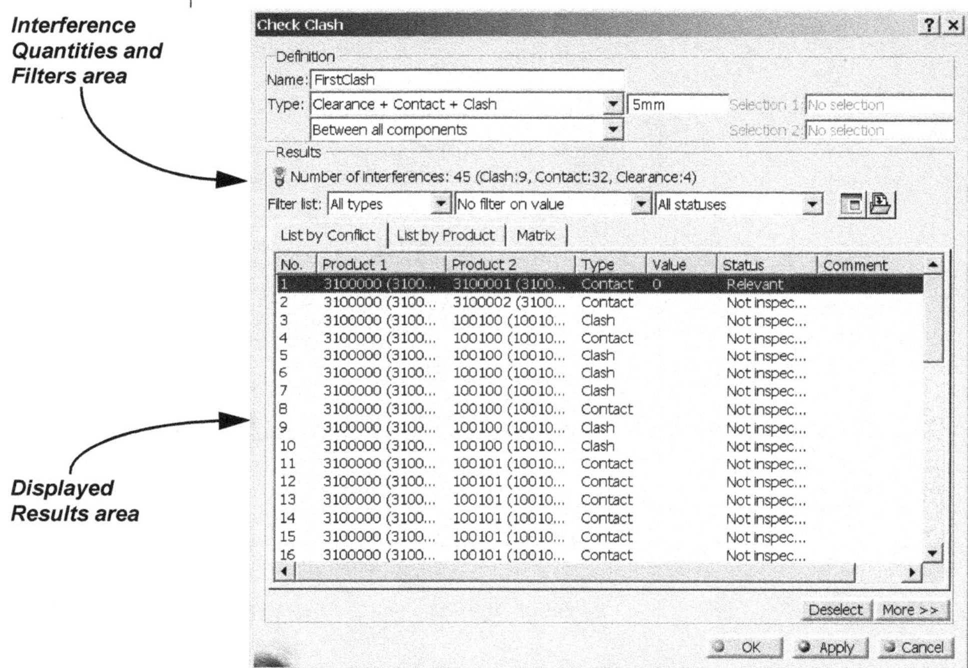

Figure 7–5

Displayed Results Area

You can display the interference results using one of three modes:

- List by Conflict
- List by Product
- Matrix

List by Conflict

The *List by Conflict* tab displays the results in the window by the number of conflicts detected, as shown in Figure 7–6.

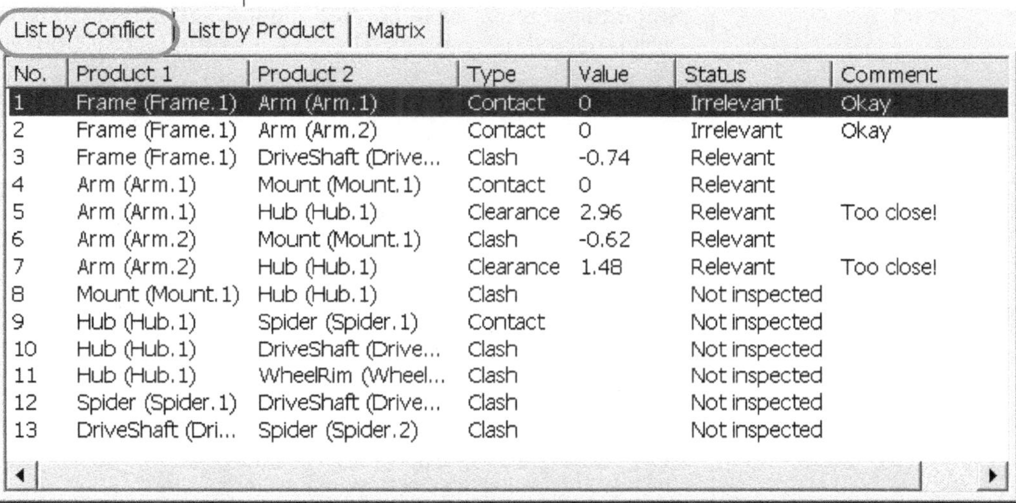

No.	Product 1	Product 2	Type	Value	Status	Comment
1	Frame (Frame.1)	Arm (Arm.1)	Contact	0	Irrelevant	Okay
2	Frame (Frame.1)	Arm (Arm.2)	Contact	0	Irrelevant	Okay
3	Frame (Frame.1)	DriveShaft (Drive...	Clash	-0.74	Relevant	
4	Arm (Arm.1)	Mount (Mount.1)	Contact	0	Relevant	
5	Arm (Arm.1)	Hub (Hub.1)	Clearance	2.96	Relevant	Too close!
6	Arm (Arm.2)	Mount (Mount.1)	Clash	-0.62	Relevant	
7	Arm (Arm.2)	Hub (Hub.1)	Clearance	1.48	Relevant	Too close!
8	Mount (Mount.1)	Hub (Hub.1)	Clash		Not inspected	
9	Hub (Hub.1)	Spider (Spider.1)	Contact		Not inspected	
10	Hub (Hub.1)	DriveShaft (Drive...	Clash		Not inspected	
11	Hub (Hub.1)	WheelRim (Wheel...	Clash		Not inspected	
12	Spider (Spider.1)	DriveShaft (Drive...	Clash		Not inspected	
13	DriveShaft (Dri...	Spider (Spider.2)	Clash		Not inspected	

Figure 7–6

Each row lists two components that have conflict, the type of conflict, and the offset distance between the two components. A negative value indicates an interference between the components in question. A positive value indicates a clearance between the two components.

The *Status* column displays **Not Inspected** until the row is highlighted. To toggle the status between **Irrelevant** and **Relevant**, highlight the row and select the status.

The *Comment* column enables the reviewer to enter comments about a specific row.

List by Product

The *List by Product* tab displays the results in the window, sorted by the product in question. It displays all of the components that conflict with a selected component, as shown in Figure 7–7. The information about each conflict and the *Status* and *Comment* columns act the same as when you use the *List by Conflict* tab.

List by Conflict | List by Product | Matrix

No.	Product 1	Product 2	Type	Value	Status	Comment
1	Frame (Frame.1)	Arm (Arm.1)	Contact	0	Irrelevant	Okay
2		Arm (Arm.2)	Contact	0	Irrelevant	Okay
3		DriveShaft (Driv...	Clash	-0.74	Relevant	
1	Arm (Arm.1)	Frame (Frame.1)	Contact	0	Irrelevant	Okay
4		Mount (Mount.1)	Contact	0	Relevant	
5		Hub (Hub.1)	Cleara...	2.96	Relevant	Too close!
2	Arm (Arm.2)	Frame (Frame.1)	Contact	0	Irrelevant	Okay
6		Mount (Mount.1)	Clash	-0.62	Relevant	
7		Hub (Hub.1)	Cleara...	1.48	Relevant	Too close!
3	DriveShaft (Driv...	Frame (Frame.1)	Clash	-0.74	Relevant	
10		Hub (Hub.1)	Clash		Not inspec...	
12		Spider (Spider.1)	Clash		Not inspec...	
13		Spider (Spider.2)	Clash		Not inspec...	

The Status can be changed and a Comment can be added by selecting the appropriate fields.

Figure 7–7

Matrix

The *Matrix* tab displays the results in a graphical chart. The chart displays the conflicts between the two components in question. The conflicts are shown at their chart intersection by shape and color-coded symbols. You can zoom the chart as you would a 3D model. The *Matrix* tab is shown in Figure 7–8.

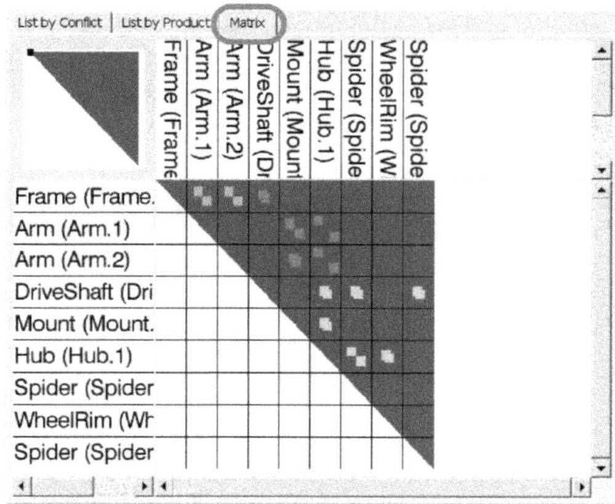

Figure 7–8

The various symbols in the Matrix chart are described as follows:

Symbol/Color	Description
	Displays a Clearance condition.
	Displays a Contact condition.
	Displays a Clash condition.
Yellow symbol	Conflict has not been inspected.
Red symbol	Conflict is inspected and relevant.
Green symbol	Conflict is inspected and irrelevant.

The Status can be changed and a Comment can be added while in this display. Select the conflict symbol, right-click, and select an option, as shown in Figure 7–9.

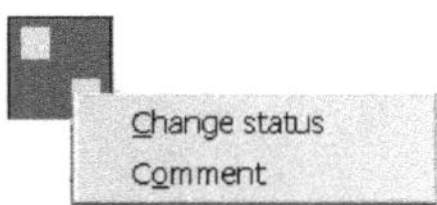

Figure 7–9

Preview Window

The **Preview** window displays the results of the conflict. The window can be resized and placed anywhere on the screen and the results can be graphically manipulated. The **Preview** window is shown in Figure 7–10, and is activated when a conflict is selected in the **Results** window.

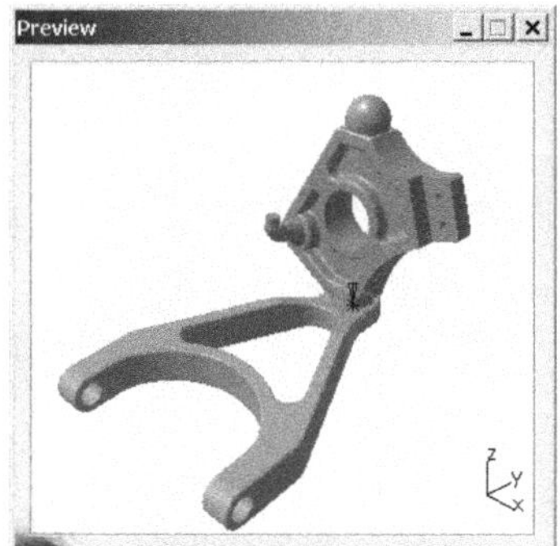

Figure 7–10

Step 4 - Export the results.

The results that are computed can be saved by storing them in an external file.

To store the results to an external file, click (Export as) in the Check Clash dialog box. Results can be saved as: XML, text, V4 model, or CGR file formats.

The XML file format generates a detailed report that includes graphics and hyperlinks to the various areas of the data. An example is shown in Figure 7–11.

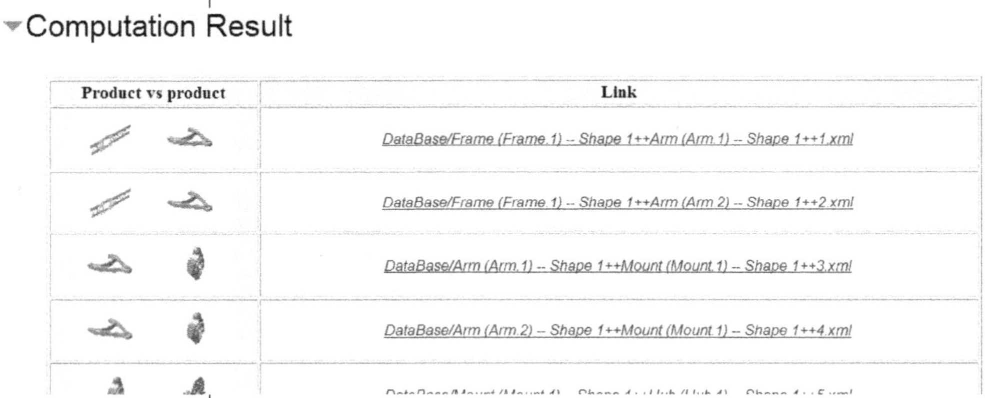

Computation Result

Product vs product	Link
	DataBase/Frame (Frame.1) -- Shape 1++Arm (Arm.1) -- Shape 1++1.xml
	DataBase/Frame (Frame.1) -- Shape 1++Arm (Arm.2) -- Shape 1++2.xml
	DataBase/Arm (Arm.1) -- Shape 1++Mount (Mount.1) -- Shape 1++3.xml
	DataBase/Arm (Arm.2) -- Shape 1++Mount (Mount.1) -- Shape 1++4.xml

Figure 7–11

Click **OK** to close the Check Clash dialog box.

7.3 Section a Model

The **Sectioning** tool enables you to cut sections in an assembly. You can use this tool to perform the following tasks:

- Examine assembly component positions.
- Display 2D complex cross-sections.
- Verify the internal design considerations of a part.

General Steps

Use the following general steps to section a model:

1. Activate the **Sectioning** tool.
2. Position the cross-section.
3. Define the output of the section.

Step 1 - Activate the Sectioning tool.

Click (Sectioning). The Sectioning Definition dialog box opens as shown in Figure 7–12.

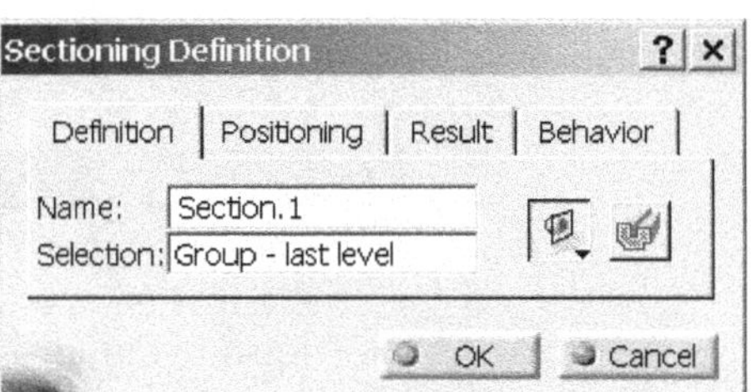

Figure 7–12

A section view is tiled vertically next to the product window, as shown in Figure 7–13.

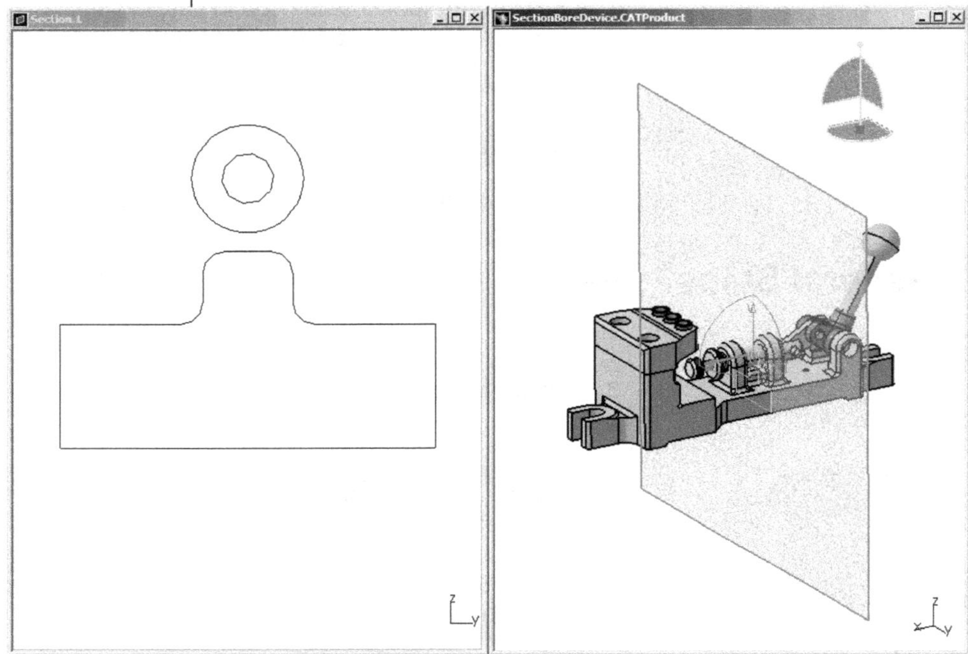

Figure 7–13

Step 2 - Position the cross-section.

Use the *Positioning* tab to position the section in different ways, as shown in Figure 7–14.

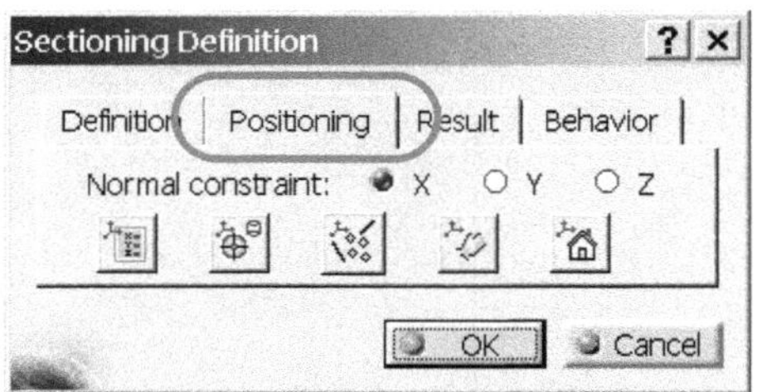

Figure 7–14

The **Normal Constraint** options enable you to determine whether the section plane is normal to the X-, Y- or Z-axis.

The four types of positioning tools available are described as follows:

Positioning Tool	Description
(Edit Position and Dimensions)	Defines precise section locations. Can set **Origin**, **Translations**, **Rotations**, and **Dimensional** sizes of the section.
(Geometrical Target)	Quickly positions the section at specific geometrical locations (e.g., cylinders, planes, faces, or edges).
(Positioning by 2/3 Selections)	Positions the section at 2 or 3 geometrical references (e.g., axes of two holes/cylinders or through three points).
(Invert Normal)	Inverts the normal direction of the master plane. If used with a **Volume Cut**, it removes the other side of the cut.
(Reset Position)	Quickly positions the section back to the starting location and orientation but does not resize the section dimensions.

Manual Section Manipulation

You can manually manipulate the section plane using any of the following methods:

- **Dragging:** Select the section plane and drag to translate the plane, as shown in Figure 7–15.

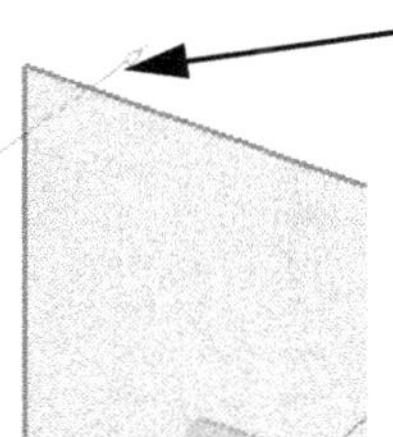

Figure 7–15

- **Rotating:** Select an arc on the section axis system and drag to rotate to a new angle, as shown in Figure 7–16.

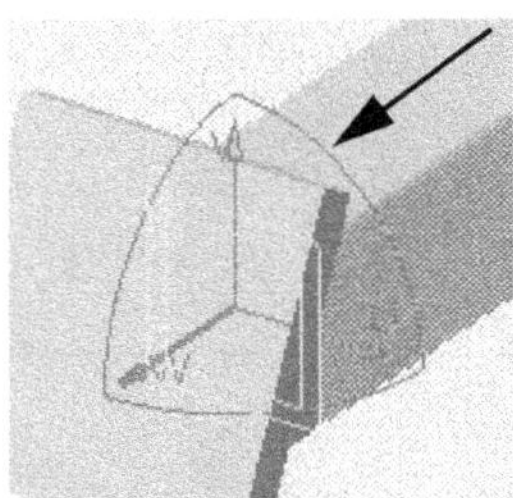

Figure 7–16

- **Resizing:** Select the sides of the section plane and drag to change the size of the section, as shown in Figure 7–17.

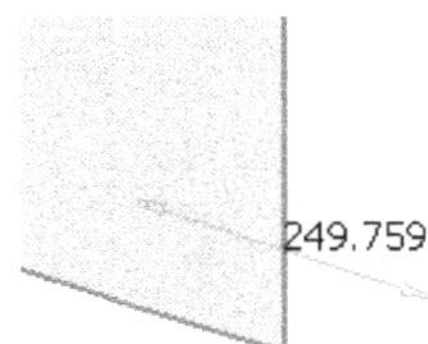

Figure 7–17

Step 3 - Define the output of the section.

Output of the section can be defined using the *Result* tab, as shown in Figure 7–18.

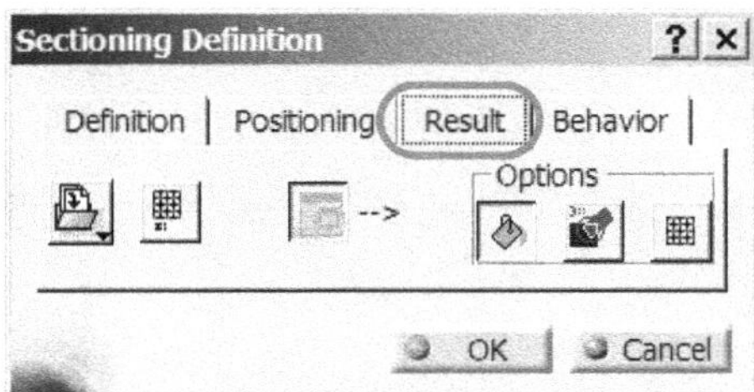

Figure 7–18

The four result information tools available are described as follows:

Result Tool			Description
		(Export and Open)	Saves the section results to either a CATPart or CATDrawing file and opens the resulting file.
		(Export As)	Saves the section results to different file formats (e.g., CATPart, CATDrawing, model, DXF, DWG, IGS, STP, or WRL).
		(Export In Existing Part)	Exports the section results to a selected part. Section results are generated in a new geometrical set in the selected part file.
	(Edit Grid)		Edits the Grid settings, such as location mode (**Absolute** or **Relative**), display style (**Lines** or **Crosses**), and spacing size.
	(Results Window)		Opens the **Results** window in which you can measure section results. The **Results** window is open by default and is tiled vertically next to the **Product** window. When this option is disabled, a **Preview** window displays. This tool must be activated to perform the following options:
		(Section Fill)	Toggles the **Section Fill** on or off. Useful for measuring section area. The **Results Window** icon must be activated to use this tool.
		(Clash Detection)	Circles all areas of clash in the current section. The **Results Window** and **Section Fill** icons must be activated to use this tool.
		(Grid)	Toggles the grid on or off in the **Results** window. Use the **Edit Grid** tool to modify the grid. The **Results Window** icon must be activated to use this tool.

When you have analyzed the section, click **OK** to close the Section Definition dialog box and the **Results** or **Preview** window.

7.4 Distance Analysis

The **Distance Analysis** tool enables you to measure the minimum distance between components in a product.

General Steps

Use the following general steps to use the **Distance Analysis** tool:

1. Activate the **Distance and Band Analysis** tool.
2. Select the method of component selection and select components.
3. Select the type of analysis.
4. Run the analysis.

Step 1 - Activate the Distance and Band Analysis tool.

Click (Distance and Band Analysis). The Edit Distance and Band Analysis dialog box opens as shown in Figure 7–19. Enter a meaningful name for the analysis in the *Name* field.

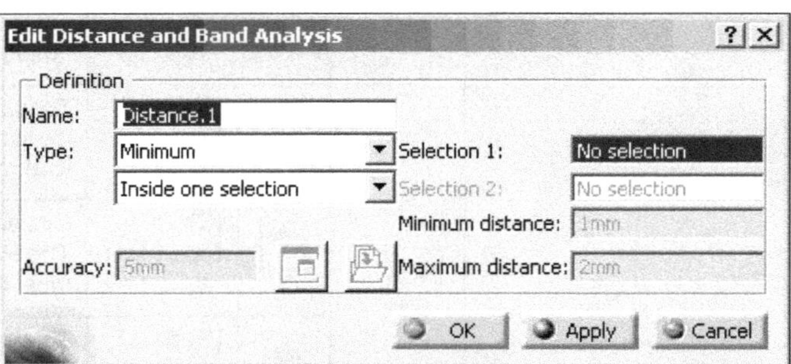

Figure 7–19

Step 2 - Select the method of component selection and select components.

Select the selection method in the Type drop-down list, as shown in Figure 7–20.

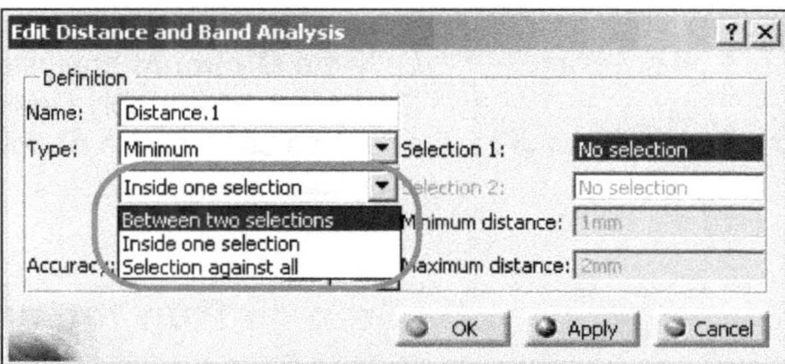

Figure 7–20

The selection methods are described as follows:

Option	Description
Between two sections	Tests each component in the first selection group against all components in the second selection group.
Inside one selection	(Default) Tests each selected component against all other selected components.
Selection against all	Tests each selected component against all other components in the assembly.

If you select a component by accident, select it again to remove it from the list.

To select a component for analysis, select the appropriate selection field and select the component in the specification tree or directly from the model. You can select as many components for each selection field as required.

Step 3 - Select the type of analysis.

Select the type of analysis to perform in the Type drop-down list. The analyses that you can perform are described as follows:

Option	Description
Minimum*	Calculates the minimum distance between selected components.
Along X	Calculates the distance between selected components in the X-direction.

Along Y	Calculates the distance between selected components in the Y-direction.
Along Z	Calculates the distance between selected components in the Z-direction.
Band Analysis	Calculates the area of minimum and maximum distance between selected components.

Only the **Minimum** analysis is available with an Assembly Design 1 or Assembly Design 2 license. Directional and Band analyses can only be performed using a DMU Space Analysis license.

Step 4 - Run the analysis.

Click **Apply** to run analysis. The Edit Distance and Band Analysis dialog box expands to display the results, as shown in Figure 7–21. If you click **OK**, it stores the interference calculation in the specification tree and does not display any results.

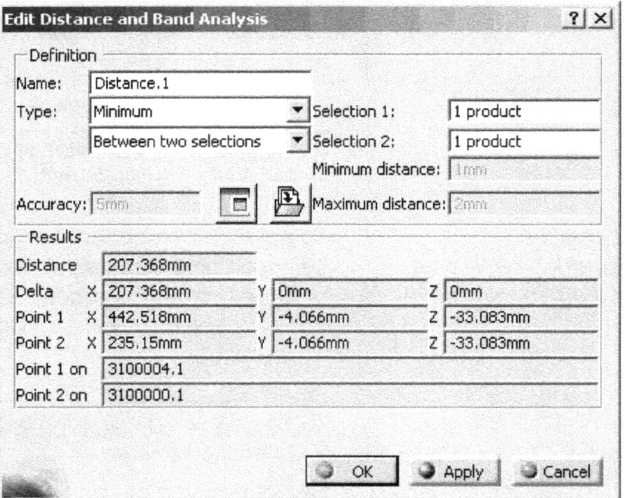

Figure 7–21

The results are also displayed directly on the model and in a **Preview** window, as shown in Figure 7–22. The **Preview** window only displays the components to which the results correspond.

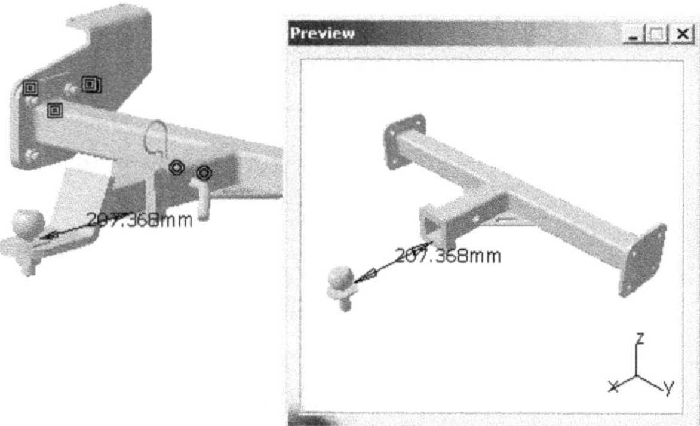

Figure 7–22

Once you have analyzed the results, click **OK** to close the dialog box.

Practice 7a Clash Analysis

Practice Objectives

- Run a clash analysis.
- Interpret the results.
- Export the results.

In this practice, you will review a product for clash and note problem areas so the designer can correct the issues.

Task 1 - Open the assembly.

1. Open **FrontWheel.CATProduct**. The assembly displays as shown in Figure 7–23.

   The files for this practice can be found in the *FrontWheel* directory.

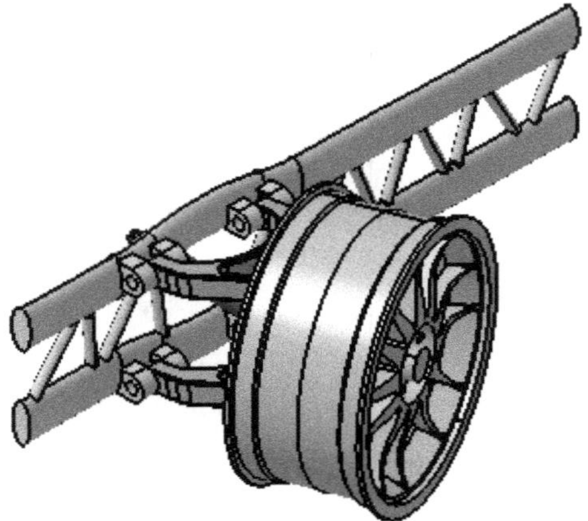

Figure 7–23

Task 2 - Run the clash analysis.

1. In the Space Analysis toolbar, click (Clash).
2. In the Type drop-down list, select **Clearance + Contact + Clash**.
3. Select **Between all components** as the selection set.
4. Set the *minimum clearance* to **4mm**. The Check Clash dialog box opens as shown in Figure 7–24.

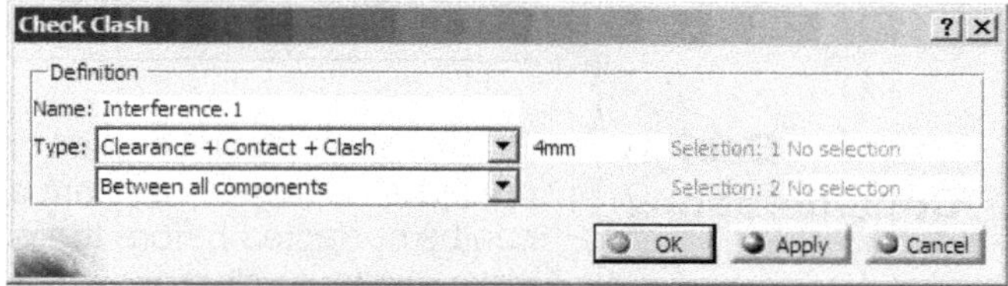

Figure 7–24

5. In the Check Clash dialog box, click **Apply** and wait for the computer to calculate the interferences.

Task 3 - Interpret results.

1. Record the total number of interferences and the total number of interferences by type. The information displays just below the *Results* area.

Interference Type	Total Number
All Interferences	
Clash	
Contact	
Clearance	

2. Select the first result in the Check Clash dialog box. It should be a contact result between **Frame** and **Arm.1**. The two parts display in the **Preview** window, as shown in Figure 7–25.

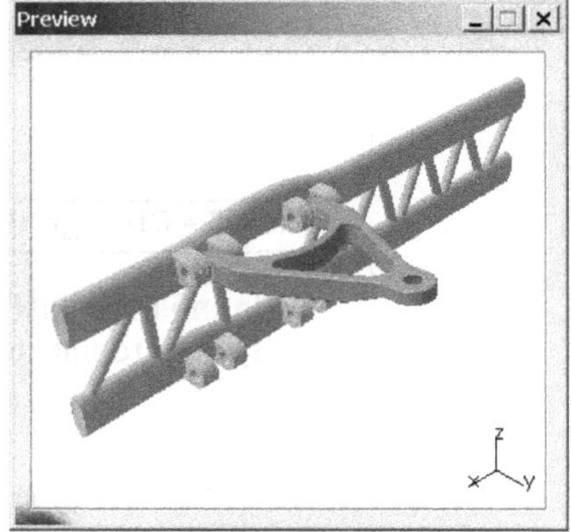

Figure 7–25

3. In the **Preview** window, pan, zoom, and rotate as required to examine the results of the conflict.

Task 4 - Make comments and change the status of a result.

Design Considerations

Once the results have been calculated, interpretation of the results is essential. Problem areas must be noted so that they can be corrected before the product goes into production. A 4mm minimum clearance between the arms and the hub is essential for the operation of the assembly. All other components can be in contact with each other but no force fits are noted for this assembly. Therefore, any clashes need to be noted for correction by the designer.

1. For first conflict, note that the type of conflict is **Contact**. Because the components are not in violation of the requirements for the assembly, place the cursor in the *Comment* column at the end of the row for the first conflict. Select the field and enter the comment shown in Figure 7–26.

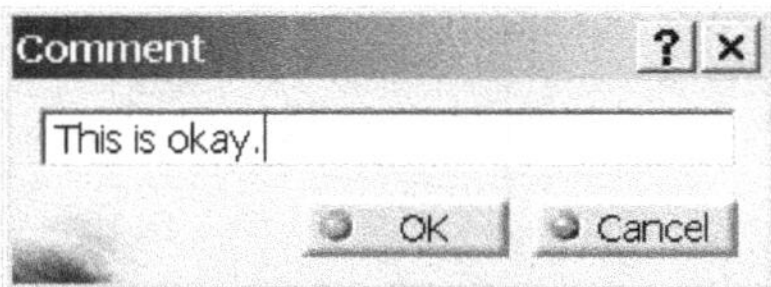

Figure 7–26

2. In the same row, to the left of the *Comment* field, select **Relevant** and change it to **Irrelevant**. This area in the Check Clash dialog box displays as shown in Figure 7–27.

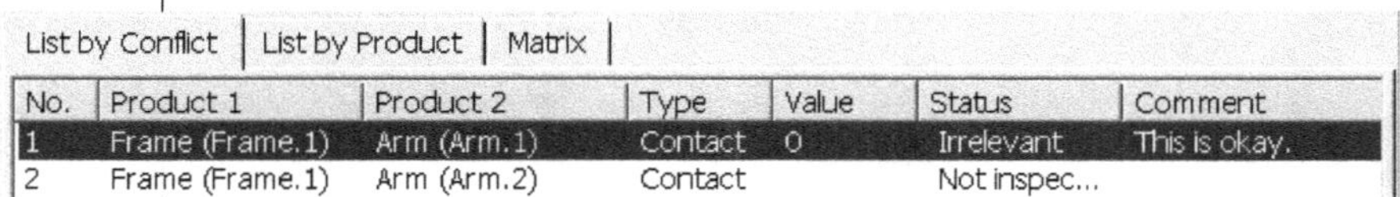

List by Conflict | List by Product | Matrix

No.	Product 1	Product 2	Type	Value	Status	Comment
1	Frame (Frame.1)	Arm (Arm.1)	Contact	0	Irrelevant	This is okay.
2	Frame (Frame.1)	Arm (Arm.2)	Contact		Not inspec...	

Figure 7–27

Task 5 - Change the Filter lists to sort the results.

1. In the Filter List drop-down list, select **Contact** to change the type of results to display, as shown in Figure 7–28.

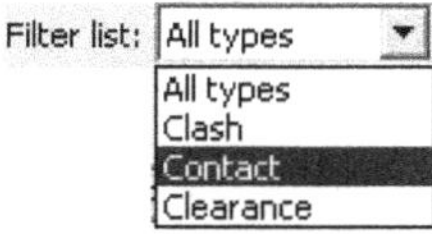

Figure 7–28

None of the contact conflicts are between the components of concern (**Hub** and **Arms**).

2. Change the *Status* of all of the contact conflicts to **Irrelevant**, as shown in Figure 7–29.

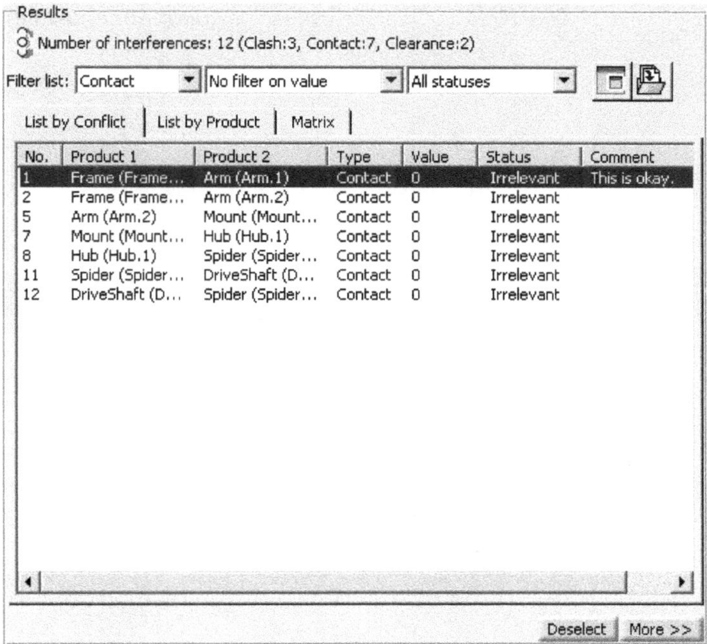

Figure 7–29

3. In the Filter List drop-down list, select **Clash** to change the type of results to display, as shown in Figure 7–30.

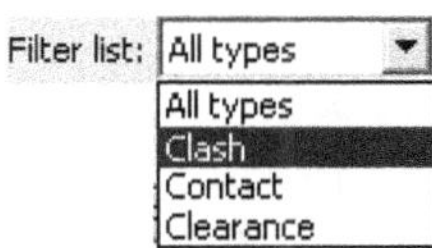

Figure 7–30

4. In the filtered list, select the first clash result and examine it in the **Preview** window. The parts in question should be **Arm** and **Mount**.

5. Zoom in on the clash area to examine it. What is the interference amount between the two parts? ____________

6. In the **Results** window, select the next conflict. The parts in question should be **Hub** and **Driveshaft**. In the **Preview** window, zoom in on the clash area. The clash exists between the two components that were constrained in the assembly. If the constraints are adjusted, the issue would be resolved.

7. Enter the comment shown in Figure 7–31 for this clash.

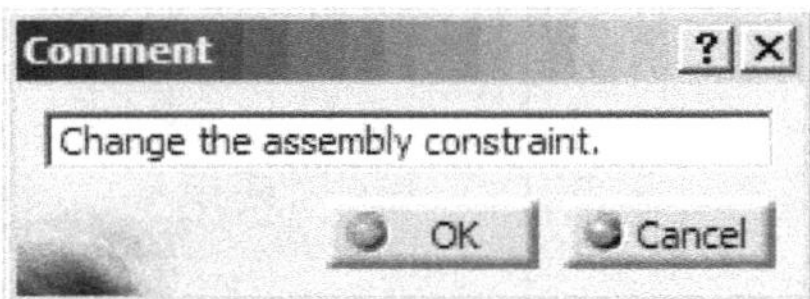

Figure 7–31

8. Review the remaining clash conflict and add a comment to propose a solution for resolving the issue.

Task 6 - Access the List by Product tab and review results.

1. In the Filter List drop-down list, select **All types** as shown in Figure 7–32.

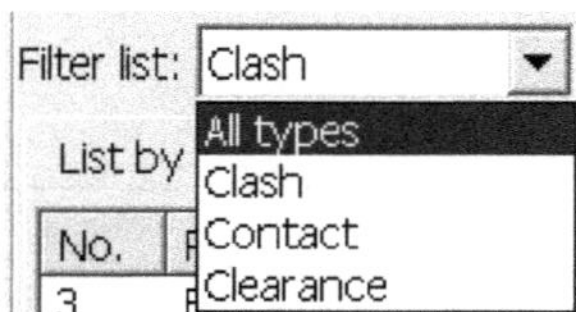

Figure 7–32

2. Select the *List by Product* tab.

3. In the *Product 1* column, select the *Hub* (*Hub.1*) field. There is a clearance between **Hub** and **Arm.1**, as shown in Figure 7–33.

4. Select in the *Product 2* column for the **Hub** (**Hub.1**)**/Arm** (**Arm.1**) row to highlight only this row as shown in Figure 7–33. Review the results of the clash in the preview window. The clearance is not the required 4mm.

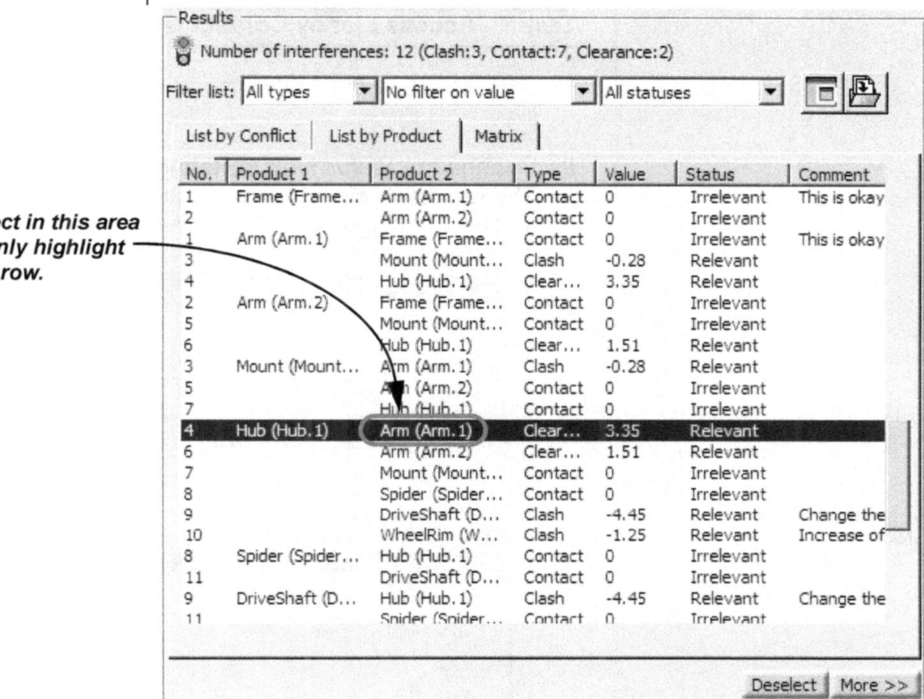

Figure 7–33

5. Enter a comment as shown in Figure 7–34.

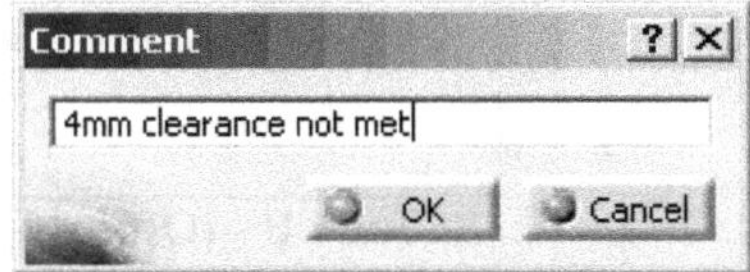

Figure 7–34

6. Inspect the conflict between the **Hub** and **Arm.2**. What type of conflict is it? Is the conflict acceptable? Make notes and change the status of the conflict to coincide with your findings.

Task 7 - Access List by Conflict tab and change filters again.

1. Select the *List by Conflict* tab to return to the original results list.

2. Change the *Status* filter to **Relevant** and note the results list. The results display the conflicts that need to be addressed, as shown in Figure 7–35.

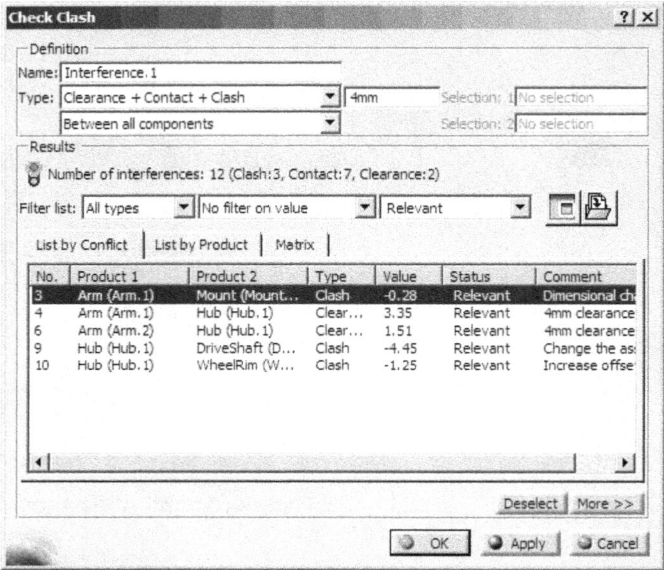

Figure 7–35

Task 8 - (Optional) Export the clash results to a text file.

1. Click (Export As).
2. In the Clash Publish - Warning dialog box, click **OK**.
3. Save the Clash analysis as a .TXT file.
4. Review the results of the export.

Task 9 - Close the Check Clash dialog box.

1. Click **OK** to close the Check Clash dialog box.
2. Save and close the model.

Practice 7b

Section Analysis

Practice Objectives

- Start a sectioning analysis.
- Set up the sectioning parameters.
- Measure in the results window.

In this practice, you will section a product file in various locations and take measurements.

Task 1 - Open the assembly.

1. Open **SectionBoreDevice.CATProduct**. The assembly displays as shown in Figure 7–36.

   The files for this practice can be found in the *BoreDevice* directory.

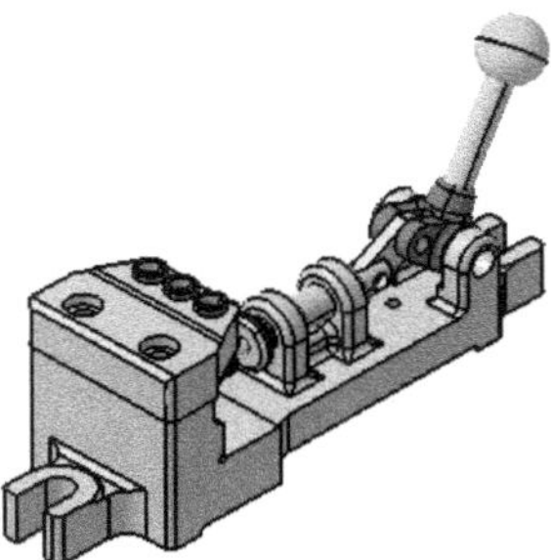

Figure 7–36

Task 2 - Start the sectioning definition.

1. In the Space Analysis toolbar, click (Sectioning). The Sectioning Definition dialog box opens as shown in Figure 7–37.

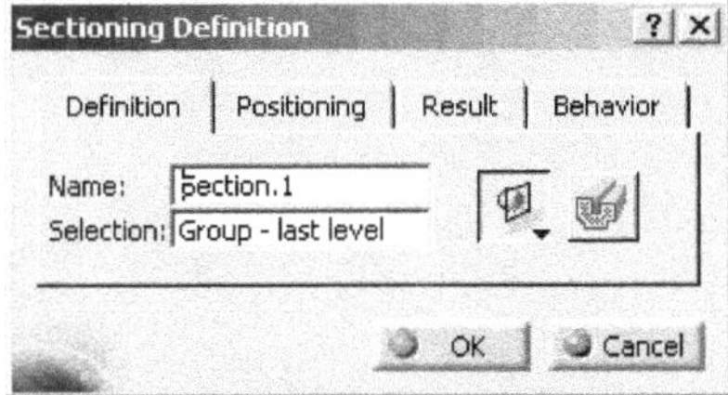

Figure 7–37

2. Select **Window>Tile Vertically** to display the **Section** and **Model** windows side by side.

Task 3 - Define the positioning settings.

1. In the Sectioning Definition dialog box, in the *Positioning* tab, change the *Normal constraint setting* to the **Y direction**, as shown in Figure 7–38.

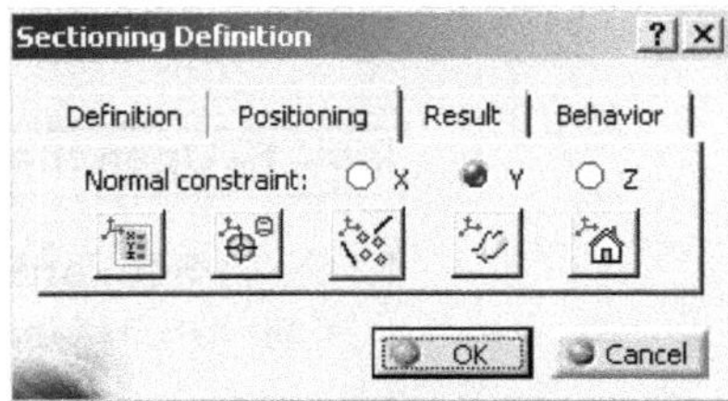

Figure 7–38

2. Move the section through the parts by selecting the cursor over the sectioning plane with the mouse button and dragging in any direction.

3. Reset the position by clicking (Reset Position). Change the *Normal constraint* back to **Y**.

4. Select the *Result* tab and click to clear (Section Fill). The section result only displays the edges of the components.

5. In the *Positioning* tab, click (Edit Position And Dimensions) to edit the exact dimensions and position of the plane.

6. Change the settings, as shown in Figure 7–39.

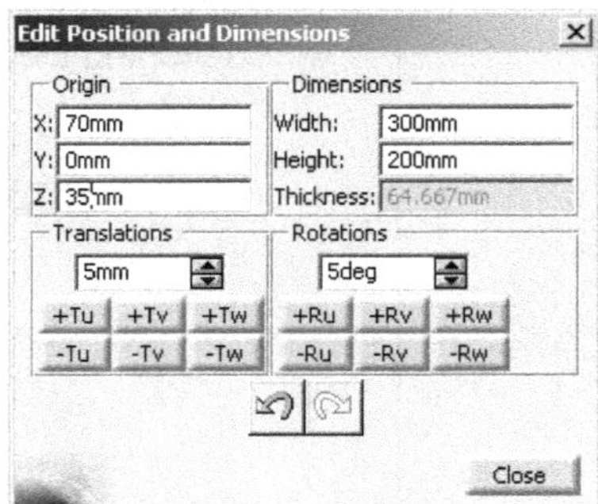

Figure 7–39

7. Click **-Tw** twice to translate the plane in 5mm increments for a total of -10mm.

8. Click **-Ru** twice and **+Rv** once to rotate the section plane in 5 degree increments. The result displays similar to those shown in Figure 7–40.

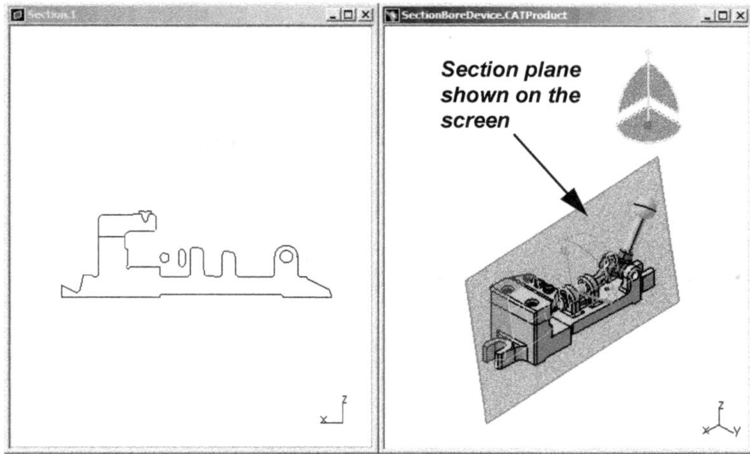

Figure 7–40

9. Click **Close** to close the Edit Position and Dimensions dialog box.

Task 4 - Take measurements.

1. Click (Reset Position).

2. Set the *Normal constraint* to **Y** and manually manipulate the section plane to ensure that it cuts through the entire model, as shown in Figure 7–41.

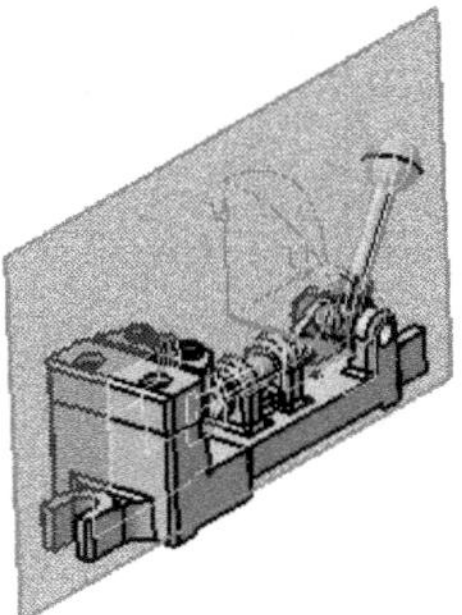

Figure 7–41

3. In the **Result** window, zoom in on the **Ball Lever**, **Pin Seized**, and **Lever Angle** components, as shown in Figure 7–42. There are two areas where clash exists.

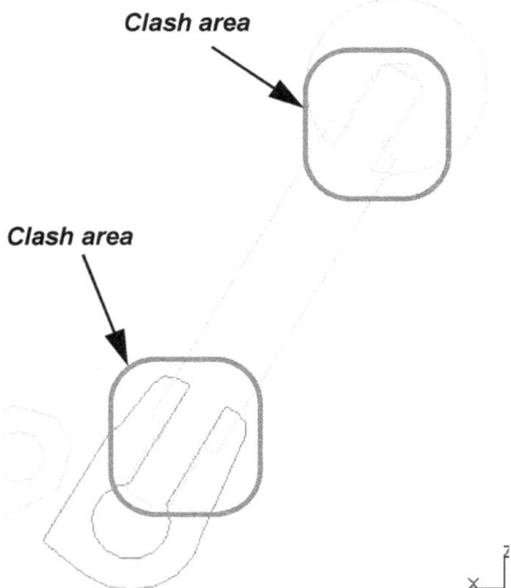

Figure 7–42

4. In the **Section.1** window, pan and zoom to display the clash areas more clearly.

5. Without closing the Sectioning Definition dialog box, in the Measure toolbar, click (Measure Between) to perform a measurement.

6. Set the *Selection 1 mode* and *Selection 2 mode settings* to **Edge only**.

7. In the **Results** window, measure the overlap distances between the **Lever Angle** part (blue) and the **Pin Seized** part (gray) as shown in Figure 7–43. You might need to pan and zoom to make measuring easier.

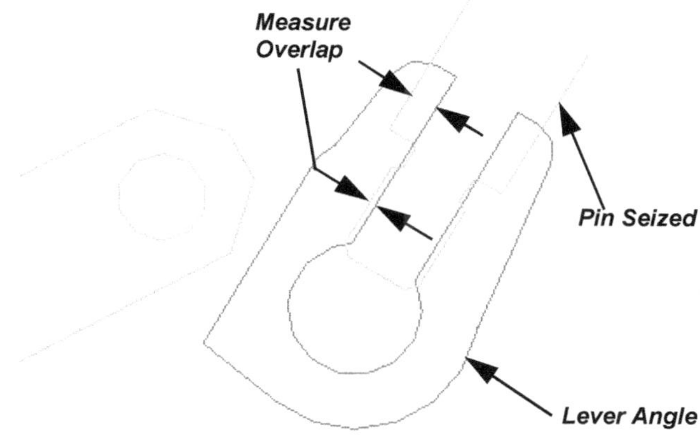

Figure 7–43

Task 5 - Analyze another section of the model.

1. Click (Reset Position) to reset the section position in the *Positioning* tab.
2. In the *Positioning* tab, click (Geometrical Target) to position the section through the features in the model.
3. Create the section shown in Figure 7–44 by selecting one of the two holes at the top of the **Feature Drill** component. Ensure that the *Normal constraint* is set to **X**.

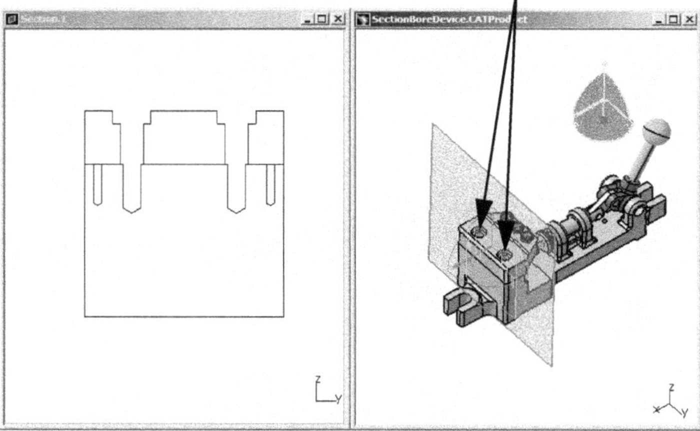

Figure 7–44

4. In the *Definition* tab, click (Volume Cut). The model is physically cut along the section plane, as shown in Figure 7–45.

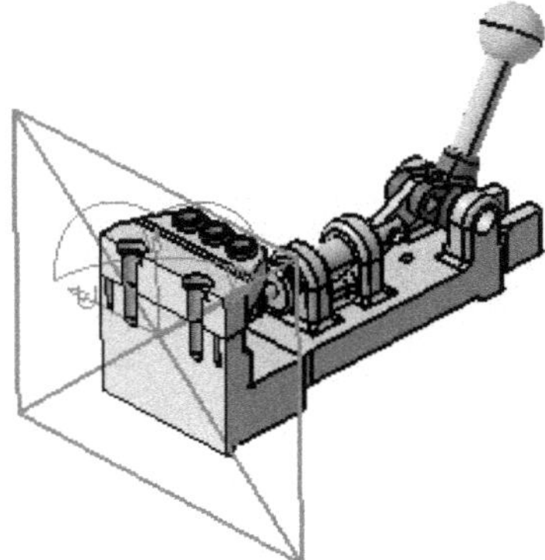

Figure 7–45

5. To close the Section Definition dialog box, click **OK**.

Task 6 - Perform a Minimum Distance analysis.

1. In the Space Analysis toolbar, click (Distance and Band Analysis).
2. Rename the analysis as **Link Analysis**.
3. In the Type drop-down lists, select **Minimum** and **Between two selections** as shown in Figure 7–46.

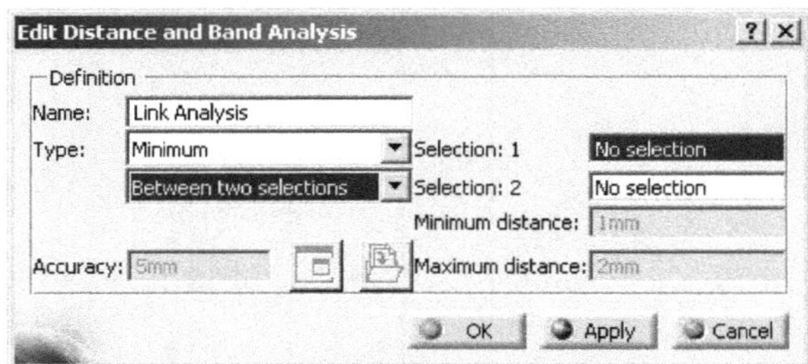

Figure 7–46

4. For *Selection 1*, select the **Lever Angle**.

5. Activate the *Selection 2* field and select **Pin Pressure**.

6. Click **Apply** to run the analysis. The results display in a **Preview** window, as shown in Figure 7–47.

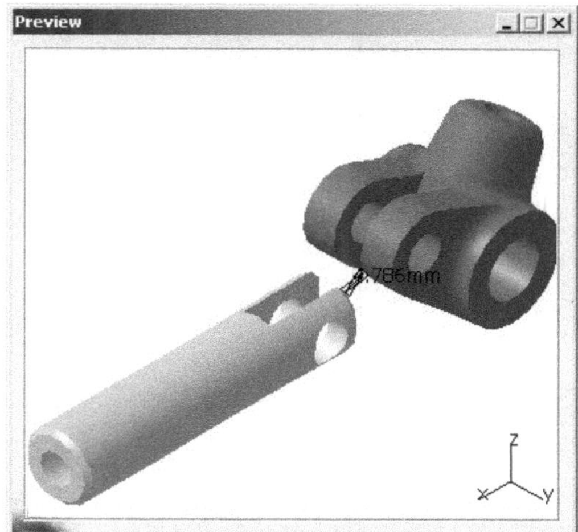

Figure 7–47

7. In the **Preview** window, review the results. The window displays the current straight line (minimum) distance between the two components.

*Remember to click **Apply** when running the analysis again. Clicking **OK** runs the analysis and closes the dialog box.*

8. Click **OK** to close the dialog box. The **LinkAnalysis** has been added to the specification tree.

9. Save and close the **SectionBoreDevice** assembly.

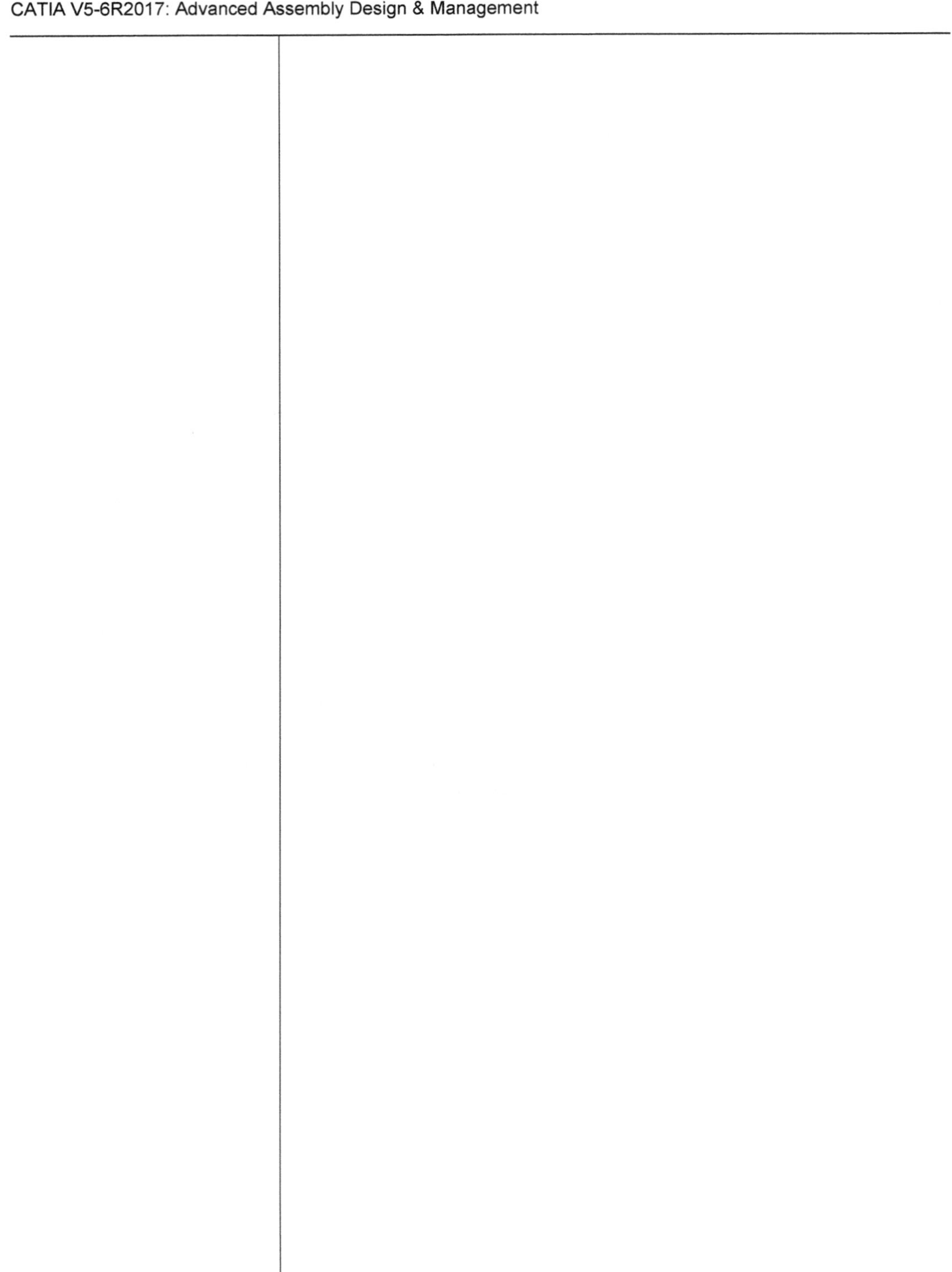

Assembly Performance Management

Large assembly management techniques minimize the amount of information brought into session, thus reducing update time. As a result, the visibility of the assembly components and overall perspective of the complete top-level assembly is reduced. You might still need to visualize and/or work with the complete top-level of a large assembly. Cache management is used to achieve this task.

Learning Objectives in this Chapter

- Understand how to use the cache system.
- Learn how to improve assembly performance.

8.1 Using the Cache System

Using the cache system reduces RAM usage. File retrieval time and update time are greatly reduced.

When the **Work with cache system** option is selected components are loaded into the system in **Visualization** mode. In **Visualization** mode, the system converts all solid geometry in the assembly to tessellated (or faceted) surfaces, resulting in a simplified representation of the geometry.

General Steps

Use the following general steps to work with the cache system:

1. Activate the cache system.
2. (Optional) Set the file path to the local cache.
3. Exit and restart CATIA.
4. Open a Product file for viewing.
5. Switch selected components to **Design** mode as required.

Step 1 - Activate the cache system.

Select **Tools>Options>Infrastructure>Product Structure** and select the *Cache Management* tab. Select **Work with the cache system** to activate the cache system, as shown in Figure 8–1.

Figure 8–1

Step 2 - (Optional) Set the file path to the local cache.

Click [icon] next to the *Path to the local cache* field and browse to the required directory, as shown in Figure 8–2. The file path only needs to be set once; if the directory changes, it must be set again.

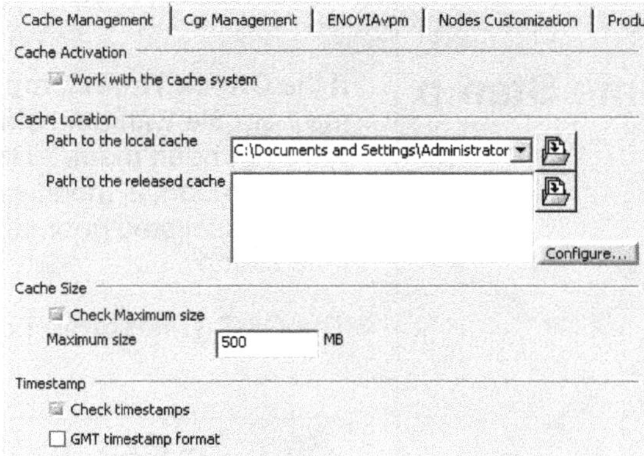

Figure 8–2

Local Cache

The local cache directory path specifies the file path to a directory on your system in which the *.cgr files are stored. The first time a component is opened, it is tessellated and the corresponding *.cgr file is computed and written to the local cache directory. The next time the component is loaded using cache management, the system searches for the corresponding *.cgr file in the local cache directory and loads it. The system default local cache directory is *C:\Documents and Settings\<user name>\Local Settings\Application Data\DassaultSystemes\CATCache* (for Windows 2000 and XP Professional) or *C:\Users\<user name>\AppData\Local\DassaultSystemes\CATCache* (for Windows 7).

Released Cache

A file path and search order can be specified for the released cache. This is a read-only cache directory that can be located anywhere on a network. Multiple released cache directories can be specified.

*Click **Configure** to configure the search order.*

If a *.cgr file is required for loading but cannot be found in the local cache directory, the system searches the released cache directories in the specified search order. If the *.cgr file is not found, the system creates one in the local cache directory. Typically, a system administrator manages released cache directories.

Cache Size

The default size of the writable cache is 500 MB. If that value is exceeded, the system automatically deletes *.cgr files on a first-in first-out basis.

Time Stamp

If the **Check Timestamps** option is enabled, the system saves the *.cgr file with a time stamp. This verifies that modifications have not been made to the model since the creation of the *.cgr file. If a model is modified, the *.cgr file is overwritten with the latest tessellated geometry data and the file contains an updated time stamp.

The **GMT Timestamp Format** option is only for global use.

Step 3 - Exit and restart CATIA.

When all of the required settings have been set, click **OK**. The system opens the Warning dialog box shown in Figure 8–3, indicating that the application must be restarted for the settings to take effect.

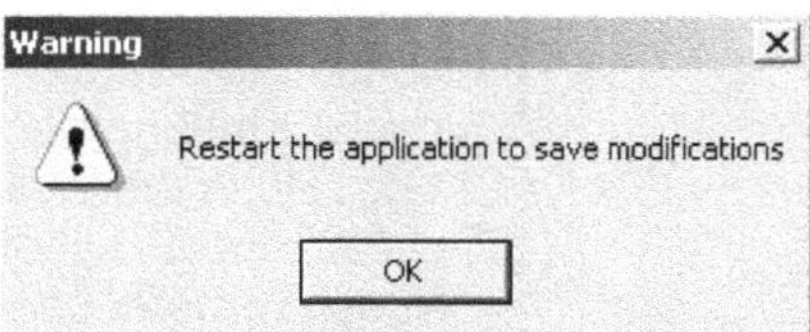

Figure 8–3

Step 4 - Open a Product file for viewing.

Open a Product file. The system loads all of the *.cgr files into the viewer. When a Product file is opened with the **Work with the cache system** option activated, all of the components are in **Visualization** mode by default.

The specification tree of a product in **Visualization** mode is shown in Figure 8–4. The component instances are listed with the name of the part or product file. It cannot be expanded to list features.

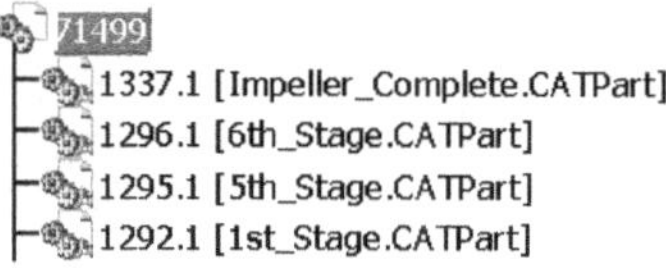

Figure 8–4

If references need to be selected while working in **Visualization** mode, the system displays a component's status, as shown in Figure 8–5.

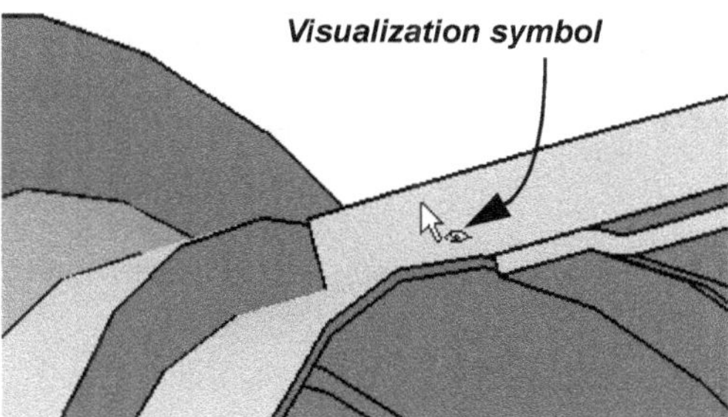

Figure 8–5

CGR File

When working with the cache system, the system displays a representation of the solid geometry. The first time a component is opened when working with the cache system, the system writes the geometry representation to a specified directory with the filename **<component name>.cgr**. A Design mode part and product names are shown in Figure 8–6.

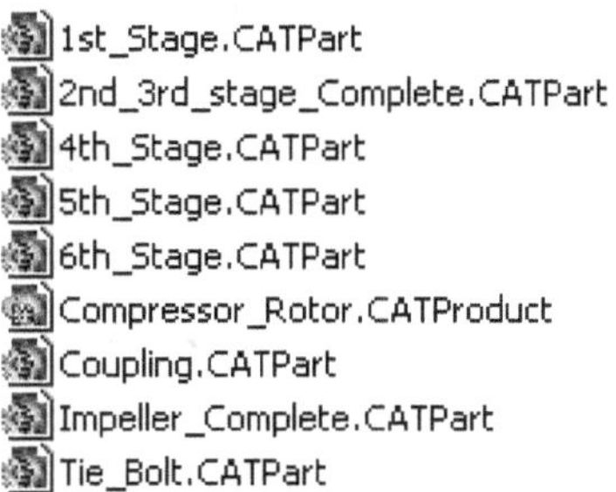

Figure 8–6

The part files shown in Figure 8–6 have been written to a *.cgr directory as a result of activating and working with the **Cache System** option. Note the *.cgr file extension and the date code preceding it, as shown in Figure 8–7.

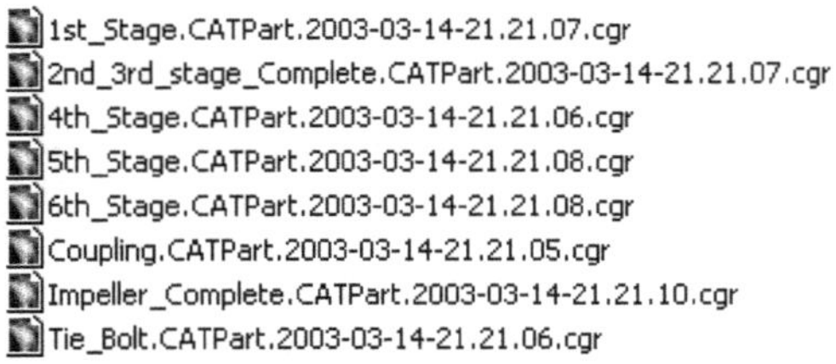

1st_Stage.CATPart.2003-03-14-21.21.07.cgr
2nd_3rd_stage_Complete.CATPart.2003-03-14-21.21.07.cgr
4th_Stage.CATPart.2003-03-14-21.21.06.cgr
5th_Stage.CATPart.2003-03-14-21.21.08.cgr
6th_Stage.CATPart.2003-03-14-21.21.08.cgr
Coupling.CATPart.2003-03-14-21.21.05.cgr
Impeller_Complete.CATPart.2003-03-14-21.21.10.cgr
Tie_Bolt.CATPart.2003-03-14-21.21.06.cgr

Figure 8–7

Step 5 - Switch selected components to Design mode as required.

Selected components can be changed to Design mode by right-clicking on the component in the specification tree and selecting **Representations>Design mode**, as shown in Figure 8–8.

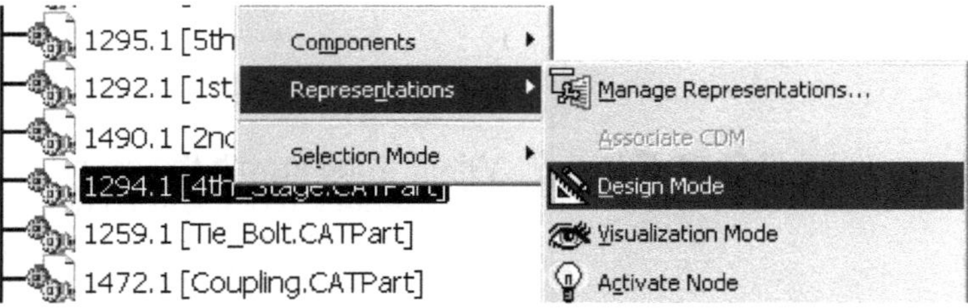

Figure 8–8

If the **Automatic switch to Design mode** option is selected (the default setting), the system automatically switches the component to Design mode.

The **Automatic switch to Design mode** option can be disabled by selecting **Tools>Options>Mechanical Design>Assembly Design**. Select the *General* tab and clear the option in the *Access to geometry* area as shown in Figure 8–9.

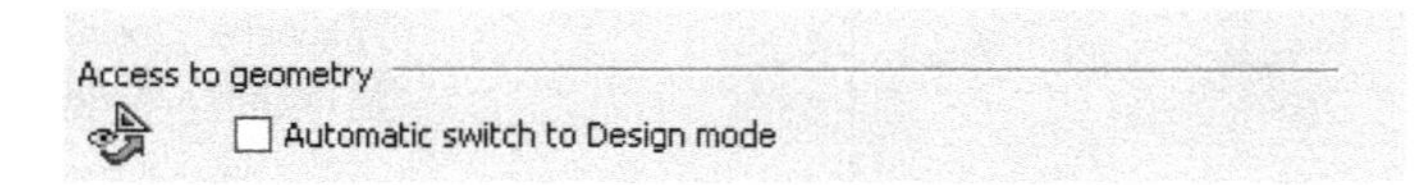

Figure 8–9

By default, all parts and products are created and manipulated in **Design** mode. When working in **Design** mode, components carry the full geometric weight of the solids they represent.

The specification tree of a product in **Design** mode is shown in Figure 8–10. The specification tree reports the part number and instance number for each part. Each part is expandable and lists its features.

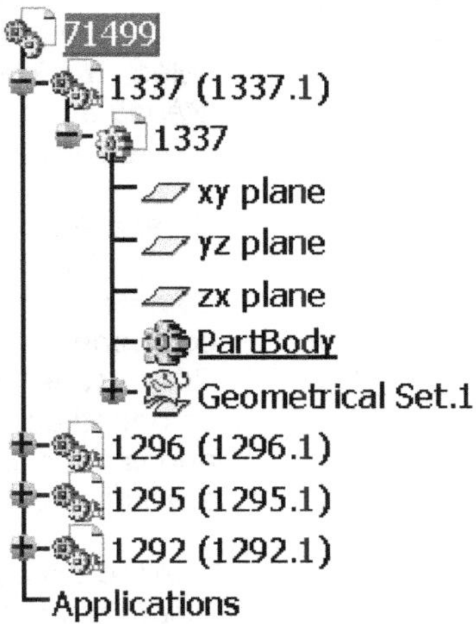

Figure 8–10

Note the following restrictions:

- If the **Work with the cache system** option is selected, components can be toggled between **Visualization** mode and **Design** mode.
- If the **Work with the cache system** option is not selected, components cannot be switched from **Design** mode to **Visualization** mode even if its *.cgr file exists in the local cache.
- If a component is automatically switched to **Design** mode, it remains in **Design** mode and must be manually switched to **Visualization** mode if the update time is affected.
- Mass properties can be calculated from a component that is in **Visualization** mode.
- CATIA must be restarted for the **Work with cache system** option to take effect.

8.2 Assembly Performance Summary

Consider the following options separately or in conjunction with each other to improve assembly performance.

Using the Cache system you can control which components are loaded into design mode.

- Use the Cache system to load assemblies in **Visualization** mode. In **Visualization** modem, file load times and RAM usage are greatly reduced. To activate the Cache system, select **Work with the cache system** in the *Cache Management* tab in the Options dialog box (**Tools>Options> Infrastructure>Product Structure**). Exit and restart CATIA.

- Clear the **Load referenced documents** option in the *General* tab in the Options dialog box (**Tools>Options> General**) to open assemblies without loading their components. Doing so improves file load times, reduces RAM usage, and improves graphical performance. An unloaded component is completely removed from memory and is not displayed in either the assembly or assembly drawing.

- Use the **Do not activate default shape** option in the *Product Visualization* tab in the Options dialog box (**Tools>Options> Infrastructure>Product Structure**) to reduce the information that is loaded when opening an assembly. When this option is selected, all components are deactivated until they are specifically activated. Using this option improves file load time, reduces RAM usage, and improves graphical performance. Although deactivation temporarily removes the model from the assembly, the model still displays in a drawing of the assembly. The system keeps a representation of the model in memory, which is used to create drawing views.

- Scenes enable you to save the various view setting configurations of your product model for reuse. You can quickly switch between scenes and view settings without having to manually configure them each time they are required. Consider using scenes to deactivate components in an assembly that do not need to be displayed for tasks and views that you require frequently.

- Use the **3D Accuracy** option in the *Performance* tab (**Tools>Options>General>Display**) to improve graphical performance. A higher number results in fewer tessellated triangles being generated. This improves graphical performance, but the quality of the model is diminished. For best performance, keep this number as high as possible. An assembly with the 3D Accuracy set to 0.01 (the minimum value) is shown on the left in Figure 8–11. The same assembly with the 3D Accuracy set to 10 (the maximum value) is shown on the right.

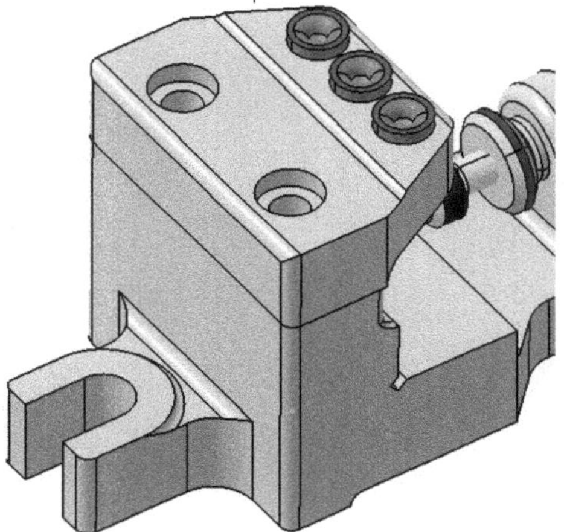

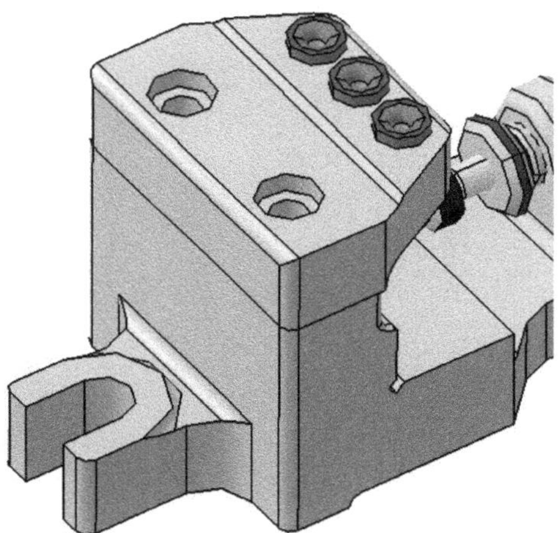

Figure 8–11

- Use the **Level of Detail** and **Pixel Culling** options in the *Performance* tab (**Tools>Options>General>Display**) to control the level of detail and pixel size of the displayed objects. To improve performance when moving a model, increase the **While Moving** value for the **Level of Detail** and **Pixel Culling** options. These options control the detail and pixel size of the model when it is being moved. For large, detailed models, increasing the value of these options can greatly help graphical performance when manipulating the model.

Create Assembly Variants if you have multiple simplified components. This enables you to quickly switch between your full assembly and simplified assembly(ies).

- Consider creating simplified versions of complex components and displaying them when the complex version is not required. Working with simplified geometry can improve graphical and RAM performance, and reduce update times. Figure 8–12 shows an example of an assembly using a simplified component.

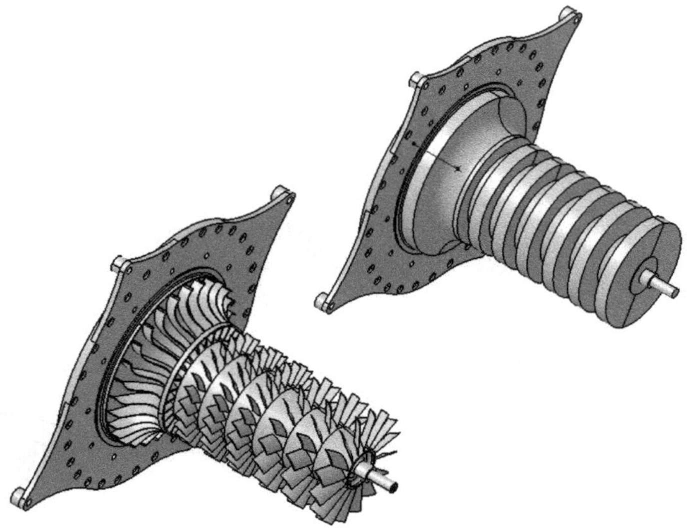

Figure 8–12

How To: Replace a Complex Component with a Simplified Version

1. Publish any element in both the simplified and the standard components that are referenced in the assembly (e.g., for constraint creation). Create reference elements to facilitate publication if required. Use the same name for the publication in both components.
2. To replace a component, select the component to be replaced, right-click and select **Components>Replace Component** or **Components>Replace Component in Session**.

Practice 8a

Working with Cache I

Practice Objectives

- Work with the cache system.
- Switch between Visualization and Design mode.

In this practice, you will work with the cache system and toggle between **Visualization** and **Design** modes to make changes to a part.

Task 1 - Open an assembly file.

1. Select **Tools>Options**. Select the *General* tab and ensure that the **Load referenced documents** option is selected.
2. Open **Engine.CATProduct** from the *Engine>Cache* directory. Note the time that it takes to load the assembly. The assembly displays as shown in Figure 8–13.

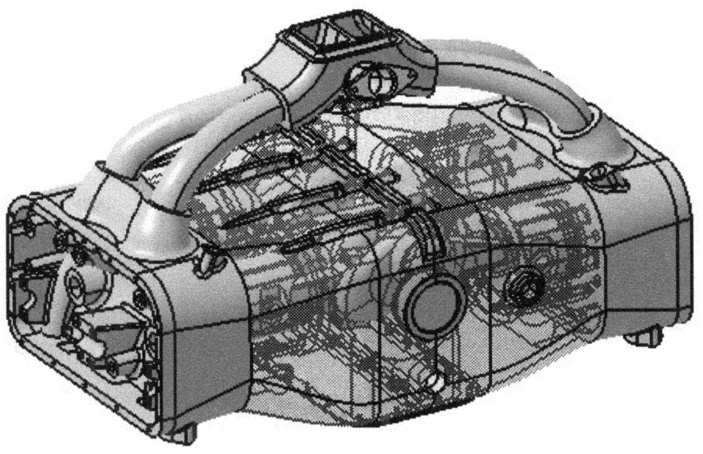

[
Figure 8–13

3. Close the assembly.

Task 2 - Activate the cache system.

1. Select **Tools>Options>Infrastructure>Product Structure** and select the *Cache Management* tab, as shown in Figure 8–14.

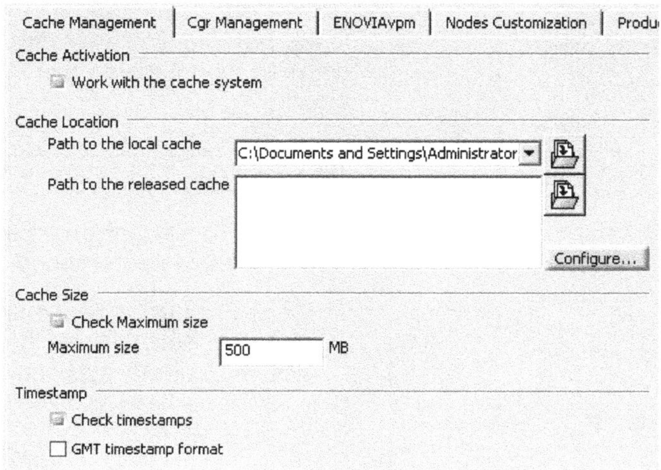

Figure 8–14

2. Select **Work with the cache system**, as shown in Figure 8–15.

Figure 8–15

3. Close the Warning dialog box.
4. Click **OK**. Exit and restart CATIA.

Task 3 - Open an assembly.

1. Open **Engine.CATProduct** from the *Engine>Cache* directory.

2. Note that it takes less time to open the model.

   You might need to close and reopen the model again to see the performance increase. The first time a model is opened using the Cache system, CGR files must be created. The next time, the model is opened, CATIA will be able to load the existing CGR files.

3. Zoom in on the **1801** part (**IntakeManifold**) and hover the cursor over the geometry as shown in Figure 8–16. The surfaces are tessellated.

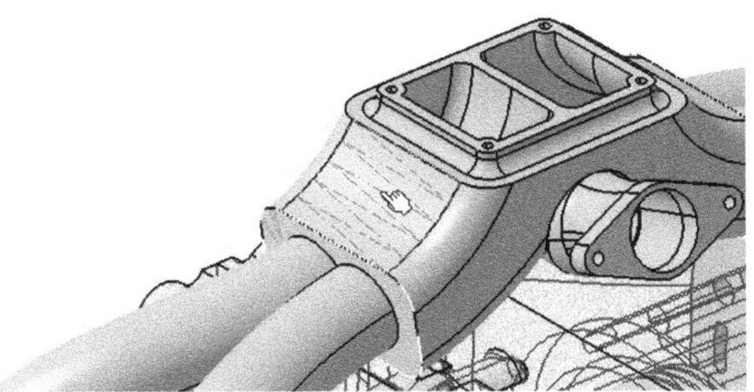

Figure 8–16

4. In the specification tree, note that when the **plus (+)** symbol that displays before each component is selected, it disappears as shown in Figure 8–17.

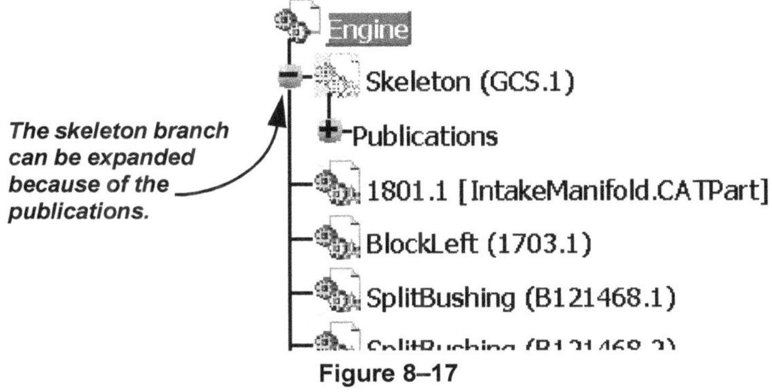

Figure 8–17

Task 4 - Switch component to Design mode.

In this task, you will make changes to a component. Components can only be modified while in Design mode.

1. In the specification tree, right-click on **IntakeManifold** and select **Representations>Design mode**.

2. **IntakeManifold** is now in **Design** mode, as shown in Figure 8–18. You can expand the **IntakeManifold** node in the specification tree to display and modify the part's features.

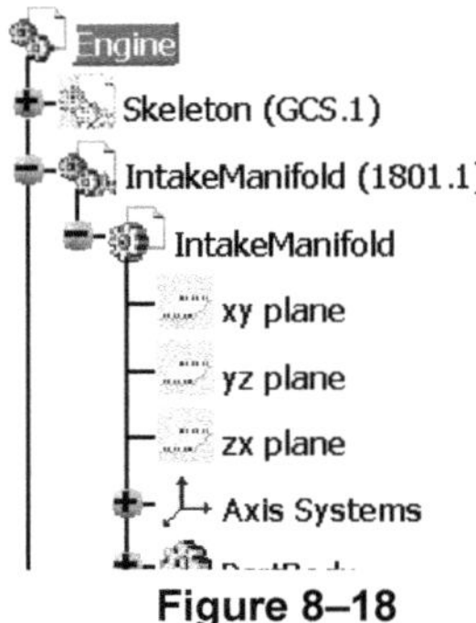

Figure 8–18

3. Activate **IntakeManifold**.

4. Right-click on **PartBody** and select **Properties**, as shown in Figure 8–19.

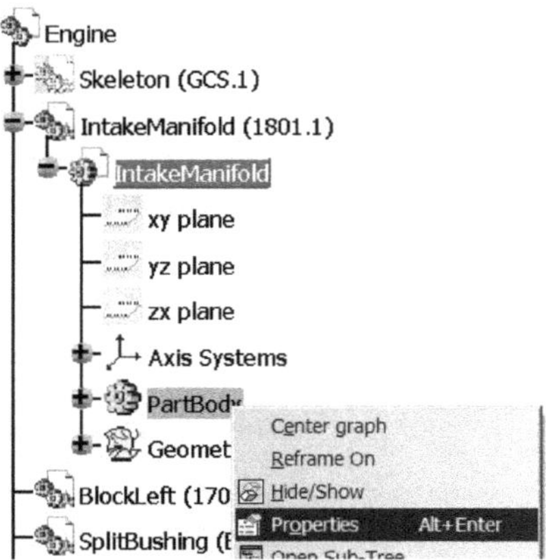

Figure 8–19

5. Select the *Graphics* tab. In the Color drop-down list, select **green** to change the Properties of **PartBody** as shown in Figure 8–20.

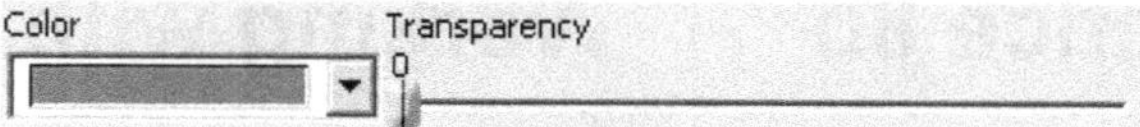

Figure 8–20

6. Save the part file.
7. Activate the top-level assembly and change **IntakeManifold** back to **Visualization** mode, as shown in Figure 8–21.

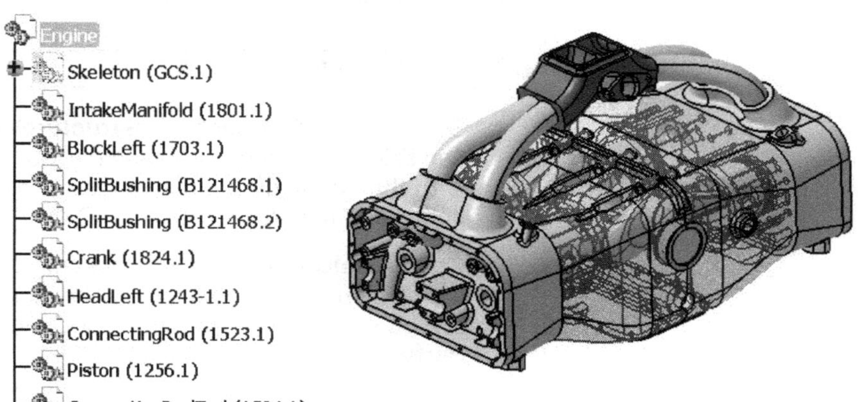

Figure 8–21

8. Save the model and close the file.

Practice 8b Working with Cache II

Practice Objectives

- Work with the cache system.
- Assemble an IGES file.
- Create features in context.

In this practice, you will work with the cache system and create a Product file in the top-level assembly.

Task 1 - Open an assembly.

1. Select **Tools>Options>Infrastructure>Product Structure** and select the *Cache Management* tab. Ensure that the **Work with the cache system** option is selected. If not, select the option and restart CATIA.

2. Open **AxialCentrifugalCompressor_Cache.CATProduct** from the *Turbine>Cache* folder. The model displays as shown in Figure 8–22 (if not all of the parts display, apply the **All Parts** scene to the assembly).

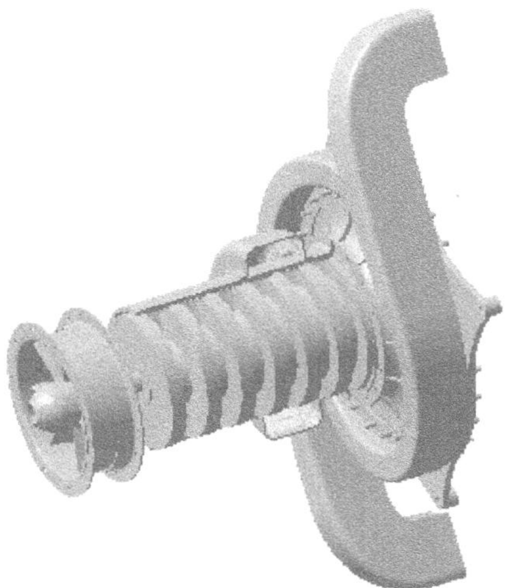

Figure 8–22

3. Click (Product) to create a product. Select **AxialCentrifugalCompressor** as the product in which to create the new Product file.

4. In the Part Number dialog box, enter **6031-1-2** as shown in Figure 8–23.

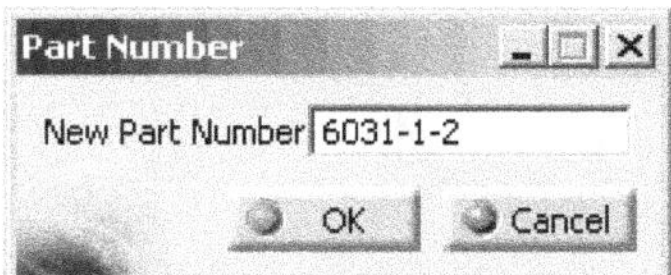

Figure 8–23

Task 2 - Assemble a component into the new product.

1. Click (Existing Component). (You might need to select **6031-1-2** as the product to assemble into.)

2. Select **1316.CATPart** in the *Turbine* folder.

3. Save the top-level assembly.

Task 3 - Change assembly management options.

1. Clear the **Work with cache system** option.

2. Exit and restart CATIA.

3. Open **AxialCentrifugalCompressor_Cache.CATProduct** from *Turbine>Cache* folder.

4. Create a new scene named **Air Bleed**.

5. Deactivate the terminal node of **AxialCentrifugalCompressor**.

6. Activate the terminal node of the **CompressorSkeleton** assembly. Also activate the **1315** and **1316** products, located under 6031-1-1 and 6031-1-2, respectively.

7. Exit the **Scene** window.

8. Apply the scene on the assembly. The model displays as shown in Figure 8–24.

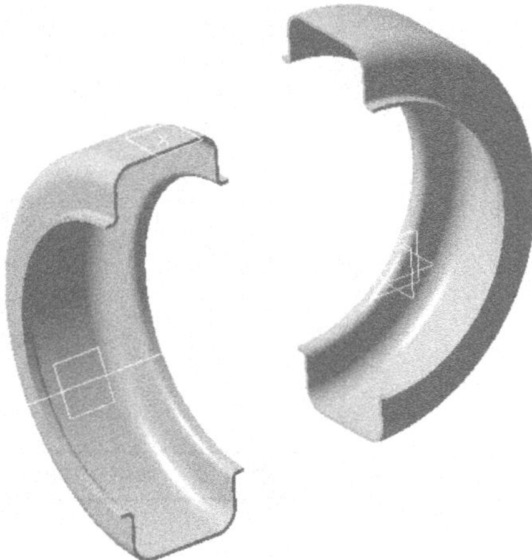

Figure 8–24

9. Snap the axes of the two parts. Orient the unconstrained part as shown in Figure 8–25, by selecting the green arrow.

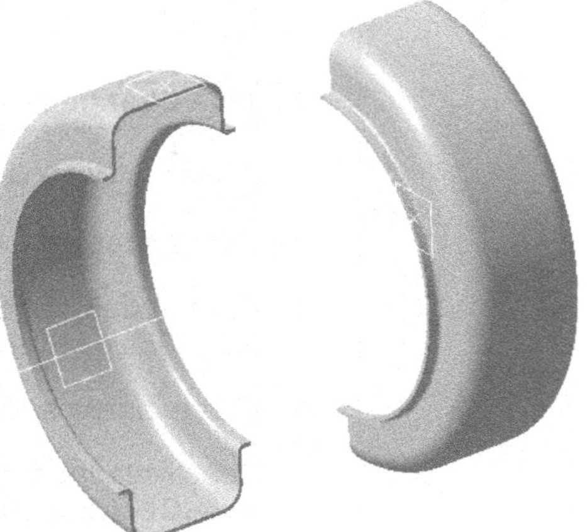

Figure 8–25

10. Snap the ZX plane of **1316** to the ZX plane of **1315**.

11. Snap the two surfaces shown in Figure 8–26.

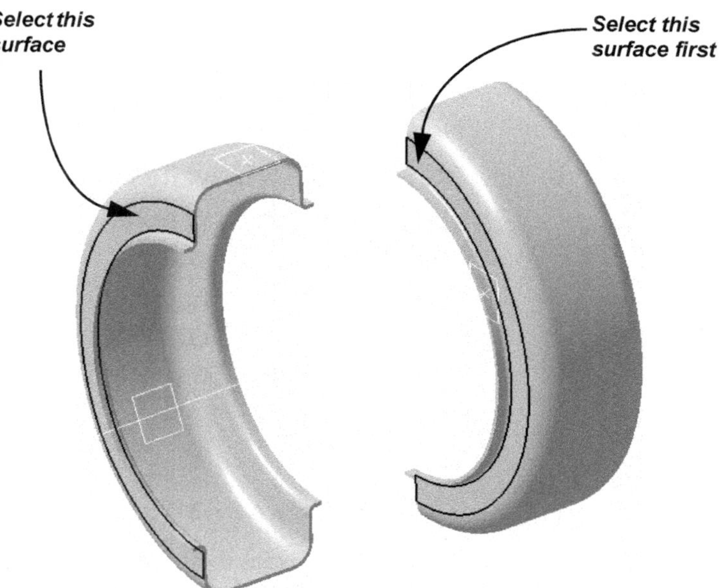

Select this surface
Select this surface first

Figure 8–26

The model displays as shown in Figure 8–27.

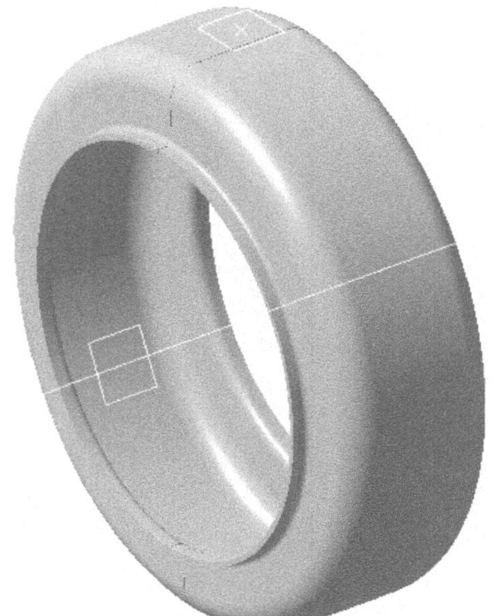

Figure 8–27

Task 4 - Assemble an IGES file.

1. Open **ABV-3185.igs** from the *Turbine* directory. The model displays as shown in Figure 8–28.

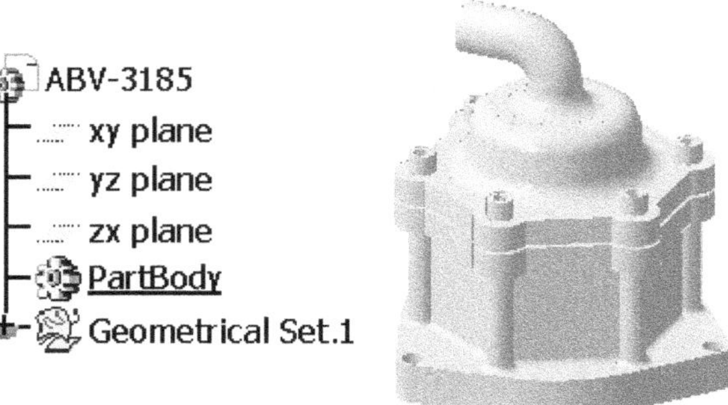

Figure 8–28

2. Copy **ABV-3185**.

3. Activate the **AxialCentrifugalCompressor_Cache** window and paste into **AxialCentrifugalCompressor**. The model displays as shown in Figure 8–29.

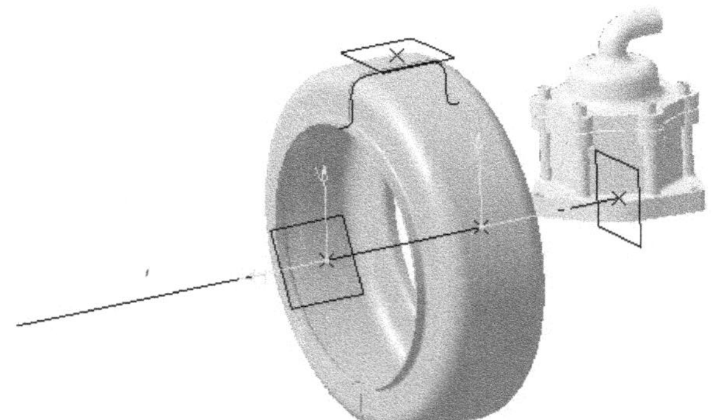

Figure 8–29

4. Constrain the surface shown in Figure 8–30 to the **AirBleed** plane of the **CompressorSkeleton**. Use the Coincidence constraint and set the *orientation* to **Same.**

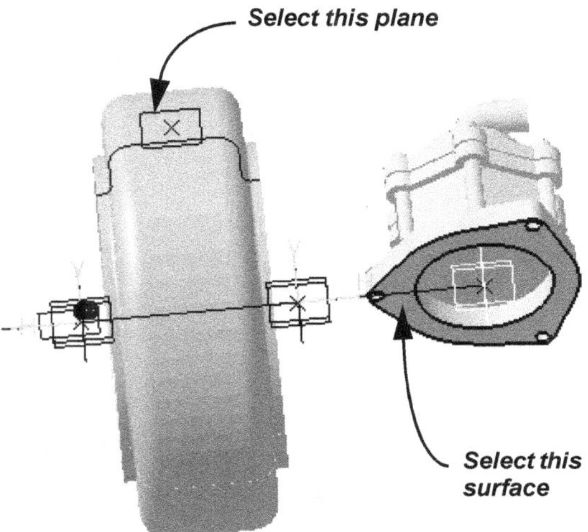

Figure 8–30

5. Click [icon].

6. Constrain the axis of **ABV-3185** to the reference point of the skeleton, as shown in Figure 8–31.

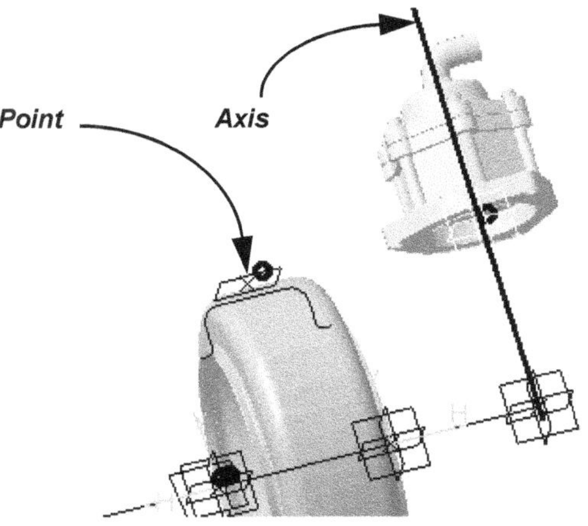

Figure 8–31

7. Click [icon].

8. Click (Isometric View).

9. Click (Angle Constraint) and select the YZ plane of the skeleton and the part surface from the IGES model shown in Figure 8–32. Specify an **Opposite** and **Parallelism** orientation.

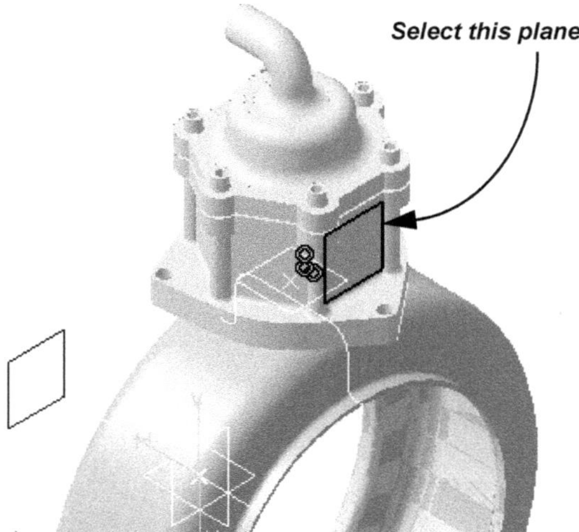

Figure 8–32

10. Update the assembly. The model displays as shown in Figure 8–33 in the Isometric view.

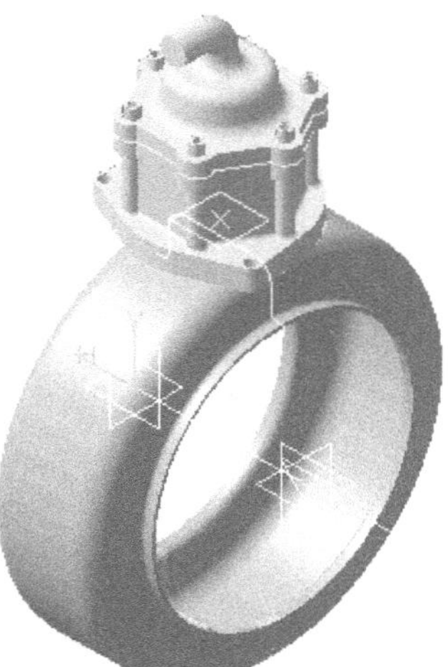

Figure 8–33

Task 5 - Modify a part in context.

1. Hide the following components using the specification tree:
   - **CompressorSkeleton**
   - **1316**
2. Orient the model to the position shown in Figure 8–34. The **Air Bleed Value** has a larger opening than the duct part (**1315**) is wide.

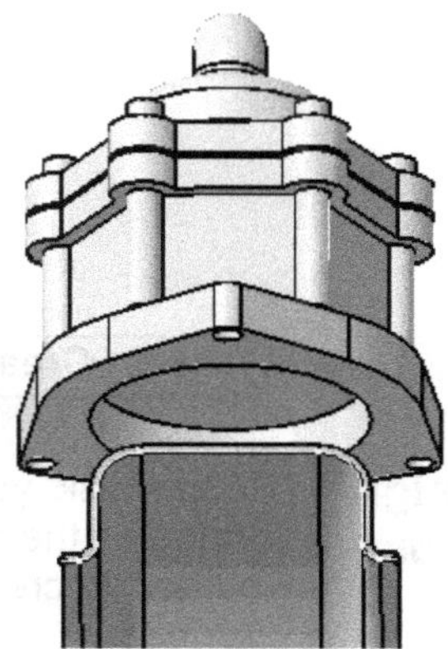

Figure 8–34

3. Activate part **1315**, and expand **Geometrical Set.2**.
4. Edit **Sketch.1** for the revolved surface feature of **1315**.
5. Change the *47.6 value* to **51.0**, as shown in Figure 8–35.

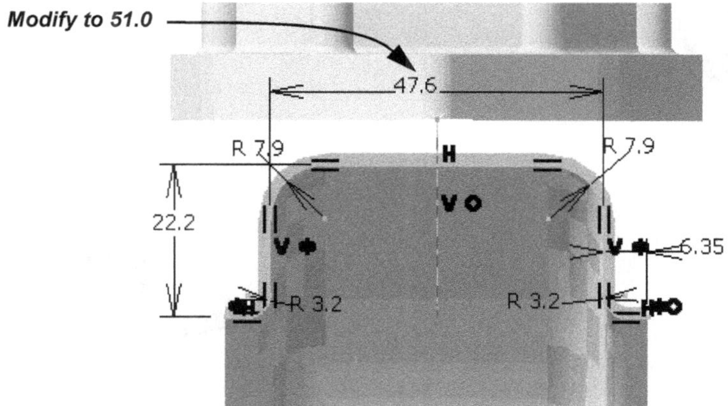

Figure 8–35

6. Exit the Sketcher workbench. The model displays as shown in Figure 8–36.

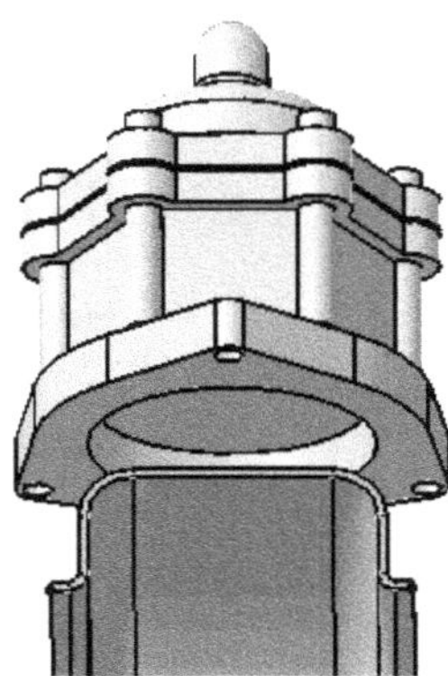

Figure 8–36

Task 6 - Create features in context.

Design Considerations

In this task, you will use the bottom surface of the **Air Bleed Value** as the profile for a Pad feature in the **1315.CATPart** model. To create this external reference, you will first publish the surface.

1. Activate part **ABV-3185**.
2. Select **Tools>Publication**.
3. Select the bottom surface of the **Air Bleed Value**, as shown in Figure 8–37.

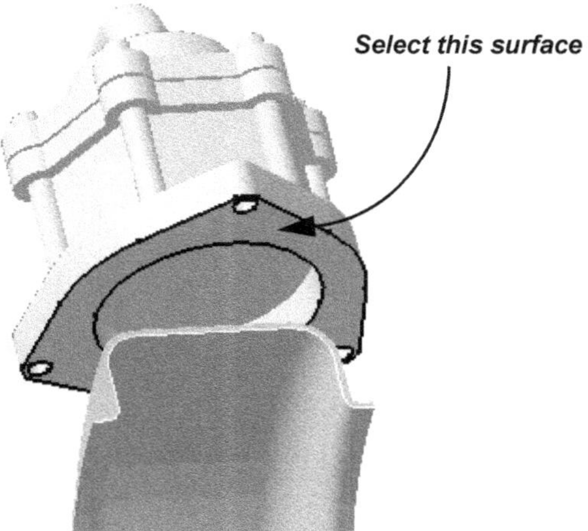

Figure 8–37

4. Change the name of the publication to **BottomSurface**, as shown in Figure 8–38.

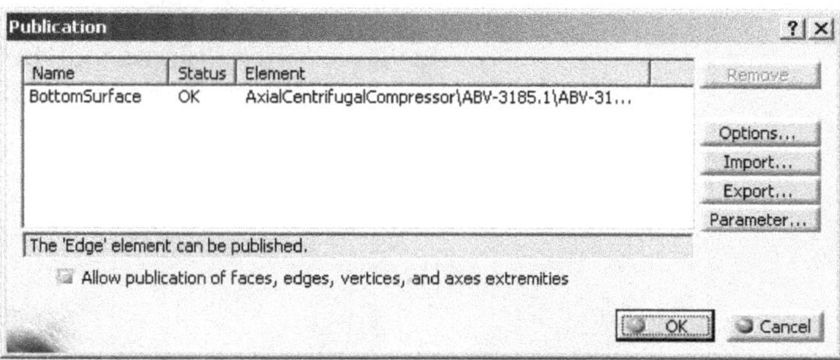

Figure 8–38

5. Click **OK** to complete the publication.
6. Activate part **1315**.
7. Activate the Wireframe and Surface workbench.

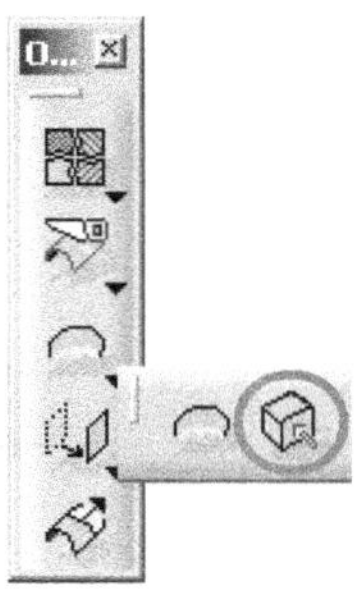

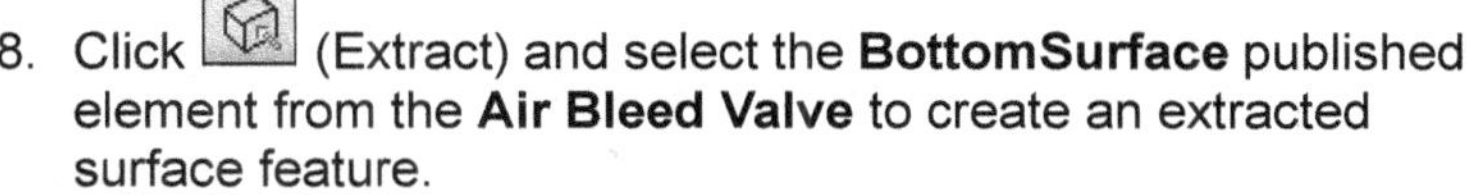

8. Click (Extract) and select the **BottomSurface** published element from the **Air Bleed Valve** to create an extracted surface feature.
9. Activate **AxialCentrifugalCompressor** and save the model.
10. In the specification tree, right-click on **1315**. Select **1315.1 object>Open in New Window**. The model displays as shown in Figure 8–39.

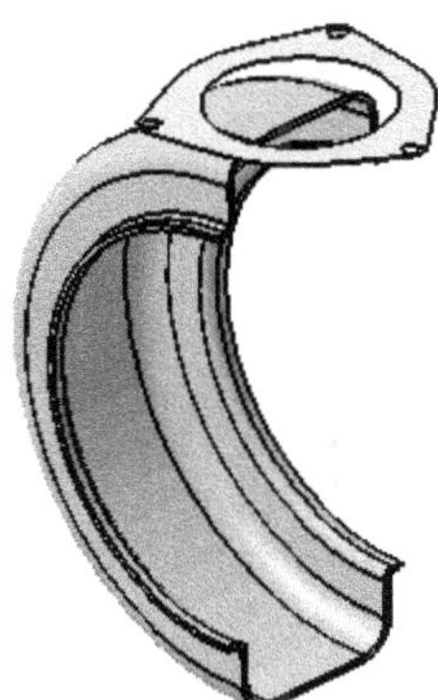

Figure 8–39

11. Hide **Sketch.1**.

12. Click (Split). Select the extract surface as the surface to cut and the ZX plane as the cutting element.

13. Click **Other Side** so that the resulting split surface is positioned over the revolved geometry.

14. Click **OK**. The model displays as shown in Figure 8–40.

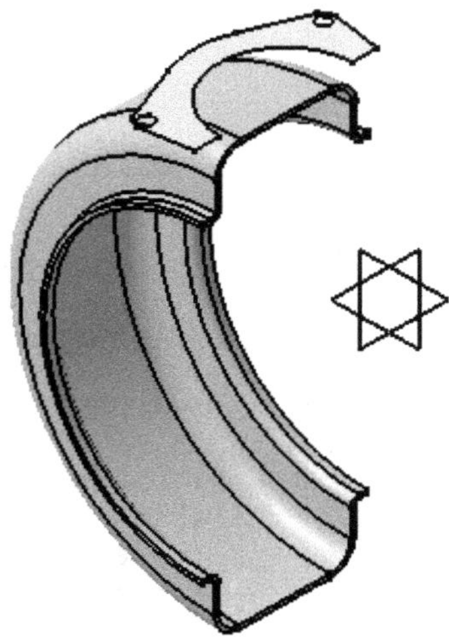

Figure 8–40

Task 7 - Create solid geometry.

1. Activate the Part Design workbench.

2. Define the **PartBody** as the work object.

3. Create a Pad and select the split surface as the profile. The system requires the selection of a directional reference when creating a Pad from an extract surface. Click **Yes** to define a direction reference.

4. Specify the XY plane as the Direction reference.

5. Fill in the Pad Definition dialog box, as shown in Figure 8–41, and complete the feature.

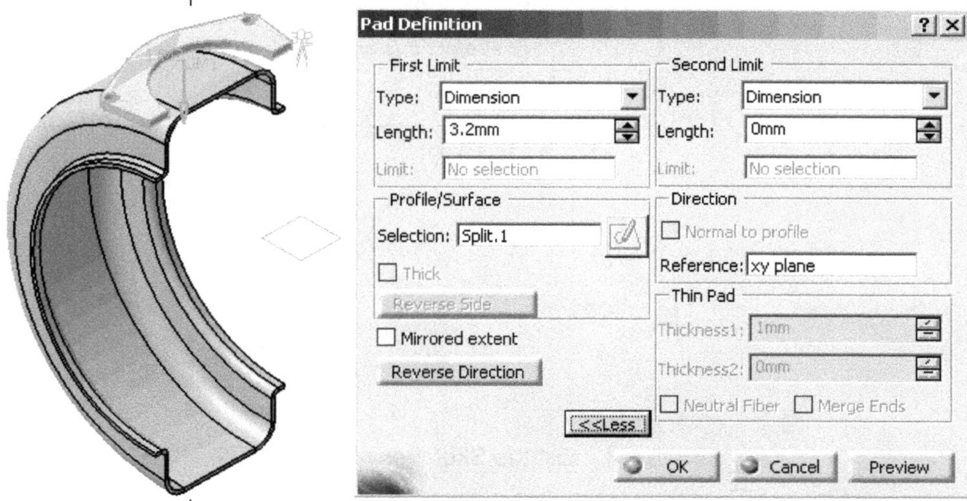

Figure 8–41

6. Create a sketch using the surface shown in Figure 8–42 as the sketch plane.

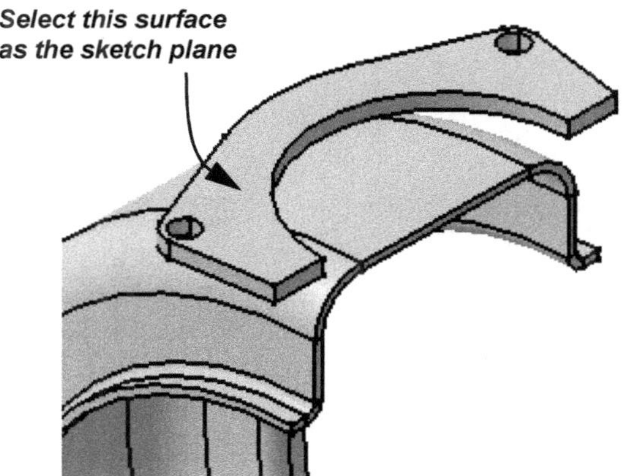

Figure 8–42

7. Click (Project 3D Elements) and select the circular edge shown in Figure 8–43.

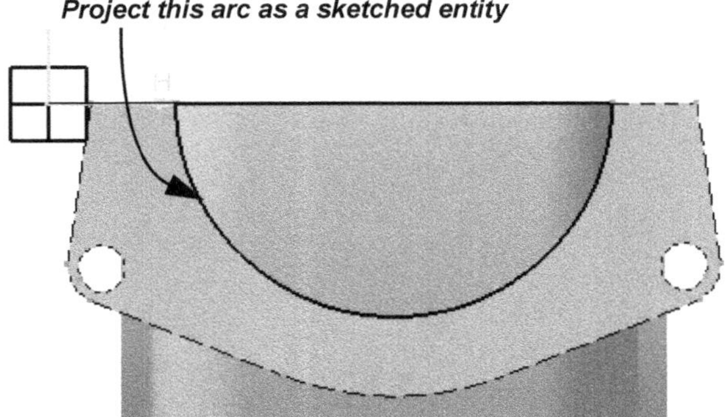

Figure 8–43

8. Exit the Sketcher workbench.

9. Create a Thick Pad up to **Revolute.1** with a *Thickness2* of **3.2**, as shown in Figure 8–44.

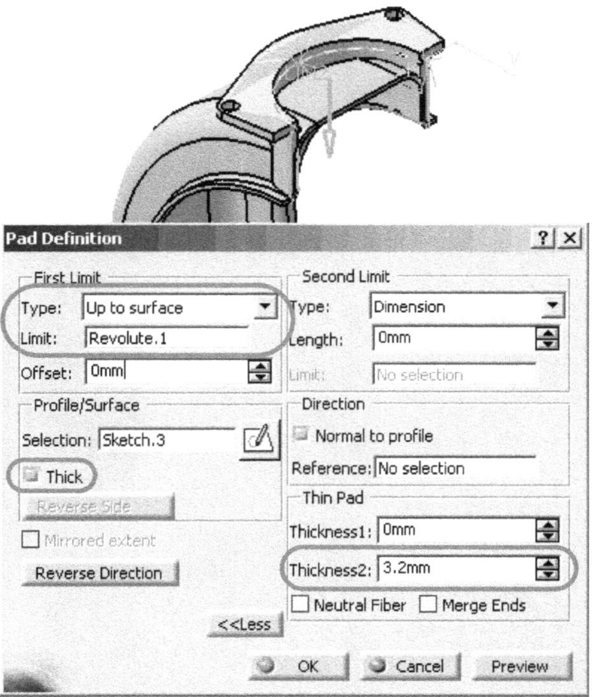

Figure 8–44

10. Create a Pocket from the same sketch using the **Up to next** depth option, as shown in Figure 8–45 and Figure 8–46.

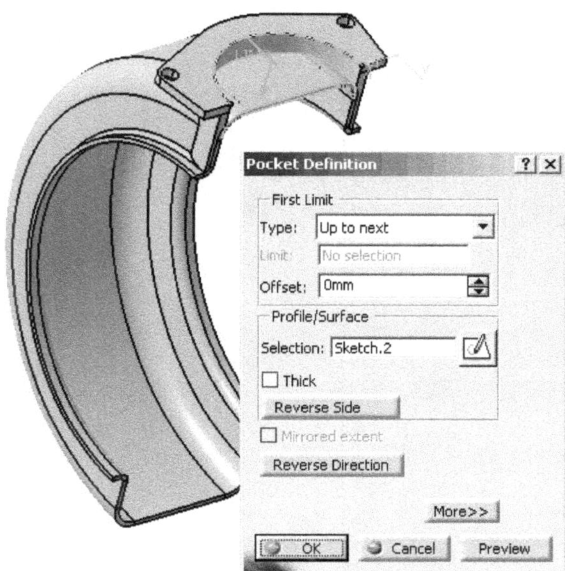

Figure 8–45

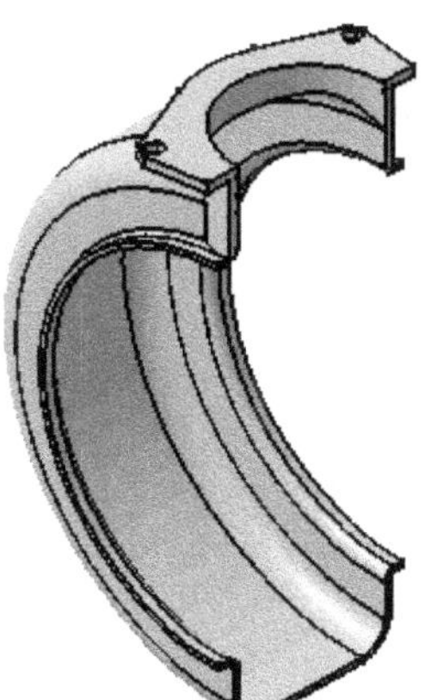

Figure 8–46

11. Save the model and close the file.

12. Display the resulting geometry in the assembly as shown in Figure 8–47.

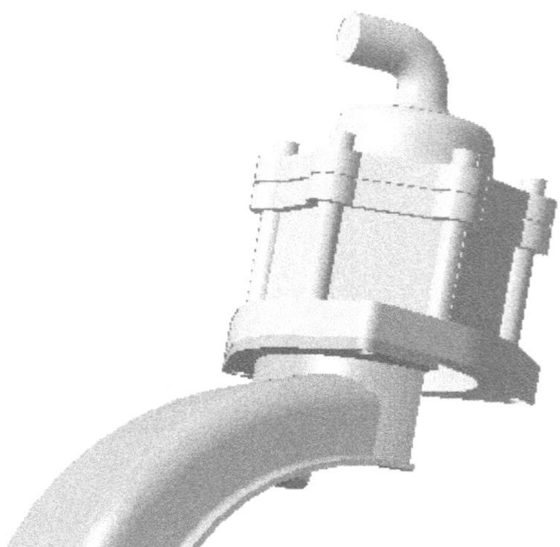

Figure 8–47

13. Save the model and close the file.

Practice 8c

Visualization and Design Modes

Practice Objectives

- Work in Visualization mode.
- Switch components to Design mode.
- Change access to geometry options.

In this practice, you will assemble a component while in **Visualization** mode. You will also practice switching components between **Visualization** and **Design** modes using different access to geometry option settings.

Task 1 - Open a Product file.

1. Select **Tools>Options>Infrastructure>Product Structure** and select the *Cache Management* tab. Select **Work with cache system**.
2. Exit and restart CATIA.
3. Open **CompressorCase_Cache.CATProduct** from the *Turbine>Cache* folder.
4. If not all of the parts display, activate terminal node of **6031-1-1**. The model displays as shown in Figure 8–48.

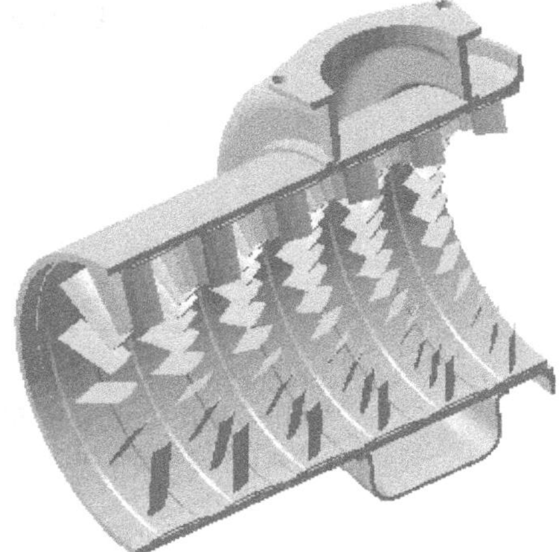

Figure 8–48

5. Assemble **1310.CATPart** from the *Turbine>Cache* folder. Drag the part to the position shown in Figure 8–49. Once repositioned, drag the compass off **1310** and select the top-level assembly in the specification tree.

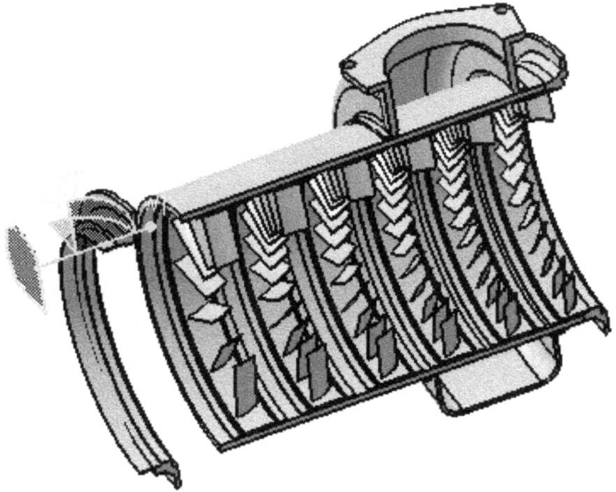

Figure 8–49

Task 2 - Change access to a geometry option.

1. Select **Tools>Options>Mechanical Design>Assembly Design**. Select the *General* tab and clear the **Automatic switch to Design mode** option, as shown in Figure 8–50.

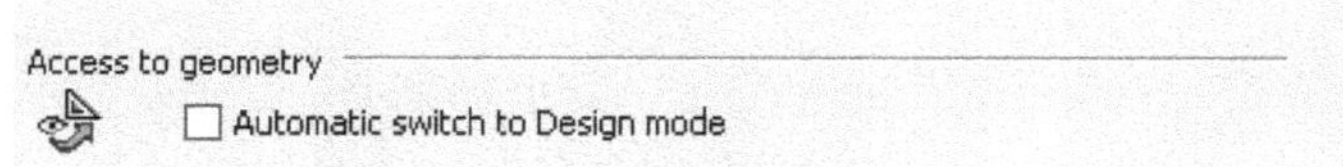

Figure 8–50

Task 3 - Set components to Design mode.

Note that most icons in the Constraints toolbar are inactive, as shown in Figure 8–51. This is because the models are in **Visualization** mode.

Figure 8–51

1. In the specification tree, right-click on **6031.1** and select **Representations>Design mode**.

2. In the specification tree, select **1310 (1310.2)** and set it to **Design** mode. The Constraints toolbar icons are now available.

3. Apply a Contact constraint as shown in Figure 8–52.

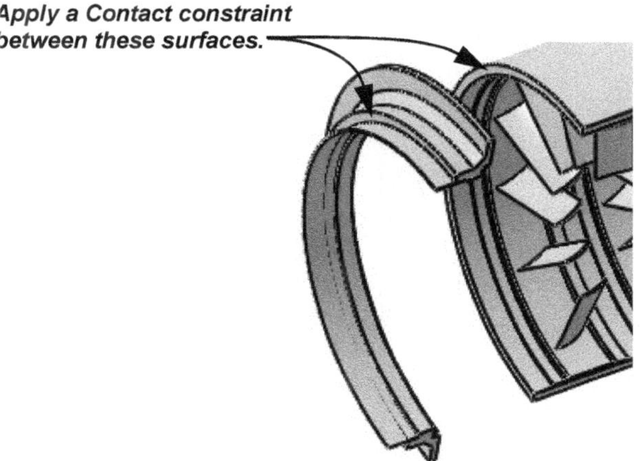

Figure 8–52

4. Click (Update All). The Update Warning box opens as shown in Figure 8–53. The system prompts you that more information is going to be loaded (increasing update time).

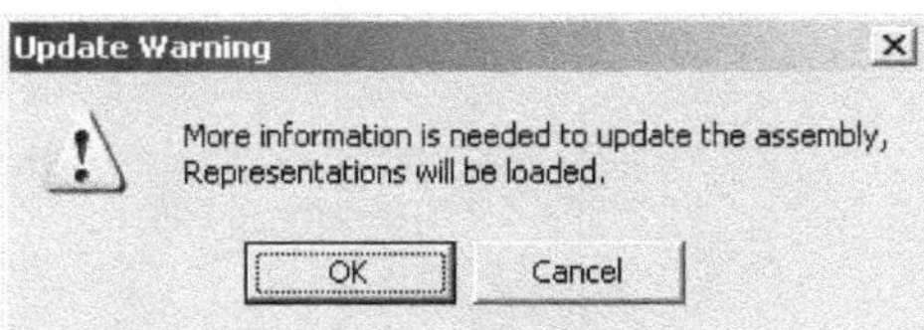

Figure 8–53

5. Click **Cancel**.

Design Considerations

displays when the constraints reference assembly components that are in **Visualization** mode. It indicates that the update status is unknown. If you were to accept the update warning CATIA would switch all components that have constraints associated with them into **Design** mode. To avoid this, a local update of just the newly created constraint can be applied.

6. In the specification tree, expand the **Constraints** branch.

7. Right-click on the last constraint (this is the Surface Contact constraint that you just created) and select **Update**, the model updates as shown in Figure 8–54.

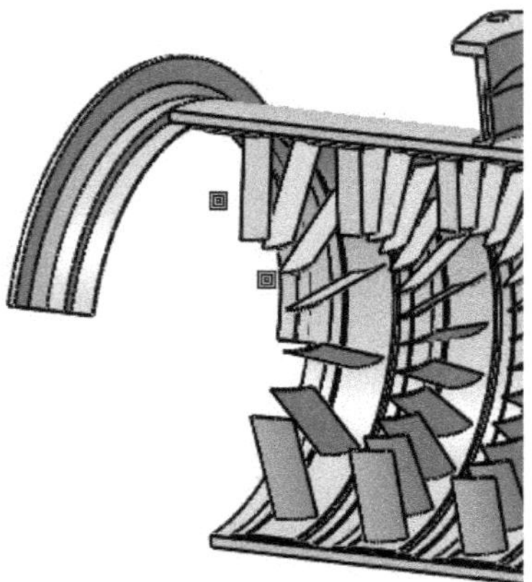

Figure 8–54

8. Set both components back to **Visualization** mode.

Task 4 - Change access to a geometry option.

1. Select **Tools>Options>Mechanical Design>Assembly Design**. In the *General* tab, select **Automatic switch to Design mode**.

2. Apply a Coincidence constraint to the surfaces shown in Figure 8–55.

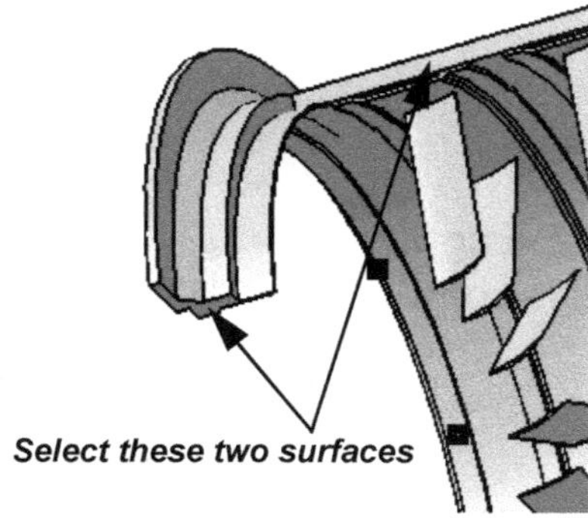

Figure 8–55

3. The Visualization symbol displays with the cursor, as shown in Figure 8–56. Select the surface. The system automatically sets the component to **Design** mode.

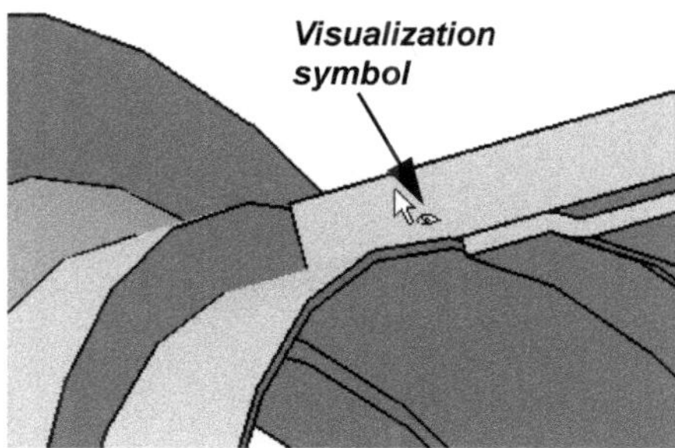

Figure 8–56

4. Select the second surface.

5. Constrain the implicit axis of both parts to fully constrain them.

6. Click (Update All) and accept the warning. The system opens all component information into session.

7. Save the model and close the file.

8. Select **Tools>Options>Infrastructure>Product Structure** and select the *Cache Management* tab. Clear the **Work with cache system** option and exit CATIA.

(Optional) Engine Project

This project is provided as additional material. Complete these optional practices if time permits during the allocated lab time. All provided models for this project can be found in the Engine directory. The units for this project are millimeters (mm). You need to save each practice after completed, because saved models are not provided. You can continue with the project at the last saved point at any time. However, please do not continue to practices relating to material not yet covered.

Learning Objective in this Chapter

- Complete an Engine assembly.

Practice 9a Engine Project

Practice Objectives

- Assemble to an axis system.
- Assemble a catalog instance.
- Control component position with a formula.

In this practice, you will create a part file to represent the global coordinate system (GCS) of a car. A coordinate system is created offset from the GCS to represent the location of the engine. You will write a formula to ensure that the crank shaft part is always centered between the bushing faces. The completed assembly is shown in Figure 9–1.

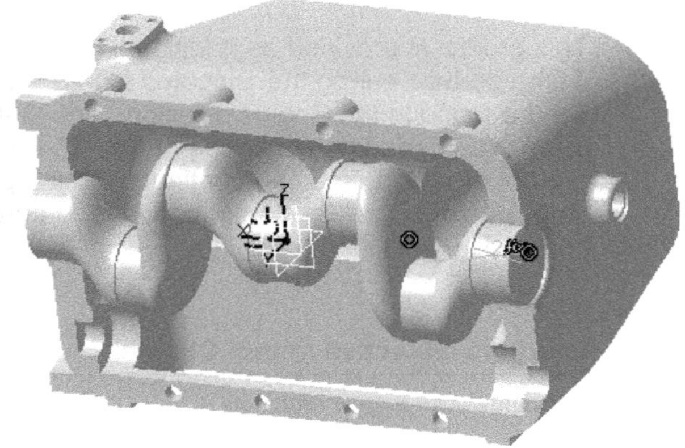

Figure 9–1

Task 1 - Create a part file.

1. Create a part file named **GCS** and set the *units* to **mm.**
2. Save the model in the *Engine* directory.

Task 2 - Create reference elements.

1. Click (Point) to create a point at (0,0,0). The Point Definition dialog box opens as shown in Figure 9–2.

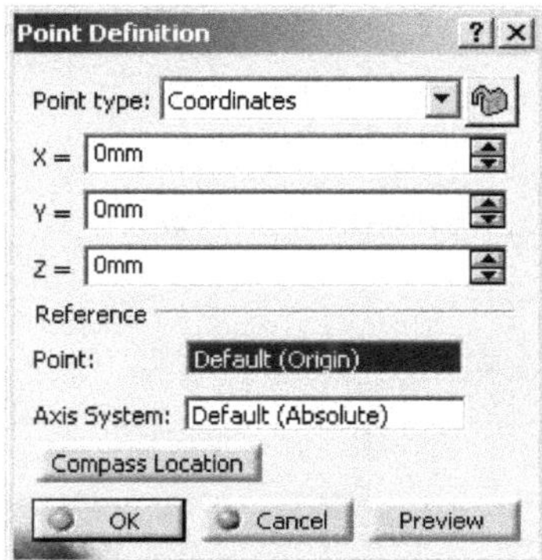

Figure 9–2

2. Ensure that **PartBody** is the work object.

3. Click (Axis System) to create an Axis System using **Point.1**. Enter the specifications shown in Figure 9–3.

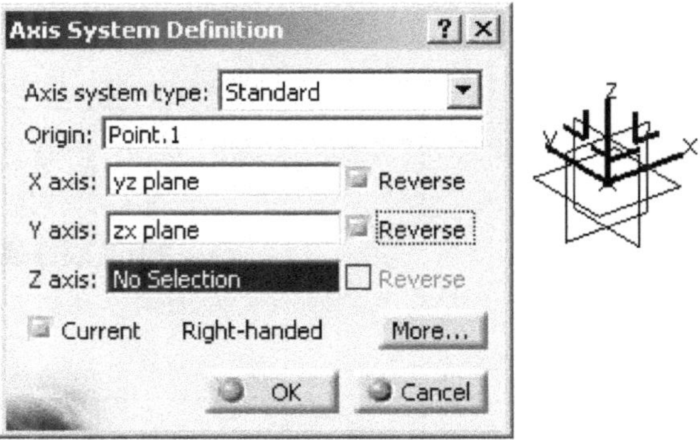

Figure 9–3

Design Considerations

When the **Reverse** option is enabled, the polarity of the resultant axis is reversed with the reference axis (e.g., the positive direction becomes negative). This effectively rotates the axis 180 degrees from the reference direction.

4. Rename the Axis System as **Global Axis System**.

5. Create a reference point by coordinates, as shown in Figure 9–4.

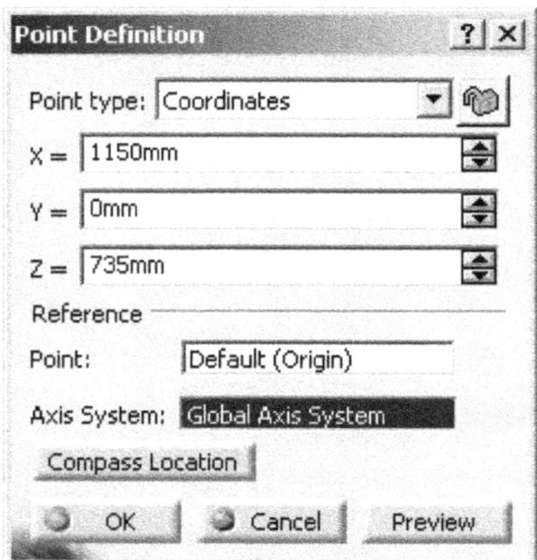

Figure 9–4

6. Ensure that **PartBody** is the work object.

7. Create an axis system using **Point.2**. Reference the Global Axis System for the orientation references, as shown in Figure 9–5.

*The **Reverse** option is not selected.*

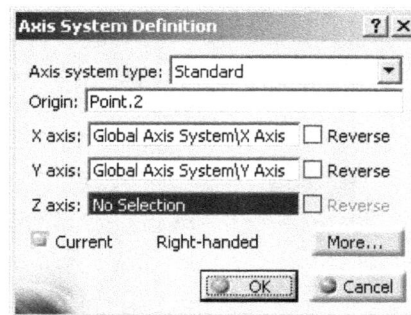

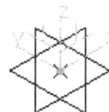

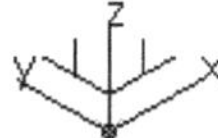

Figure 9–5

8. Rename the axis system as **Axis System Engine**.

   The specification tree opens as shown in Figure 9–6.

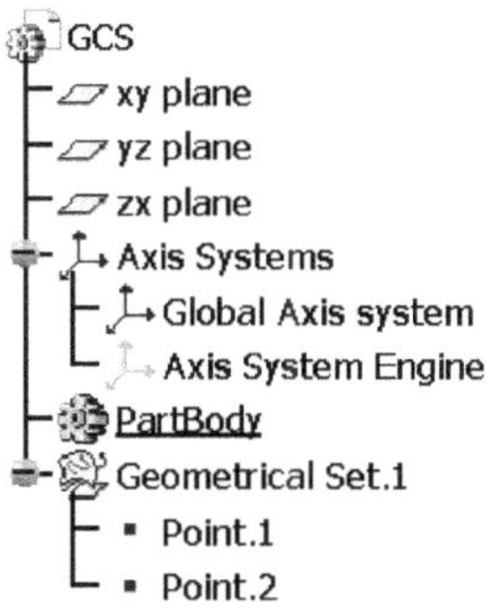

Figure 9–6

9. Save the model and close the file.

Task 3 - Create a Product file.

1. Create a new Product file. Rename the part number as **Engine**.
2. Save the product with the default name of **Engine** in the *Engine* directory.

Task 4 - Assemble a part file.

1. Assemble **GCS.CATPart** into the Engine product.
2. Apply a Fix constraint. The model displays as shown in Figure 9–7.

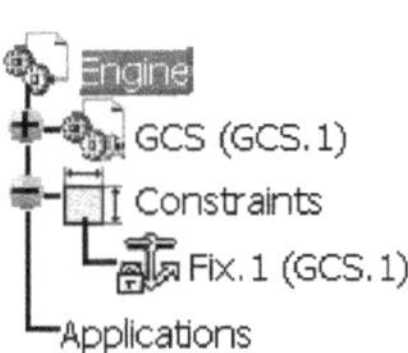

Figure 9–7

3. Assemble **BlockLeft**.

4. You must reset the snap settings for the compass. Right-click on the red box and select **Snap Automatically to Selected Object**.

5. In the specification tree, select **1703** and drag the model toward the Axis System Engine, as shown in Figure 9–8.

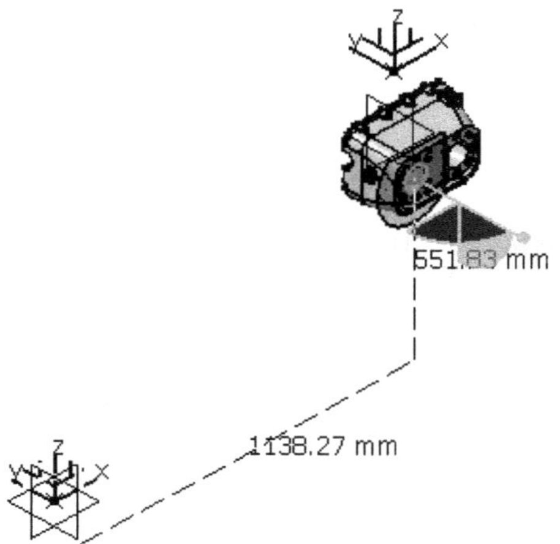

Figure 9–8

6. Move the compass off **BlockLeft**.

7. Create three Coincidence constraints using the information listed in the table below. By constraining a reference plane to each axis of the **Axis System Engine**, the **BlockLeft** model is completely constrained in 3D space.

Item	Selection from Axis System Engine	Selection from BlockLeft (Part Number 1703)
1	X-Axis of Axis System Engine	ZX plane
2	Y-Axis of Axis System Engine	XY plane
3	Z-Axis of Axis System Engine	YZ plane

8. Update the assembly. The model displays as shown in Figure 9–9.

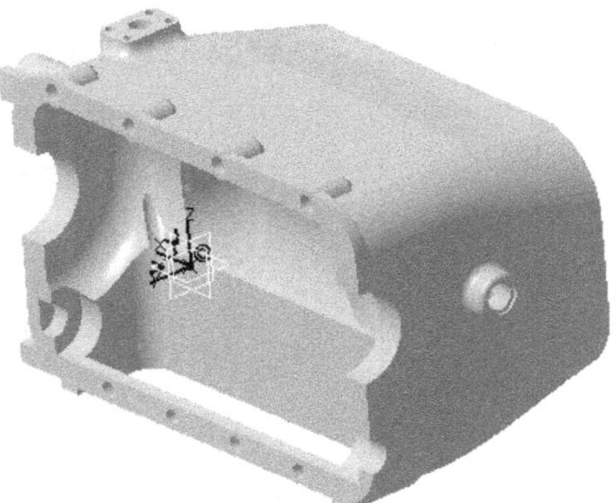

Figure 9–9

Task 5 - Assemble a component from a catalog.

In this task, you will assemble a configuration of a split bushing model from a catalog. To select the correct configuration, you must take some measurements from **BlockLeft**.

1. In the Measure toolbar, click [icon] and select the cylindrical surface shown in Figure 9–10.

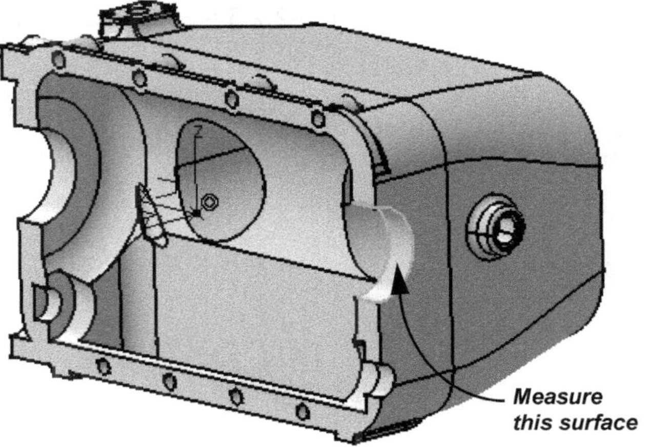

Figure 9–10

2. The surface has a diameter of 30mm. Ensure that the **Keep Measure** option is not selected and click **OK**.

3. Measure the width of the wall at the cylindrical surface, as shown in Figure 9–11. The width is 20mm.

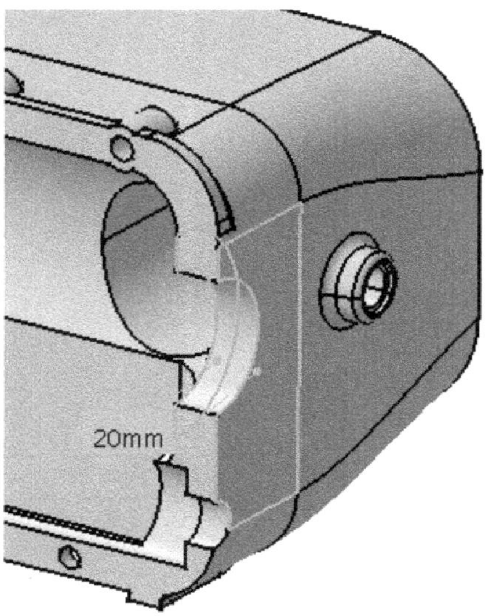

Figure 9–11

Design Considerations

The split bushing configurations are measured using the inside diameter. The thickness of the bushing is 2.5mm. Therefore, you need a configuration of the bushing with a diameter of 25mm (30-2*2.5 = 25) and a width of 20mm.

4. Click (Catalog Browser) and open **engine.catalog** from the *Engine* folder.

5. Browse to the **SplitBushing** group. The configurations of **SplitBushing** are listed at the bottom of the dialog box, as shown in Figure 9–12.

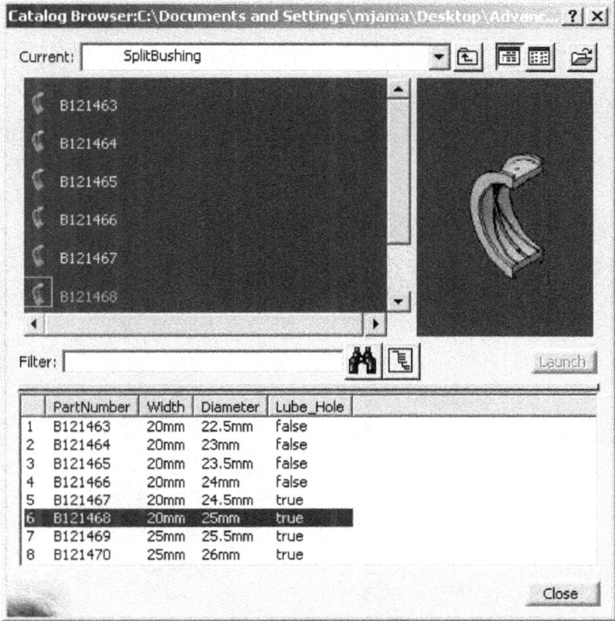

Figure 9–12

6. The part number **B121468** has the correct **Width** and **Diameter** values. Double-click on line 6 to bring the model into the assembly.

7. A **Catalog** window opens in the bottom right corner, as shown in Figure 9–13.

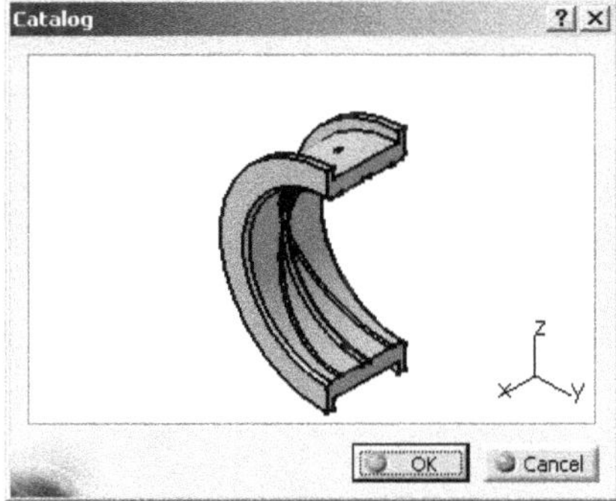

Figure 9–13

8. Confirm the selected model before adding it to the assembly. Click **OK** to add the model.

9. Close the catalog browser.

10. In the specification tree. right-click on **B121468**. Copy and paste the model into the assembly to create a second instance of the bushing.

11. Constrain the two instances of **B121463** using Coincidence, Contact, and Parallelism Angle constraints. The assembly displays as shown in Figure 9–14.

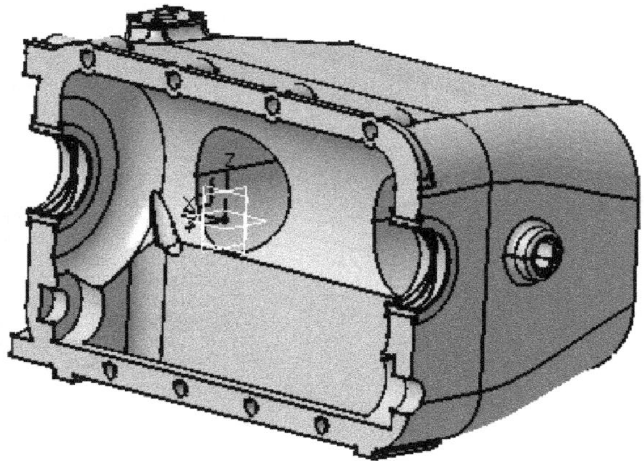

Figure 9–14

12. Assemble **Crank.CATPart** from the *Engine* directory and drag it to a location next to **BlockLeft**, as shown in Figure 9–15.

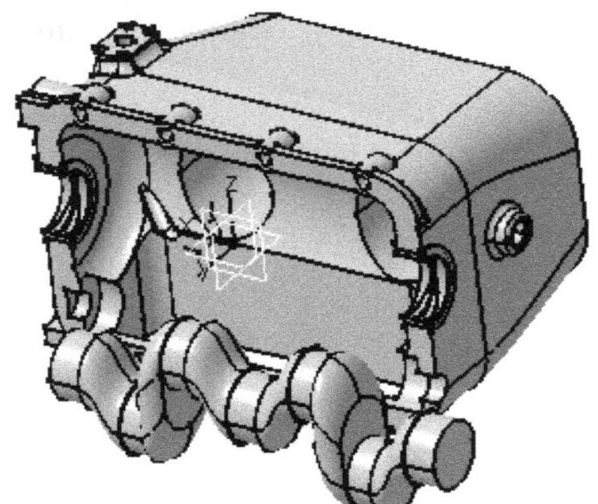

Figure 9–15

Task 6 - Create a formula to ensure that the crank remains centered.

1. Click (Measure Between).
2. Measure the distance between the inside faces of the bushings, as shown in Figure 9–16.

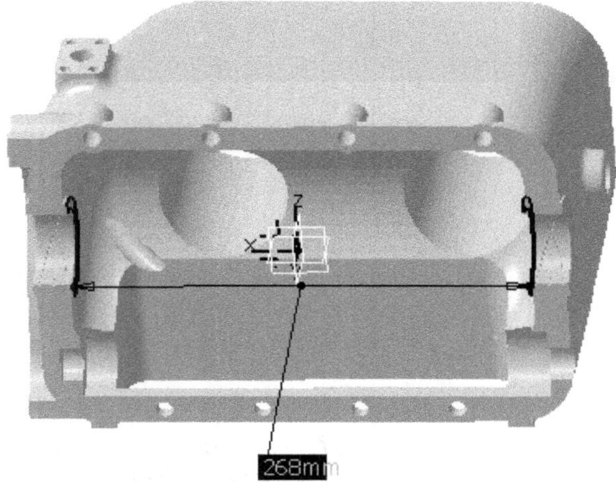

Figure 9–16

3. Select **Keep measure** to save the measurement and click **OK**.
4. Measure the distance between the outside faces of the main journal bearings of the crank, as shown in Figure 9–17. Ensure that the **Keep measure** option is selected.

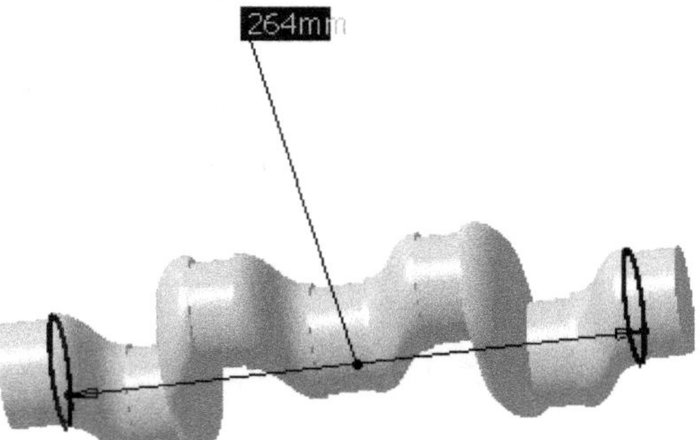

Figure 9–17

5. Hide the two measurements that were just created.
6. Apply an Offset constraint between the surfaces shown in Figure 9–18.

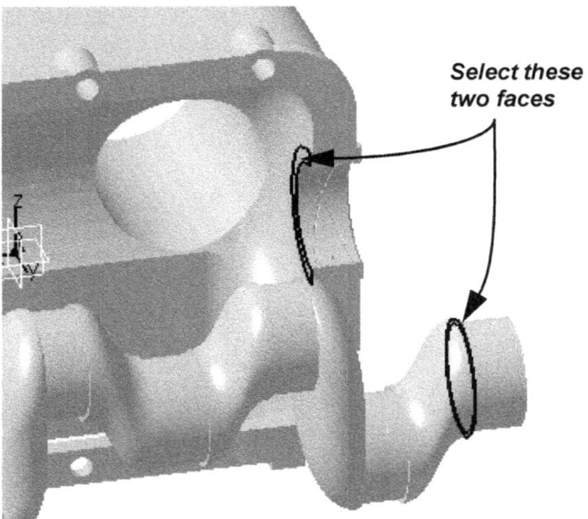

Figure 9–18

7. Right-click in the *Offset* field and select **Edit formula**, as shown in Figure 9–19.

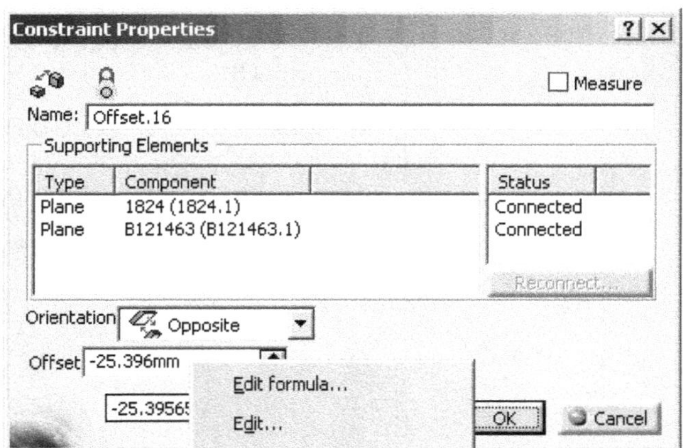

Figure 9–19

8. In the formula window, enter **(** as shown in Figure 9–20.

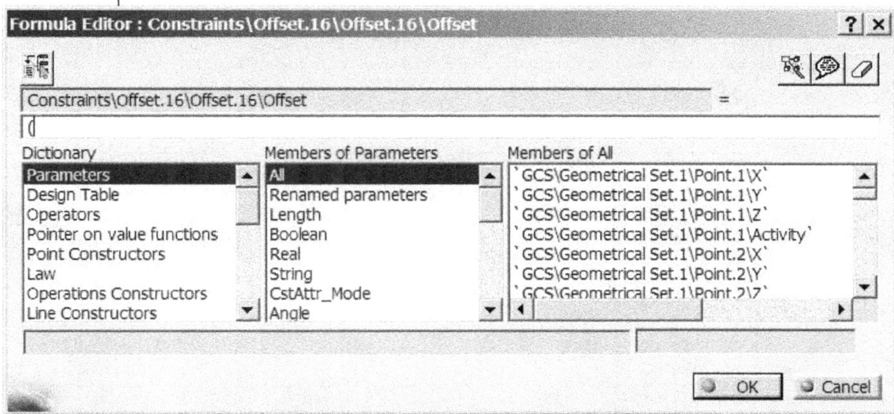

Figure 9–20

9. In the specification tree, expand **MeasureBetween.1** and double-click on the Length parameter to add it to the formula, as shown in Figure 9–21.

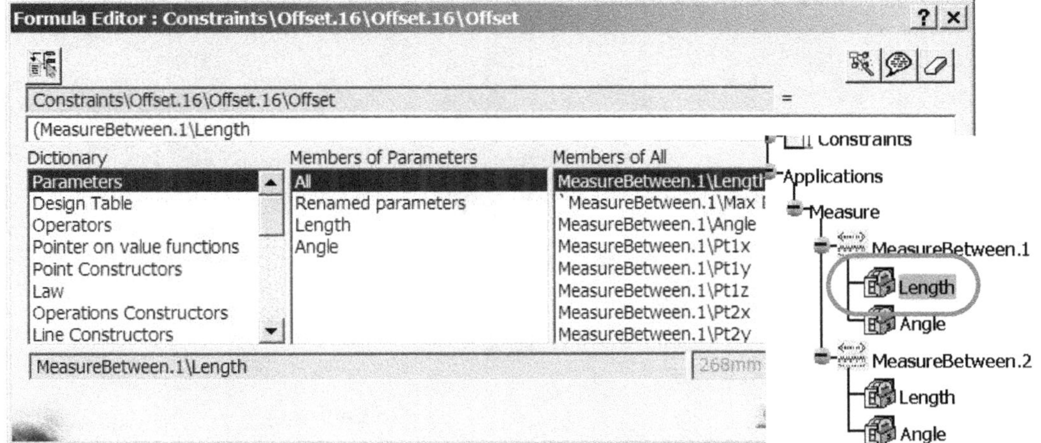

Figure 9–21

10. In the formula window, enter **-**.

11. In the specification tree, expand **MeasureBetween.2** and double-click on the Length parameter to add it to the formula.

12. Complete the formula by entering **) /2)**. The formula displays as shown in Figure 9–22.

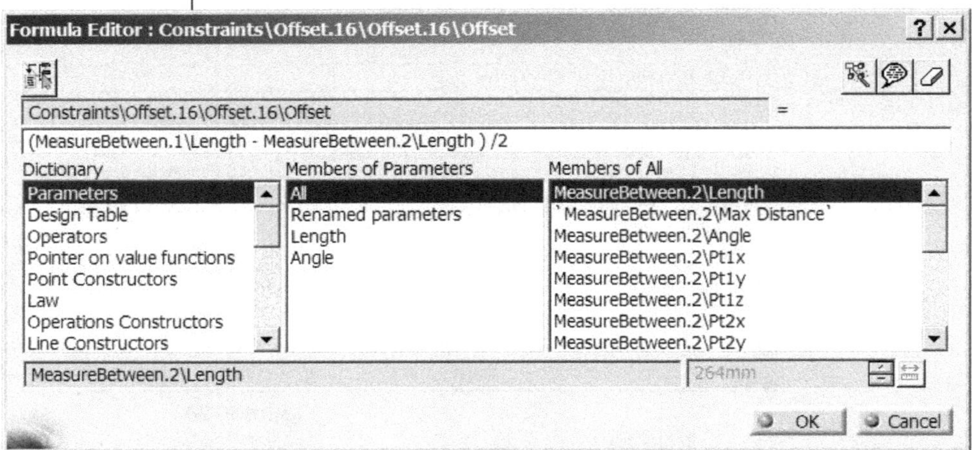

Figure 9–22

13. Constrain the axis of the **Crank** to the axis of a **Bushing**. The assembly displays as shown in Figure 9–23.

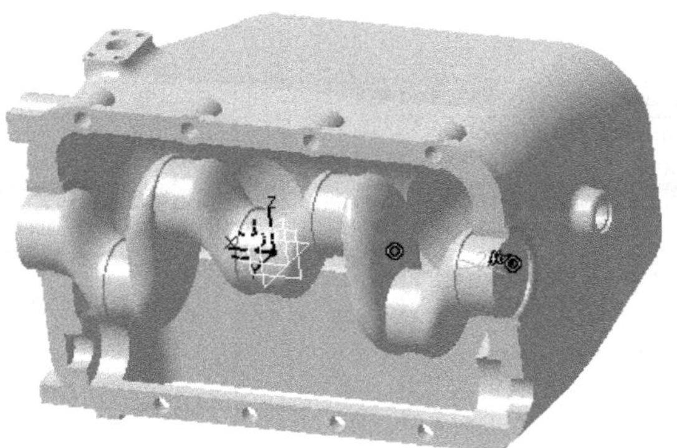

Figure 9–23

14. Save the model and close the window.

Practice 9b

Engine Project II

Practice Objective

- Create a spatial skeleton.

In this practice, you will create reference elements and a surface feature to define the volume for a part. These features are placed in the **GCS.CATPart** model created in the last practice. The model is used as the skeleton model for the **Engine.CATProduct** assembly.

Task 1 - Open GSC.CATPart.

1. Open **GCS.CATPart** from the *Engine* directory. The model mainly consists of reference geometry, as shown in Figure 9–24.

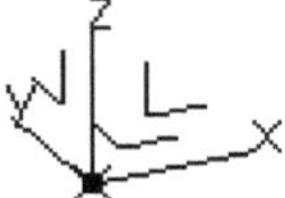

Figure 9–24

2. Set the *units* to **millimeters**.

3. Ensure sure that the **Axis System Engine** is set as current, which is identified by an orange symbol in the specification tree. If the axis system is not current, double-click on it in the specification tree and select **Current**, as shown in Figure 9–25.

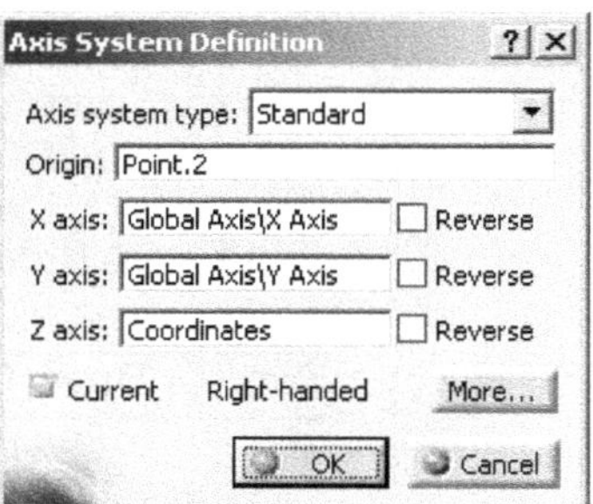

Figure 9–25

4. Create a **Coordinates** reference point offset from **Point.2** by **110** in the Z-direction, as shown in Figure 9–26.

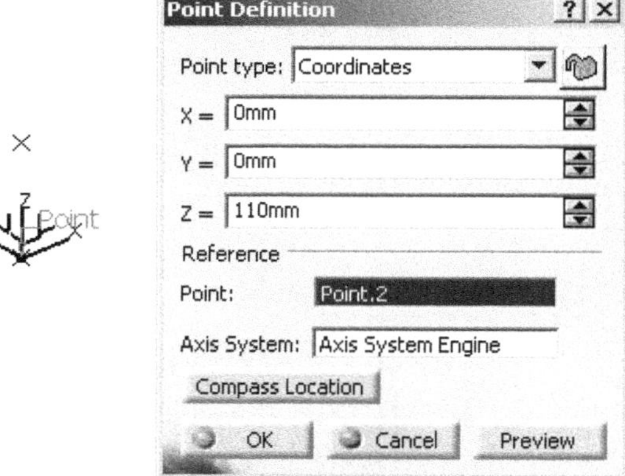

Figure 9–26

5. Create a second **Coordinates** reference point, offset from **Point.3** by **120** in the Z-direction.

6. Create two **Parallel Through Point** reference planes using **Point.3** and **Point.4**. Make the planes parallel to the XY plane, as shown in Figure 9–27.

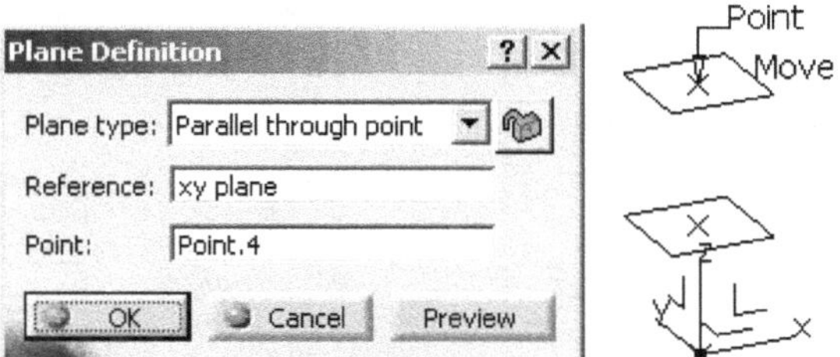

Figure 9–27

7. Rename the two reference planes as shown in Figure 9–28.

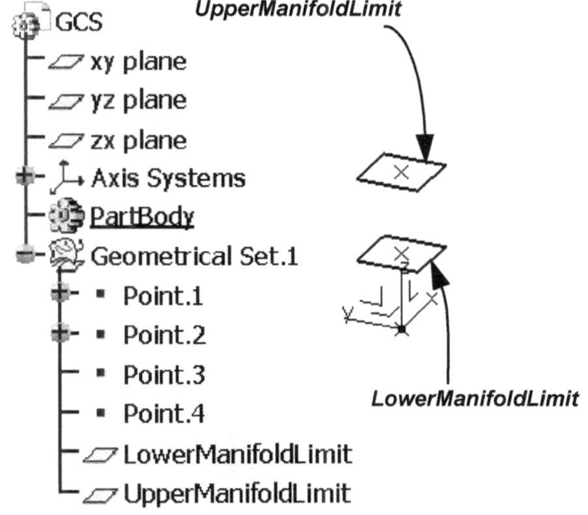

Figure 9–28

8. Double-click on Axis System Engine and clear the **Current** option.

9. Set the view to (Isometric View) and save the model.

Task 2 - Create a surface feature.

1. Select **LowerManifoldLimit** plane as the sketching plane and create the sketch shown in Figure 9–29. Add Symmetry constraints relative to the Axis System Engine.

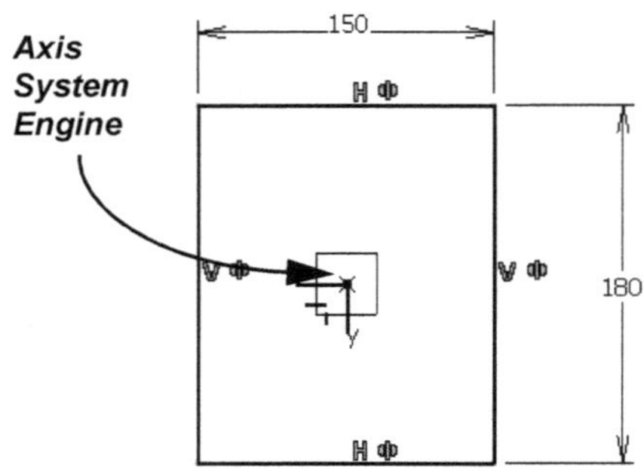

Figure 9–29

2. Activate the Wireframe and Surface workbench.

3. Click  (Extrude) to create an Extruded surface feature using the sketch created in Step 1, as shown in Figure 9–30.

Extrude the surface up to the ***UpperManifoldLimit****.*

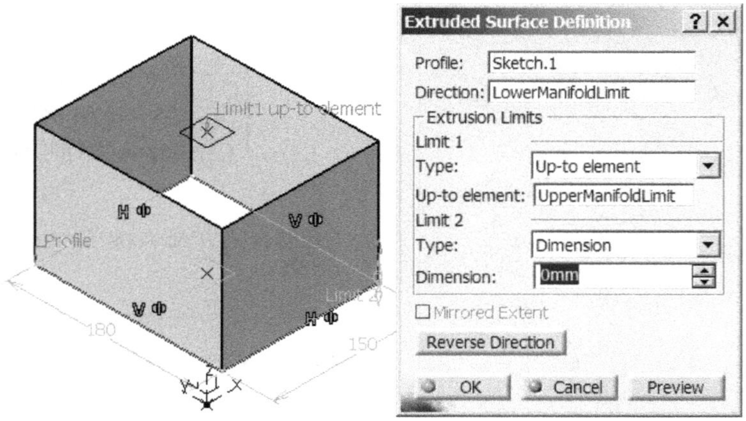

Figure 9–30

4. Rename the *Extrude.1* feature as **ManifoldSpaceClaim**.

5. Rename the part number from *GCS* to **Skeleton**.

6. Save the model and close the window.

Practice 9c

Constraints Analysis

Practice Objective

- Analyze constraints.

In this practice, you will assemble parts to a product and perform a constraints analysis.

Task 1 - Open the Engine Product file.

1. Open **Engine.CATProduct** from the *Engine* directory. The model displays as shown in Figure 9–31.

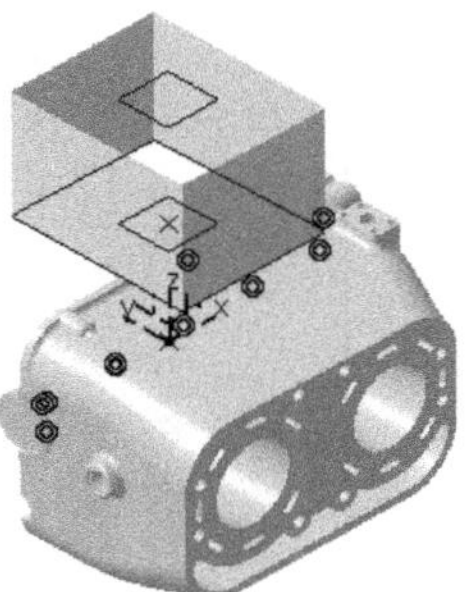

Figure 9–31

2. Set the *units* to **millimeters**.

Task 2 - Assemble IntakeManifold.CATPart.

1. Bring **IntakeManifold.CATPart** into the assembly. The model displays as shown in Figure 9–32.

Figure 9–32

2. Enable the compass by activating the **Snap Automatically to Selected Object** option.

3. In the specification tree, select **1801**. Switch to (Right View).

4. Using the compass, translate the **Intake Manifold** to a new position so that it is hidden by the **ManifoldSpaceClaim** surface, as shown in Figure 9–33.

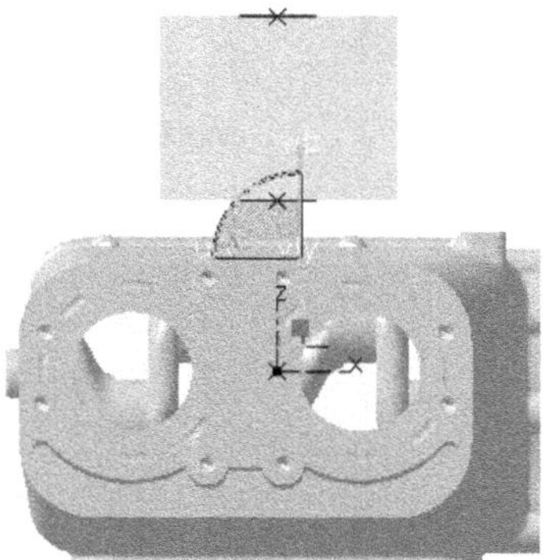

Figure 9–33

5. Switch to the (Front View) and translate the **Intake Manifold** so that it is hidden by the **ManifoldSpaceClaim** surface. This ensures that the **Intake Manifold** is positioned in the space claim surface in 3D space.

6. Return to the Isometric view. The model displays as shown in Figure 9–34.

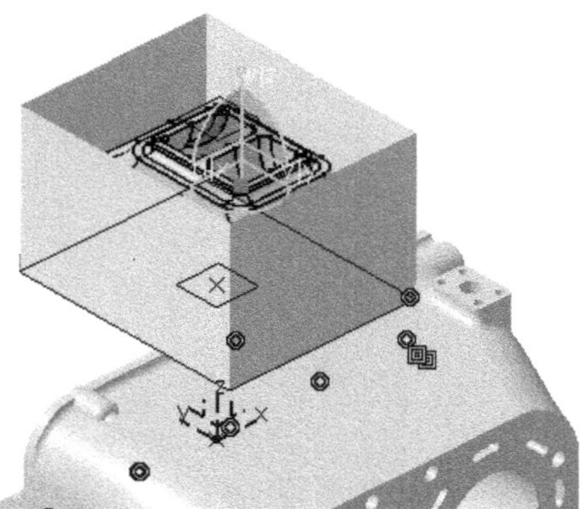

Figure 9–34

Task 3 - Change the graphic display.

1. Right-click on **ManifoldSpaceClaim** in the Skeleton part and select **Properties**. Move the Transparency slider to an approximate value of **121**, as shown in Figure 9–35.

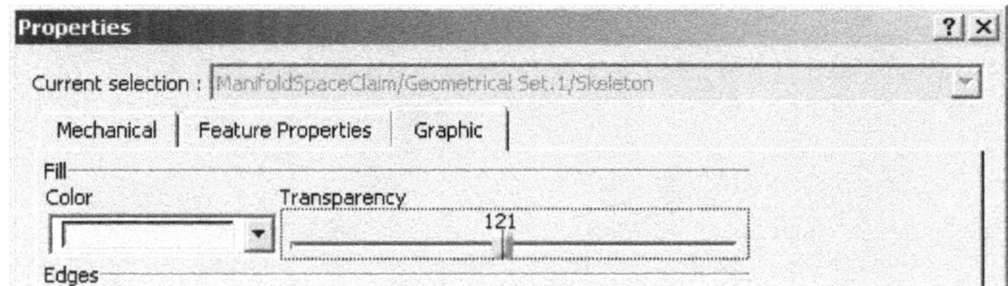

Figure 9–35

2. Click **OK**. The model displays as shown in Figure 9–36.

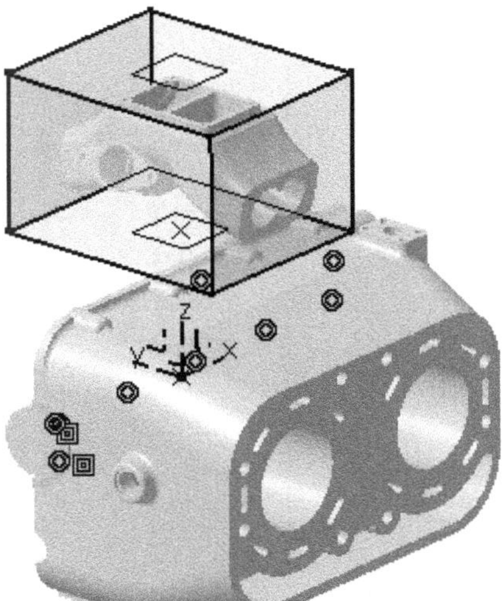

Figure 9–36

Task 4 - Assemble the cylinder head.

1. Bring **HeadLeft.CATPart** into the assembly.
2. Constrain **HeadLeft** to the **BlockLeft** component using a combination of Contact and Coincidence constraints.
3. Update the assembly and check the degrees of freedom for **HeadLeft** (1243-1) to ensure that it is fully constrained. The model displays as shown in Figure 9–37.

Figure 9–37

4. Save the model and close the window.

Practice 9d

Component Symmetry

Practice Objectives

- Copy and paste components.
- Create a component by symmetry.

In this practice, you will assemble a piston and connecting rod for the **Engine** assembly. You will instantiate multiple instances of the piston and connecting rod components. The **Cylinder Head** component for the engine assembly is identical in geometry. However, it is a one-sided component. Component symmetry is used to create a new part that is a mirror of the existing **Cylinder Head** component.

Task 1 - Open Engine.CATProduct.

1. Open **Engine.CATProduct** from the *Engine* directory.
2. Hide **1243-1**. The model displays as shown in Figure 9–38.

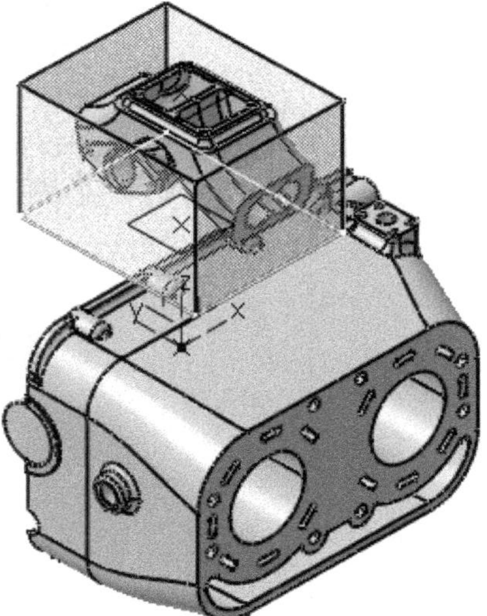

Figure 9–38

Task 2 - Assemble the connecting rod and piston components.

1. Bring **ConnectingRod.CATPart** and **Piston.CATPart** into the assembly.
2. Move the new components to the locations shown in Figure 9–39.

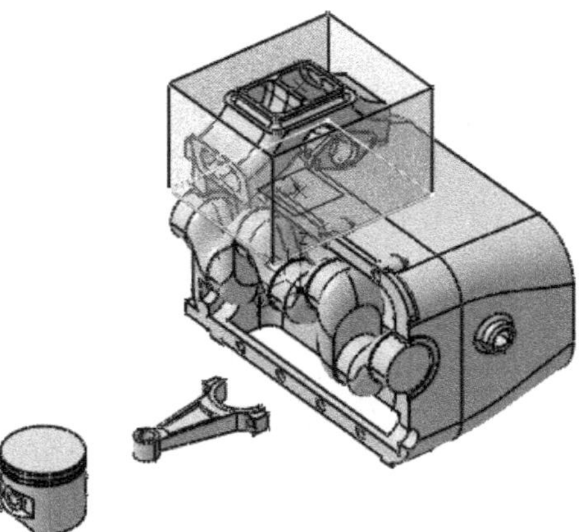

Figure 9–39

3. Add a Coincidence constraint between the **Connecting Rod** and **Crank** axis references, as shown in Figure 9–40.

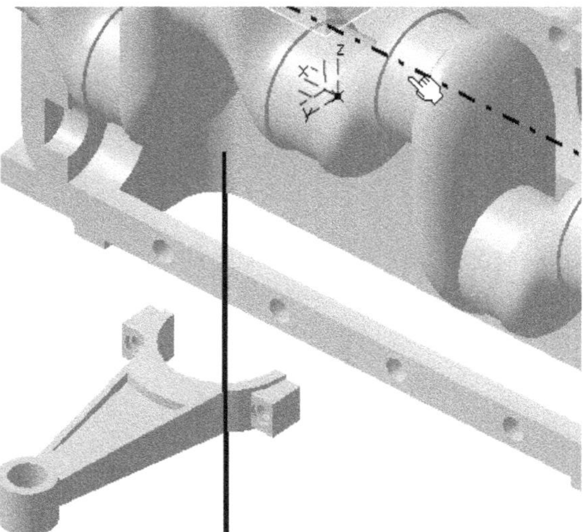

Figure 9–40

4. Create a Contact constraint using the faces shown in Figure 9–41.

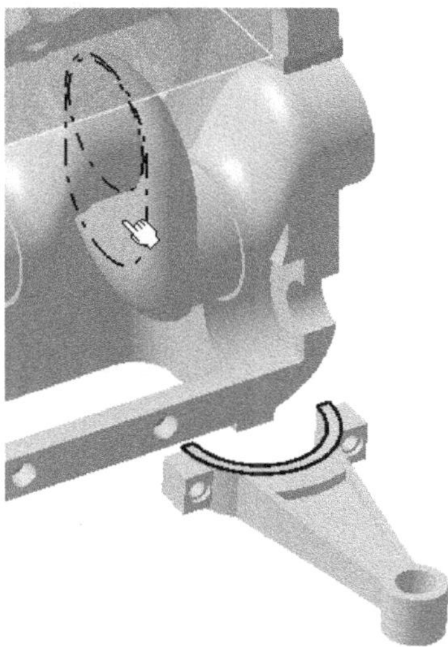

Figure 9–41

5. Update the assembly.

6. Assemble the piston to the connecting rod using a Coincidence, and a Contact constraint.

7. Create a Parallel constraint between the top face of the piston and **BlockLeft**. The assembled model displays as shown in Figure 9–42. If the model does not update correctly, move the **Connecting Rod** to a similar position and then update the assembly.

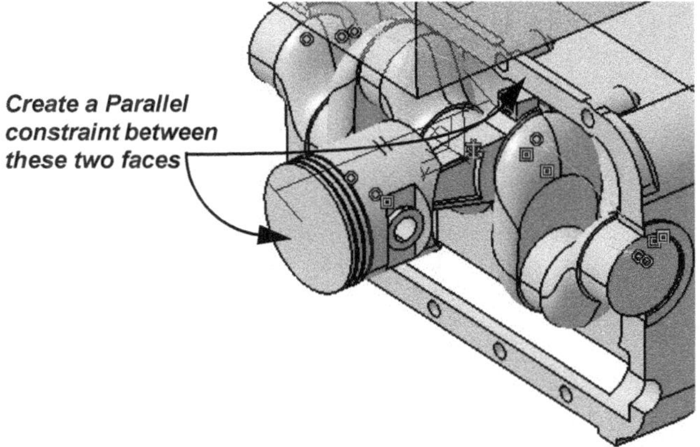

Figure 9–42

Task 3 - Set Paste options for constraints.

1. Select **Tools>Options>Mechanical Design>Assembly Design** and select the *Constraints* tab.
2. In the *Paste Components* area, select **With the assembly constraints only after a Copy**, as shown in Figure 9–43.

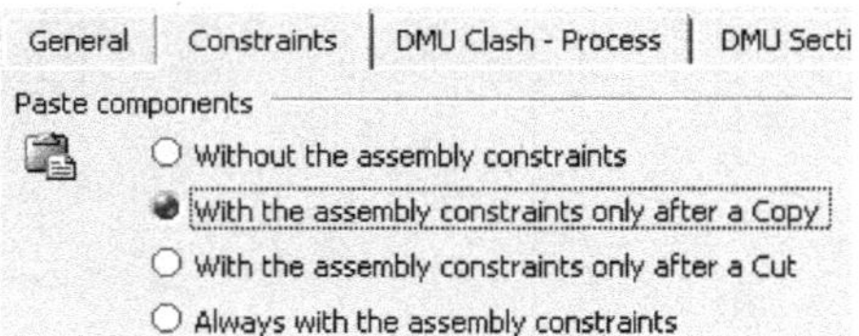

Figure 9–43

Task 4 - Copy and paste with constraints.

1. In the specification tree, use <Ctrl> to select **1523 (ConnectingRod)** and **1256 (Piston)**.
2. Copy the components.
3. Paste these models into the Engine as shown in Figure 9–44. The pasted models display on top of the copied components. The constraints were also pasted in the specification tree.

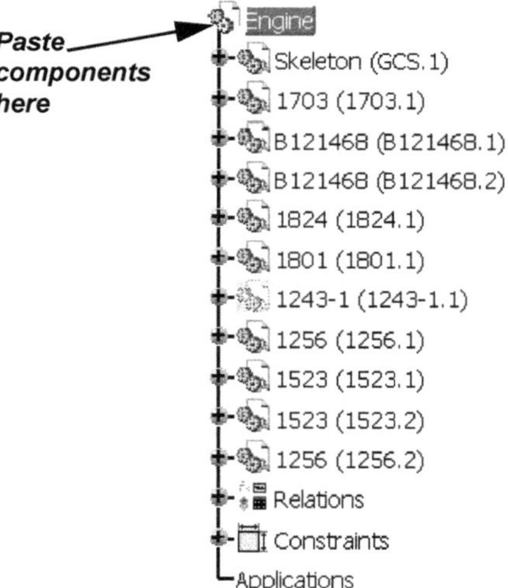

Figure 9–44

The additional five constraints have been pasted from the copied components, as shown in Figure 9–45.

The names of the constraints in your model might differ from those shown in Figure 9–45.

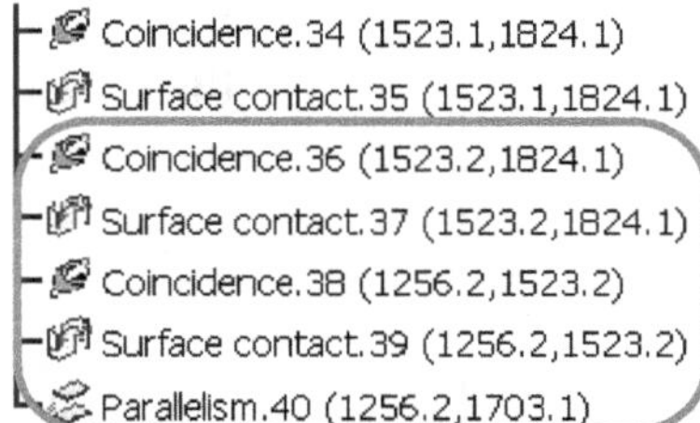

Figure 9–45

Design Considerations

Copying components and their respective constraints is a fast way of duplicating the components and constraint information. Once pasted, the duplicated constraints can be modified to reference different geometry as required.

Task 5 - Modify the pasted constraints.

The goal of this task is to adjust the pasted constraints so that the assembly displays as shown in Figure 9–46. **Skeleton**, **1703**, and **1801** have been hidden. This was done to clarify Figure 9–46 so that it shows the pasted components.

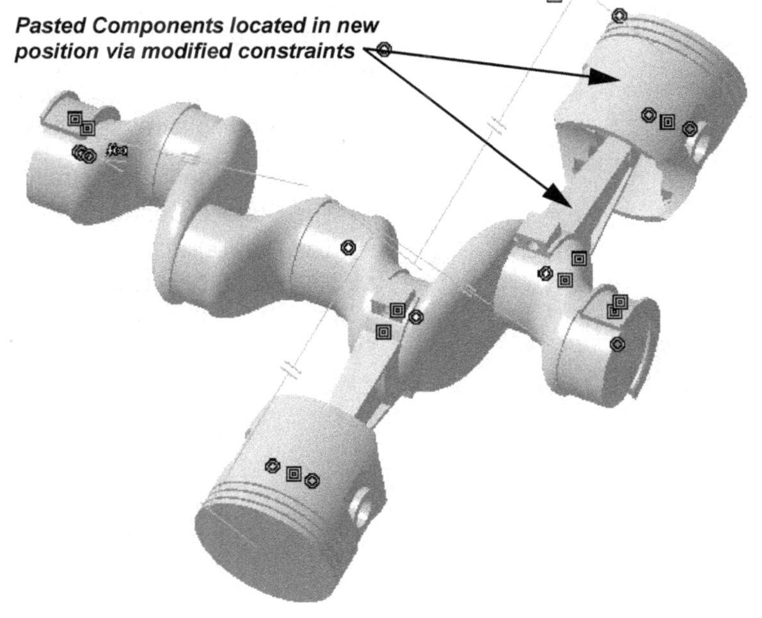

Figure 9–46

1. Hide the following components:
   - **Skeleton**
   - **1703**
   - **1801**

   The model displays as shown in Figure 9–47.

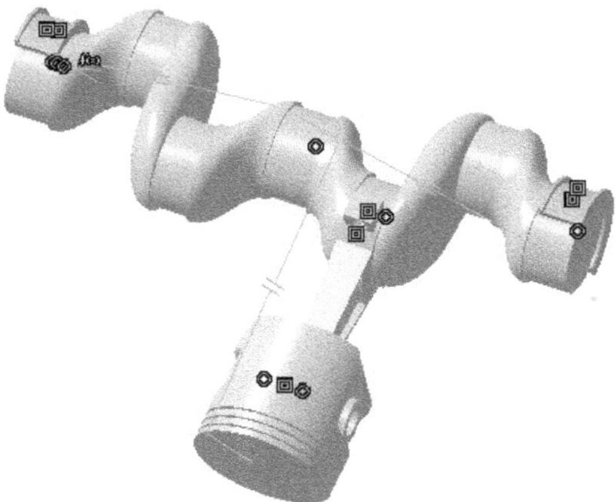

Figure 9–47

2. Hover the cursor over each of the pasted constraints. The geometric references used to define each constraint display on the model. This will give you an idea of the geometric references that are currently used in each pasted constraint. To correctly locate the pasted **Piston** and **Connecting Rod**, the following constraints will be modified:
   - The Coincidence constraint between **1523.2, 1824.1**
   - The Surface Contact constraint between **1523.2, 1824.1**
   - The Parallelism constraint between **1256.2, 1703.1**

The names of the constraints in your model might differ from those shown in Figure 9–48.

3. Modify the Surface Contact constraint between **1523.2, 1824.1** shown in Figure 9–48 by double-clicking on the constraint in the specification tree.

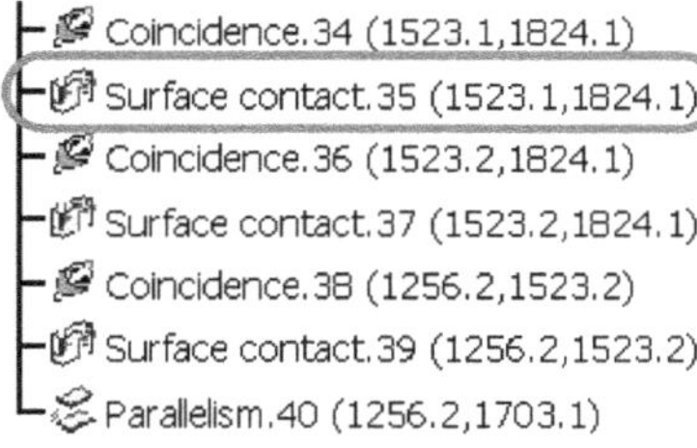

Figure 9–48

4. In the Constraint Definition dialog box, click **More**. The dialog box displays the two components referenced in the Surface Contact constraint.
5. Select **1824.1**, as shown in Figure 9–49.
6. In the Constraint Definition dialog box, click **Reconnect** as shown in Figure 9–49. This tells CATIA that you will be selecting a new geometric reference for **1824.1**.

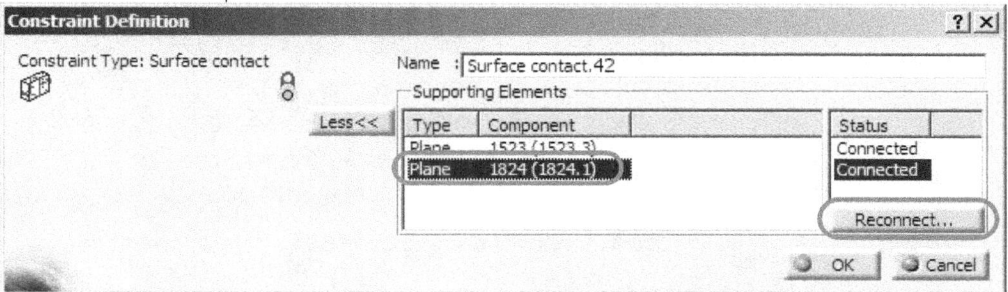

Figure 9–49

7. Select the face shown in Figure 9–50 as the new reference.

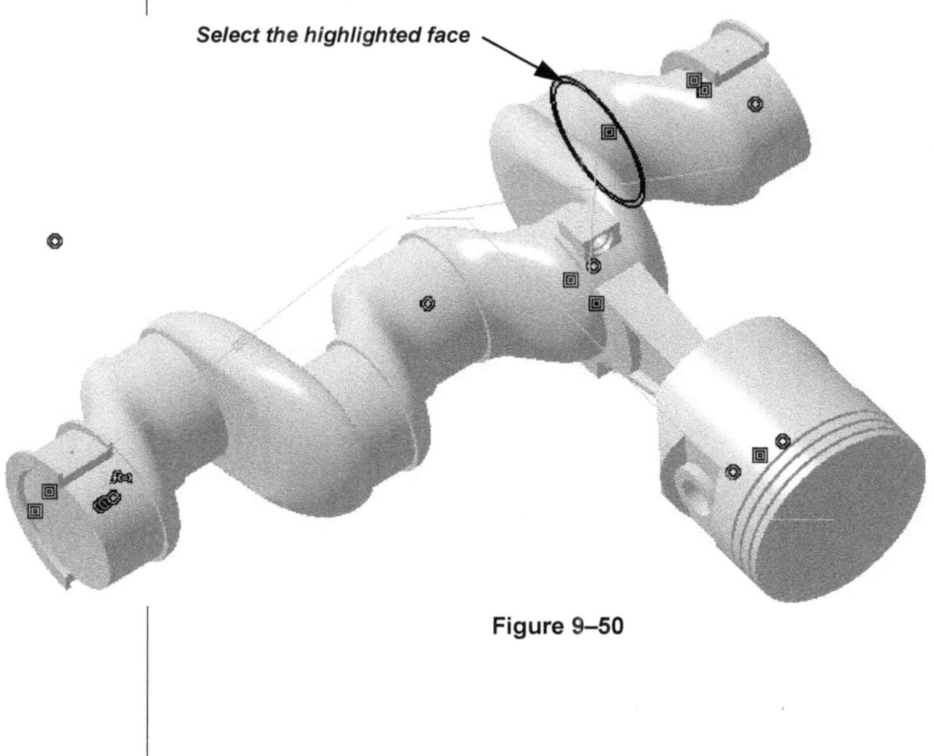

Figure 9–50

The names of your constraints might be different. Use the constraint names you entered previously in the chapter.

8. Click **OK** to complete the modification of the constraint. The Surface Contact constraint between **1523.2, 1824.1** will now reference the new face you selected in the Step 8.

9. Modify the Coincidence constraint between **1523.2, 1824.1** highlighted in Figure 9–51.

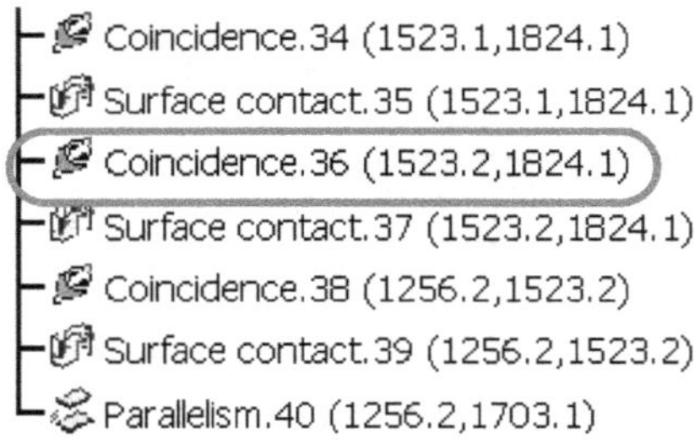

- Coincidence.34 (1523.1,1824.1)
- Surface contact.35 (1523.1,1824.1)
- Coincidence.36 (1523.2,1824.1)
- Surface contact.37 (1523.2,1824.1)
- Coincidence.38 (1256.2,1523.2)
- Surface contact.39 (1256.2,1523.2)
- Parallelism.40 (1256.2,1703.1)

Figure 9–51

10. Reconnect component **1824's** reference to the axis shown in Figure 9–52.

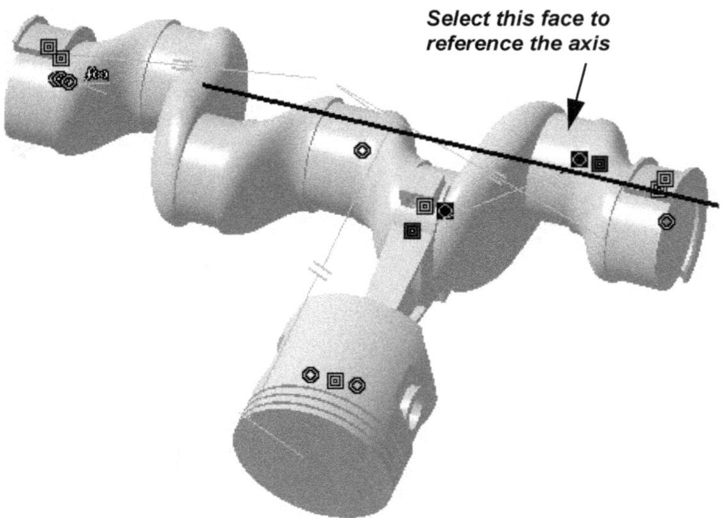

Figure 9–52

11. Click **OK** to complete the modification of the constraint.

12. Modify the Parallelism constraint between **1256.2, 1703.1** as shown in Figure 9–53.

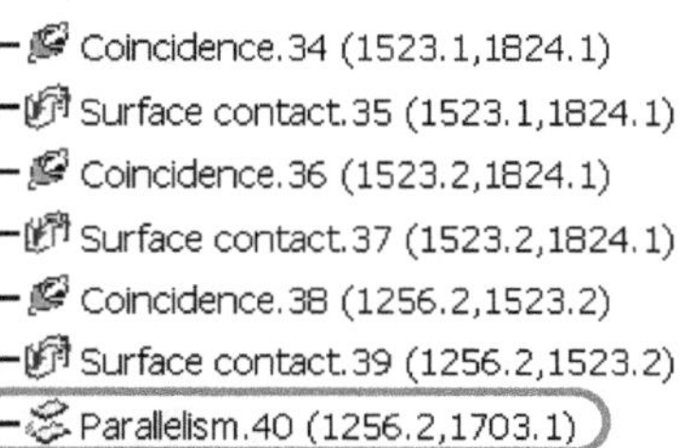

Figure 9–53

13. Instead of reconnecting a geometric reference as in the last two constraints modified, you will change the orientation of the Parallel constraint. Set the *orientation* to **Opposite**.

14. Click **OK** to complete the modification of the constraint.

15. Update the assembly. It displays as shown in Figure 9–54. Note where the pasted piston and connecting rod update. If your assembly did not update correctly, use the compass or **Manipulate** tool to locate the **Piston** and **Connecting Rod**. Try updating the assembly again.

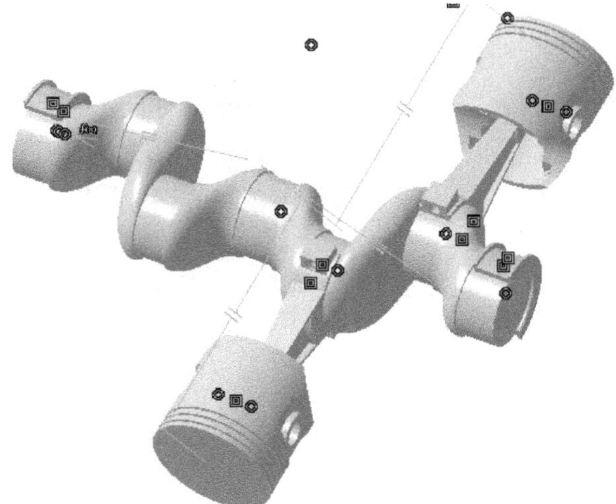

Figure 9–54

16. Show component **1703**. Components **1256.2** and the **1703** do not line up correctly.

17. Create a Coincident constraint between **1256.2** and **1703** using the references shown in Figure 9–55. Components have been hidden to display the references required to create the constraint more clearly.

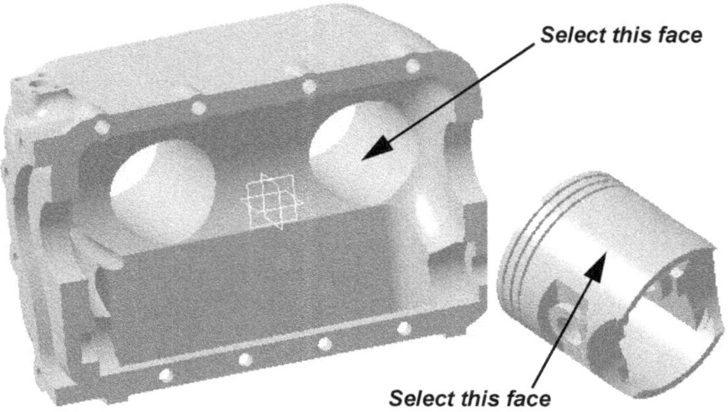

Figure 9–55

Task 6 - Manipulate the assembly to line up the piston.

1. Show the following components:
   - **Skeleton**
   - **1801**
2. Set the transparency of **BlockLeft** (part number **1703**) to approximately **130**.
3. Click (Manipulation). The Manipulate Parameters dialog box opens as shown in Figure 9–56.

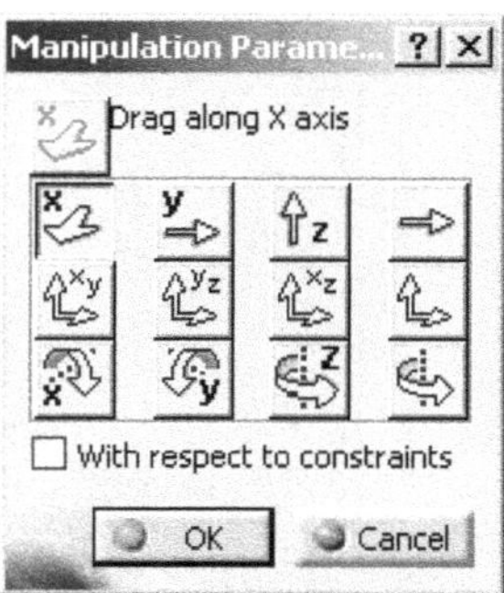

Figure 9–56

4. Select **With respect to constraints**. Click .
5. Switch the model to the **Front** saved view. In the window, select the **Crank model** (part number **1824**) and drag the component to the position shown in Figure 9–57.

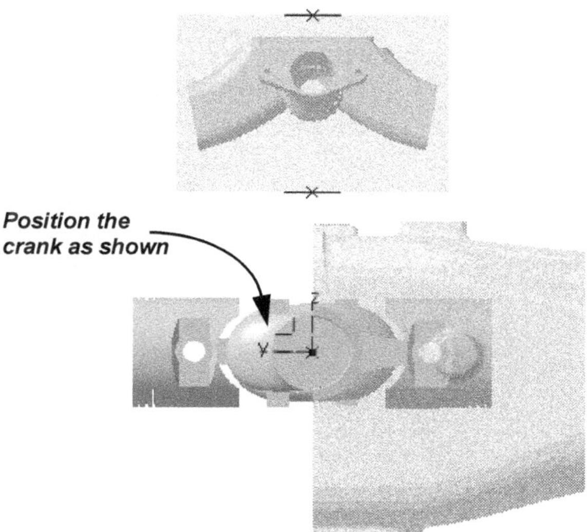

Figure 9–57

6. Return to the Isometric view. The model displays as shown in Figure 9–58.

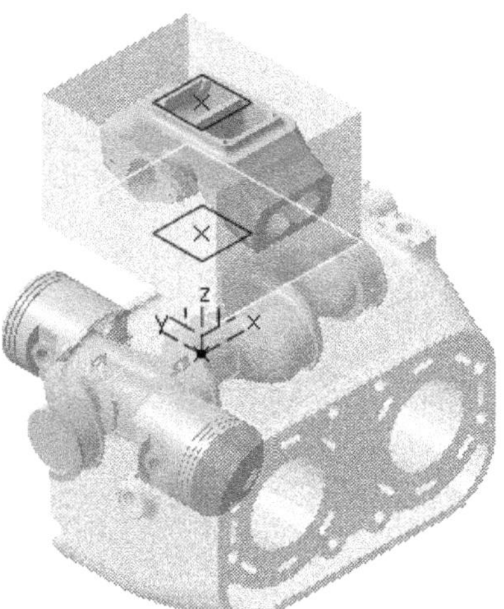

Figure 9–58

7. Set the *transparency* of **BlockLeft** (part number **1703**) back to **0**.

8. Save the model and close the window.

Task 7 - Create a symmetrical component.

1. Create a new Product file with the default name.

2. Assemble **HeadLeft.CATPart**. Do not apply any constraints to the model.

3. Click (Symmetry). The Assembly Symmetry Wizard dialog box opens and prompts for a symmetry plane. Select the face shown in Figure 9–59.

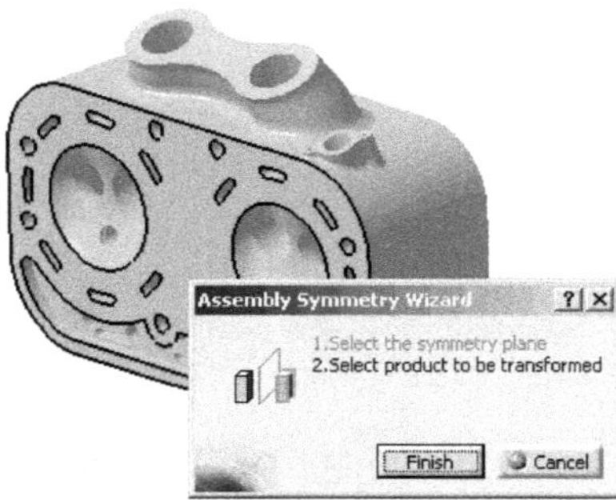

Figure 9–59

4. Select **HeadLeft (1243-1)** to transform. The dialog box opens as shown in Figure 9–60.

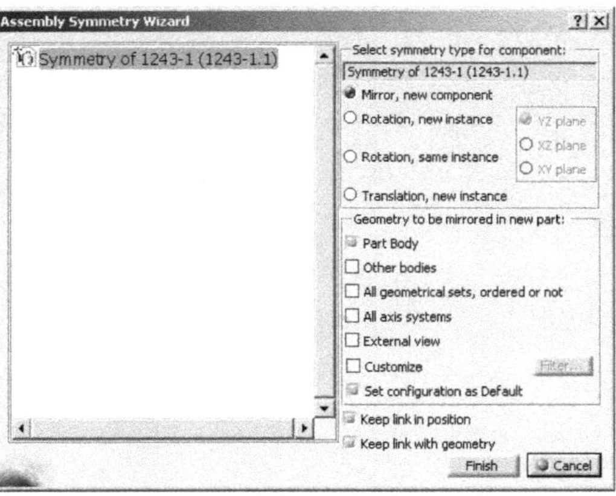

Figure 9–60

5. Accept the default values and click **Finish** to create the symmetrical component. The system updates the progress of the geometry creation, as shown in Figure 9–61.

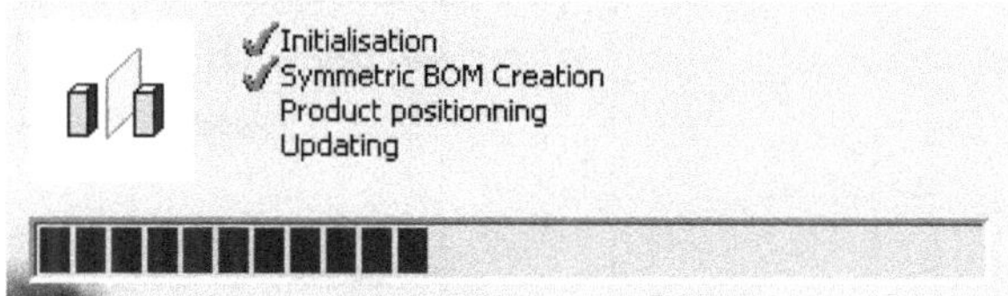

Figure 9–61

6. Once the process is complete, the Assembly Symmetry Result dialog box reports the creation of one new component, as shown in Figure 9–62.

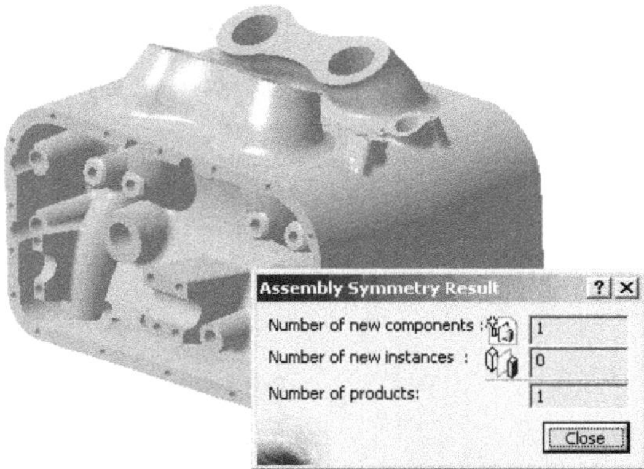

Figure 9–62

7. Close the dialog box.

8. The Assembly features component has been added to the specification tree. Expand it to display the **Assembly Symmetry.1** feature, as shown in Figure 9–63.

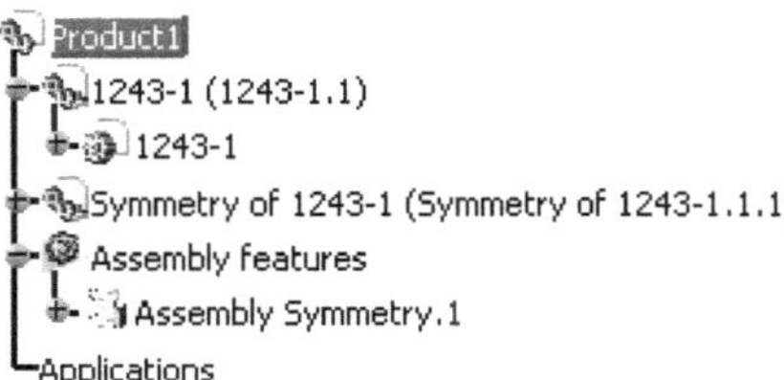

Figure 9–63

9. Rename the part number of the new component as **1243-2**, as shown in Figure 9–64.

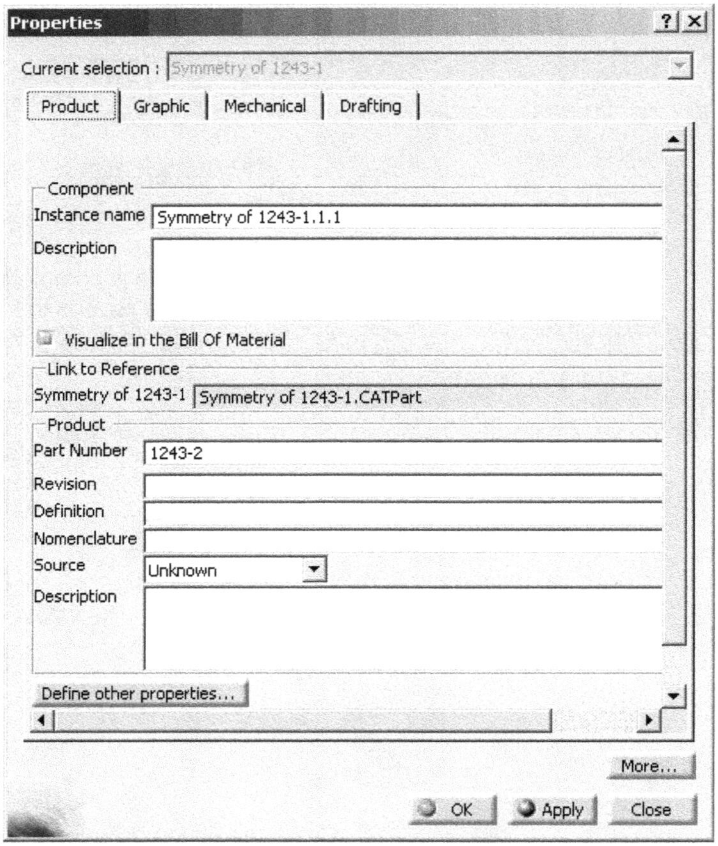

Figure 9–64

10. Save the new component as **HeadRight** in the *Engine* directory.

11. Close the Product file without saving it.

Task 8 - Open the new component.

1. Open **HeadRight** from the *Engine* directory. The model displays as shown in Figure 9–65.

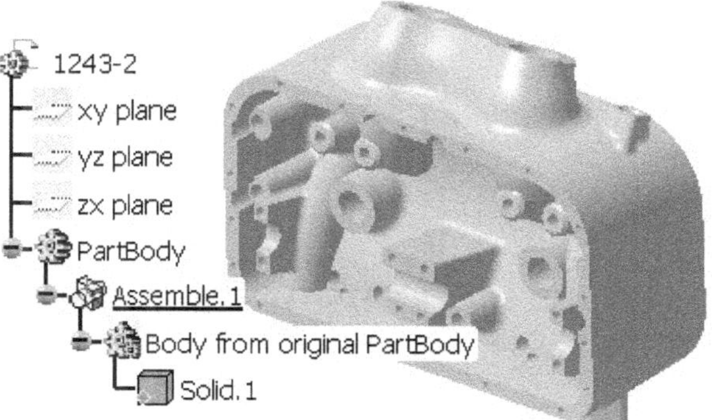

Figure 9–65

The feature information is linked to **HeadLeft** part, indicated by the symbol on **Solid.1**. The information is linked because the **Keep link with geometry option** was selected during the creation of the symmetrical component.

2. Close the file.

Proceed to the next practice if you have already covered the content on Assembly Performance Management.

Practice 9e Selective Load

Practice Objectives

- Use the Desk command.
- Manage an assembly by selective loading.

In this practice, you will use the **Desk** command to locate a renamed file. Manage the amount of information loaded into the session using the **Selective Load** functionality.

practice

Task 1 - Rename a part file.

1. Select **File>Open** and browse to the *Engine* directory.
2. Right-click on **GCS.CATPart** and select **Rename**, as shown in Figure 9–66.

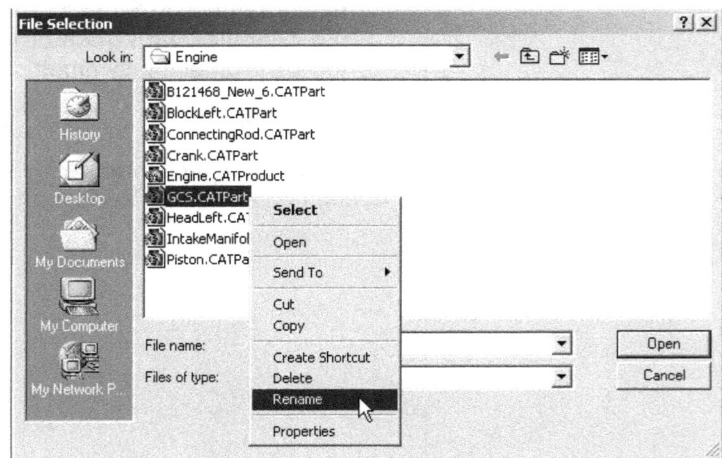

Figure 9–66

3. For the new model name, enter **Skeleton.CATPart** and press <Enter> to accept the change.

Task 2 - Open the Engine Product file.

1. Open **Engine.CATProduct** from the *Engine* directory.

2. The Open dialog box opens as shown in Figure 9–67. The Product file is unable to locate **GCS.CATPart** because it was renamed as **Skeleton.CATPart**.

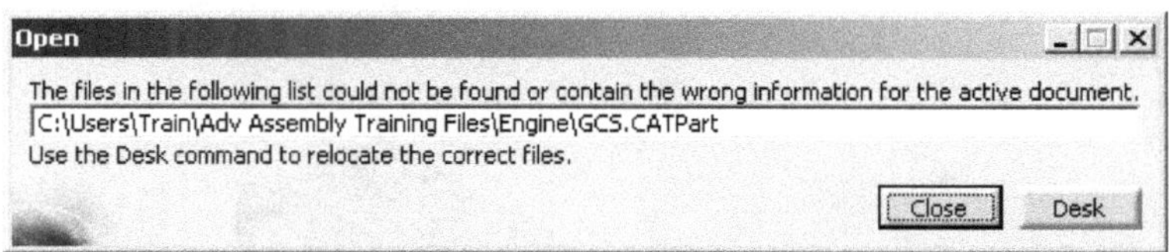

Figure 9–67

3. Click **Desk**. The Desk workbench opens, displaying all of the parts and the missing part file, as shown in Figure 9–68.

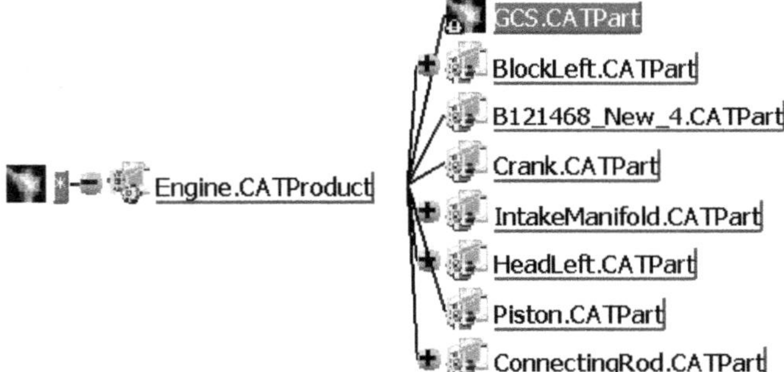

Figure 9–68

4. Right-click on GGS.CATPart and select **Find**, as shown in Figure 9–69.

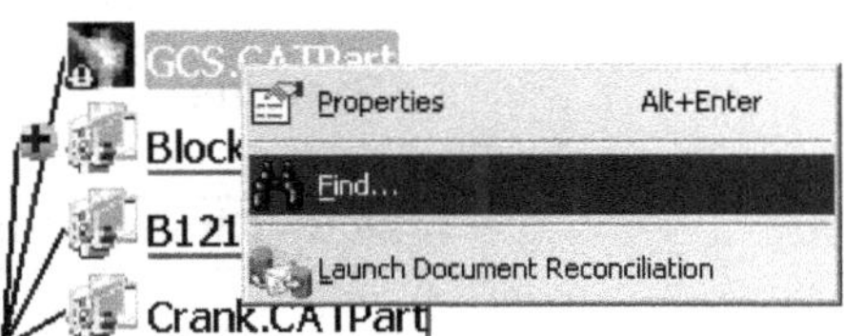

Figure 9–69

5. Double-click on **Skeleton.CATPart** in the *Engine* directory. **Skeleton.CATPart** is now listed in the Desk workbench and the red warning status is cleared.

6. Close the Desk workbench.

7. The assembly displays with the skeleton model in place. Update the assembly as required.

Task 3 - Assemble BlockRight and HeadRight.

1. Bring **BlockRight** and **HeadRight** into the assembly and use the compass to position the models, as shown in Figure 9–70.

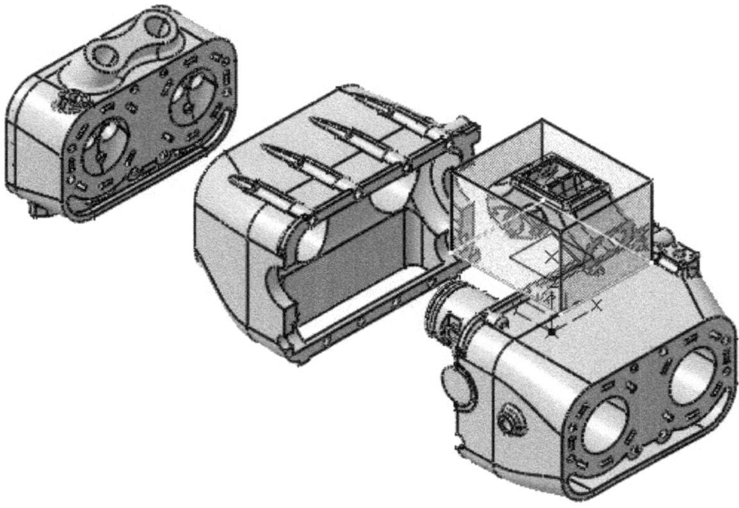

Figure 9–70

Task 4 - Deactivate the top-level assembly.

1. In the specification tree, right-click on *Engine* and select **Representations>Deactivate Terminal Node**.
2. Save the model and close the file.

Task 5 - Change document loading options.

1. Select **Tools>Options** and select the *General* tab.
2. Clear the **Load referenced documents** option and click **OK**.

Task 6 - Use Selective Load to load components into the assembly.

1. Open **Engine.CATProduct**.

2. Click (Selective Load). The Product Load Management dialog box opens.

3. Select **GCS.1 (Skeleton.CATPart)**. In the Product Load Management dialog box, click .

4. Repeat this process to load **1705.1** (**BlockRight.CATPart**) and **1243-2.1** (**HeadRight.CATPart**). The selected items are listed in the *Delayed Actions* area with the status **will be loaded**, as shown in Figure 9–71.

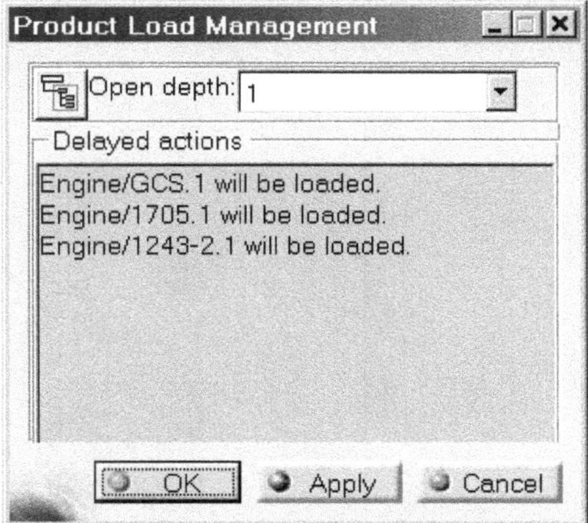

Figure 9–71

5. Click **Apply**. The system loads the selected documents. Click **OK**.

6. Update the assembly.

Task 7 - Assemble components.

1. Assemble **BlockRight** to the **Axis System Engine**. Create three Coincidence constraints using the information listed in the table below.

Item	Selection from Axis System Engine	Selection from BlockRight (Part Number 1705)
1	X-Axis of Axis System Engine	ZX plane
2	Y-Axis of Axis System Engine	XY plane
3	Z-Axis of Axis System Engine	YZ plane

2. Assemble **HeadRight** to **BlockRight**, as shown in Figure 9–72.

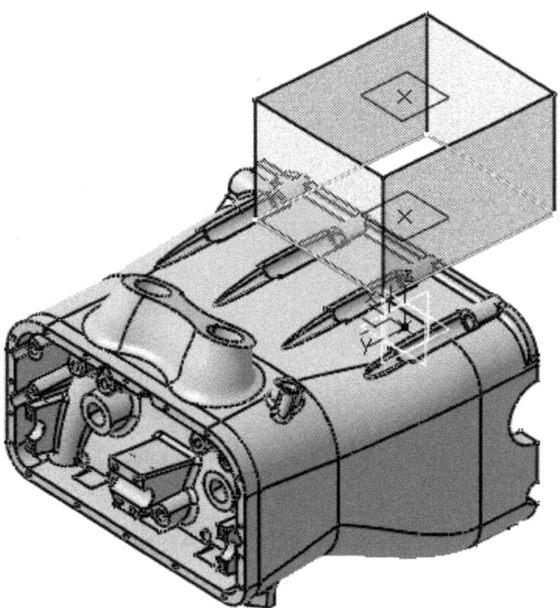

Figure 9–72

3. Ensure that both components do not have any degrees of freedom.

Task 8 - Load the entire top-level assembly.

1. Select the top-level assembly and activate the terminal node.
2. Load the remaining components of the assembly by right-clicking on the components highlighted in Figure 9–73 and selecting **Components>Load**.

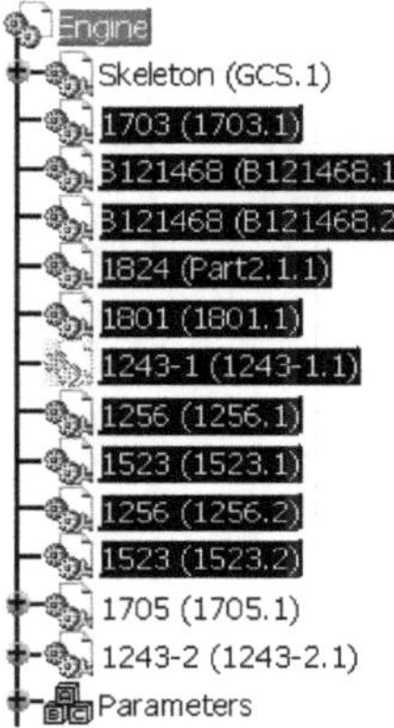

Figure 9–73

3. Select **Tools>Options** and select **Load referenced objects**.

Task 9 - Unload a component.

1. Right-click on part **1705** and select **Components>Unload**, as shown in Figure 9–74.

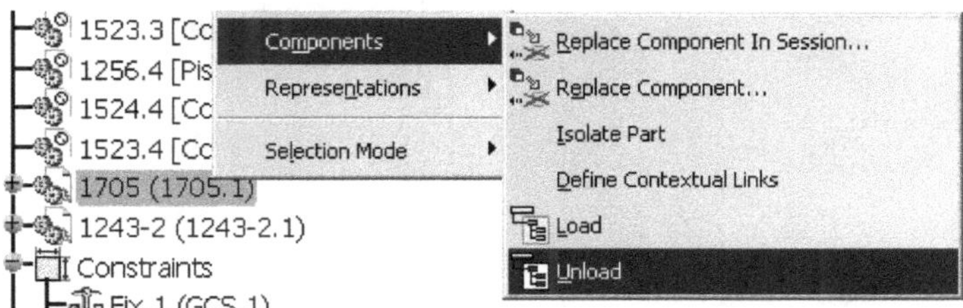

Figure 9–74

2. Save the model and close the file.
3. Open **Engine.CATProduct**. A load or unload status cannot be saved.
4. Close the model.

www.ingramcontent.com/pod-product-compliance
Lightning Source LLC
Chambersburg PA
CBHW080709220326
41598CB00033B/5359

* 9 7 8 1 9 4 7 4 5 6 0 0 6 *